USAGE-BASED MODELS OF LANGUAGE

USAGE-BASED MODELS OF LANGUAGE

MICHAEL BARLOW
&
SUZANNE KEMMER
editors

CSLI Publications
Center for the Study of Language and Information
Stanford, California

Copyright ©2000
CSLI Publications
Center for the Study of Language and Information
Leland Stanford Junior University
Printed in the United States
04 03 02 01 00   1 2 3 4 5

Library of Congress Cataloging-in-Publication Data

Usage-based models of language / [edited by] Suzanne Kemmer and Michael
    Barlow.
    p.cm.
    Includes bibliographical references and index.
    ISBN 1-57586-219-0 (alk. paper) -- ISBN 1-57586-220-4 (pbk. : alk. paper)
        I. Linguistic models. 2. Linguistic analysis (Linguistics) I.Kemmer, Suzanne.
    II. Barlow, Michael, 1950-

    P128.M6 U8 1999
    418--dc21   99-059368

∞ The acid-free paper used in this book meets the minimum requirements of the American
National Standard for Information Sciences – Permanence of Paper for Printed Library
                        Materials, ansi z39.48-1984.

Visit our web site at
http://cslipublications.stanford.edu/
for comments on this and other titles, as well as for changes and
corrections by the author and publisher.

Contents

Introduction: A Usage-Based Conception of Language

SUZANNE KEMMER AND MICHAEL BARLOW
Rice University

This volume is designed to bring together various approaches to the theory and description of human language which, despite numerous differences in methodology and focus, we see as similar in a fundamental way: All share a commitment to **usage-based** models and theories of language. Since this term, introduced in Langacker (1987) (and defined in more detail in Langacker 1988) has only recently gained currency, and is liable to be misunderstood or, more probably, overly broadly applied, it will be useful to describe what this notion entails. Many of the individual authors of these papers describe their specific idea of what it means for an approach to be usage-based; we will gather up the main strands of these conceptions below, showing their interrelation and at the same time highlighting the ways in which they contrast with assumptions (explicit or tacit), methods, and aims that have been characteristic of much work in modern linguistics.

There are at least two major traditions that are usage-based in the sense of focusing on acts of language use: the Firthian tradition, which has emphasized the importance of context, including its social aspects (see for example Firth 1957); and what might be called enunciativist linguistics, in which theories of language structure are based on the speech act (e.g. Benveniste 1971, Ducrot 1984, Culioli 1995). Both of these have unbroken traditions of influence in modern linguistics, including but not limited to some of the usage-based approaches described in this volume. But the most dominant trends in linguistics in the last generation have been squarely focused on language as a more or less fixed system, which can be studied independently of context and use and independently of its interactions with other aspects of cognition.

Recently, the field of linguistics at large has been moving towards more usage-based kinds of frameworks. The mechanics of formal linguistic theories have shifted, new methodologies have been applied, and the idea has taken root that a very narrow conception of what has to be accounted for in language is not satisfying. There are signs of increasing convergence between a number of formal models of language and approaches that have long insisted on a usage-based perspective.

In the following section we describe explicitly what it means for an approach to be usage-based, by laying out what we see as the most fundamental characteristics of that notion. The papers in the volume then illustrate how various approaches and models constructed around language use lead to fruitful generalizations and insights about the nature of language.

Aspects of a Usage-based Model

Usage-based models share a number of characteristic assumptions, discussed under the headings below.

The intimate relation between linguistic structures and instances of use of language. All the authors in this volume would agree on the need for basing posited linguistic structures on language use. However, 'linguistic structure' is ambiguous: it can refer to hypothesized structures derived by the analyst from observation of linguistic data, with no expectation that such structures are cognitively instantiated (the 'external' linguistic system, or what Lamb in this volume terms the 'theory of the linguistic extension'); or alternatively, to structures posited by the analyst as a claim about mental structure and operation (the 'internal' linguistic system). On either reading, the heading above points to a shared methodological assumption about what kinds of data to use (cf. the introductory remarks in Dickinson and Givón's paper). This aspect will be considered further below in the discussion of usage data. The second reading is the one focused on by most, but not all, of the authors, and the discussion below refers to this cognitively-oriented view of the linguistic system as a mental system.

A usage-based model is one in which the speaker's linguistic system is fundamentally grounded in 'usage events': instances of a speaker's producing and understanding language. 'Grounded in' means that linguistic representations are tightly linked to usage events in three ways: First, such instances are the basis on which a speaker's linguistic system is formed, i.e. they are experience from which the system itself is initially abstracted (discussed further below). Second, the relation between the more abstract representations in the speaker's grammar and the usage events experienced by the speaker is much more direct than usually assumed. The abstract and the particular remain tightly linked, for the following reason. Usage events are necessarily specific in nature, in that, for example, any given linguistic utterance has lexical content. The linguistic system is built up from such lexically specific instances, only gradually abstracting more general representations, such as phonemes, morphemes, and syntactic patterns, from the repetition of similar instances of use (cf. Langacker 1987, this volume). This means that any general representations that emerge from the operation of the system necessarily are tied to, i.e. activated in concert with, specific instances of those patterns. Abstract utterances without any phonetic or lexical content do not exist.

Such links between general patterns, often called **schemas**,[1] and their instantiations have important consequences. For one thing, units of language (from phonemes to constructions) are not fixed but dynamic, subject to creative extension and reshaping with use. This leads to the third way in which representations relate to usage: Usage events are crucial to the ongoing structuring and operation of the linguistic system. Language productions are not only products of the speaker's linguistic system, but they also provide input for other speakers' systems (as well as, reflexively, for the speaker's own), not just in initial acquisition but in language use throughout life. Thus, usage events play a double role in the system: they both result from, and also shape, the linguistic system itself in a kind of feedback loop.

Langacker's paper presents a particularly explicit and detailed conception of the workings of a usage-based model, specifically the framework of Cognitive Grammar, which he has been developing over the last two decades. In his 1988 paper "A Usage-Based Model," Langacker identified three key characteristics of a usage-based model which Cognitive Grammar instantiates: it is maximalist, non-reductive, and bottom up. The first two of these properties pertain to the view, consistent with what is known about cognitive processing, that grammar is massive and highly redundant, rather than stripped down and economical. There is no need to choose between unanalyzed listings and analytical treatment of a complex language structure; the mind can potentially represent the same structure in multiple ways, and hence the grammar includes both specific items and the more general patterns they are instances of. The specific and the general are mutually linked through usage. The bottom up property adds that the specific and idiosyncratic elements of the system are privileged over the general in the acquisition and operation of the system: the general arises out of the specific, and the specific is what is most directly taken from experience.

In his paper in this volume, Langacker develops his original vision further to include a detailed description of the mechanics of individual usage events in terms of acts of categorization. A usage event can be precisely defined as "the pairing of a vocalization, in all its specificity, with a conceptualization representing its full contextual understanding" (p. 9). He describes how usage events relate to conventionalized (entrenched) linguistic units of various degrees of specificity through cognitive processes that are not strictly linguistic. His paper shows how the usage-based nature of Cognitive Grammar provides a natural account for a number of the most fundamental problems in linguistics, including not only the creation and understanding of novel expressions, but also the assignment of structural descriptions, judgments of well- and ill-formedness, distributional restrictions, and differences in the degree of compositionality, productivity and generality of linguistic units. In addition he describes a wide range of descriptive applications of the model, covering all aspects of linguistic systems, from phonology to syntax and semantics/pragmatics. The book-length treatments in Langacker (1987, 1991) present the theory and applications in more comprehensive detail.

The other central properties of usage-based models follow from various aspects of the close relation between structure and use described above.

The importance of frequency. Because the system is largely an experience-driven one, frequency of instances is a prime factor in its structure and operation. Since frequency of a particular usage pattern is both a result and a shaping force of the system, frequency has an indispensable role in any explanatory account of language (cf. Bybee 1988, Haiman 1991, 1994). Higher frequency of a unit or pattern results in a greater degree of what Langacker terms **entrenchment**, i.e. cognitive routinization, which affects the processing of the unit. This idea of the fundamental importance of frequency, expressed in many of the papers in this volume, sharply distinguishes usage-based models from other approaches in which frequency is an insignificant artifact, unconnected with speakers' linguistic knowledge. The role of frequency in leading to entrenchment of units in the linguistic system is a crucial aspect of Langacker's and Bybee's models. In addition the papers of Barlow and Biber in particular stress the importance of frequency in the organization of the linguistic system (although unlike the others', Biber's conception of 'linguistic system' is external, rather than internal). Frequency also plays a fundamental role in connectionist simulations of the sort described in MacWhinney's contribution, discussed below.

Bybee's paper is centrally focused on the effects of frequency. Her paper, a reexamination of the problem of *t/d* deletion, presents strong empirical evidence of the effects of lexical frequency in the phonological (and morphological) system. Using a corpus of phonological productions, she shows that the phonetic properties of lexical items are significantly influenced by language use, in that repeated use of a word affects its lexical representation. Her results highlight the dynamic interplay between language use and the speaker's linguistic system.

Comprehension and production as integral, rather than peripheral, to the linguistic system. Given that usage events drive the formation and operation of the internal linguistic system, the structure of this system is not separate in any significant way from the (cumulative) acts of mental processing that occur in language use. The speaker's linguistic ability, in fact, is *constituted* by regularities in the mental processing of language. On this view, it does not make sense to draw a sharp distinction between what is traditionally called 'competence' and 'performance,' since performance is itself part of a speaker's competence. Instead of viewing language processing as something external to the system, which happens only to the outputs of competence, processing is rather to be seen as an intrinsic part of the linguistic knowledge system, which cannot be treated separately from it.[2] 'Performance errors,' for example, are not viewed as due exclusively to 'processing factors,' and thus are not treated as a completely separate phenomenon from other utterances not licensed by competence. Instead, all linguistic productions are seen as simply in conformance, or non-conformance, with linguistic norms to differing degrees. All of the papers in the volume contribute in some measure to closing the traditional theoretical gap between language system and language use.

Focus on the role of learning and experience in language acquisition. Since in a usage-based model instances of producing and understanding language are of central importance to the structuring of the linguistic system, they must be especially significant in the acquisition of language, when the system is in the process of taking form.

For many cognitive scientists, it is obvious that learning is central to language acquisition. Many linguists, however, would dispute this. In the recent history of linguistics, the fact of children's language acquisition has been given as *the* fundamental problem of language to be explained (Chomsky 1972). This problem is extremely intractable given the kind of deductive linguistic system traditionally envisaged (discussed further under the next heading). The solution offered has been to posit highly specific innate linguistic structures that lead to the putative development of an adult linguistic system within a few short years of a child's life. As we might expect with such a view, the role of learning and experience has consequently been minimized to an extreme extent, in favor of an 'input as trigger' model (see Chomsky 1988, Crain 1991 for strong statements of these views).

A usage-based model, which stresses the importance of instances of use and consequent cognitive entrenchment, places learning at the forefront of language acquisition. This type of model reconceives the nature of the linguistic system, such that it is far easier to see how it could be learnable. If instances of use are the prime input driving the system's formation, then positing genetically-specified guiding linguistic structures is unnecessary. A well-conceived mechanism for learning, which is also applicable to the learning of other kinds of cognitive patterns besides language, is what is needed for a basic understanding of language acquisition and its relation to general cognition. Such a mechanism does not have to be conceived of as applying to a 'blank slate' (the kinds of brain structures that support the learning mechanism are presumably themselves genetically guided, after all); but the necessity for pre-existing, hard-wired structures is minimized, a great advantage given what is known about neural development. (See Elman et al. 1998 for a thorough discussion of the issues surrounding 'innate structures'and of acquisition models.)

There are a number of strands of research emphasizing a usage-based, learning-driven perspective on acquisition. In one of these, it is shown just how little in the way of grammatical structures children actually start out with; their first complex utterances are based on specific lexical items, notably verbs. Only later do they start to abstract more general constructional patterns (Tomasello 1992; Pine and Lieven 1993; Tomasello, Lieven, Behrens and Forwergk, Forthcoming). Another line of research focuses on how children learn linguistic patterns based on their everyday bodily and social experience (e.g. Bates 1976, Bowerman 1982, Slobin 1985, Johnson 1999, MacWhinney 1999a). A related strand concentrates specifically on the structure and operation of the learning mechanism, investigating how the acquisition of particular linguistic systems can be modeled with a connectionist architecture. MacWhinney's paper in this volume is an example of this approach (see next heading).

Linguistic representations as emergent, rather than stored as fixed entities. The view of language as consisting of a set of stored units which are operated on by a set of (also stored) procedures or instructions, producing some output, is rejected by cognitively-oriented theorists of usage-based approaches. Instead, linguistic units are seen as cognitive routines. Such units are nothing more than recurrent patterns of mental (ultimately neural) activation; as such they are not 'stored' in any particular neural location, nor is it useful to think of them as being located in the types of memory 'storage devices' often posited in the psychological literature. During linguistic processing, linguistic units are part and parcel of the system's processing activity: they exist as activation patterns. When no processing is occurring, the information represented by such units simply resides in patterns of connectivity (including differential connection strengths) resulting from previous activations. Emergence as a property of linguistic systems, and the distributed nature of representations, has been argued for on linguistic grounds by linguists such as Hopper (1988, 1998) and Fox (1994). Researchers such as Elman, McClelland, MacWhinney and others have been building explicit simulative models of linguistic subsystems with these properties for some time (see below). For exploration of the notion of emergence and its implications for language and mind, see the collection in MacWhinney (1999b).

In general, those usage-based theorists who have striven for an explicit model of the internal linguistic system have based it on some form of an activation network, which is a well-known type of psychological model. A specific type of such model is a connectionist network, which has several desirable properties for a model of mind. Because it is an emergence-based system, as described above, there is no separate set of processing algorithms or rules, independent of units in the system. This accords with a well-known property of the human brain: its lack of a central processing unit that directs mental operations. Instead, each neuron is its own processor and functions by activating (or inhibiting) links to other neurons. In a connectionist network, information resides in patterns of connection weights that link (essentially contentless) nodes. Nodes can be thought of as analogous to neurons or at least complex subnetworks of neurons.

Three of the papers in the volume utilize a network representation that can be applied directly to the description of linguistic structure. Langacker, in describing the basic constructs and processes of Cognitive Grammar, also includes a connectionist interpretation of the theory, explaining in general terms how the abstract descriptive representations he utilizes can be ultimately related to an explicitly connectionist model (see also Langacker 1990). The model made reference to in Bybee's paper (described in more detail in Bybee 1988, 1994 and 1995) stresses the cognitive links between lexical items, from which phonological and morphological regularities emerge. The paper by Lamb sketches still another theoretical architecture for a connectionist linguistic/conceptual network that directly refers to and conforms as far as possible with known properties of neurons (described in greater detail in Lamb 1998). He incorporates a mechanism for bidirectional processing which captures the neural properties necessary to account for both comprehension and production in the same network. With this model Lamb goes much further than many others in directly relating the properties of linguistic and other conceptual networks to the properties of neural structure itself, one of the ultimate, albeit distant, goals of cognitive research.

Comparing these three proposed network models is instructive; the similarities are fundamental, yet the differences highlight the different foci of interest of each model's originator and the consequent difference in levels of representation at which they operate.[3]

Other properties of connectionist models are that they are analogy driven (but see Section 6 of Langacker's paper for clarification of what this means); they involve competition among possible candidates for activation (see also Deane 1992); and their output is the result of simultaneous constraint satisfaction rather than a rule-like process. Constraint satisfaction is also characteristic of some formal linguistic theories (e.g. HPSG, Optimality Theory), although these do not go as far in the direction of eliminating the fundamental division between symbols in the system and the operations, principles or constraints such symbolic units are subject to.

Connectionist models have the advantage of being computationally implementable in principle. Thus such models can be used to simulate acquisition of specific linguistic systems, such as English past tense verb forms or German noun categories. In a connectionist learning simulation, a basic network structure without any specific information to start with is fed exemplars and in the process organizes itself into a system that produces output which (in a successful simulation) matches the patterns in the input. Specific connectionist implementations vary in the computational algorithms and architecture used; manipulating such variations allows for testing of various properties of the model, with the aim of maximal conformity with attested patterns of human learning. There is a large literature on the application of such models to linguistic problems, see for example Elman and McClelland (1984), Rumelhart and McClelland (1986), McClelland and Rumelhart (1986), and Gupta and MacWhinney (1992).

The paper by MacWhinney in this volume situates the basic ideas underlying connectionist learning simulation models in the context of developments in cognitive science. He highlights the two essential characteristics that mark their advance over the rule-based systems developed in the 60s and 70s: the lack of symbol-passing in connectionist architecture and the self-organizing nature of the systems, both of which are attractive to those seriously committed to compatibility with brain architecture. He describes a number of innovations—lexical mapping, argument frames, and systems for phonological and semantic modification—that have been applied to linguistic problems of ever greater complexity, from acquisition of morphological systems such as tense and agreement, to verb argument structure, to even more complex syntactic structures, with results in many cases rivalling those of traditional algorithmic architectures. Although connectionist models still deal with restricted systems with relatively small numbers of units, MacWhinney's contribution suggests the potential for ultimately relating such simulations to the more complex, hand-wired theoretical models of linguists described above, as well as, perhaps, to the more scalable, but less self-organizing simulations such as found in Regier (1996).

Importance of usage data in theory construction and description. Because the linguistic system is so closely tied to usage, it follows that theories of language should be grounded in an observation of data from actual uses of language. In linguistics, the standard methodology relies on constructed examples with no naturally occurring context of production (or comprehension). This practice derives from the basic assumption, referred to above in the discussion of the competence/performance distinction, of a very indirect relation between linguistic knowledge and acts of language use. Observation of data from actual language production has been typically confined to subfields of linguistics often deemed 'peripheral': phonetics, sociolinguistics, historical linguistics, and other fields which have in practice had minimal impact on the development of linguistic theory. The study of syntax in particular, long treated as the 'core' of linguistics, has almost exclusively relied on judgments of 'grammaticality' of constructed examples.

Speaker intuitions about constructed examples are an invaluable tool, provided that such data are treated with all appropriate care. Their use requires at least the following: an acceptance and appreciation of the cline of acceptability and the interspeaker variability that is typically associated with such examples; an understanding of the nature of 'deviance' from linguistic norms; and most generally, some serious reflection on what such judgments actually tell us. But even with such judicious use, intuitions about constructed data cannot be treated as the sole, or even primary, source of evidence as to the nature and properties of the linguistic system.

A usage-based theory, whether its object of study is the internal or external linguistic system, takes seriously the notion that the primary object of study is the language people actually produce and understand. Language in use is the best evidence we have for determining the nature and specific organization of linguistic systems.[4] Thus, an ideal usage-based analysis is one that emerges from observation of such bodies of usage data, called corpora. But even if not based primarily on such data, at a minimum, analyses must ultimately be at least consistent with production data.

One often-used type of corpus is a collection of production data comprising many texts produced by many speakers or writers. Such a corpus is not, of course, a mirror of the exact input that has shaped a particular individual's linguistic system. For one thing such corpora, as they are currently structured, typically omit almost all the context of use of the language captured by the corpus, and context, as discussed below, is an indispensable component of usage-based approaches. In addition, there is a danger that a corpus containing a mixture of text-types will neutralize genre-specific patterns of the kind discussed in Biber's paper. These caveats notwithstanding, textual corpus data provide a sampling of usage that can reflect general patterns very faithfully. Used sensibly, such data can give an insight into such questions as which units are most entrenched in speakers' linguistic systems (via examination of frequency of constructions, collocations etc.) and how such units relate to each other in the grammatical system. For an account along these lines based on the frequency of English reflexive constructions of various types in spoken and written corpora, see Barlow (1996).

The papers in this volume by Verhagen, Biber and Barlow all use linguistic corpora to search for patterns in usage events. Verhagen and Barlow are interested in the nature of linguistic representations, while Biber seeks to provide empirically well-grounded descriptions of such aspects of language as words, grammatical features, text types, and the relations between these.

Verhagen's paper uses corpus data from three centuries to investigate differences between older and modern Dutch in relation to the use of the causative verbs *laten* and *doen*. By looking at frequency data in various genres of texts and with various types of participants (e.g., causers and causees that are animate vs. inanimate, male vs. female), he is able to demonstrate that *laten* and *doen* have undergone a complex set of changes in variation patterns over the centuries (see further below). His main methodological point is that in order to arrive at insights about cognitive and cultural models invoked by the use of *laten* and *doen*, investigation of corpora of actual usage events is indispensable.

Biber in his corpus-based investigations concentrates not so much on individual constructions, but on quantitative association patterns, i.e. clusters of cooccurring lexical and grammatical features, which he relates to different genres (i.e. different types of usage situations). In this volume, Biber reveals associations between different lexical items (*promise* and *tell*) and different argument structures (intransitive, transitive, etc.), which are in turned linked to specific genres or registers (e.g. Academic Prose and Conversation). He shows that strong linguistic associations in one register may represent rather weak associations in other registers, highlighting the intimate connection between choice of forms and context of use.

Barlow investigates the relation of patterns of usage to grammatical structure. It is clear that highly frequent, fixed collocations found in corpora, such as *from time to time*, can be tied to well-entrenched schemas or constructions. But what of the patterns in corpora that do not appear to be equivalent either to fixed units, on the one hand, or completely novel, creative utterances, on the other hand? Barlow explores the idea that the semi-fixed, semi-creative structures found in language use may be the result of a merger or blending process (Fauconnier and Turner 1996), which takes entrenched forms as one input in the creation of a blended structure. Evidence for this notion is based in Barlow's paper on the corpus-based analysis of idioms such as *make hay while the sun shines,* which turn out to display a surprising range of variability in form. The intimate intertwining of such idioms with other grammatical patterns calls for a rethinking of the often assumed division between productive syntax vs. fixed expressions.

A number of other studies in this volume investigate quantitative patterns in linguistic production data. Bybee, as already mentioned, uses a phonetically-transcribed corpus to study the effects of frequency on phonological variation. Ariel examines quantitative patterns in referential expressions and agreement marking in a variety of written and spoken texts of English and Hebrew. She compares occurrences, in various person and other categories, of a range of forms along a portion of what she has elsewhere identified as the Accessibility Hierarchy (Ariel 1990): here, the continuum from full NPs, to pronominal elements of various degrees of reduction, to 'pure agreement' forms, to no agreement.[5] Ariel shows that the predominant typological agreement pattern of first and second person agreement marking vs. no third person marking is motivated by the consistently greater referential accessibility (high salience) of the speech act participants compared to third person referents. Previous generalizations about the motivations for reduction and fusion processes, particularly by Bybee (1985), pointed to two factors, the conceptual coherence of adjacent morphemes ('relevance'), and the degree of frequency of phonological adjacency. Ariel's paper thus points to a more complex interaction between frequency and cognitive factors in the domain of reference than previously recognized.

Dickinson and Givón utilize still another data-oriented methodology to study linguistic productions. They investigate the recall of events in visually observed 'stories' under a range of experimental conditions. Their ultimate aim is to determine whether interactional vs. informational aspects of an ongoing communicative process are processed and entrenched in episodic memory in different ways. In this study they find that verbal interaction after a viewing episode significantly affects the recall of events, with different types of interaction (e.g. cooperative vs. uncooperative) affecting the degree of recall of the events. They suggest that cooperative interaction facilitates the coherent consolidation of information in memory. Dickinson and Givón's investigation illustrates the potential usefulness of manipulating cognitive variables under controlled conditions for discourse production. Most generally, it provides a valuable corrective to the often-assumed dichotomy between cognitively-oriented studies, which often ignore the interactional aspects of discourse, vs. interaction models, which often deemphasize cognitive processes.

Thus, the papers in this volume offer an eclectic array of different methodologies and data sources, each with its own advantages (and disadvantages). In our view, there is nothing to be gained by an insistence on, or rejection of, one particular method or type of data, even if we are far from a complete methodological synthesis. The most immediate aim is to determine how the various sorts of evidence relate to what speakers do in natural usage of language, and to understand what each kind of data can tell us about how ordinary comprehension and production of language work.

The intimate relation between usage, synchronic variation, and diachronic change. Patterns in usage data are in general patterns of variation along different dimensions of various kinds, from formal to social. In a cognitive usage-based model, variant linguistic forms can be thought of as alternate possibilities licensed by the linguistic network. The selection of a given entrenched variant for activation is governed by a complex set of motivating factors, including system-internal as well as contextual, situational factors. As observed in the seminal work of Labov, variation is highly structured, not only in the individual's system, but across groups of speakers. The effects of usage on the linguistic system as described earlier lead us to expect that speakers' language will be influenced by the productions they hear in particular speech communities of which they are members. As noted in Kemmer and Israel (1994: 167), "the more speakers talk to each other the more they will talk alike, and so linguistic variation will pattern along lines of social contact and interaction."

Bybee's paper demonstrates that greater frequency of a word correlates with greater phonological reduction in final consonant clusters. She makes the important claim that reduction occurs as a gradual diachronic process in the systems of individual speakers, by virtue of frequent repetition. Thus, linguistic usage is seen to be the locus of language change. Bybee sees speakers as initiating, and responding to, diachronic microchanges in their own and others' linguistic systems in the form of introductions of motivated variants and (lexically-influenced) change in the frequency of those variants that they hear around them. This influence is relatively weak, since learned conventional patterns, particularly with a system as automated as phonology, are strong.[6] But it is in principle measurable over time and with enough usage events.

Different speakers will not have precisely the same experience and will thus differ somewhat in the frequency of variants they exhibit. But speakers who interact with each other more are predicted to have more similar patterns of variation. Looking across groups defined by degree of interaction, rather than simply across individuals, we can see that the inevitable result, as well as reinforcer, of the kinds of microchanges Bybee envisages, is sociolinguistic variation, as speakers are influenced by those they interact with most and also influence them in turn.

In the case at least of motivated phonetic reductions, the change in proportion of variants typically proceeds in the direction of increase in the occurrence of the reduced variant(s), as the articulatory motivation for the change is reinforced by the increasing conventionalization of the reduced variant. When the proportion of 'non-reduced' variants has dropped to insignificance, historical linguists will refer to a diachronic change (reduction or loss); but clearly, the whole process has been characterized by change, and both children and adults have participated in it. At every stage also, the same motivations are operative: cognitive, articulatory, and social, affecting the perception and production acts of individuals. The effects of these motivations on each usage event are very slight, but cumulative over many usage events over time. Bybee's paper, in empirically linking lexical frequency with low-level synchronic variation, provides a new view of the relation between variation and lexical diffusion.

In a usage-based model of language change,[7] specific instances are extremely significant. Lexical items are important in syntax as well as phonology and morphology, and in syntax likewise we expect to find a similar relation between synchronic usage patterns and diachronic change. For example, it has been shown for English that basic clause-level constructions are linked with specific classes of verbs, and that particularly frequent verbs have a special relationship to their characteristic constructions (Goldberg 1998). Links between constructions and lexical items that frequently occur in them also appear to drive creative extensions of syntactic constructions, both synchronically and with cumulative diachronic effects over time (Israel and Kemmer 1993, Israel 1996).

Two other papers in the volume that relate synchronic patterns of variation in linguistic usage to patterns of diachronic change are those by Ariel and Verhagen. Ariel's paper addresses in comprehensive detail the question of why and how agreement markers develop out of personal pronouns. The data she provides on patterns of pronoun and agreement use in Hebrew in various genres is an excellent illustration of particular phases in the development of agreement markers, as well as a demonstration of the importance of referential accessibility as a motivation for forms and choice of variants in person paradigms. Verhagen's paper gives insight into how subtle changes in meaning of *laten* and *doen* in causative constructions can be tracked by observing shifts in frequency of these elements across various linguistic categories and genres.

The contributions of Bybee, Ariel, and Verhagen all illustrate that a dynamic, usage-based conception of the internal linguistic system provides a natural framework for understanding why variation and change exist in the first place, as well as for understanding the mechanisms that produce and propagate patterns of variation and change.[8] Acquisition, variation, and diachronic change are all reflexes of the dynamics of linguistic usage.

The interconnectedness of the linguistic system with non-linguistic cognitive systems. It is plausible, indeed a null-hypothesis, to assume that the process of abstracting what is similar in recurrent experiences (**schema abstraction** in Langacker's terms) is not intrinsically different in language from what happens for other types of experience. Humans are sensitive to patterns in experience, and learned patterns can be of many different types, constrained in particular ways by general properties of our cognitive makeup and our earliest pre-linguistic experience. Linguistic structure in this view is a subset of conceptual structure. The field of Cognitive Linguistics in general has elaborated this point in great detail, emphasizing, for example, the encyclopedic nature of linguistic concepts (Haiman 1980, Lakoff 1987, Langacker 1987, Lamb 1998). The work of Charles Fillmore on frame semantics is particularly important in showing how conventional linguistic units like words and grammatical constructions are understood against the background of conventional situations of use which include far more than linguistic information. He demonstrates, for example, that the semantic roles of participants in verbal events cannot be described solely in terms of generalized 'case roles', but instead emerge from highly structured frames of knowledge about particular kinds of actions and interactions (Fillmore 1977, Fillmore and Atkins 1992). These ideas lead to the notion of cognitive and cultural models as frameworks of understanding for the meanings of linguistic expressions. Such models are coherent systems of knowledge of varying degrees of complexity, from the simple and basic image schemas discussed in Lakoff (1990) to highly intricate and culture-specific models extracted from cultural and social experience, as in the paper by Verhagen.

Verhagen's paper takes as its starting point the general conceptual system of 'force dynamics' proposed in Talmy (1988), a cluster of related cognitive models which structure the expression of causation and interpersonal manipulation in language (see also Kemmer and Verhagen 1994). In Verhagen's diachronic study of Dutch *laten* and *doen* causative constructions, he demonstrates the centrality of language- and culture-specific force dynamic models in the functioning and change of the system of expression of causation. He argues that the changes in these constructions are linked with a set of changes in the models of personal and social interaction which form the underpinning for the meanings of the two verbs. For example, certain changes in the frequency of use of the two verbs relate to changes in the relations of authority between people in Dutch culture in the last two centuries. Verhagen's paper leads to some thought-provoking (re)consideration of the relation between language and culture.

The crucial role of context in the operation of the linguistic system. If as suggested above the processes of linguistic abstraction and categorization are not different in kind from such processes in other cognitive domains, then it is highly likely that both linguistic and non-linguistic patterns will be processed and learned in an integrated way. All aspects of language, from phonetics to semantics, are open to influence from both linguistic and non-linguistic context. Moreover, there is always the potential for regular aspects of context to become conventionalized and thus part of the linguistic system itself. In phonology, for example, both recurrent aspects of the articulatory and the social context are abstracted together and conventionally linked with phonological variants (Kemmer and Israel 1994). In semantics, it is well known that elements from pragmatic contexts in which an expression typically occurs can become part of its conventional meaning (Traugott, Forthcoming; see also Langacker, this volume Section 4.3).

There is always a complex interaction between cognitive representations (which have themselves been abstracted from many similar contextualized experiences) and contextual factors in the immediate situation of use. Verhagen in his paper highlights the indirectness of this relation as follows:

> Usage always involves specific speakers/writers, hearers/readers, at a specific time, in specific contexts; and since these influence production and understanding, facts of production and understanding do not in themselves relate immediately and unambiguously to the abstract models invoked by the words. (Verhagen, this volume: 270)

The context-dependent nature of linguistic production and understanding entails, among other things, the inevitable underspecification of linguistic forms. Language does not hold or "convey" meaning per se, but simply provides *cues* for meaning construction in context. A conceptualization occurring in a specific instance of language use is evoked by the linguistic forms used, but is necessarily far richer than any information specifically associated with those forms; such information, as noted above, is merely an abstraction from experience or use of the forms. This general view has been emphasized particularly by Fauconnier (e.g. Fauconnier 1997), influenced by Ducrot, referred to earlier; and it is a prominent feature in Langacker's work as well. Langacker, in his analysis of the mechanics of individual usage events in this volume, provides in effect a precise description of the relation between conventional linguistic categories and how speakers employ them to create meaning in context. The paper by Verhagen provides rich detail on the intimate interaction of contextual factors with the conventionalized cognitive models associated with linguistic forms.

The importance of context and in particular the social aspects of context for understanding the form and nature of language has historically been more of a major feature of British and other European linguistic traditions than traditions dominant in the U.S. such as American structuralism and Chomskyan linguistics. In Firthian linguistics in particular, as mentioned earlier, context plays a key role. This tradition has been continued in work by linguists such as John Sinclair and Michael Stubbs (e.g. Sinclair 1991, Stubbs 1996), who not only examine textual patterns such as collocations, but also the context of use of such patterns, whether relating to register, institutions, or culture. The work of Biber likewise emphasizes the connection between language use and situational, social and textual factors, with a concentration in the paper in this volume on the latter.

*   *   *   *

With this volume, our intent is to bring together a wide range of approaches in a context that highlights the importance of a fundamentally usage-based conception of language. In doing so we wish to make these ideas available not only for mutual cross-fertilization of the approaches represented but also to researchers working with other linguistic frameworks. This volume will be of interest not only to linguists but also to those in allied disciplines—psychologists, cultural and social anthropologists, applied linguists, computer scientists, artificial intelligence researchers, and others concerned with the nature of language and how it relates to cognitive functioning and social interaction. The study of language use, as illustrated in this volume, has a great deal to tell us about the way human language works.

Acknowledgments

We would like to thank the Rice University Department of Linguistics and the Rice School of Humanities for generous support for the Sixth Rice Biennial Symposium on Language in March 1995, the conference on which this volume is based. We particularly appreciate the support of our department chair, Professor James Copeland. The conference would not have been a success without the additional help and cooperation of the Rice graduate students in Linguistics, especially Polly Washburn, who assisted in making the conference arrangements. Many thanks to the staff at CSLI Publications, especially Dikran Karagueuzian and Kim Lewis for helping to guide this publication through to fruition. A special debt of gratitude goes to Sue-Wen Chiao for her hard work and attention to detail in making corrections on the proofs and her invaluable skills in computer-typesetting the manuscript. Her work was supported by a summer grant to the editors from the Rice School of Humanities. Equally heartfelt thanks to Vicki Suchanek, for similar tasks at an earlier phase of the production. Thanks to John Benjamins B.V. for permission to reprint a revised version of the Biber paper from *International Journal of Corpus Linguistics* 1(2), 171-197, 1996.

Notes

We are indebted to Michael Israel for insightful comments on an earlier draft of this Introduction. Any errors of interpretation of the work of authors cited is our sole responsibility.

1. A schema can be defined as a cognitive representation comprising a generalization over perceived similarities among instances of usage. Schemas arise via repeated activation of a set of cooccurring properties, and are used to produce and understand linguistic expressions. Langacker's paper describes how schemas are used to categorize (or license) utterances. In syntax schemas go by the name of constructional schemas or constructions. For various modes of representation of linguistic schemas, see in addition Bybee and Slobin (1982), Fillmore et al. (1988), Barlow and Kemmer (1994).

2. As Croft shows in his empirical study of the relation between intonation units and syntactic constructions, "the units employed for spoken communication are basically the units stored as constructions in the mind" (Croft 1995: 872-3).

3. Difference in level of analysis gives rise to apparent differences that on closer inspection fade in significance. For example, Bybee rejects the existence of linguistic units such as 'phonemes.' Langacker's representations make reference to such units, but as his discussion of the

connectionist interpretation of his model makes clear, he also views them as being reducible to patterns of activation and connection weights, immanent in the network, rather than separately-stored entities. His linguistic units have status in the network as higher-order representations similar to Lamb's higher-level nections (i.e., linking points for distributed information); they represent cognitive routines, i.e. entrenched patterns of co-activation. Bybee's networks have only lexical nodes, whose connections capture the same distributed information at a lower level. In both Langacker's and Bybee's models, phonemes ultimately reduce to motor routines at the lowest level, affected by the preceding and subsequent motor processes in speech. It remains to be seen if there are any empirical consequences that follow from whether entrenched units other than lexical items are redundantly represented as nodes in the network.

4. The work of Chafe (e.g. Chafe 1994) has contributed greatly to an understanding of how cognitive processing of language, particularly regarding focus of attention and topic development, relates to naturalistic language production (crucially including intonation) in discourse.

5. Pioneering work on reference and topicality which also studied quantitative patterns of referential forms in discourse was carried out by T. Givón and his associates (e.g. Givón 1983).

6. Moreover, in phonological production particularly, early experience may lead to greater entrenchment than later learning, due to greater plasticity in the motor cortex during childhood.

7. See Croft (2000) for theory of language change that is fundamentally usage-based.

8. Ferguson (1990) also stresses the close relation between patterns of variation and change. He shows how examining the differing probabilities of occurrence of phonological variants and their respective favoring conditions gives clues to what type of general diachronic process is underway, since superficially similar patterns of change can be distinguished by looking at their different associated patterns of synchronic variation.

References

Ariel, Mira. 1990. *Accessing NP Antecedents.* (Croom Helm Linguistic Series.) London: Routledge.

Barlow, Michael. 1996. Corpora for theory and practice. *International Journal of Corpus Linguistics* 1(1), 1-37.

Barlow, Michael, and Suzanne Kemmer. 1994. A schema-based approach to grammatical description. In Roberta Corrigan, Gregory Iverson and Susan Lima (eds.), *The Reality of Linguistic Rules,* 19-42. Amsterdam: John Benjamins.

Bates, Elizabeth. 1976. *Language and Context: Studies in the Acquisition of Pragmatics.* New York: Academic Press.

Benveniste, Emile. 1971. *Problems in General Linguistics.* Translated by Mary Elizabeth Meek. Coral Gables, Florida: University of Miami Press.

Bowerman, Melissa. 1982. Reorganizational processes in lexical and syntactic development. In Eric Wanner and Lila R. Gleitman (eds.), *Language Acquisition: The State of the Art,* 319-346. Cambridge: Cambridge University Press.

Bybee, Joan L. 1985. *Morphology: A Study of the Relation Between Meaning and Form.* (Typological Studies in Language 9.) Amsterdam: Benjamins.

Bybee, Joan L. 1988. Morphology as lexical organization. In Michael Hammond and Michael Noonan (eds.), *Theoretical Morphology: Approaches in Modern Linguistics,* 119-41. San Diego: Academic Press.

Bybee, Joan L. 1994. A view of phonology from a cognitive and functional perspective. *Cognitive Linguistics* 5(4), 285-305.

Bybee, Joan L. 1995. Regular morphology and the lexicon. *Language and Cognitive Processes* 10(5), 425-55.

Bybee, Joan L. and Dan I. Slobin. 1982. Rules and schemas in the development and use of the English past tense. *Language* 58, 265-89.

Chafe, Wallace. 1994. *Discourse, Consciousness, and Time: The Flow and Displacement of Conscious Experience in Speaking and Writing.* Chicago, IL: University of Chicago Press.

Chomsky, Noam. 1972. *Language and Mind.* New York: Harcourt Brace Jovanovich.

Chomsky, Noam. 1988. *Language and Problems of Knowledge: The Managua Lectures.* Cambridge, MA: MIT Press.

Crain, Stephen. 1991. Language acquisition in the absence of experience. *Behavioral and Brain Sciences* 14, 597-611.

Croft, William. 1995. Intonation units and grammatical structure. *Linguistics* 33, 839-882.

Croft, William. 2000. *Explaining Language Change: An Evolutionary Approach.* Harlow: Longman.

Culioli, Antoine. 1995. *Cognition and Representation in Linguistic Theory.* Texts selected, edited, and introduced by Michel Liddle, translated with the assistance of John T. Stonham. (Current Issues in Linguistic Theory, Vol. 112.) Amsterdam: Benjamins.

Deane, Paul. 1992. *Grammar in Mind and Brain: Explorations in Cognitive Syntax.* (Cognitive Linguistics Research 2.) Berlin: Mouton de Gruyter.

Ducrot, Oswald. 1984. *Le Dire et le Dit.* Paris: Minuit.

Elman, Jeffrey L. and James L. McClelland. 1984. Speech perception as a cognitive process: The interactive activation model. In Norman Lass (ed.), *Speech and Language,* Vol. 10, 337-74. New York: Academic Press.

Elman, Jeffrey L., Elizabeth Bates, Mark H. Johnson, Annette Karmiloff-Smith, Domenico Parisi, and Kim Plunkett. 1998. *Rethinking Innateness: A Connectionist Perspective on Development.* (Neural Network Modeling and Connectionism series.) Cambridge, MA: MIT Press.

Fauconnier, Gilles. 1997. *Mappings in Thought and Language.* Cambridge: Cambridge University Press.

Fauconnier, Gilles and Mark Turner. 1996. Blending as a central process of grammar. In Adele E. Goldberg (ed.), *Conceptual Structure, Discourse, and Language,* 113-130. Stanford: CSLI Publications.

Ferguson, Charles. 1990. From esses to aitches: Identifying pathways of diachronic change. In Croft, William, Keith Denning and Suzanne Kemmer (eds.), *Studies in Typology and Diachrony for Joseph H. Greenberg,* 59-78. (Typological Studies in Language 20.) Amsterdam: Benjamins.

Fillmore, Charles J. 1977. The case for case reopened. In Peter Cole and Jerry Sadock, (eds.), *Syntax and Semantics 8: Grammatical Relations,* 59-82. New York: Academic Press.

Fillmore, Charles J. and B.T.S. Atkins. 1992. Towards a frame-based lexicon: The semantics of *risk* and its neighbors. In Lehrer, Adrienne, and Eva Feder Kittay (eds.), *Frames, Fields, and Contrasts: New Essays in Semantic and Lexical Organization,* 75-102. Hillsdale, NJ: Lawrence Erlbaum.

Fillmore, Charles J., Paul Kay, and Mary Catherine O'Connor. 1988. Regularity and idiomaticity in grammatical constructions: The case of *let alone. Language* 64, 501-38.

Firth, John Rupert. 1957. A synopsis of linguistic theory. *Studies in Linguistic Analysis,* 1-32. Special Volume. London: Philological Society.

Fox, Barbara. 1994. Contextualization, indexicality, and the distributed nature of grammar. *Language Sciences* 16, 1-38.

Givón, T. (ed.). 1983. *Topic Continuity in Discourse: A Quantitative Cross-Linguistic Study.* (Typological Studies in Language 3.) Amsterdam: Benjamins.

Goldberg, Adele E. 1998. Patterns of experience in patterns of language. In Tomasello (ed.), 203-219.

Gupta, Prahlad and Brian MacWhinney. 1992. Integrating category acquisition with inflectional marking: A model of the German nominal system. *Proceedings of the Fourteenth Annual Conference of the Cognitive Science Society,* 253-8. Hillsdale, NJ: Lawrence Erlbaum.

Haiman, John. 1980. Dictionaries and encyclopedias. *Lingua* 50: 329-57.

Haiman, John. 1991. Motivation, repetition and emancipation: The bureaucratisation of language. In H. Christoph Wolfart, ed., *Linguistic Studies Presented to John L. Finlay,* 45-70. Winnipeg, Manitoba: Algonquian and Iroquoian Linguistics.

Haiman, John. 1994. Ritualization and the development of language. In William Pagliuca (ed.), *Perspectives on Grammaticalization*, 3-28. Amsterdam: Benjamins.

Hopper, Paul J. 1988. Emergent grammar and the a priori grammar postulate. In Deborah Tannen (ed.), *Linguistics in Context*, 117-134. Norwood, NJ: Ablex.

Hopper, Paul J. 1998. Emergent grammar. In Tomasello (ed.), 155-175.

Israel, Michael. 1996. The Way constructions grow. In Adele E. Goldberg (ed.), *Conceptual Structure, Discourse, and Language*, 217-230. Stanford: CSLI Publications.

Israel, Michael, and Suzanne Kemmer. 1993. Repetition is a form of change: A usage-based model of historical analogy. Presented at the Eleventh International Conference on Historical Linguistics, UCLA, August 1993.

Johnson, Christopher. 1999. *Constructional Grounding: The Role of Interpretational Overlap in Lexical and Constructional Acquisition*. Doctoral dissertation, University of California at Berkeley.

Kemmer, Suzanne and Michael Israel. 1994. Variation and the usage-based model. In Katherine Beals, et al. (eds.), *CLS 30: Papers from the 30th Regional Meeting of the Chicago Linguistic Society*, Vol. 2: *Parasession on Variation and Linguistic Theory*, 165-79. Chicago: CLS.

Kemmer, Suzanne, and Arie Verhagen. 1994. The grammar of causatives and the conceptual structure of events. *Cognitive Linguistics* 5(2), 115-156.

Lakoff, George. 1987. *Women, Fire, and Dangerous Things: What Categories Reveal About the Mind*. Chicago: University of Chicago Press.

Lakoff, George. 1990. The invariance hypothesis: Is abstract reason based on image-schemas? *Cognitive Linguistics* 1, 39-74.

Lamb, Sydney. 1998. *Pathways of the Brain. The Neurocognitive Basis of Language*. (Current Issues in Linguistic Theory, Vol. 170.) Amsterdam: Benjamins.

Langacker, Ronald W. 1987. *Foundations of Cognitive Grammar*, Vol. 1: *Theoretical Prerequisites*. Stanford, CA: Stanford University Press.

Langacker, Ronald W. 1988. A usage-based model. In Brygida Rudzka-Ostyn (ed.), *Topics in Cognitive Linguistics* (Current Issues in Linguistic Theory 50), 127-61. Amsterdam: Benjamins.

Langacker, Ronald W. 1990. The rule controversy: A Cognitive Grammar perspective. *Center for Research in Language Newsletter* 4(3), 4-15.

Langacker, Ronald W. 1991. *Foundations of Cognitive Grammar*, Vol. 2: *Descriptive Application*. Stanford, CA: Stanford University Press.

McClelland, James L. and David E. Rumelhart (eds.). 1986. *Parallel Distributed Processing: Explorations in the Microstructure of Cognition*, Vol. 2: *Psychological and Biological Models*. Cambridge, MA and London: MIT Press and Bradford.

MacWhinney, Brian. 1999a. The emergence of language from embodiment. In MacWhinney (ed.), 213-256.

MacWhinney, Brian (ed.). 1999b. *The Emergence of Language.* (Carnegie Mellon Symposia on Cognition.) Mahwah, NJ and London: Lawrence Erlbaum.

Pine, Julian and Elena Lieven. 1993. Reanalysing rote-learned phrases: Individual differences in the transition to multi-word speech. *Journal of Child Language* 20, 551-571.

Regier, Terry. 1996. *The Human Semantic Potential: Spatial Language and Constrained Connectionism.* Cambridge, MA: MIT Press.

Rumelhart, David E. and James L. McClelland (eds.). 1986. *Parallel Distributed Processing: Explorations in the Microstructure of Cognition*, Vol. 1: *Foundations.* Cambridge, MA and London: MIT Press and Bradford.

Sinclair, John. 1991. *Corpus, Concordance, Collocation.* Oxford: Oxford University Press.

Slobin, Dan I. 1985. Cross-linguistic evidence for the language-making capacity. In Dan Slobin (ed.), *A Cross-Linguistic Study of Language Acquisition,* Vol. 2, 1157-1256. Hillsdale, NJ: Lawrence Erlbaum.

Stubbs, Michael. 1996. *Text and Corpus Analysis: Computer-Assisted Studies of Language and Culture.* Oxford: Blackwell.

Talmy, Leonard. 1988. Force dynamics in language and cognition. *Cognitive Science* 12, 49-100.

Tomasello, Michael. 1992. *First Verbs: A Case Study of Early Grammatical Development.* New York and Cambridge: Cambridge University Press.

Tomasello, Michael (ed.). 1998. *The New Psychology of Language: Cognitive and Functional Approaches to Language Structure.* Mahwah, NJ and London: Lawrence Erlbaum.

Tomasello, Michael, Elena Lieven, Heike Behrens and Heike Forwergk. Forthcoming. Early syntactic creativity: A usage-based approach. Submitted for publication.

Traugott, Elizabeth. Forthcoming. The role of pragmatics in semantic change. In Jef Verschueren (ed.), *Pragmatics in 1998,* Vol. 2. Antwerp: International Pragmatics Association.

A Dynamic Usage-Based Model

RONALD W. LANGACKER
University of California, San Diego

1. The Usage-Based Conception

For better or for worse, I admit to having coined the term **usage-based model**. In *Foundations of Cognitive Grammar*, I described such a model as follows: "Substantial importance is given to the actual use of the linguistic system and a speaker's knowledge of this use; the grammar is held responsible for a speaker's knowledge of the full range of linguistic conventions, regardless of whether these conventions can be subsumed under more general statements. [It is a] nonreductive approach to linguistic structure that employs fully articulated schematic networks and emphasizes the importance of low-level schemas" (Langacker 1987a: 494). Subsequently, in the paper titled "A Usage-Based Model" (Langacker 1988), I described the "maximalist," "non-reductive," "bottom-up" nature of Cognitive Grammar. In these respects it stood in contrast to the "minimalist," "reductive," "top-down" spirit of generative theory, at least in its original (archetypal) formulation. Let me start by briefly describing each property.

Generative theory has always tried to minimize what a speaker has to learn and mentally represent in acquiring a language. Its minimalism was originally based on economy: the best grammar was the one that did the job with the fewest symbols. In recent years, the emphasis has shifted to posit-

1

ing a richly specified universal grammar, so that the role of experience in learning a language involves little more than the setting of parameters. By contrast, Cognitive Grammar accepts that becoming a fluent speaker involves a prodigious amount of actual learning, and tries to minimize the postulation of innate structures specific to language. I consider these to be empirical issues. If one aims for psychological reality, it cannot be maintained on purely methodological grounds that the most parsimonious grammar is the best one. Should it prove that the cognitive representation of language is in fact massive and highly redundant, the most accurate description of it (as a psychological entity) will reflect that size and redundancy. Regarding the issue of innate specification I make no apriori claims. I do however subscribe to the general strategy in cognitive and functional linguistics of deriving language structure insofar as possible from more general psychological capacities (e.g. perception, memory, categorization), positing inborn language-specific structures only as a last resort. I anticipate, moreover, that any such structures would constitute specialized adaptations of more general abilities, and thus be continuous with them rather than separate and *sui generis*.

The issue of reductionism pertains to the relation between general statements and more specific statements that amount to special cases of them. Suppose a speaker has learned both a general "rule" (such as the pattern for combining prepositions with their objects) and certain specific expressions which instantiate the pattern (e.g. *for me*, *on the floor*, *in the garage*). Traditionally, in generative accounts, the instantiating expressions would be excluded from the grammar on grounds of economy. Since they are regularly derivable by rule, to list them individually would be to miss a generalization. This reasoning however rests on the spurious assumption that rules and lists are mutually exclusive (the **rule/list fallacy**). There is a viable alternative: to include in the grammar both rules and instantiating expressions. This option allows any valid generalizations to be captured (by means of rules), and while the descriptions it affords may not be maximally economical, they have to be preferred on grounds of psychological accuracy to the extent that specific expressions do in fact become established as well-rehearsed units. Such units are cognitive entities in their own right whose existence is not reducible to that of the general patterns they instantiate.

The "top-down" spirit of generative grammar is evident in its emphasis on general rules and universal principles, as well as its historic neglect of lexicon, low-level subpatterns, and the patient enumeration of idiosyncrasies. Less-than-fully-general phenomena were in fact embarrassing and problematic from the outset, handled by a series of ad hoc devices (e.g. the "rule features" proposed in Lakoff 1970) appended to the rule-based system. Now certainly an objective in Cognitive Grammar is to capture whatever generalizations the data will support. There are nonetheless several respects in which the framework manifests a "bottom-up" orientation. For one thing, it recognizes that linguistic patterns occupy the entire spectrum ranging from the wholly idiosyncratic to the maximally general. In a complete account of language structure, fully general rules stand out as being atypical rather than paradigmatic. Another facet of Cognitive Grammar's bottom-up orientation is the claim that "rules" can only arise as schematizations of overtly occurring expressions. However far this abstraction may proceed, the schemas that emerge spring from the soil of actual usage. Finally, there is reason to believe that lower-level schemas, expressing regularities of only limited scope, may on balance be more essential to language structure than high-level schemas representing the broadest generalizations.

As I articulate the usage-based conception in the following sections, two basic themes ought to be borne in mind. First, the assumptions made about mental abilities and cognitive processing are, I think, both minimal and relatively non-controversial. If the approach proves adequate from the linguistic standpoint (and I take the entire body of work in Cognitive Grammar as suggesting that it is), then its psychological plausibility argues strongly in its favor. Second, this usage-based model achieves a high degree of conceptual unification: a few basic mechanisms are operative in all domains of language structure and afford a unified account of phenomena traditionally handled separately and in very different ways. Provided once more that the model is shown to be linguistically adequate, its unifying nature is another strong point in its favor. These factors, together with the austerity they entail in the positing of both psychological and linguistic entities, render the model intrinsically desirable. It seems to me that linguistic theorists should want to make it work as their first option and should abandon it only with great reluctance.

2. Psychological Phenomena

I start by recognizing a number of basic and very general psychological phenomena that are essential to language but certainly not limited to it. The first of these, which I refer to as **entrenchment**, has also borne such labels as "routinization," "automatization," and "habit formation." The occurrence of psychological events leaves some kind of trace that facilitates their re-occurrence. Through repetition, even a highly complex event can coalesce into a well-rehearsed routine that is easily elicited and reliably executed. When a complex structure comes to be manipulable as a "pre-packaged" assembly, no longer requiring conscious attention to its parts or their arrangement, I say that it has the status of a **unit**. It is convenient notationally to indicate unit status by means of boxes or square brackets, enclosing non-unit structures with closed curves or parentheses: [A] vs. (A).

A second basic phenomenon, **abstraction**, is the emergence of a structure through reinforcement of the commonality inherent in multiple experiences. By its very nature, this abstractive process "filters out" those facets of the individual experiences which do not recur. We will mostly be concerned with a special case of abstraction, namely **schematization**, involving our capacity to operate at varying levels of "granularity" (or "resolution"). Structures that appear very different when examined in fine-grained detail may nonetheless be quite comparable in a coarse-grained view. A **schema** is the commonality that emerges from distinct structures when one abstracts away from their points of difference by portraying them with lesser precision and specificity. I use a solid arrow for the relationship between a schema and a more specific structure that **instantiates** or **elaborates** it: A → B. The formula indicates that B conforms to the specifications of A but is characterized in finer-grained detail.

Also fundamental to cognition is the ability to **compare** two structures and detect any discrepancy between them. This operation involves an inherent asymmetry, whereby one structure functions as a **standard** of comparison, the other as its **target**. We can reasonably consider **categorization** to be a special case of comparison, obtaining when the standard represents an established unit and the target (at least originally) is novel. Categorization is most straightforward when there is no discrepancy, i.e. when the standard can be recognized in the target because the latter fully satisfies its specifications. In this case the two structures stand in an elaborative relationship: [A] → (B). An act of categorization may also register some disparity between the categorizing structure and the target. In this case I speak of **extension**, indicated with a dashed arrow: [A] ---> (B).

Yet another basic phenomenon is the combination of simpler structures to yield a more complex structure. Let us call this **composition**. It involves the **integration** of two or more **component** structures to form a **composite** structure. If [A] and [B] are units, not previously combined, their integration to produce the novel composite structure (C) can be given as follows: ([A] [B])$_C$. The formula should not however be taken as implying that (C) is merely the union of [A] and [B], nor that [A] and [B] occur unmodified in (C). When motor routines are chained together into a complex action, their coordination entails that no component routine is manifested in precisely the form it would have in isolation; typing *kl*, for instance, is not just the same as typing *k* then typing *l*. The same is clearly true of speech sounds, and (I would argue) of most any kind of conceptual integration. A composite structure has to be regarded as an entity in its own right, not strictly reducible to it components. For this reason I speak of **partial compositionality**.

Let us mention, finally, the well-known phenomenon of **association**, in which one kind of experience is able to evoke another. The particular kind of association that concerns us is **symbolization**: the association of conceptualizations with the mental representations of observable entities such as sounds, gestures, and written marks. An established symbolic relationship—a **symbolic unit**—is conveniently given as [[A] / [a]], where upper and lower case stand respectively for a conceptualization and a symbolizing structure. A symbolic structure is said to be **bipolar**: [A] is the **semantic pole**, and [a] the **phonological pole** (in the case of sounds).

While there may be differences in approach and terminology, I consider it self-evident that something akin to each phenomenon has to be ascribed to cognition generally and to language in particular. It should also be evident that these operations occur in various combinations, some applying to the results of others. Composition, for example, is applicable to its own output—composite structures can in turn function as components integrated to form a more elaborate composite structure. Repeated episodes of composition yield constituency hierarchies having indefinitely many levels of organization. Here is another plausible sequence of operations: $(A_1), (A_2), (A_3) >$ $[A] > ([A] \rightarrow (A_4)) > [[A] \rightarrow [A_4]]$. From a series of similar experiences, represented as $(A_1), (A_2),$ and (A_3), a schema emerges that embodies their commonality and achieves the status of a unit, [A]. This structure is subsequently used to categorize a new experience, (A_4), which instantiates it. If (A_4) recurs and continues to be recognized as an instance of [A], both it and the categorizing relationship undergo entrenchment and gain unit status. $[[A] \rightarrow [A_4]]$ then constitutes an established categorization.

I suggest that repeated applications of such processes, occurring in different combinations at many levels of organization, result in cognitive assemblies of enormous complexity. The vision that emerges is one of massive networks in which structures with varying degrees of entrenchment, and representing different levels of abstraction, are linked together in relationships of categorization, composition, and symbolization. This is precisely the view of language that I advocate, and for many years I have been trying to demonstrate that all facets of linguistic structure can be reasonably described in these terms.

3. Processing Interpretation

The network model just presented deserves to be handled with caution, for like any metaphor it has the potential to mislead. In particular, the network metaphor encourages us to think of linguistic structures as discrete, object-like entities forming a static assembly observable as a simultaneously available whole. All of these features are problematic in regard to the neural implementation of language. From the processing standpoint, language must ultimately reside in patterns of neurological activity. It does not consist of discrete objects lodged in the brain, and it cannot all be manifested at any one time. An important question, then, is whether and how these two perspectives can be reconciled.

As a general orientation, I incline to the **connectionist** style of computation based on **parallel distributed processing** (McClelland and Rumelhart 1986; Rumelhart and McClelland 1986). This mode of processing has the advantage of resembling what the brain actually does, at least at a basic level, and I believe it to be both realistic and revelatory with respect to language. I realize how enormous the gap is between existing PDP models and a system that would approximate the actual complexity of linguistic structure, even in limited domains. This huge discrepancy reflects the fact that the PDP-style processing constitutive of human language occurs in the context of a highly-structured brain of unfathomable complexity, and draws upon the structures that progressively emerge over the course of many years through continuous and multifaceted interaction with a rich environment. Since actual connectionist systems are not embedded in such a matrix, there are severe limitations on how close they can come to realistically modeling linguistic structure. That is not *per se* an argument against connectionist-type processing, however.

Here I will merely try to indicate that the psychological phenomena discussed in the previous section can all be given a connectionist interpretation. For analytical purposes, it is helpful (if not necessary) to think in terms of discrete structures represented by distinct symbols enclosed in brackets or boxes. Such reifications are not too harmful so long as we do not lose sight of the dynamic reality they conceal. In the final analysis, linguistic structures and relationships reside in cognitive processing, identified as neurological activity.

Entrenchment is straightforwardly identifiable as an adjustment in connection weights, brought about by the occurrence of a pattern of activation, which renders more likely the re-occurrence of the same or a comparable pattern. With respect to the system's movement through state space, entrenchment amounts to the emergence of an attractor. The term fits quite well with the topographical conception of state space, where attractors of different strength are thought of as wells or valleys of varying depth that the system tends to settle into as it relaxes into a state of minimum energy.

Connectionist systems are well known for their ability to extract whatever regularities are inherent in their input. I have previously discussed the extraction of schemas in connectionist terms (Langacker 1990; 1991: 12.3). Let me first reiterate that discrete representations such as A → B are not to be taken as implying that a schema and its instantiation are wholly distinct and separately stored. Rather, I think of schemas as being **immanent** in their instantiations, and while a schema may in some cases be independently accessible (e.g. the schematic notion common to *apple, orange, banana*, etc. is individually symbolized by *fruit*), there is no supposition that this is true in general. In saying that a schema is extracted, what is necessarily being claimed is actually fairly minimal: that the commonality inherent in multiple experiences is reinforced and attains some kind of cognitive status, so that it has the potential to influence further processing. This is, I think, equivalent to Bybee's (1988) notion of "connections" established between overlapping portions of stored units.

In offering a connectionist interpretation of schema extraction, we can first equate a particular experience (or "structure") with either a point in state space or a trajectory through it (cf. Elman 1990). To the extent that two experiences are similar, their constitutive patterns of neural activation will be neighbors in state space: either points in close proximity, or trajectories following roughly parallel courses. We can focus on the simpler case of points, since a trajectory reduces to a series of points ordered in processing time. Suppose, then, that the patterns representing a number of similar structures all cluster in the same general region of state space. Call this region R. The occurrence of a given pattern will impact connection weights in such a way that the occurrence of any pattern close to it in state space will tend to be facilitated. The repeated use of similar structures will thus facilitate the occurrence of any pattern within the general region R. This amounts to the extraction of a schema. With reference to state space, a schema is describable as a basin of attraction (R) which subsumes a number of more point-like locations corresponding to its instantiations. A schema is immanent in its instantiations in the sense that being located in a point-like region of state space entails being located in a broader region that encompasses it.

Categorization is then interpretable as capture by an attractor. Presenting the system with a certain input tends to activate a variety of previously established patterns, some of which may be mutually inhibitory. When an input (B) results in the full activation of pattern [A]—which may have won out over numerous competitors—we can reasonably say that [A] is used to categorize (B). Of course, if the input is only fragmentary, categorization via the activation of [A] may serve to reconstitute the full, familiar experience it represents. The categorizing experience will also be qualitatively different depending on whether (B) is compatible with [A] or succeeds in eliciting [A] despite some discrepancy between them. We will return to these matters in the following section.

With respect to composition, it can plausibly be suggested that component structures are to some degree activated in the process of carrying out the more elaborate pattern of activation constitutive of the composite conception. Ultimately I would like to argue that composition reduces to categorization (Langacker 1987a: 12.2). I have already noted that component structures are not appropriately conceived as "building blocks" stacked together to form the composite structure. The latter is an entity in its own right, facets of which correspond to the components but either elaborate or diverge from their specifications. I believe the component structures are properly thought of as categorizing those facets of the composite structure to which they correspond. Like other categorizing structures, the components are in some sense prior, most obviously in cases where they represent established units while the composite structure is novel. Moreover, a composite structure resembles the target of categorization in being the structure of concern, the one being assessed in relation to others having some kind of prior standing. Yet another resemblance between composition and categorization is that in each case the quality of the target experience is partially shaped and (re)-constituted by the structures activated for its assessment.

Finally, symbolization is readily interpretable as one pattern of activation reliably serving to elicit another. If semantic structures are represented as patterns occurring in one bank of processing units, and phonological structures in another, a connectionist system can easily be trained to establish the proper correlations.

4. Basic Linguistic Problems

In Cognitive Grammar, a language is described as a **structured inventory of conventional linguistic units**. The units (cognitive "routines") comprising a speaker's linguistic knowledge are limited to semantic, phonological, and symbolic structures which are either directly manifested as parts of actual expressions, or else emerge from such structures by the processes of abstraction (schematization) and categorization (this restriction is called the **content requirement**). In describing these units as an inventory, I am indicating the non-generative and non-constructive nature of a linguistic system. Linguistic knowledge is not conceived or modeled as an algorithmic device enumerating a well-defined set of formal objects, but simply as an extensive collection of semantic, phonological, and symbolic resources which can be brought to bear in language processing. This inventory of resources is structured in the sense that some units are incorporated as parts of larger units, specifically in relationships of categorization, composition, and symbolization: [[A] ---> [B]]; [[A] [B]]$_C$; [[A] / [a]]. For some purposes it may be helpful to reify linguistic knowledge or ability as something called the "grammar" of a language. We must however resist the temptation to think of it as a separate or sharply bounded cognitive entity, if only because a structure's characterization as being conventional, linguistic, or a unit is inherently a matter of degree (Langacker 1987a: 2.1).

Can a grammar of this sort actually do the job? We somehow have to deal with a number of basic problems: the creation and understanding of novel expressions; the ascription of particular structures to such expressions; judgments of well- and ill-formedness; distributional restrictions; and the varying degrees of compositionality, productivity, and generality exhibited by linguistic structures and patterns. At least some of these problems were straightforwardly handled by classic generative grammars formulated as constructive devices. That kind of grammar defines an "output" containing an infinite set of sentences (mostly novel) which are by definition well-formed ("all and only the grammatical sentences of a language"). Moreover, an expression's "structural description" is recoverable from the sequence of rules that apply in its derivation. The question, then, is how a grammar that is neither generative nor constructive—a mere inventory of semantic, phonological, and symbolic resources—can deal with the problems mentioned. How can the units constitutive of established linguistic knowledge be related to actual expressions, especially novel ones?

4.1 Categorization of Usage Events

It is not the linguistic system *per se* that constructs and understands novel expressions, but rather the language user, who marshals for this purpose the full panoply of available resources. In addition to linguistic units, these resources include such factors as memory, planning, problem-solving ability, general knowledge, short- and longer-term goals, as well as full apprehension of the physical, social, cultural, and linguistic context. An actual instance of language use, resulting from all these factors, constitutes what I call a **usage event**: the pairing of a vocalization, in all its specificity, with a conceptualization representing its full contextual understanding. A usage event is thus an utterance characterized in all the phonetic and conceptual detail a language user is capable of apprehending. For immediate purposes it makes no difference whether we consider the speaker or the addressee, since each has to establish some connection between the linguistic system and a usage event that supposedly manifests it. In comprehension, the hearer has to interpret the event as the intended realization of particular linguistic structures. In production, the speaker has to select linguistic structures capable of evoking the desired contextual understanding, and has to then ensure that the event can indeed be so interpreted.

In both production and comprehension, therefore, facets of a usage event must somehow be assessed in relation to linguistic units. I take this to be a matter of categorization. Let us consider the minimal case, in which a single linguistic unit, [A], is used to categorize a particular facet, (B), of a usage event. There are two basic possibilities, depicted in Figure 1, where the box labeled L represents the linguistic system (i.e. the inventory of conventional units), and the overall usage event is given as the circle labeled U. On the one hand, [A] can be recognized in (B), which thus instantiates [A], as seen in Figure 1(a). This amounts to the judgment that (B) is **well-formed** with respect to [A]. We can also describe it as being **conventional**, in the sense of conforming to the linguistic convention embodied in [A]. On the other hand, there may be some discrepancy between the two structures. In this case (B) is not perceived as an elaboration of [A], but rather as an extension from it, as shown in 1(b). This amounts to the judgment that (B) is **ill-formed**, or **non-conventional**, with respect to [A].

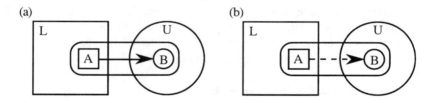

Figure 1. Categorizing Usage Events

We have already noted the oversimplification inherent in representing the linguistic system, L, as a discrete box. For example, since entrenchment is a matter of degree, there is no clear line of demarcation between novel structures and those with the status of units. Moreover, a boundary imposed at any particular threshold will continually fluctuate, since every use of a structure reinforces it and entrenches it more deeply, whereas non-use has the opposite effect. Even the first occurrence of a novel structure constitutes an

initial step along the path of progressive entrenchment and conventionalization, assuming that it leaves some kind of trace in at least one member of
the speech community. Suppose, then, that structure (B) begins to occur
with some frequency in a speech community, and that speakers consistently
invoke unit [A] to categorize it. For example, [A] might be the basic meaning of a lexical item, and (B) a semantic extension (as when *mouse* first
started being applied to a piece of computer equipment). With frequent recur-
rence, both (B) and ([A] ---> (B)), i.e. (B)'s categorization as an extension
from [A], will become progressively entrenched and eventually achieve the
status of units. To the extent that this happens, both [B] and the categorizing relationship [[A] ---> [B]] become members of L as a matter of definition. Figure 2 diagrams the expansion of L to incorporate these new conventional units.

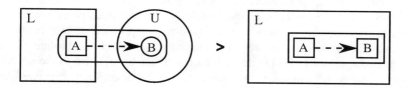

Figure 2. Entrenchment and Conventionalization of a Categorizing Relationship

Actually, a slight refinement of Figure 2 should be noted. Since (B) is
part of a usage event, it represents a conceptual or phonetic structure in the
full detail of its contextual apprehension. Numerous fine-grained details, as
well as contingent features of the context, are bound to vary from one usage
event to the next. On successive occasions, for example, the referents of
mouse may be slightly different shades of gray and occupy different positions vis-à-vis the computer. Failing to recur consistently, such details will
not be reinforced and hence will not be included in the new conventional
unit that emerges. The categorizing judgments that occur on particular occasions can thus be given as ([A] ---> (B_1)), ([A] ---> (B_2)), ([A] --->
(B_3)), etc., where the subscripts indicate divergence in the targets. The
structures that undergo entrenchment and achieve the status of conventional
units are schematic relative to those which figure in any actual usage event:
[B] is schematic with respect to (B_1), (B_2), and (B_3), and [[A] ---> [B]] with
respect to ([A] ---> (B_1)), ([A] ---> (B_2)), and ([A] ---> (B_3)). The point

is a general one—linguistic units are always schematic in relation to their instantiations in actual usage events.

Repeated occurrences of the processes sketched in Figures 1 and 2 can naturally be expected, and a unit added to L at any point is then eligible to serve as a categorizing structure in subsequent occurrences. Thus, from a single structure [A], there may eventually develop an elaborate **network** comprising any number of conventional units linked by categorizing relationships. These structures and relationships are said to form a **complex category**. To the extent that the network consists of chains of extensions radiating outward from [A] (thereby identifiable as the prototype), it constitutes a "radial category" (Lakoff 1987).

While accepting the insight and basic validity of the radial model based on extension (i.e. A ---> B), I also emphasize schematization and relationships of instantiation (A → B), if only because the latter correspond to essential linguistic phenomena: the extraction of generalizations, and judgments of well-formedness (conventionality). The two kinds of categorization are in any case very intimately related (and may in practice be hard to distinguish). Both involve an act of comparison in which a standard (S) is matched against a target (T). Instantiation can then be regarded as the special, limiting case of extension that arises when the discrepancy registered between S and T happens to be zero. Conversely, if categorization is interpreted as the attempt to "recognize" S in T, then instantiation represents the privileged case where this happens unproblematically, and extension constitutes recognition accomplished only with a certain amount of "strain." The source of the strain is that, for S to be recognized in a target which does not fully conform to its specifications, the conflicting features of S somehow have to be suppressed or abstracted away from.

Extension can thus be thought of as recognition achieved at the cost of invoking a schematized version of the categorizing structure, one whose coarser-grained specifications are satisfied by the target. For this reason I suggest that extension tends to be accompanied by schematization, that the "outward" growth of a network by extensions from a prototype tends to induce its "upward" growth via the extraction of higher-level schemas. The general mechanism is diagrammed in Figure 3. I presume that extension does not occur at random; there is always some basis for it. The categorization of (B) as an extension from [A] implies some abstract commonality—however limited or tenuous—which enables [A] to be evoked for that purpose in the first place and to successfully categorize (B) despite a conflict in their properties. By definition, that commonality amounts to a schema, labeled (A') in the diagram, having both [A] and (B) as instantiations. It is not necessary that (A') be salient or separately apprehended, or that it endure beyond its fleeing occurrence as an implicit facet of the categorizing event

([A] ---> (B)). Still, the very fact that [A] and (B) occur together tends to reinforce their commonality and thus facilitates (A')'s emergence as an established cognitive entity. Should (A') attain the status of a unit, it is validly describable as both a schema instantiated by [A] and (since the latter is prior) as an extension from it: [[A'] → [A]]; [[A] ---> [A']].

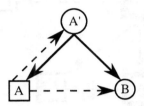

Figure 3. Extension and Schematization

I assume, then, that linguistic categories are usually complex, developing from prototypical structures via such processes as extension, the extraction of schemas, and the articulation of coarse-grained units into more specific ones (as finer discriminations are made and particular instantiations gain unit status). Bearing in mind the limitations of the metaphor, we can view complex categories as **networks** in which linguistic structures of any kind and any size are linked in pairwise fashion by categorizing relationships (Langacker 1987a: ch. 10). These structures—the "nodes" or vertices of the network—might consist, for example, of the allophones of a phoneme, the alternate senses of a lexical item, a family of related metaphors, or variant forms of an elaborate grammatical construction. There is more to such a network, however, than just a set of nodes and a set of arcs connecting them. Additionally, each structure and each categorizing relationship has some degree of entrenchment and ease of activation. Moreover, the target of categorization in each case lies at a certain "distance" from the standard, depending on how far T elaborates S or how many features of S it violates. Entrenchment and distance are respectively indicated in Figure 4 by the thickness of boxes and the length of arrows. In general, though, my diagrams will not attempt to represent these parameters.

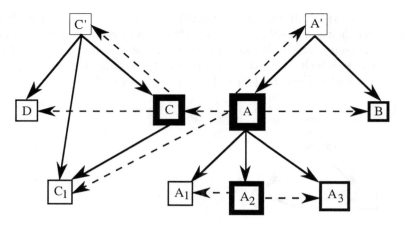

Figure 4. Complex Category Network

4.2 Selection of Categorizing Structures

At this juncture a basic problem arises. I have suggested that the units constitutive of linguistic knowledge are related to actual expressions by means
of categorization, as shown in Figure 1. Yet even a single category may
well contain a large number of units all of which are in principle available
to categorize some particular facet of a usage event. They cannot all do so at
once, for chaos would then ensue. A given target is well-formed with respect
to certain potential categorizing units and ill-formed with respect to others.
Unless these units are recruited in some specific way to assess the target (on
any one occasion), there will be no basis for the clear judgments of well-
and ill-formedness that commonly occur. I assume, in fact, that primary
categorization is effected by just one unit at any given moment. How, then,
does a particular target manage to be categorized by a single unit selected
from a large network of potential categorizing structures?

Let me first point out that this is a general problem in cognition, not
specifically a linguistic one. Consider the recognition of a familiar face.
Among others, I possess schematized representations of both Suzanne
Kemmer's face and Sydney Lamb's. When Suzanne walks into the room, I
usually manage to correctly recognize her as Suzanne and not confuse her
with Syd. To do so, I have to activate the Kemmer schema for the categorization of my visual experience, not the Lamb schema—otherwise I would
see her as Sydney Lamb and marvel at how much he had changed. Suzanne
is, after all, a very good instance of Suzanne, but a rather poor instance of

Syd. Depending on which schema I activate, therefore, the episode of facial recognition will yield a judgment of either well-formedness or deviance, as sketched in Figure 5.

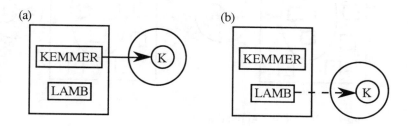

Figure 5. Face Recognition

For both linguistic and non-linguistic input, I assume we have to tell a certain kind of story. It has no claim to novelty, being basically what is envisaged in the interactive activation model (Elman and McClelland 1984; McClelland and Elman 1986a; McClelland and Elman 1986b), the competition model (MacWhinney 1987), and for that matter in connectionist processing generally. The story runs more or less as follows. A particular target of categorization tends to activate a variety of established units, any one of which could in principle serve to categorize it. Let us call this set of units (which may belong to a single complex category or to multiple categories) the **activation set** of the target. Initially, as shown in Figure 6(a), the members of the activation set are all activated by T to some degree. (Observe that here the thickness of boxes corresponds to level of activation rather than entrenchment.) Since we usually interpret an expression in a particular way, presumably only one member actually categorizes T on a given occasion. The members of the activation set must in effect compete for this privilege; some are no doubt mutually inhibitory and tend to suppress one another. One member of the activation set eventually wins the competition in the sense of becoming highly active relative to all the others. It is this unit—termed the **active structure**—which serves to categorize the target, as seen in 6(b).

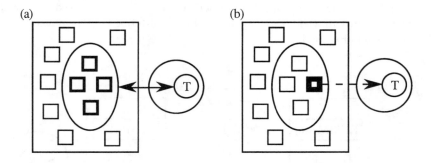

Figure 6. Interactive Activation

Several factors interact to determine which particular member of the activation set wins the competition and emerges as the active structure evoked to categorize the target. The first is level of entrenchment, or inherent likelihood of activation. In a neutral context, for example, *Bali* would more easily be misheard as *belly* than conversely. A second factor is contextual priming, which can override the effects of familiarity. Suppose we are discussing our upcoming trip to Bali and (my mind wandering) I happen to say—out of the blue—that I would like to see some *belly dancers*. The context might well lead you to misinterpret me as saying that I want to see some *Bali dancers*. A third factor is the amount of overlap between the target and a potential categorizing structure. We can reasonably assume that the sharing of features is what enables the target to stimulate members of the activation set in the first place, and that the degree of stimulation is roughly proportional to the number of features shared. This has the important consequence that lower-level schemas, i.e. structures with greater specificity, have a built-in advantage in the competition with respect to higher-level schemas. Other things being equal, the finer-grained detail of a low-level schema affords it a larger number of features potentially shared by the target.

We can now describe, in very general terms, how expressions are evaluated with respect to the linguistic system. A usage event has many facets susceptible to categorization by conventional linguistic units, which in Cognitive Grammar are limited to semantic, phonological, and symbolic structures. The potential categorizing units are entrenched to varying degrees and form a vast, structured inventory through relationships of symbolization, composition, and categorization. These units can be of any size, represent any dimension of linguistic structure, and are characterized at all levels of specificity. By virtue of overlapping content, each facet of the usage event serves to activate a set of potential categorizing structures—its activation set—which then compete for the right to categorize it. The winner of each competition is determined by a dynamic interactive process on the basis of degree of overlap, inherent ease of activation (correlated with entrenchment), contextual priming, and mutual inhibition. The resulting set of categorizations, in which the winners (the active structures) categorize the facets of the usage event which elicit them, constitute the expression's **structural description** (i.e. its interpretation with respect to the linguistic system). The expression is fully well-formed (conventional) provided that all of these categorizations are elaborative in nature. It is ill-formed (non-conventional) to the extent that any of them involve extension rather than elaboration. We can expect many extensions to pass unnoticed in normal language use. It is only when a conflict is egregious, or when small conflicts have a cumulative effect, that the strain they produce rises to the level of conscious awareness (cf. Ross 1987). In principle, then, a linguistic system conceived as being non-generative and non-constructive can nonetheless support the ascription of structural descriptions to expressions and provide the basis for judgments of well- and ill-formedness. One need only envisage this inventory of semantic, phonological, and symbolic resources as being embedded in a dynamic processing system which operates in accordance with minimal and highly plausible assumptions.

4.3 Categorization vs. Construction

I have posed the question of whether the linguistic system *per se* specifies in full detail how expressions are constructed (thus characterizing a well-defined set of expressions as its "output"), or whether it is merely an inventory of units invoked for the categorization of usage events. Should responsibility for constructing expressions be assigned to the "grammar," or to the language user drawing upon a full range of psychological and contextual resources? Though it may seem slight, this distinction has important consequences for how we think about linguistic problems. At stake are basic questions such as the scope of linguistic meaning, how rules are related to instantiating expressions, and whether the linguistic system constitutes a discrete, well-delimited cognitive entity.

The difference between construction and categorization can first be illustrated by a simple case of semantic extension, e.g. the extension of *mouse* to indicate a piece of computer equipment. Prior to the first occurrence of this usage, the linguistic system (for a representative speaker of English) contained the symbolic unit [[MOUSE] / [mouse]], where the semantic structure given as [MOUSE] designates a type of rodent, and [mouse] stands for the phonological structure that symbolizes it. Consider now a speaker who—for the very first time—faced a usage event in which the same term was used in reference to a computer device. We can represent this novel expression as ((MOUSE') / [mouse]), where (MOUSE') is the conception of the new referent. Now, in either producing or comprehending this novel usage, the speaker must somehow relate it to the conventional unit [[MOUSE] / [mouse]], from which it derives via the metaphorical extension ([MOUSE] ---> (MOUSE')). It is evident that the linguistic system *per se* cannot be responsible for constructing the new expression ((MOUSE') / [mouse]), if only because the concept (MOUSE') is (by assumption) a novel one. It is clearly the speaker who, from the context (e.g. seeing the device on a desk) and by means of abilities that are not specifically linguistic, entertains the new conception and apprehends the resemblance that motivates the extension. The role of the conventional unit [[MOUSE] / [mouse]] is not to construct but simply to categorize the new expression, which it motivates by serving as the basis for metaphorical extension. Of course, once the usage becomes familiar and conventionalized, it is incorporated in the language as the new symbolic unit [[MOUSE'] / [mouse]], in the manner of Figure 2.

In terms of this scenario, what can we identify as the meaning of *mouse* at different stages? According to standard doctrine, its linguistic meaning was simply [MOUSE] when first applied to the novel conception (MOUSE'), since the latter was not yet a conventional semantic value; its metaphorical understanding in the context of the initial usage event lies beyond the scope of linguistic semantics. Yet standard practice would accept [MOUSE'] as a conventional meaning of *mouse* at the present time. When did this change in status occur? When did (MOUSE') go from being an extra-linguistic understanding of *mouse* to being one of its linguistic semantic values? Does such a transition occur after one usage event? After seven? After *m* usage events involving each of *n* speakers? We could certainly adopt a threshold number to determine when new senses will be described as "linguistic" and admitted to the mental lexicon. This would allow us to maintain a strict dichotomy between linguistic and non-linguistic meanings, consistent with the notion that a language is a discrete and well-delimited cognitive entity. I submit, however, that any particular threshold would be arbitrary, in which case the claim that linguistic meanings are clearly distinguishable from contextual understandings is vacuous, rendered true just as a matter of definition.

I prefer to view things in a rather different manner. The very first time the term *mouse* is used in regard to a piece of computer equipment, it is contextually understood by the interlocutors as referring to that device. It is also so understood (in appropriate contexts) once the new sense is fully established as a conventional semantic value. Since *mouse* is understood with the value (MOUSE') from the very outset, and winds up having [MOUSE'] as

an indisputably linguistic meaning, it seems pointless to say that (MOUSE')
was ever non-linguistic (though it did start out being non-conventional).
Stated more precisely, and in positive terms, I would want to say the following. On the occasion of the initial usage event, *mouse* has the meaning
([MOUSE] ---> (MOUSE')), i.e. the conception of the computer device construed metaphorically as a kind of rodent. Through continued usage, this
complex meaning undergoes progressive entrenchment and conventionalization, and eventually the metaphorical value [[MOUSE] ---> [MOUSE']]
emerges as a fully conventional meaning of *mouse* with unit status. The
only thing special about the initial usage event is that the linguistic meaning's prior entrenchment and conventionality lie at the zero end of the scale.
However, the very first use starts to move it away from the endpoint, and to
the extent this happens it becomes part of the linguistic system.

By limiting the role of linguistic units to categorization, we can thus
account for extension in a straightforward way that avoids the imposition of
artificial boundaries. Of course, since a grammar is not usually thought of
as "constructing" extended meanings, this may not seem terribly consequen-
tial. I would argue, however, that the same considerations apply in the formation of complex expressions in accordance with grammatical rules. Here
the distinction between a categorizing and a constructive role for linguistic
units leads to more tangible results.

Consider the grammatical pattern of deriving nouns from verbs with the
suffix *-er*. Since the actual semantic complexity of the phenomenon need
not concern us (cf. Ryder 1991), we can focus on the basic pattern whereby
a verb with the meaning 'do X' yields a noun which means 'something that
does X.' Thus an *eraser* is 'something that erases,' a *printer* is 'something
that prints,' etc. The process is of course productive. Whereas *eraser*, *printer*,
and many others are now well-established lexical items, novel expressions
on the same pattern are freely coined and readily understood.

Clearly, though, an *eraser* is not just 'something that erases,' and a
printer is more than just 'something that prints.' In what is now its primary
meaning, for example, *printer* specifically indicates an electronic device, of a
certain approximate size, which is run by a computer to record its output on
paper (hence the word would not be applied to a traditional mechanical printing press). That meaning clearly represents a substantial elaboration vis-à-
vis the expression's **compositional meaning**, i.e. the one predictable on
the basis of the grammatical pattern it instantiates. Moreover, a novel *V-er*
expression can perfectly well be understood in such a highly specific way on
the very first occasion of its use. Imagine a computer novice who is shown
a printer in operation and hears it called by that term. The context will allow
this person to understand *printer* as referring specifically to an electronic device of this kind, even in the absence of prior exposure to the usage.

In such cases, a constructive view of grammatical rules engenders conceptual difficulties. Since the grammar itself is incapable of conceptual understanding, it can only yield the compositional meaning of a novel expression, not the full **contextual meaning** it actually has for a speaker. The same problems then arise as before (with *mouse*) concerning the discrepancy between what the grammar says an expression means and how speakers actually understand it from the very outset, as well as the arbitrariness of deciding when the contextual meaning should properly be accepted as the expression's conventional semantic value. Moreover, with compositional patterns a further difficulty ensues. If the *V-er* pattern is constructive in nature, it gives as "output" an open-ended set of forms such as *computer, printer, eraser, enabler, visualizer, freezer, deepener, stretcher, recycler,* etc. Many of these forms clearly exist as established lexical units whose conventional meanings are either elaborations or extensions with respect to their compositional meanings. What, then, does a constructive grammar say about the relationship between a compositional pattern and a particular lexical item with such a value? How, for example, is the *V-er* pattern related to the lexical unit *printer* that specifically designates a computer accessory? There are two options, neither of them descriptively adequate: *printer* can simply be listed as a lexical item completely unrelated to the pattern; alternatively, it can be treated as an instance of the pattern (included in the output of the rule), in which case its linguistic meaning would have to be simply 'something that prints.' In a purely constructive approach, it cannot simultaneously instantiate the pattern and have a semantic value that diverges from its compositional meaning.

I realize that a purely constructive view of grammar is no longer fashionable, and that the problem can be avoided by such devices as full lexical listings and redundancy rules (e.g. as in Jackendoff 1975). The essential point is that a usage-based model of the sort I advocate avoids the problem altogether. If all linguistic regularities are embodied in schematized templates whose role is merely to categorize expressions, special apparatus is not required since the problem never arises in the first place. Let me note in passing, without pausing to argue the matter in detail, that precisely the same issues arise in syntax. What we intuitively feel to be the linguistic meaning of a complex syntactic structure (e.g. a clause or a sentence) is usually more elaborate than its compositional value, or else diverges from it. The only real difference is that syntactic structures are less likely than morphological ones to recur and establish themselves as conventional units with extra-compositional meanings.

4.4 Composition

Let us take a closer look at how a non-constructive model deals with complex novel expressions and their relation to established grammatical patterns. In Cognitive Grammar, complex expressions are described as **assemblies of symbolic structures**. These assemblies consist primarily of compositional relationships, wherein two or more component symbolic structures are integrated—semantically and phonologically—to form a composite symbolic structure. For example, the component symbolic units [[JAR] / [jar]] and [[LID] / [lid]] are integrated to form the composite symbolic structure [[JAR LID] / [jar lid]]. An assembly of this kind, involving composition at one level of organization, is a **minimal construction**. Larger assemblies arise when the composite structure of one minimal construction functions in turn as a component structure in another, representing a higher level of organization (e.g. *jar lid* might be pluralized to form *jar lids*). Naturally this can happen repeatedly, at progressively higher levels, yielding composite symbolic structures of ever greater semantic and phonological complexity. Expressions of any size can thus be assembled.

Grammar consists of patterns for creating symbolic assemblies. In accordance with basic principles of Cognitive Grammar (in particular the content requirement), these patterns can only assume the form of **schematized expressions**: templates abstracted from a set of complex expressions to embody whatever commonality is inherent in them. Hence grammatical patterns are themselves assemblies of symbolic structures comprising compositional relationships at various levels of organization. These assemblies are directly analogous to their instantiating expressions, except that the symbolic structures which form them are more schematic. In particular, the schematic template corresponding to a construction—a **constructional schema**—itself resides in component symbolic structures integrated to form a composite symbolic structure. For example, the compositional pattern instantiated by *jar lid*, *garage door*, and countless other noun-noun compounds is merely a symbolic assembly in which two schematic nouns, [[A] / [a]] and [[B] / [b]], are integrated in a certain manner to yield the composite symbolic structure [[AB] / [ab]] (Langacker 1993: 326-327). This entire symbolic assembly serves to categorize either a fixed or a novel expression that instantiates it. Moreover, the global categorizing relationship is resolvable into local categorizing relationships between particular substructures. The categorization of *jar lid* as an instance of the noun-noun compounding pattern therefore subsumes the local categorizations:

[[[A] / [a]] → [[JAR] / [jar]]],
[[[B] / [b]] → [[LID] / [lid]]], and
[[[AB] / [ab]] → [[JAR LID] / [jar lid]]].

Consider, then, the construction of a novel expression in accordance with an established grammatical pattern. We may suppose that at the time of the utterance the linguistic system (L) contains the various conventional units indicated in Figure 7(a). One such unit is a constructional schema comprising two component symbolic structures, [A] and [B], as well as the composite symbolic structure, [C]. We can further suppose the existence of two lexical items, [A'] and [B'], which respectively instantiate the schematic units [A] and [B]. Assuming that these instantiating relationships represent established categorizations, they constitute the categorizing units [[A] → [A']] and [[B] → [B']].

Together, these units implicitly define a complex expression, assumed to be novel, which in Figure 7(b) is thus surrounded by a closed curve (rather than a box) to indicate its non-unit status. The latent composite structure, (C'), represents the expression's **compositional value**: the structure that emerges if [A'] and [B'] are integrated precisely as the constructional schema specifies, at both the semantic and the phonological poles. In this case (C') elaborates [C], and the complex expression ([A'] [B'])$_{C'}$ elaborates the constructional schema [[A] [B]]$_C$.

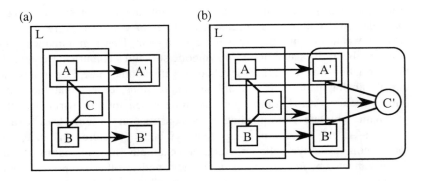

Figure 7. Actualization

In referring to (C') as merely "latent," and saying that the conventional units "implicitly" define the complex expression, I am once more emphasizing the non-constructive nature of a grammar. Novel expressions are not created by the linguistic system *per se*, but rather by the speaker, drawing on all available resources. Of course, the distinction is of little moment provided that we confine our attention to the (possibly hypothetical) situation of full compositionality. Assuming full compositionality, both (C') and the entire assembly ([A'] [B'])$_{C'}$ are wholly prefigured by conventional units of L: [A'] and [B'] are established units, in which the schematic units [A] and [B] are respectively immanent; the constructional schema [[A] [B]]$_C$ represents an established pattern for integrating [A] and [B] to form [C]; therefore, constructing ([A'] [B'])$_{C'}$—with composite structure (C')—is simply a matter of carrying out the established pattern of integration when [A] and [B] are embedded in the more elaborate structures [A'] and [B']. In effect, the potential structure ([A'] [B'])$_{C'}$ is rendered actual just by co-activating the conventional units in question. I call this **actualization** (Langacker 1987a: 11.3).

I have argued, however, that full compositionality is uncharacteristic of normal language use. In a typical usage event, the contextual understanding and phonetic rendition of a complex expression diverge from its compositional value if only by being more specific, and often in more drastic ways. This is shown in Figure 8, where the expression's **contextual value**, (C"), is depicted as an extension vis-à-vis its compositional value, (C'). To be sure, those facets of the expression that are extra-compositional (i.e. the discrepancies between (C') and (C")) start out as being non-conventional, but it is only by terminological fiat that they are also considered non-linguistic, for the usage event begins their conventionalization. Indeed, prior to actualization in a usage event, (C') itself lies beyond the scope of established convention, a non-unit prefigured by L but unexploited and unfamiliar to speakers.

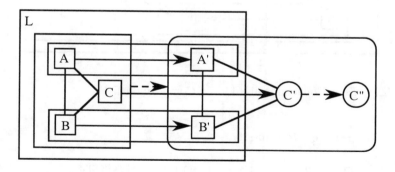

Figure 8. Partial Compositionality

Because (C") represents the way the expression is actually understood (and may eventually become its conventional meaning, as we saw in the case of *printer*), it is only (C') whose status is reasonably called into question. I believe it does have both linguistic status and some kind of cognitive presence. Since it represents the latent potential inherent in an assembly of conventional units, we can reasonably suppose that (C') is activated when those units are invoked in a usage event. It thus embodies whatever motivation conventional units provide for (C") and serves as a kind of stepping-stone on the way to it. The expression's actual value, then, is neither (C') alone nor (C"), but (C") construed in relation to (C'), which categorizes it: ((C') ---> (C")). I would say, for example, that the compositional value 'something that prints' does figure in the meaning of *printer* as a computer term. More obviously, a metaphorical expression like *chopper* (for 'helicopter') retains the compositional value 'something that chops' as a secondary facet of its meaning; an expression is metaphorical just by virtue of construing the target domain against the background of the source domain. If (C') and the categorizing relationship ((C') ---> (C")) do indeed have some cognitive presence, they might well retain it as the expression coalesces into an established unit, as shown in Figure 9.

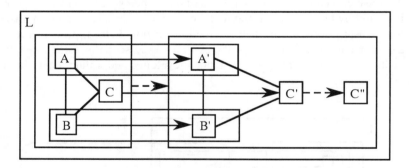

Figure 9. Conventionalized Extra-Compositionality

4.5 Degrees of Regularity

If all grammatical patterns reside in constructional schemas, they nonetheless vary considerably in the nature and extent of their regularity. At least three parameters need to be distinguished: compositionality, generality, and productivity. While there is some tendency for these properties to be associated with syntactic patterns, and their opposites with morphological ones, I see no empirical grounds for believing that position along these scales correlates in any absolute way with whether a pattern obtains above or below the word level. The lack of absolute correlations is one reason for a basic claim of Cognitive Grammar, namely that morphology and syntax form a continuum (fully describable as assemblies of symbolic structures). Nor is grammar distinct from lexicon, defined in the theory as the set of "fixed" expressions in a language (i.e. expressions with unit status), regardless of size or type.

Compositionality pertains to how closely an expression approximates the result predicted for the integration of particular component structures in the manner specified by a constructional schema. To be completely compositional, therefore, an expression can exhibit no discrepancy between its predicted value and its actual composite structure. In terms of Figures 7-9, the complex expression $([A'] [B'])_{C'}$ is compositional with respect to pattern $[[A] [B]]_C$ just in case the predicted value (C') and the contextual value (C'') precisely coincide; their identity entails that the composite structure $((C') \longrightarrow (C''))$ collapses onto (C'). Previous discussion raises the question of whether an expression is ever completely compositional. One can plausibly argue that an expression's contextual understanding always diverges to some extent (however minimally) from its predicted value, and that a residue of such divergence is retained even when the expression coalesces into an established lexical unit. However, in this non-constructive framework nothing much hinges on whether the limiting case of zero divergence is ever actually attained.

As defined, degree of compositionality is not a property of grammatical patterns *per se*, but rather of particular expressions that they categorize. The other two parameters do pertain to the patterns themselves and are thus reflected in the constructional schemas which embody them. **Generality** relates to the level of specificity at which such schemas are characterized. A given pattern has greater or lesser generality depending on whether it is potentially applicable to a wider or a narrower range of elements. In English, for example, tense marking is applicable to essentially any verb, whereas only "perfective" verbs enter into the progressive construction (Langacker 1987b). Constructions can also be limited to smaller classes that I likewise consider to be semantically definable, e.g. change-of-state verbs, verbs of transfer, "unaccusative" verbs, etc. Limitations of this sort are readily accommodated by the proper formulation of constructional schemas. Thus, whereas the schemas describing tense marking identify one component structure just as a verb, the progressive schema is more specific by virtue of requiring a perfective verb in particular. There is no inherent limit to the level of specificity at which a constructional schema can characterize its components. Indeed, a schema can incorporate a particular lexical item, even a specific variant of a lexical item, as one of its component structures.

Productivity is a matter of how available a pattern is for the sanction of novel expressions. Though productivity tends to correlate with generality, they are often dissociated and have to be distinguished. Patterns of comparable generality can easily differ in their degree of productivity. For example, a causative construction applicable (say) to intransitive verbs might be fully productive, applying to any such verb if the result is semantically coherent, or it might be limited to particular lexical combinations and unavailable for the creation of new expressions. Conversely, a pattern representing any level of generality has the potential to be fully productive. For instance, a certain plural marker might be restricted to a small class of nouns (such as animal names) but be freely applicable to any noun in that class.

In a usage-based model with dynamic processing (of the sort described previously), productivity amounts to likelihood of being selected as the active structure used to categorize a novel expression. The constructional schema representing a highly productive pattern must be well-entrenched and easily activated for this purpose. The schema representing a non-productive pattern presumably expresses a valid generalization, but if it cannot compete successfully for selection as an active structure, this pattern cannot extend beyond the range of data from which it is extracted. For example, English past-tense formation subsumes both the productive, default-case pattern with the conditioned variants [-d], [-t], and [-´d] (as in *rowed*, *kicked*, and *goaded*), and also a variety of largely non-productive patterns restricted to fixed sets of verbs, such as the ablaut pattern which changes everything after the initial consonant cluster to [Ot] (as in *bought*, *brought*, *caught*, and a number of others). We must therefore posit a deeply entrenched, easily elicited past-tense schema that we can abbreviate as [[V/...] [PAST/-D]], whose phonological pole specifies the suffixation of an alveolar stop, as well as various non-salient schemas, among them [[V/C(C)...] [PAST/C(C)Ot]]. We must further assume their difference in salience to be such that, even though they are both quite non-specific in their characterization of the verb stem, the former will virtually always win the competition for the privilege of categorizing a novel form.

Suppose, then, that *leached* is offered as the past-tense form of *leach*. Its interpretation as a past-tense form tends to activate both [[V/...] [PAST/-D]] and [[V/C(C)...] [PAST/C(C)Ot]] as possible categorizing schemas. By assumption, [[V/...] [PAST/-D]] will win the competition and be selected as the active structure, so the expression is judged well-formed (since *leached* conforms to its specifications). On the other hand, suppose that *lought* is offered as the past-tense form. While this does conform to a pattern in the language, namely [[V/C(C)...] [PAST/C(C)Ot]], that alone is not sufficient to guarantee its well-formedness. A judgment of well-formedness additionally requires that the schema an expression instantiates be in fact selected as the active structure with respect to which the assessment is made. The situation in English is such that usually the default-case pattern suppresses less salient patterns even when the latter have a greater degree of overlap with the target (this tendency is however less than absolute, as discussed in Bybee and Moder 1983). As a consequence, *lought* will not be categorized by [[V/C(C)...] [PAST/C(C)Ot]], but rather by [[V/...] [PAST/-D]], whose specifications it violates. Only established past-tense forms like *bought*, *brought*, *caught*, etc. are accepted as well-formed. Since they are themselves entrenched conventional units, they require no sanction from constructional schemas.

I conclude that a usage-based model with dynamic processing is able in principle to accommodate the full range of regularity encountered in natural language. Degree of compositionality is free to vary owing to the non-constructive nature of constructional schemas (whose role is merely to categorize target expressions), while generality and productivity are respectively determined by the level of specificity at which such schemas are characterized and their ease of selection as an active (categorizing) structure. It should be emphasized that nothing precludes the emergence of patterns that are highly general and fully productive. For example, a schema that we can abbreviate as [[V] [NP]] might describe the semantic integration of a verb with an object noun phrase and specify phonologically that this NP immediately follows V in the temporal sequence. The pattern has full generality: since V and NP are schematic characterizations, it refers to the combination of any verb with any noun phrase. The pattern is productive to the extent that entrenchment assures its activation in preference to any lower-level constructional schemas making conflicting specifications. A dynamic usage-based model is therefore perfectly capable of handling productive general rules whose application is exceptionless for all intents and purposes.

At the same time, Cognitive Grammar agrees with Construction Grammar (Fillmore, Kay, and O'Connor 1988; Goldberg 1995) in viewing such rules as special and actually rather atypical cases in the overall spectrum of linguistic patterns, most of which exhibit some lesser degree of generality and/or productivity. Even with respect to word order, there will usually be alternatives to the basic pattern that are able to preempt it in specific circumstances. A language might have, for example, both the general constructional schema [[V] [NP]] and also the more specific schema [[PRON] [V]], which describes the verb's semantic integration with an object pronoun and specifies phonologically that a pronominal NP precedes V in the temporal sequence rather than following it. Assuming that [[V] [NP]] and [[PRON] [V]] are comparable in their degree of entrenchment, it is [[PRON] [V]] that will be elicited to categorize an expression with a verb and an object pronoun, by virtue of its greater overlap with the target. The sequence *PRON V* will thus be judged grammatical, and *V PRON* ill-formed, despite the fact that only the latter conforms to the higher-level schema [[V] [NP]]. The pattern described by this high-level schema is rendered less productive by the existence of a more specific pattern that preempts it.

4.6 Distribution

Like most linguistic phenomena, grammatical patterns usually arrange themselves in complex categories comprising numerous related variants (see, for example, Lakoff 1987: Case Study 3). Such families of patterns are describable as networks, as in Figure 4, where each node in a network consists of an entire constructional schema. The patterns are thus characterized at different levels of specificity, some are special cases of others (constructional subschemas), some constitute extensions relative to more prototypical variants, and so on. At the extreme, the lowest-level subschemas in such a network incorporate particular lexical items (even lexical variants) as component structures. If, for example, the schema [[V] [NP] [NP]] describes the English ditransitive pattern in general terms, the constructional subschema [[SEND/send] [NP] [NP]] represents the lower-level generalization that *send* in particular conventionally occurs in this construction (e.g. *I sent my mother a birthday card*). It is perhaps more obvious that particular instantiations of morphological patterns have the status of conventional units. The English past tense, for instance, requires a family of constructional schemas including the category prototype, [[V/...] [PAST/-D]], as well as various schemas representing minor patterns, e.g. [[V/C(C)...] [PAST/C(C)Ot]], which can be regarded as extensions from the prototype. Clearly, it is part of a speaker's conventional knowledge of the language that particular verbs like *buy*, *bring*, and *catch* occur in this latter pattern. This knowledge takes the form of lower-level subschemas in which these specific stems function as component structures:

[[BUY/buy] [PAST/C(C)Ot]];
[[BRING/bring] [PAST/C(C)Ot]];
[[CATCH/catch] [PAST/C(C)Ot]].

In fact, although it might not be apparent from this notation (which omits the composite structures), these subschemas are nothing other than the specific forms *bought*, *brought*, and *caught*. Experimental evidence suggests that instantiations of even productive morphological patterns are stored as units provided that they occur with sufficient frequency (Stemberger and MacWhinney 1988).

It is in this manner that a usage-based framework accommodates distributional restrictions. The fact that *send* participates in the ditransitive construction is not indicated by means of an arbitrary device such as a "rule feature" or a diacritic, but merely by the inclusion of the constructional subschema [[SEND/send] [NP] [NP]] among the conventional units comprising the linguistic system. The fact that *buy* occurs in the morphological pattern [[V/C(C)...] [PAST/C(C)Ot]] is likewise given by the inclusion in L of the instantiating subschema [[BUY/buy] [PAST/C(C)Ot]] (i.e. *bought*). I conclude that idiosyncrasies such as these are readily described in a theory that posits only assemblies of symbolic structures for the characterization of lexical and grammatical structure (they fail to establish that grammar is "autonomous" in the sense of requiring descriptive devices not reducible to symbolic assemblies). Moreover, the examples illustrate the "bottom-up" orientation of Cognitive Grammar and the observation that lower-level schemas, expressing regularities of only limited scope, may on balance be more essential to language structure than high-level schemas representing the broadest generalizations. A higher-level schema implicitly defines a large "space" of potential instantiations. Often, however, its actual instantiations cluster in certain regions of that space, leaving other regions sparsely inhabited or uninhabited altogether. An adequate description of linguistic convention must therefore provide the details of how the space has actually been colonized. Providing this information is an elaborate network of conventional units including both constructional subschemas at various levels and instantiating expressions with unit status. For many constructions, the essential distributional information is supplied by lower-level schemas and specific instantiations. High-level schemas may either not exist or not be accessible for the sanction of novel expressions.

A simple example is provided by postpositional phrases in Luiseño (Uto-Aztecan, southern California). In this language postpositions occur suffixed to either inanimate nouns or pronouns, as in *ki-yk* 'to the house' and *po-yk* 'to him,' but not to animate nouns: **hunwu-yk* 'to the bear.' For the latter we instead find expressions like *hunwut po-yk* (bear it-to), where the postposition attaches to a coreferential pronoun. Forms like *ki-yk* 'to the house' give rise to the constructional schema $[N_{inan}\text{-}P]$, and those like *po-yk* 'to him,' to the schema [PRON-P]. From these two patterns, moreover, the higher-level schema [N-P] is presumably capable of emerging to embody the generalization that postpositions attach to nouns of any sort: they occur on both pronouns and non-pronouns, and they are not limited to inanimates (since the pronouns are usually animate in reference). [N-P] is thus an expected outcome of the usual process of abstraction, whereby commonalities are reinforced and points of divergence effectively cancel out. Additionally, forms like *hunwut po-yk* 'to the bear' permit the extraction of the more complex constructional schema $[N_{an} \text{ [PRON-P] }]$, which incorporates [PRON-P] as a component structure.

It is readily seen that the crucial distributional information resides in the lower-level schemas $[N_{inan}-P]$, [PRON-P], and $[N_{an} [PRON-P]]$. If the high-level schema [N-P] were accessible for the categorization of novel forms, expressions like *hunwu-yk* 'to the bear,' which conform to its abstract specifications, would be accepted as conventional. We must therefore suppose that [N-P] always loses the competition to be selected as the active structure; it is consistently superseded by the lower-level schemas as a function of its own non-salience and the inherent advantage accruing to more specific structures through their greater overlap with the target. Hence a form like *hunwu-yk* 'to the bear' would not be categorized by [N-P], but rather by either $[N_{inan}-P]$, [PRON-P], or $[N_{an} [PRON-P]]$, all of whose specifications it violates.

We can say that the space of potential structures defined by the high-level generalization [N-P] is only partially inhabited. In particular, the region corresponding to expressions with non-pronominal animate nouns is completely unoccupied; the notions potentially coded by forms in this region are instead handled by another, more complex construction, namely $[N_{an} [PRON-P]]$. A constructive model might account for this unexpected "gap" in the general pattern by positing a rule which transforms the non-occurring "underlying" forms into those which actually surface in their stead: $[N_{an}-P] ===> [N_{an} [PRON-P]]$. Alternatively, one could remove the non-occurrent forms from the grammar's output by means of a filter: $*[N_{an}-P]$. (The pattern $[N_{an} [PRON-P]]$ would then have to be dealt with separately.) We have just seen, however, that a dynamic usage-based model straightforwardly accommodates the data without resorting to either filters or underlying structures. The distributional gap simply results from the existence of $[N_{an} [PRON-P]]$ as a possible sanctioning unit, and the non-existence of $[N_{an}-P]$. That in turn reflects the respective occurrence and non-occurrence in the input data of expressions like *hunwut po-yk* and *hunwu-yk*. The schemas speakers extract are those supported by the expressions they are exposed to.

If it is workable, a theory that does not posit filters or derivations from underlying structures should definitely be preferred. Their avoidance simplifies the problem of language acquisition, which in essence then reduces to reinforcement of the commonality inherent in expressions that actually occur. I emphasize in particular that descriptions comprising only positive statements of what does occur are in principle able to account for distributional gaps. To be sure, a systematic attempt has not yet been made in Cognitive Grammar to show in precise detail how every known type of distributional restriction could be dealt with, and every proposed filter eliminated. The working hypothesis that only positive specifications are needed could be weakened if necessary without undermining the essential claims of the theory. Yet I see little reason to doubt that appropriate arrays of constructional schemas, varying in their degree of specificity and ease of activation, are capable of handling actual distributional phenomena.

This expectation extends to general constraints, such as those advanced for movement rules (Ross 1967 [1986]; Chomsky 1973) and pronoun-antecedent relationships (for a detailed account of the latter in Cognitive Grammar, see van Hoek 1992). Such constraints pertain to constructions in which corresponding entities lie at some distance, so that in their most general form the patterns describe the intervening material only in schematic terms. When the corresponding entities occur in certain "structural" configurations—e.g. when one occurs inside a tensed clause, or when they are separated by more than one boundary of a certain kind—deviance ensues, the details being in some measure language-specific. It is reasonably supposed that the restrictions partially reflect processing difficulties associated with simultaneously activating particular sorts of complex structures and selectively accessing their substructures. Still, the processing limitations are not absolute, and a given language manifests them in conventionally determined ways.

In Cognitive Grammar, the constructions in question are described by families of constructional schemas characterized at varying levels of specificity. A relative clause construction, for example, will have multiple variants differing as to whether the argument corresponding to the head noun is a subject, an object, or has some other grammatical relation within its clause, whether that clause combines directly with the head or is part of a larger clause which does so, whether the clause is finite or non-finite, and so on. The highest-level constructional schema may define a vast space of structural possibilities, but occurring expressions will not be distributed evenly within it. As with the other kinds of patterns described above, constructional subschemas specify which regions of that space are actually used, and with what degree of likelihood. If well-entrenched subschemas sanction particular configurational relationships between the corresponding entities, they can consistently win out over higher-level schemas for the privilege of categorizing novel expressions. Configurations not covered by the subschemas will consequently result in judgments of ill-formedness.

It can even happen that comparable sets of configurational relationships become conventionally established for multiple constructions (e.g. for multiple "extraction rules"). If, in one construction, speakers learn to effect a dependency between two elements in a particular kind of structural configuration, that itself constitutes a pattern which might be extended to other constructions. For instance, once a speaker learns to make a correspondence between the object argument in a finite clause and a nominal in the clause containing it (say for relative clauses), it might subsequently be easier to make an analogous correspondence in another type of construction (e.g. in clefting). Conventionalized dependencies of this sort can themselves be represented as constructional schemas which abstract away from the differences between the types of constructions involved. Thus, although a detailed study has not yet been undertaken, I believe that even such "parameter setting" is susceptible to characterization in a dynamic usage-based model.

5. Structural Applications

The usage-based model described above is applicable to all domains of language structure: semantics, phonology, lexicon, morphology, syntax. A linguistic system comprises large numbers of conventional units in each domain, and a target expression is simultaneously categorized by numerous active units, each assessing a particular facet of its structure. A few basic psychological phenomena (listed in Section 2), applying repeatedly in all domains and at many levels of organization, give rise to structures of indefinite complexity, which categorizing relationships—each pertaining to a particular structural dimension—link into cross-cutting networks. A description of this sort is further unified in that seemingly diverse phenomena are seen as residing in different aspects of the same or comparable structural assemblies, or the same aspects "viewed" in alternate ways.

5.1 Lexicon and Grammar

Cognitive Grammar itself offers conceptual unification. It posits only semantic, phonological, and symbolic structures. Lexicon, morphology, and syntax form a gradation claimed to be fully describable as assemblies of symbolic structures. The distinction between grammatical rules and symbolically complex expressions is only a matter of whether (or the degree to which) the symbolic assemblies constituting them are schematic rather than specific. While there is some tendency for morphological and syntactic rules to differ in terms of generality and productivity, the only consistent basis for distinguishing them is whether the phonological composition they specify takes place within a word or involves word sequences. Expressions constructed in accordance with grammatical schemas can also be of any size. With repeated use, an expression of any size or degree of compositionality can be entrenched and conventionalized. The lexicon of a language is then definable as the set of expressions with the status of conventional units.

Constructional schemas and complex lexical items both consist of symbolic assemblies with unit status, often comprising component and composite symbolic structures at multiple levels of organization. The reason for referring to such an assembly as a rule or constructional schema, rather than as a lexical item, is the incorporation of one or more symbolic components too schematic—especially phonologically—to actually be expressed as such. There are however degrees of schematicity, even at the phonological pole, and in a complex structure different numbers of components can be characterized schematically. The fixed expression *crane one's neck* would generally be considered a lexical item, yet the possessive element is actually schematic: *one's* is just a placeholder for *my*, *your*, *his*, etc., all of which are monosyllabic. Does *crane one's neck* count as a grammatical pattern instead of a lexical item by virtue of this schematic component? What about *X take Y over X's knee and spank Y*, which is schematic in several positions? If these are still considered lexical rather than grammatical, there is no evident reason why a constructional schema that incorporates a specific element, e.g. [[send] [NP] [NP]], should not also be a lexical item. That in turn is only one step away from according lexical status to assemblies like [[V] [NP] [NP]], all of whose components are schematic. My point, of course, is that lexicon and grammar grade into one another so that any specific line of demarcation would be arbitrary.

To make the same point in another way, let us consider more carefully the status of the ditransitive pattern [[send] [NP] [NP]], i.e. the commonality inherent in complex expressions like *send me a package*, *send your mother an eviction notice*, *send Washington a message*, etc. On the left in Figure 10, enclosed in a circle, is a fragment of the network of constructional schemas and subschemas constituting conventional knowledge of the English ditransitive construction. Verbs of transfer function as a prototype giving rise to various extensions (Goldberg 1992). Subschemas specify the occurrence of particular verbs in this pattern, *give* and *send* of course being common and well-entrenched. Special cases of these subpatterns may themselves be established as familiar units, e.g. [[give] [me] [NP]] (note the contraction *gimme*).

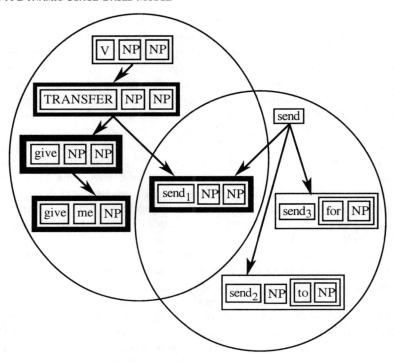

Figure 10. Constructional and Lexical Networks

At the same time, however, the subschema [[send] [NP] [NP]] represents a lexical property of *send* and belongs to a network of constructional schemas describing its grammatical behavior. Some of these are shown in the circle on the right in Figure 10. In both Construction Grammar and Cognitive Grammar, a lexical item's characterization includes a set of "structural frames" in which it conventionally occurs. While comparable in function to the "syntactic features" used in generative theory to specify the permitted contexts of lexical insertion, these frames are actually just partially schematic symbolic assemblies representing the commonality of certain complex expressions. They are, moreover, inherent and essential to a lexeme's value. Lexical items arise through a process of progressive decontextualization, where non-recurring aspects of usage events are filtered out through lack of reinforcement. Part of the relevant context is their occurrence in larger symbolic assemblies. To the extent that a form like *send* has any cognitive status independently of the structural frames in which it appears, it emerges by abstraction from these larger assemblies. Figure 10 should not be read as indicating that *send* is a distinct element which merely happens to be incorporated in a set of constructional subschemas. Rather, it is immanent in these assemblies and apprehended as a separate entity only by suppressing them.

What, then, is the status of [[send] [NP] [NP]]? Does it belong to the ditransitive construction or to the lexical item *send*? The answer, of course, is that the question is wrong: it is simultaneously part of both. Viewed in relation to the construction, it constitutes a subschema helping to specify the conventional distribution of a more general grammatical pattern. Viewed in relation to the lexical item, it specifies one grammatical environment in which the form occurs. In the present model, it is unproblematic (and certainly usual) for the same element to participate in multiple networks, which thereby intersect.

5.2 Lexical Semantics

A lexeme is not precisely the same in all its environments. Since elements are always shaped by the contexts in which they occur, it is only by abstracting away from contextual variation that a constant representation emerges. *Send* is thus shown in Figure 10 as having the contextual variants [$send_1$], [$send_2$], and [$send_3$]. In particular, [$send_1$] chooses the recipient as its direct object—defined in Cognitive Grammar as a participant receiving a secondary degree of "focal prominence"—and further highlights the resultant possessive relationship. On the other hand, [$send_2$] confers object status on the mover and highlights the path it follows, whereas [$send_3$] downplays both the mover and the recipient, focusing instead on the entity the sender hopes to obtain. It is I think pointless to ask whether these differences in relative prominence are responsible for the variants occurring in distinct structural frames, or whether the frames themselves induce the differences by virtue of what they explicitly encode. In any case a variant enters into a kind of "ecological system" with its structural context and does not necessarily exist outside that habitat. I am suggesting that these context-dependent variants may be more fundamental than the context-neutral schematization we tend to regard as primary.

In a "bottom up" account of this sort, the polysemy of lexical items should be expected as the normal state of affairs. Whether the contexts are structural, collocational, or pragmatic, they inevitably shape the construal of symbolic structures and thus give rise to semantic variants. Polysemy results when multiple variants become entrenched as units, provided of course that some connection is established between them (otherwise we speak of homonymy). Often a particular variant is both prior and sufficiently salient to serve as the basis for extension to other contexts, in which case we anoint it as the lexical item's prototypical semantic value. Through the reinforcement of common features, schemas emerge at different levels of abstraction to represent the commonality inherent in sets of variants. These alternate semantic values constitute a complex category describable as a network (as in Figure 4).

A classic problem of lexical semantics is whether an expression is truly "ambiguous," so that we must indeed posit two senses, or whether it is only "vague," in which case there may be just one. In practice the line is often hard to draw, with standard tests (Zwicky and Sadock 1975) failing to produce a clear-cut distinction. Consider the question of whether the verb *paint* is ambiguous between designating an artistic endeavor and a utilitarian one, or whether it is merely vague in this regard. One way to test this is by ascertaining whether a sentence like *Bill has been painting and so has Jane* is semantically coherent or anomalous when the two clauses are construed as differing on this point. Thus, if Bill is painting a portrait while Jane is putting lines on a highway, the sentence feels zeugmatic. This suggests two distinct meanings, whereas the anaphoric expression *so has* requires that the two clauses be semantically parallel. However, Tuggy (1993) has argued convincingly that judgments like these are often graded, making the test results indeterminate. The above example is less zeugmatic if Jane is instead painting a wall, and virtually normal if Bill is covering a wall for artistic purposes (say with a mural) and Jane for purely utilitarian purposes.

Tuggy shows that graded judgments like these, as well as clear-cut assessments of vagueness or ambiguity, are expected and readily accommodated in a dynamic usage-based model using networks for the description of complex categories. The nodes in such a network vary in their entrenchment and ease of activation, hence in the extent of their accessibility for specific grammatical purposes. The issue of vagueness vs. ambiguity hinges on the relative status of three structures: the putative specific senses (e.g. 'paint for artistic purposes' and 'paint for utilitarian purposes'), and also the schematic meaning representing their commonality ('paint'). Each structure is established to some degree as a conventional meaning of the lexical item in question. The possibilities range from being relatively unfamiliar and lacking unit status, at one extreme, to being very well-entrenched and easily elicited, at the other. As shown in Figure 11, clear-cut cases of ambiguity are those where only the specific senses are entrenched and accessible. If *paint* were like this, a neutral sense would be unavailable for anaphora, and one could not say *Bill has been painting and so has Jane* in mixed circumstances comparing artistic and utilitarian intent. Conversely, definite cases of vagueness are those where only the schematic meaning is entrenched and accessible. If this were true of *paint*, it should always be felicitous to use the sentence in mixed circumstances (even with portraits and lines on a highway). The actual situation appears to fall somewhere in between. When the two instances of painting are similar enough, the neutral value is able to emerge for anaphoric purposes. However, egregious differences call attention to themselves and make it harder to suppress the specific senses in favor of the neutral one. Thus, if Bill has been painting a portrait, Jane's having done so with lines on a highway can only be zeugmatic.

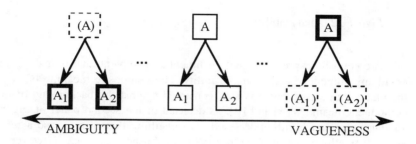

Figure 11. The Vagueness/Ambiguity Cline

Comparable differences in salience and likelihood of activation are responsible for another important dimension of lexical semantics, namely degree of **analyzability**. By analyzability I mean the extent to which speakers are cognizant of the presence and the semantic contribution of component symbolic elements. A novel combination is by definition fully analyzable, since a speaker has to actively manipulate the components in constructing it. Its meaning then is not just the novel composite conception (C), but (C) construed in relation to the component meanings [A] and [B], which categorize different facets of it. If I coin the term *flinger* to describe a new device, I necessarily recognize the contribution of *fling* and *-er*, thereby understanding it to mean 'something that flings.' That is the situation shown on the left in Figure 12.

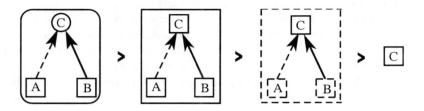

Figure 12. Analyzability

A composite expression's entrenchment as a conventional unit does not entail any immediate loss of analyzability. The composite meaning [C] will then have unit status, but it is still construed against the background of the component meanings [A] and [B], as depicted in the second panel of Figure 12. Thus a *printer* is still understood as 'something that prints,' and a *scanner* as 'something that scans.' Once [C] is established as a unit, however, it has at least the potential to be activated independently of [A] and [B]. There is an overall long-term tendency for the analyzability of composite lexical units to gradually decline: I do not always think of a *computer* as 'something that computes,' I am less likely to think of a *freezer* as 'something that freezes,' and a *propeller* is hardly ever thought of as 'something that propels.' We can interpret this lessening analyzability as a reduction in the likelihood of [A] and [B] being activated along with [C] and/or as a decrease in their level of activation. This is shown in the third panel of the diagram. The final step is for [A] and [B] to remain completely inert when [C] is activated. Linguistically we can then describe the expression as having lost its original symbolic complexity via reanalysis.

One factor facilitating a decline in analyzability is the usual discrepancy between an expression's expected compositional meaning and the actual contextual meaning that eventually becomes its conventional value. In accordance with the discussion of Figures 7-9, the structure given as [C] in Figure 12 is resolvable into [[C'] ---> [C'']], in which the compositional value [C'] is merely a stepping-stone for arriving at the contextual value [C'']. Thus a *printer* is not just 'something that prints' but a specific kind of computer equipment. More drastically, a *ruler* is less commonly understood as a device used for ruling lines than as an instrument of measurement. The more [C''] diverges from [C'], the less it is motivated by [C'], and the easier it becomes for [C''] to be activated autonomously. Hence a decline in analyzability involves [C'] gradually fading out the picture along with [A] and [B].

Because mainstream theories have little to say about analyzability, it has largely been ignored by linguistic theorists despite its omnipresence as a significant dimension of meaning and a recurring problem in lexical and grammatical description. The one context where degrees of analyzability are often noted is in the discussion of "fading" metaphors. In yachting, for example, there is a crew member who turns a crank in a manner resembling that involved in grinding meat. This person is metaphorically called a *grinder*, but for those immersed in the sport the term's familiarity has no doubt substantially reduced the salience of its metaphorical basis. We can describe this fading of the metaphor as a gradual decrease in the likelihood of the "literal" meaning [C'] being activated along with the "figurative" meaning [C"], as well as in its level of activation.

5.3 Metaphor

Metaphor is a vast subject that I can mention only briefly, in order to indicate how it fits into the overall picture being presented. Most basically, the entire scheme rests on a general notion of comparison, and specifically categorization, in which established structures are used for assessing novel structures. Metaphor can be seen as the special case in which the two structures represent different domains of experience, the target domain being understood with reference to the source domain. This entails two basic properties of a metaphorical relationship: its directionality, as well as its dependence on correspondences between elements of the source and target domains. Using one structure to categorize another is inherently directional, and any act of comparison presupposes that the standard of comparison be aligned with the target in some specific fashion.

Starting with Lakoff and Johnson (1980), theorists have emphasized that metaphor is a conceptual phenomenon not necessarily tied to any particular linguistic expressions. Often the same correspondences between two domains support a number of conventional metaphorical expressions and can further be exploited for novel ones. Since Cognitive Grammar makes the general claim that linguistic meanings are multifaceted conceptualizations, drawing on numerous cognitive domains which correspond in various ways, expressions invoking domains linked in a metaphorical relationship are accommodated with no special apparatus. Of course, some metaphors are in fact limited to particular expressions, the yachting term *grinder* providing one example. The difference between a general conceptual metaphor (e.g. LOVE IS A JOURNEY) and one tied to a specific lexical item is simply a matter of context: whether the metaphorical mapping occurs and becomes conventionalized as the semantic pole of a particular symbolic structure (hence invoked only in that context), or whether it occurs in numerous symbolic contexts and thus becomes independent of any one of them via the usual process of abstraction and decontextualization.

Metaphors also vary in their level of specificity, some being schematic relative to others (Lakoff and Turner 1989). We thus find hierarchies like the following, where successive instantiations lead from a highly "generic" metaphor down to a highly specific one coded in a particular expression: LIFE IS A JOURNEY → LOVE IS A JOURNEY → LOVE IS A JOURNEY IN A VEHICLE → LOVE IS A JOURNEY IN A CAR → *Our relationship is spinning its wheels*. Such hierarchies reflect the same process of abstraction we have been considering all along. However, they can also be used to illustrate an essential point that has not yet been emphasized: that parallel categorizing relationships are themselves subject to abstraction and schematic representation (in the same way that parallel compositional relationships give rise to constructional schemas). We can therefore posit schemas describing the commonality of more specific metaphorical mappings. To the extent that the metaphors are associated with particular expressions, these schemas characterize established **patterns of metaphorical extension**. More broadly, we can postulate **conventional patterns of semantic extension**, not limited to metaphor (also included, for example, are standard patterns of metonymy).

Consider the use of terms designating animals in reference to people exhibiting salient stereotypical characteristics of those animals. We refer to a sloppy, voracious eater as a *pig*, to a fierce competitor as a *tiger*, to people who merely follow the lead of others as *sheep*, etc. Each conventional usage of this sort constitutes a semantic extension vis-à-vis the basic sense of the lexical item. The semantic pole of *pig*, when applied metaphorically to people, can thus be given very roughly as [[PIG] ---> [PERSON RESEMBLING PIG]]. It is a complex structure of the form [[C'] ---> [C'']], in which a person is categorized (by extension) as a kind of pig. The metaphorical sense of *tiger* is similarly represented as [[TIGER] ---> [PERSON RESEMBLING TIGER]], and so on. These categorizing relationships are of course structurally parallel. On the assumption that abstraction occurs ubiquitously (by the reinforcement of commonalities), we expect the emergence of the schematized structure [[ANIMAL] ---> [[PERSON RESEMBLING ANIMAL]]. This schematic categorizing relationship constitutes a conventional pattern of metaphorical extension.

Let me quickly review another class of issues raised by metaphor. They pertain to the number of structures that have to be posited to describe a particular metaphorical relationship, as well as their relative status. Following Lakoff and Johnson, a standard practice in recent years has been to posit just two basic structures (connected by correspondences), the source domain and the target domain: [[S] ---> [T]]. These authors in fact argue against an "abstractionist" account in which a schematic conception common to both domains is posited in lieu of a metaphorical connection between them (Lakoff and Johnson 1980: 107-110). A related issue is whether even the target domain has any existence independently of the metaphor. It is often intimated that certain targets are essentially "constituted" by metaphor and without it either do not exist or are too amorphous to be easily apprehended. On the other hand, Fauconnier and Turner (1994; Turner and Fauconnier 1995) have shown the need to posit, in addition to S and T, a third "space" comprising a "blend" of their properties.

I would not propose an abstractionist account as an alternative to metaphor. There is no doubt that metaphorical projection from source to target domains is prevalent and of fundamental cognitive importance. At the same time, it seems to me that most if not all metaphorical extension presupposes not only some prior understanding of the target (cf. Quinn 1991), but also some apprehension of an abstract commonality which motivates the extension. I noted earlier (in regard to Figure 3) that while this commonality amounts to a schema which both the standard and the target instantiate, it need not be salient or separately apprehended, and may have only fleeting occurrence as an implicit facet of the categorizing event. I have further stated that schemas are immanent in their instantiations (discrete notations notwithstanding), so that even if they have some permanent cognitive status they are not necessarily individually accessible. In my view this conception of the role of schemas in metaphor is fully compatible with that implied by the **invariance hypothesis**. Lakoff (1990) claimed that metaphorical mappings preserve the image-schematic structure of the source domain. Turner (1990) subsequently offered an amended and more precisely formulated version: for those components of the source and target domains involved in the mapping, the image-schematic structure of the target is preserved, and as much image-schematic structure as possible is imported from the source, consistent with that preservation. Turner's statement at least implies that the target domain usually has some structure not created by the metaphor. Moreover, both formulations presume the importance of schematic representations, and neither denies the possibility that the source and target domains might initially share certain image-schematic properties.

I therefore propose a synthesis along the following lines. In principle, the description of a metaphor always involves at least three structures: the source, the target, and a schema. The latter two structures do however show substantial variation in their nature and status, thus contributing to the impressive qualitative diversity of metaphors. The target domain ranges along the entire spectrum from being fully apprehended independently of the metaphor, as when people are likened to animals, to being wholly constituted by the metaphor for all intents and purposes (e.g. a layperson's understanding of the Big Bang). The schematic commonality of the source and target domains likewise ranges from the blatantly obvious (people and animals have a lot in common), through the tenuous and hard to articulate (e.g. an argument as a building), to the limiting case where any commonality is negligible. This would at least be so for instances where the target domain is wholly constituted by the metaphor.

Yet even three structures are not enough. Also essential to the metaphorical experience is what Fong (1988) referred to as a **hybrid domain**. This is the structure that results when the target domain is construed against the background of the source domain and structured in accordance with its specifications. Equivalent to neither the source nor the target, it "blends" their properties to yield a distinct structure that may itself be accessed for purposes of inference (as discussed by Fauconnier and Turner 1994) or linguistic coding. If I describe a person as a *tiger*, for instance, I may actually conceive of a hybrid creature, person-like but with fangs and claws, pursuing human objectives with the strength, energy, and ferocity characteristic of the tiger stereotype. If I say that someone *demolished my argument*, I may actually imagine an ethereal yet building-like entity that collapses into a heap when subjected to destructive force. Like the relation between component and composite structures, the hybrid domain (or "blended space") is in a sense constituted by the source and target domains being construed in relation to one another, but may well emerge as a cognitive entity in its own right, with its own distinctive properties. Applied to the hybrid conception just described, an expression like *demolished my argument* could be regarded as non-anomalous, even literal.

A metaphorical extension like [[TIGER] ---> [PERSON RESEMBLING TIGER]] is thus resolvable into the tripartite structure [[[TIGER] ---> [PERSON]] = [PERSON RESEMBLING TIGER]], where [PERSON] represents the target domain prior to its metaphorical construal, and [PERSON RESEMBLING TIGER] is the hybrid domain that results. The relation between S, T, and H actually amounts to a special case of composition: S and T are component structures, and H the composite structure resulting from their integration. It differs from ordinary (grammatical) composition primarily in being limited to the semantic pole. Whereas a compound like *tiger person* might yield a comparable hybrid notion by integrating [TIGER/tiger] and [PERSON/person] both semantically and phonologically, in the metaphor the component and composite conceptions are all facets of the meaning symbolized by the single form *tiger*. This difference is sketched in Figure 13.

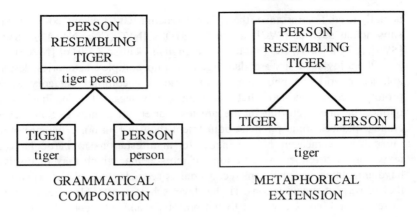

Figure 13. Composition vs. Metaphor

5.4 Phonology

Let us now turn to phonology and to the phonological aspects of morphology. Phonological structures are one of the three kinds of units permitted by the content requirement, the others being semantic and symbolic units. The difference between phonology and morphology resides in whether we consider phonological organization in its own terms or with respect to its role in symbolic structures. While I cannot yet claim to have seriously dealt with phonology in Cognitive Grammar, insightful preliminary studies have been carried out by Farrell (1990) on Spanish stress and by Rubba (1993) on modern Aramaic. I would also subscribe in both spirit and detail to Bybee's prolegomena for a cognitive/functional phonology (Bybee 1994). Kemmer and Israel (1994) discuss phonological variation from a usage-based perspective.

Purely phonological structures include such elements as segments, syllables, words, feet, and intonation groups. These can all be represented at various levels of specificity. A form like *pot*, for example, can be characterized phonologically in precise phonetic detail as a sequence of "phones" ([pʰát]), more abstractly as a series of phonemes (/pat/), or schematically as a syllabic template ([CVC]). From the usage-based perspective, we can reasonably anticipate that structures of any size and any level of abstraction are capable of being learned and represented as conventional units. A schema that describes a general pattern, thus defining a space of possible structures, co-exists with instantiating units that specify which regions of the space are actually used. For instance, the syllable schema [CVC] might co-exist with subschemas such as [SVC] (where S = STOP), [NVC] (N = NASAL), [SVN], [SVS], [pVC], [NVt], etc. (but not—for English—either [CVh] or [NVC]).

Phonological units are also organized into complex categories describable as networks. A phoneme, for example, is a complex category whose prototype corresponds to what was traditionally regarded as its basic allophone, the one occurring in the greatest variety of contexts. Since every context induces some phonetic adjustment (however minor), the prototype must in some measure be schematic. Its manifestations in particular contexts constitute either instantiations of the schema, which may themselves have unit status, or extensions recognized as secondary allophones owing to their divergent specifications. Higher-level schemas may also be abstracted to represent what is common to the prototype and different sets of extensions.

A variety of basic phonological entities can be seen as naturally arising via the same process of abstraction that we have been discussing throughout. Consider sound segments. At the phonetic level, segments have no independent existence. To the extent that we need to posit them, we can regard them as being abstracted from syllables—perhaps to be modeled as constellations of articulatory gestures, as proposed by Browman and Goldstein (e.g. 1992)—which have some claim to being the minimal units of speech. It is only through phonological decontextualization that a segmental phoneme like /p/ emerges as a distinct cognitive entity. From actual syllables, an array of schemas are presumably extracted representing a p-like sound in various syllabic contexts: syllable initial, syllable final, before or after particular vowels, as part of certain consonant clusters, etc. We can identify these p-like sounds with phones or allophones of the complex category defining /p/, and the syllabic schemas as their conditioning environments. If these phonological variants have enough in common, and occur in enough distinct environments, a schematized segment arises which embodies their commonality but makes no specific reference to syllabic position or the surrounding context.

Likewise, classificatory phonological features constitute abstractions from sounds (or sound sequences). To the extent that we need to posit them, they are merely the schematic characterizations of "natural classes" of sounds. Representing the feature [STOP], for example, would be a stop consonant schematic in regard to such properties as voicing and place of articulation. Of course, sounds vary in the nature and the degree of their commonality, so alternate sets give rise to schemas with different numbers and combinations of specific properties: [STOP], [ALVEOLAR STOP], [HIGH FRONT VOWEL], [CONSONANT], [NASAL], etc. Standard features can then be described as schemas that are specific in regard to just a single phonological parameter. In the same vein, the "tiers" employed in contemporary phonological description amount to sequences of segmental schemas all of which are specific in regard to certain parameters while abstracting away from the others.

What about phonological rules? As in grammar, rules are limited to schemas abstracted from actual expressions. This conception of phonological rules is quite straightforward in the case of phonotactics. Consider the constraints a language imposes on the form of permitted syllables. An array of syllable schemas—[nVt], [NVt], [NVS], [CVS], [CVC], etc.—represent the patterns inherent in occurring syllables, described at various levels of generality. When embedded in a dynamic processing model based on interactive activation, these schemas specify the actual syllabic distribution of segments, certain combinations being assessed as non-conventional. For example, we can posit for English the low-level schemas [mVC] and [nVC], as well as the higher-level generalization [NVC], but not the non-occurring pattern [NVC]. To account for the judgment that a syllable like (Næk) is un-English, we need only assume that a lower-level schema wins out over [NVC] for the privilege of categorizing it, e.g. ([nVC] ---> (Næk)).

Less obvious is the treatment of phonological rules traditionally formulated in process terms as derivations from underlying representations. Although the content requirement proscribes derivations from underlying structures, it does permit relationships of categorization, including extension (for some differences between derivation and categorization, see Langacker 1987a: 443-444). Moreover, from other domains of linguistic structure we know that chains of extensions often occur, that extensions are sometimes limited to particular contexts, and that analogous categorizing relationships can themselves give rise to schemas describing their abstract commonality. These properties suggest an analysis of derivational phonological rules as **patterns of phonological extension**.

Consider, for example, a rule voicing [t] to [d] intervocalically. We can posit such a rule when there is evidence that speakers pronounce certain forms with a [d] which they nonetheless categorize as instantiating /t/. For instance, variants with [t] and [d] might co-exist as the careful and fast-speech pronunciations of numerous lexical items: [fita]~[fida], [oti]~[odi], [ketul]~[kedul], etc. I follow Bybee (1994) in supposing that each habitual pronunciation is mentally represented in considerable phonetic detail. Assuming, then, that [t] is felt to be "basic," phonological characterizations of the lexical items in question include categorizing relationships between their prototypical and extended phonetic variants: [[fita] ---> [fida]], [[oti] ---> [odi]], and [[ketul] ---> [kedul]]. Like any other regularity, the commonality inherent in these alternations can be extracted as a schema: [[...VtV...]

---> [...VdV...]]. We can describe this schema in a number of mutually consistent ways. First, it is immanent in the networks describing the phonological variants of individual lexical items. Second, it is part of the complex category representing the phoneme /t/. It specifies that the basic allophone [t] is extended to [d] in the context [...V_V...]. Finally, the schema can be regarded as a phonological rule (which may or may not be productive, i.e. accessible for the sanction of new instances). These are not competing analyses, but a matter of the same cognitive entity being considered from alternate perspectives.

5.5 Morphology

As we turn to morphology, I must pause to acknowledge the visionary work of Joan Bybee (1985; 1988; Bybee and Slobin 1982), who was advocating a usage-based approach long before that term was coined. Many of her ideas have direct analogs in the conception presented here, including the extraction of schemas, the storage of specific complex forms (even some that appear to be regular), degrees of entrenchment and ease of activation ("lexical strength"), and the importance of viewing morphological structure as networks of "connections" (as opposed to discrete "building blocks"). I must also highlight the more recent contribution of Jo Rubba (1993), who has given extensive thought to how traditional morphological problems can be handled in Cognitive Grammar, providing illustration with a detailed description of verb morphology in modern Aramaic.

A number of classic problems pertain to the notion "morpheme." We present the concept to students by means of data sets like {*fast, faster, fastest, cool, cooler, coolest, red, redder, reddest*}, where words are exhaustively decomposable into discrete chunks from which they derive in a transparently regular way. However, linguists are well aware that this archetypal conception of morphemes as building blocks has severe limitations—with any representative array of data, the metaphor breaks down immediately. The difficulties lie with the metaphor itself. When the same phenomena are examined from the usage-based perspective, the problems simply fail to arise.

Just as segments are abstracted from syllables, morphemes are abstracted from words. Though some stand alone (just as vowels can stand alone as syllables), there are many morphemes—in some languages the vast majority—which only occur as part of larger words. By and large, it seems fair to say that speakers are more intuitively aware of words than of their parts, and that large numbers of complex forms are initially learned as wholes and analyzed only subsequently (if at all). Words, then, have some claim to primacy.

In the usage-based perspective, morphemes are naturally seen as arising by the usual process of abstraction. The interpretation of abstraction as the reinforcement of recurring commonalities echoes the basic technique of classic morphemic analysis, where the objective is to identify recurrent pairings between particular conceptual and phonological structures. The pairing observed in *fast* is also inherent in *faster* and *fastest*. Analysts therefore posit the symbolic unit [FAST/fast], just as speakers abstract it from usage events. From forms like *fastest*, *coolest*, and *reddest*, both linguists and speakers extract the morpheme [MOST/-est] to represent the systematic co-occurrence of the concept 'most' (with respect to a property) and the phonological sequence *-est*. In straightforward cases like *fastest*, the symbolic units thus extracted are exhaustive of the word and readily taken as yielding it compositionally.

We have seen, however, that complex words are not in general fully compositional, whether we look at their initial use or their established conventional value. The morphemic analysis of *printer* into [PRINT/print] and [ER/-er] does not (in conjunction with compositional patterns) provide a full characterization of its linguistic meaning (where it specifically indicates a piece of computer equipment). We saw earlier how this is a natural consequence of learning via schematization based on contextual understanding (Figures 7-9). From the standpoint of morphemic analysis, this typical situation is nonetheless problematic if one thinks of words as being built out of morphemes (where does the extra material come from?). On the other hand, it is unproblematic if words have a status of their own and morphemes are abstracted from them. While [PRINT] and [ER] do not exhaust the specialized meaning of *printer*, they are discernible in that meaning. [PRINT/print] can thus be extracted from *printer, printing, printed*, etc. by reinforcing their commonality, and [ER/-er] from *printer, freezer, eraser*, etc., regardless of whether any particular word is fully compositional. This is the morphemic consequence of the distinction previously discussed between construction and categorization.

Once the abstractive nature of morphemes is recognized, a raft of other classic problems evaporate. Degrees of analyzability are readily accommodated. If forms like *propeller, ruler*, and *stretcher* are originally learned as unanalyzed wholes, it makes little difference to their efficacious use whether speakers ever make a connection with *propel, rule*, and *stretch*, acquired from other contexts. If they do establish a connection, the extent to which the composite expressions activate these components is likewise inessential and no doubt variable. Should we then say that words like *propeller, ruler*, and *stretcher* are polymorphemic? Either a positive or a negative answer would, I think, be simplistic. In the present framework it is both reasonable and coherent to say instead that their analyzability into component morphemes is a matter of degree.

The extraction of morphemic components need not be uniform for all portions of a word. For example, since *-er* occurs in so many nouns, particularly those indicating agentive or instrumental participants in actions, it is sufficiently entrenched and salient that appropriate forms strongly tend to be analyzed in terms of it. Intuitively, I would judge that *-er* is more clearly apparent in *propeller*, *ruler*, and *stretcher* than are *propel*, *rule*, and *stretch*. The disparity is even more evident in *pliers* and *plumber*, where *ply* and *plumb* cast a faint shadow at best. The limiting case of such disparity is when morphemic analysis touches only part of a word, leaving the remainder as an unanalyzed residue. There are of course numerous examples involving *-er*: *father*, *mother*, *brother*, *sister*, *hammer*, *roster*, *sliver*, *master*, *geyser*, *crater*, *miser*, and so on. Bybee (1988: 128) notes the residues *Mon*, *Tues*, *Wednes*, etc. left when an obvious commonality is observed in the names for days of the week. An account of morphemes based on the reinforcing of common features renders it unproblematic for only portions of words to participate in such associations.

Bybee correctly notes that this account extends to phonaesthemes, e.g. the *str* of *strip*, *stripe*, *strap*, *strop*, *street*, *stretch*, *strand*, *string*, etc., which indicates length and thinness. Whether it has iconic motivation or comes about merely by historical accident, a recurring sound/meaning association of this kind allows the extraction of a schema with the potential to be used in coining or analyzing other expressions. Elaborate systems of sound symbolism might arise in this fashion (cf. Langacker 1987a: 399-401). On the other hand, the schema may have little salience if only because so many forms containing the phonological sequence lack the meaning component, and conversely. Still, the basic process is the same one operative in canonical morphemic analysis. What varies is how far the intrinsic organization of the data allows this process to proceed—how close it comes to the "ideal" situation where the morphemic components are salient and exhaust the content of the words from which they are extracted.

In her description of modern Aramaic verb morphology, Rubba (1993) shows that with this kind of approach non-concatenative morphology poses no special problems. A simple illustration is given in Figure 14. The symbolic units shown at the bottom are specific words and stems: the infinitival, third feminine singular jussive, and agentive forms of 'work,' and the agentive forms of 'lie' and 'study' (the agentive stems are further inflected for gender and number). If morphemes are abstracted from words by a process of schematization, the data straightforwardly yields the symbolic units shown at the top. The stem [WORK/p...l...x...] comprises the consonants [p], [l], and [x], occurring in a particular linear sequence, but abstracts away from the placement (and also the identity) of vowels—since the vocalism is variable, it is filtered out as common features are reinforced. Conversely, the agentive morpheme [AG/CaCaC] is specific in regard to vocalism but schematic with respect to the surrounding consonants. Such morphemes are non-prototypical in the sense that their specified segments are not all contiguous in the temporal sequence. However, the process of schematization does not itself require any particular distribution of shared and canceled properties. While there is often a partitioning between specific and schematic substructures, their interdigitation is not at all unusual (cf. *X take Y over X's knee and spank Y*).

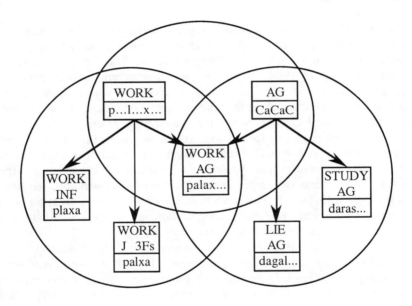

Figure 14. Abstraction Yielding Discontinuous Morphemes

Figure 14 further illustrates the point that the same network of structures can be viewed in different ways, corresponding to different linguistic constructs. I noted earlier that part of the overall characterization of a lexical item is a set of structural frames in which it conventionally occurs. While these frames were identified earlier as constructional subschemas (as in Figure 10), they also include specific complex expressions with unit status (constructional subschemas and complex expressions form a gradation in any case). Hence the structures in the circle on the left are part of the overall characterization of the lexical item [WORK/p...l...x...], and those in the circle on the right help define the agentive morpheme. At the same time, many specific forms like *palax-* 'worker' have the status of conventional units and thus constitute lexical items (fixed expressions). A form like *palax-* is of course polymorphemic, comprising the two morphemes under discussion. The structures in the middle circle are thus interpretable as a construction, in which two component structures categorize and motivate the composite expression. This construction in turn instantiates (or has immanent in it) a constructional schema describing the formation of agentive noun stems.

5.6 Morphophonemics

Rubba (1993) has also examined in preliminary terms the treatment of phonological rules in a network account of morphology. Recall that phonotactic rules are simply schematized representations of occurring phonological sequences, whereas "derivational" rules are schemas representing patterns of phonological extension. The examples given previously were purely phonological in the sense that the schemas made no reference to any particular morphological context. Sometimes patterns of extension are however limited to certain morphological contexts, in which case the rules are considered "morphophonemic." Their description in Cognitive Grammar remains the same except that appropriate reference to the context is incorporated in the schema characterizing the extension (for illustration, see Langacker 1988: 143-145). The example to be considered here involves a phonotactic constraint and a rule that is morphophonemic in the sense that extension affects a segment's phonemic categorization.

Rubba documents for modern Aramaic a phonotactic constraint to the effect that obstruent clusters agree in voicing. For our purposes, it is sufficient to posit the cluster template [TT], reflecting the frequent co-occurrence of voiceless obstruents, as well as the absence of the schema [DT], which speakers do not extract since clusters consisting of a voiced and a voiceless obstruent do not occur. There are however verb roots, such as [HEAL/b...s...m...], where voiced and voiceless obstruents occur in consecutive consonantal slots. These are abstracted from specific occurrent forms in which a vowel appears between the two obstruents, so that the phonotactic constraint is not violated. Now certain stem forms, including the infinitive, involve patterns of vocalization that leave the first two root consonants adjacent to one another. The composite expression is then pronounced with a voiceless initial obstruent, e.g. *psama* 'to heal' (not *bsama*). In process terms, one could say that a rule changes /b/ to /p/ to agree in voicing with the following consonant. Of course, it has sometimes been taken as problematic that the assimilation rule effectively duplicates the phonotactic constraint, which has to be posited for independent reasons. Much has also been made of the fact that such a rule can either be phonological or morphophonemic depending on whether the phoneme it applies to happens to have a counterpart with the opposite voicing (Halle 1959).

A partial description of the situation is given in Figure 15, adapted from Rubba (1993: 499). At the top in this diagram are three symbolic structures: the root [HEAL/b...s...m...], the infinitival morpheme [INF/CCaCa], and the composite infinitival expression [HEAL INF/psama]. Collectively these make up a construction, in which the two component morphemes categorize the composite structure. The box labeled (i) is part of the overall characterization of the lexeme *b-s-m* 'heal.' Its full description comprises not only the root morpheme, but also an array of structural frames, including various specific composite expressions in which it conventionally appears. One of these is the infinitive *psama* 'to heal.' At the phonological pole, the relation between [b...s...m...] and [ps...m...] (inherent in [psama]) is a fragment of the complex category representing the variant phonological shapes of the root morpheme. It is in particular a relationship of extension from the presumed prototype [b...s...m...] to the variant that appears in the context of the infinitival construction.

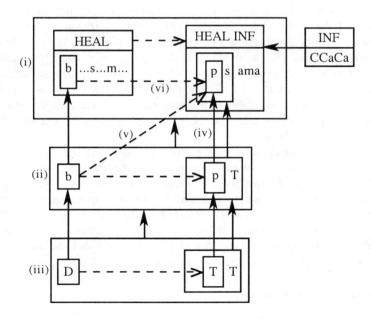

Figure 15. Morphophonemic Alternation

Also apparent in the diagram is the schema [TT], which specifies the conventionality of a cluster of voiceless obstruents. This is instantiated by [pT], representing a special case of the general pattern, in turn elaborated by the specific cluster [ps] (as part of [psama]). These units and categorizing relationships are a fragment of the network describing permissible consonant clusters in the language. Moreover, these elements also function as components of the structures in boxes (ii) and (iii), which belong to another network describing a family of phonological extensions. Extracted from numerous specific extensions like [[b...s...m...] ---> [ps...m...]], schema (ii) represents the pattern of [b] extending to [p] before a voiceless obstruent. Since the analogous extension occurs with other voiced obstruents, the higher-level schema (iii) is extracted to embody the generalization that any such obstruent devoices in this context. Observe that (ii) is a subschema with respect to (iii), and that the relevant portions of (i) are a specific instantiation of (ii).

Yet other facets of the diagram pertain to the phonemes /b/ and /p/. The elements [b] and [p] in (ii) are more or less identifiable with the basic allophones of these respective categories. The relationship [[D] → [b]] shows [b] as a member of the more inclusive class of voiced obstruents, while [[T] → [p]] relates [p] to the class of voiceless obstruents. The existence of both voiced and voiceless obstruent phonemes has the consequence that the systematic extension [[b] ---> [p]] (before T) effects a change in category membership: one variant of /b/ coincides with the basic (or at least a central) allophone of /p/. That, however, is a contingent matter which depends on the specific inventory of phonemes the language happens to have—the extension in (ii), and its generalized version in (iii), are not intrinsically either phonological or morphophonemic. Another instantiation of (iii) in the same language could perfectly well be purely phonological (this is in fact the case in Aramaic).

How, then, do we characterize the [p] or [psama]? It is shown in Figure 15 as both an instantiation of the phoneme /p/ (note the arrow labeled (iv)) and also an extension vis-à-vis the phoneme /b/ (arrow (v)). The former categorization has a phonetic basis, and the latter a morphological one, [psama] being understood as a manifestation of [b...s...m...] (arrow (vi)). While phonologists will have to determine the relative salience and the consequences of the alternate categorizations, it seems to me that the framework portrays the complex situation in a realistic way.

5.7 Larger Assemblies

Diagrams like Figures 14 and 15 are initially rather forbidding. To be sure, they are no more so than a set of algebraic rules or formulas providing comparable information, and probably less so once certain notational conventions become familiar. Complex representations such as these can only be avoided at the price of failing to be even minimally explicit about essential aspects of linguistic organization. These diagrams are in any case drastically oversimplified relative to the actual complexity of the linguistic reality they seek to model. At best they depict only small fragments of pertinent structures and networks, selected for minimal illustration of some particular point.

These fragmentary representations afford at least a hint of the large coalitions of structures and relationships that are brought to bear in shaping even the smallest portions of expressions and determining their linguistic interpretation. Coalitions of diverse character and indefinite complexity have the potential to coalesce into higher-order structures having some kind of cognitive status in their own right. The most obvious examples are lexical items (fixed expressions), which in principle have no upper bound on their possible size. While *X take Y over X's knee and spank Y* is longer than lexical items are traditionally thought of as being, it is certainly a conventionally established unit, and by no means the largest conventional expression to be found. Complex expressions can also give rise to constructional schemas spanning multiple levels of organization, i.e. not just a single pattern for integrating two component structures to form a composite structure, but multi-level assemblies of such patterns defining constituency hierarchies.

For example, English has both a morphological pattern deriving adjectives from nouns by means of *-ful*, and one deriving adverbs from adjectives by means of *-ly*. We can represent the two constructional schemas as $[[\ldots]_N$ -ful$]_{ADJ}$ and $[[\ldots]_{ADJ}$ -ly$]_{ADV}$. On the basis of a large set of well-established forms—*artfully, carefully, hopefully, sinfully, dutifully, shamefully, deceitfully, beautifully, playfully, cheerfully, successfully, lawfully, scornfully, zestfully*, etc.—it is evident that the combination of these two patterns in successive layers of morphological organization also represents a conventional pattern. We can therefore posit the higher-order constructional schema $[[[\ldots]_N$ -ful$]_{ADJ}$ -ly$]_{ADV}$ to capture the generalization. Immanent in particular forms like those cited, this structure is both a complex pattern in its own right and a subschema of $[[\ldots]_{ADJ}$ -ly$]_{ADV}$ in the network spelling out its conventional exploitation. Even a morphologically impoverished language like English has still more elaborate assemblies of this kind, e.g. $[[[[\ldots]$ -al$]_{ADJ}$ -iz$]_V$ -ation$]_N$, from *centralization, normalization, nationalization, radicalization, marginalization, lexicalization, grammaticalization*, and so on (cf. Chapin 1967). Without going into any detail, let me suggest that comparable assemblies of constructional schemas correspond to such traditional descriptive devices as morpheme-order charts and templates specifying permitted clitic sequences.

I should also mention higher-order coalitions such as paradigms and conjugation classes. I make no apriori claims about the proportion of specific inflected forms that are learned and stored as units, nor about the nature and extent of their organization into psychological assemblies analogous to the paradigms described by grammarians. However, as Bybee has long maintained, we can reasonably suppose that speakers learn and store large numbers of specific forms, especially those that are idiosyncratic or represent minor patterns, but no doubt also including high-frequency forms instantiating major patterns. A particular stem is abstracted from an array of inflected forms, many of which may have unit status, as shown in Figure 14 for Aramaic *p...l...x...* 'work.' Through the categorizing relationships thus established, a stem provides access to a set of inflected forms which—if complete enough in relation to the structural patterns of the language—we can recognize as a paradigm. Like a grammarian's paradigm, moreover, it is a structured set in which forms are connected to one another in myriad ways. Schematized forms capture similarities observable with respect to various parameters at different levels of abstraction. With a verb, for instance, schemas might be extracted to represent the commonalities of singular forms, non-future forms, third-person plurals, etc.

At the same time, other schemas are extracted to capture what is shared by analogous forms in the paradigms of different lexemes. These amount to constructional schemas and subschemas. For instance, Figure 16 depicts a constructional subschema describing one pattern of agentive-noun formation in modern Aramaic. It specifies how a root is integrated with the agentive morpheme to yield the composite agentive expression which interdigitates the root consonants with the agentive morpheme's vocalism. Three instantiations are shown, the same ones as in Figure 14, which however did not give the constructional schema or the component structures for *dagal...* 'liar' or *daras...* 'studier.' Hence the two diagrams offer different partial views of the same elaborate web of structures and relationships.

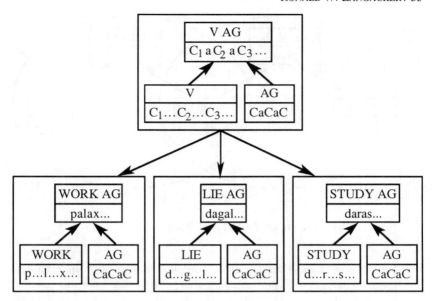

Figure 16. A Morphological Schema

Figure 16 is a fragment of the network of constructional schemas, sub-schemas, and specific instantiations describing agentive-noun formation in Aramaic. Comparable networks describe the patterns for other forms appearing in verbal paradigms (see Rubba 1993 for details). Consider now a particular verb root, e.g. *p...l...x...* 'work.' A given root functions as a component structure in numerous constructions, corresponding to the different inflected forms in its paradigm. Just two of these are shown (enclosed in circles) in Figure 17: *p...l...x...* 'work' is a component of both the agentive *palax...* and the infinitival form *plaxa*. We can think of this diagram as abbreviating a much larger array of constructions in which the root occurs. This larger collection of symbolic assemblies constitutes a higher-order coalition of the sort whose cognitive status is under discussion.

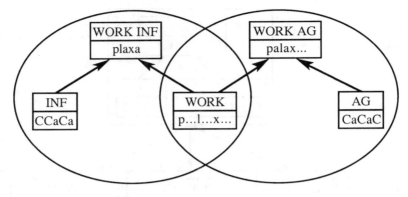

Figure 17. Conjugation of a Specific Root

Let me now suggest that the entire complex configuration in Figure 17 (and even the larger configuration that it abbreviates) may have the status of a conventional linguistic unit. It may in any case provide a basis for schematization. Suppose a number of other verb roots participate in precisely the same inflectional patterns. For each of them a higher-level symbolic assembly directly analogous to Figure 17 can thus be posited. The usual process of abstraction could then apply, resulting in the schematized higher-order assembly depicted in Figure 18. This is a coalition of particular constructional subschemas, describing inflectional patterns all of which are conventionally applicable to the same root. In other words, this higher-order schema defines a *conjugation class*. It is a set of associated inflectional patterns, which certain verbs plug into, and which might have sufficient entrenchment and salience to exert an influence on others. If accessible for the sanction of novel expressions, it can simultaneously specify all the inflected forms of a newly minted root.

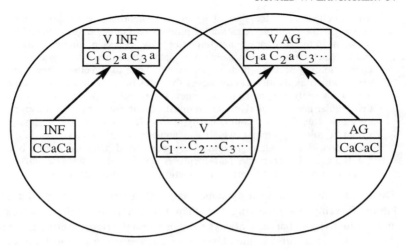

Figure 18. Schemas Defining a Conjugation Class

6. A Final Issue

One of my central objectives has been to indicate that the vast assemblies comprising a speaker's conventional linguistic knowledge can in principle be ascribed to a few basic psychological phenomena, applying repeatedly in many domains and at many levels of organization. Obviously, I have only been able to sketch this vision here. Even the substantial body of work done to date in Cognitive Grammar puts only limited flesh on this skeleton. Perhaps the foregoing discussion at least affords some grounds for suspecting that a dynamic usage-based model of the sort described stands a chance of proving adequate.

I would like to conclude by comparing this model to two alternate proposals with respect to the nature of linguistic "rules." One proposal, recently advanced by Pinker and Prince (1991), is that regular and irregular expressions are handled by distinct systems very different in nature:

> *Regular inflection* (e.g., *walk-walked*) is perfectly rule-governed, and thus looks like a paradigm case of a grammatical rule implemented in human brains. Irregular inflection (e.g., *sing-sang*) shows varying degrees of unpredictability and thus would seem to involve brute-force memory...The regular process seems to be the very essence of the symbol-manipulating, algorithmic approach to language underlying most theories of grammar, whereas the irregular process seems to involve a quite different kind of memory-driven processing.... (230-231)

> The conclusion we draw is that generative theories are fundamentally correct in their characterization of productive rules and structures, but deficient in the way they characterize memory of less predictable material, which must be associative and dynamic, somewhat as connectionism portrays it. It is necessary, then, to develop a new theory ...which explicitly acknowledges the roles of rules on the one hand and of associative memory on the other. From such a theory, it follows that regular and irregular inflection must be computed by two different systems. Regulars are computed by an implementation of a classic symbolic rule of grammar, which concatenates an affix with a variable that stands for the stem. Irregulars are memorized pairs of words, but the linkages between the pair members are stored in an associative memory structure with certain connectionist-like properties. (233)

Thus, something akin to a dynamic usage-based model is accepted for the kinds of examples—involving less than full compositionality, generality, and productivity—that have always been problematic in generative grammar. At the same time, rules in the classic constructive sense (algorithmic operations on strings of discrete symbols) are held necessary for truly systematic phenomena.

In one respect Pinker and Prince are no doubt correct: there is a difference in processing between regular and irregular forms. The latter are indeed stored and retrieved from memory, whereas the former are assembled in accordance with productive patterns (an option available even for high-frequency forms also learned as units). The two modes of processing are qualitatively distinct in ways that might very well explain the psycholinguistic and neurological evidence the authors advance to support their dichotomous view. Still, I am mystified by their apparent inclination to seek a dichotomous account in preference to a unified one. This inverts the usual scientific practice of seeking a unified account for seemingly diverse phenomena. I should think that positing two distinct cognitive systems would be done only reluctantly and as a last resort, after all other options have been thoroughly explored.

The linguistic facts do not suggest a strictly dichotomous organization, since sporadic exceptions are possible even for highly productive general rules, and since minor patterns often show a certain measure of productivity (Bybee and Slobin 1982). Research from the usage-based perspective consistently reinforces the idea that linguistic patterns run the full gamut in terms of systematicity, that rules approximate full generality and productivity more commonly than they actually reach it, and that such rules are at best a small minority in any case. The question, then, is whether a unified account can be given for the entire spectrum of patterns, including those which approach full systematicity. I have tried to show that a dynamic usage-based model offers a realistic prospect of achieving this. Under the right circumstances, a dynamic system of the sort envisaged is capable of crisp, reliable behavior representing any desired approximation to categorical rules. I see no reason to doubt that the observed degrees and kinds of systematicity can all be accommodated by positing appropriately configured networks in which conventional units vary in their specificity and inherent ease of activation.

The other alternate proposal is for linguistic regularities and the creation of novel expressions to be described in terms of "analogy" rather than "rules." This is, of course, a classic issue (see, for example, Bloomfield 1933: 16.6; Householder 1971: ch. 5), which appears to be reviving as alternatives to the generative paradigm are increasingly being sought. What the issue amounts to naturally depends on how the key terms are defined. For example, if "rules" are equated with constructive statements and "analogy" with schemas or templates, then the model proposed here is purely analogical. My own practice, however, is to use the term "rule" for extracted regularities with some kind of enduring cognitive presence, regardless of their specific nature. I will understand "analogy" as referring to expressions being directly formed on the model of others, not on the basis of stored abstracted patterns. By these definitions, the dynamic usage-based model I propose is rule-based rather than analogical. The rules, though, are templatic schemas (as opposed to constructive statements), and are immanent in their instantiations (as opposed to being represented as distinct cognitive entities).

The question, then, is whether rules (schemas) can be wholly dispensed with in favor of the direct modeling of novel expressions on the basis of familiar ones. I think the answer is clearly negative. An exclusively analogical account—one that posits no abstraction or schematization—runs directly counter to the usage-based notion that language exhibits patterns at all levels of generality. It is also internally inconsistent, since even the learning of specific expressions (required as the basis for analogy) involves abstraction and schematization from actual usage events. Moreover, the standard argument against analogy is still a forceful one: if only analogy is posited, how is the distinction drawn between those analogical formations we find acceptable and those we do not? If the past tense of *swim* is *swam*, why can I not analogize and use *tram* as the past tense of *trim*? One cannot merely say that there are relatively few pairs like *swim/swam* to analogize from, and many more like *film/filmed*, since nothing would ensure that only the latter would be chosen as the model. If one were to claim that the much more numerous pairs like *film/filmed* reinforce one another and thus offer an irresistible model for analogy, the analogical position becomes indistinguishable from one which posits schemas. As I have characterized them, schemas are simply reinforced commonalities with the potential to influence subsequent processing.

As this example shows, the distinction between an analogical and a schema-based account is not necessarily a drastic one (Langacker 1987a: 11.3.4). For one thing, schemas can represent any level of abstraction, and low-level schemas are preferentially invoked (other things being equal) for the categorization of novel expressions. An expression sanctioned by a low-level schema rather than a higher-level generalization is likely to be considered "analogical," but a schema abstracted from just a handful of forms is a schema nonetheless. Moreover, analogy itself presupposes structural parallelism. In solving a proportion—e.g. in computing *trimmed* as the value of X in the formula *film/filmed* = *trim/X*—one must first determine that *film* and *filmed* are related in a specific way, and then find an X such that *trim* and X are related in the same way. But what is "the same way"? It is an abstract commonality, which the two pairs share. It is therefore a schema which they both instantiate, and if made explicit it would actually constitute a constructional schema of the sort proposed in Cognitive Grammar. I have no doubt that true analogies do occur, where new expressions are modeled on others without the prior extraction and enduring cognitive presence of any schema. However, the very process of analogizing induces the apprehension of an abstract commonality, at least as a fleeting occurrence. The distinction between rule and analogy then reduces to whether the operative schema has already achieved the status of a unit. This is at most a matter of timing and may well be one of degree.

Notes

I am grateful to Joan Bybee for helpful comments on an earlier version of this paper.

References

Bloomfield, Leonard. 1933. *Language*. New York: Holt.

Browman, Catherine P. and Louis M. Goldstein. 1992. Articulatory phonology: An overview. *Phonetica* 49, 155-80.

Bybee, Joan L. 1985. *Morphology: A Study of the Relation Between Meaning and Form* (Typological Studies in Language 9). Amsterdam: Benjamins.

Bybee, Joan L. 1988. Morphology as lexical organization. In Michael Hammond and Michael Noonan (eds.), *Theoretical Morphology: Approaches in Modern Linguistics*, 119-41. San Diego: Academic Press.

Bybee, Joan L. 1994. A view of phonology from a cognitive and functional perspective. *Cognitive Linguistics* 5, 285-305.

Bybee, Joan L. and Carol L. Moder. 1983. Morphological classes as natural categories. *Language* 59, 251-70.

Bybee, Joan L. and Dan I. Slobin. 1982. Rules and schemas in the development and use of the English past tense. *Language* 58, 265-89.

Chapin, Paul G. 1967. On the syntax of word-derivation in English. *Information System Language Studies, Report no. 16.* MITRE Corporation.

Chomsky, Noam. 1973. Conditions on transformations. In Stephen R. Anderson and Paul Kiparsky (eds.), *A Festschrift for Morris Halle*, 232-86. New York: Holt.

Elman, Jeffrey L. 1990. Finding structure in time. *Cognitive Science* 14, 179-211.

Elman, Jeffrey L. and James L. McClelland. 1984. Speech perception as a cognitive process: The interactive activation model. In Norman Lass (ed.), *Speech and Language*, Vol. 10, 337-74. New York: Academic Press.

Farrell, Patrick. 1990. Spanish stress: A cognitive analysis. *Hispanic Linguistics* 4, 21-56.

Fauconnier, Gilles and Mark Turner. 1994. Conceptual projection and middle spaces. *Dept. of Cognitive Science, Report no. 9401.* San Diego, CA: University of California.

Fillmore, Charles J., Paul Kay, and Mary Catherine O'Connor. 1988. Regularity and idiomaticity in grammatical constructions: The case of *let alone. Language* 64, 501-38.

Fong, Heatherbell. 1988. *The Stony Idiom of the Brain: A Study in the Syntax and Semantics of Metaphors.* San Diego: University of California doctoral dissertation.

Goldberg, Adele E. 1992. The inherent semantics of argument structure: The case of the English ditransitive construction. *Cognitive Linguistics* 3, 37-74.

Goldberg, Adele E. 1995. *Constructions: A Construction Grammar Approach to Argument Structure.* Chicago: University of Chicago Press.

Halle, Morris. 1959. *The Sound Pattern of Russian.* The Hague: Mouton.

Householder, Frederick W. 1971. *Linguistic Speculations.* Cambridge: Cambridge University Press.

Jackendoff, Ray. 1975. Morphological and semantic regularities in the lexicon. *Language* 51, 639-71.

Kemmer, Suzanne and Michael Israel. 1994. Variation and the usage-based model. *Papers from the 30th Annual Regional Meeting of the Chicago Linguistic Society: Parasession on Variation and Linguistic Theory*, 165-79. Chicago: CLS.

Lakoff, George. 1970. *Irregularity in Syntax.* New York: Holt.

Lakoff, George. 1987. *Women, Fire, and Dangerous Things: What Categories Reveal About the Mind.* Chicago: University of Chicago Press.

Lakoff, George. 1990. The invariance hypothesis: Is abstract reason based on image-schemas? *Cognitive Linguistics* 1, 39-74.

Lakoff, George and Mark Johnson. 1980. *Metaphors We Live By.* Chicago: University of Chicago Press.

Lakoff, Geroge and Mark Turner. 1989. *More than Cool Reason: A Field Guide to Poetic Metaphor.* Chicago: University of Chicago Press.

Langacker, Ronald W. 1987a. *Foundations of Cognitive Grammar*, Vol. 1: *Theoretical Prerequisites*. Stanford: Stanford University Press.

Langacker, Ronald W. 1987b. Nouns and verbs. *Language* 63, 53-94.

Langacker, Ronald W. 1988. A usage-based model. In Brygida Rudzka-Ostyn (ed.), *Topics in Cognitive Linguistics* (Current Issues in Linguistic Theory 50), 127-61. Amsterdam: Benjamins.

Langacker, Ronald W. 1990. The rule controversy: A Cognitive Grammar perspective. *Center for Research in Language Newsletter* 4(3), 4-15.

Langacker, Ronald W. 1991. *Foundations of Cognitive Grammar*, Vol. 2: *Descriptive Application*. Stanford: Stanford University Press.

Langacker, Ronald W. 1993. Grammatical traces of some "invisible" semantic constructs. *Language Sciences* 15, 323-55.

MacWhinney, Brian. 1987. The competition model. In Brian MacWhinney (ed.), *Mechanisms of Language Acquisition*, 249-308. Hillsdale, NJ: Erlbaum.

McClelland, James L. and Jeffrey L. Elman. 1986a. Interactive processes in speech perception: The TRACE model. In McClelland and Rumelhart (eds.), 58-121. Cambridge, MA/London: MIT Press/Bradford.

McClelland, James L. and Jeffrey L. Elman. 1986b. The TRACE model of speech perception. *Cognitive Psychology* 18, 1-86.

McClelland, James L. and David E. Rumelhart (eds.). 1986. *Parallel Distributed Processing: Explorations in the Microstructure of Cognition*, Vol. 2: *Psychological and Biological Models*. Cambridge, MA/London: MIT Press/Bradford.

Pinker, Steven and Alan Prince. 1991. Regular and irregular morphology and the psychological status of rules of grammar. *Proceedings of the 17th Annual Meeting of the Berkeley Linguistics Society*, 230-51. Berkeley, CA: BLS.

Quinn, Naomi. 1991. The cultural basis of metaphor. In James W. Fernandez (ed.), *Beyond Metaphor: The Theory of Tropes in Anthropology*, 56-93. Stanford: Stanford University Press.

Ross, John R. 1967. *Constraints on Variables in Syntax*. Cambridge, MA: MIT doctoral dissertation. [Published as Ross 1986.]

Ross, John R. 1986. *Infinite Syntax!* Norwood, NJ: Ablex.

Ross, John R. 1987. Islands and syntactic prototypes. *Papers from the 23rd Annual Regional Meeting of the Chicago Linguistic Society*, 309-20. Chicago: CLS.

Rubba, Johanna E. 1993. *Discontinuous Morphology in Modern Aramaic*. San Diego: University of California doctoral dissertation.

Rumelhart, David E. and James L. McClelland (eds.). 1986. *Parallel Distributed Processing: Explorations in the Microstructure of Cognition*, Vol. 1: *Foundations*. Cambridge, MA/London: MIT Press/Bradford.

Ryder, Mary Ellen. 1991. Mixers, mufflers and mousers: The extending of the *-er* suffix as a case of prototype reanalysis. *Proceedings of the 17th Annual Meeting of the Berkeley Linguistics Society*, 299-311. Berkeley, CA: BLS.

Stemberger, Joseph P. and Brian MacWhinney. 1988. Are inflected forms stored in the lexicon? In Michael Hammond and Michael Noonan (eds.), *Theoretical Morphology: Approaches in Modern Linguistics*, 101-16. San Diego: Academic Press.

Tuggy, David. 1993. Ambiguity, polysemy, and vagueness. *Cognitive Linguistics* 4, 273-90.

Turner, Mark. 1990. Aspects of the invariance hypothesis. *Cognitive Linguistics* 1, 247-55.

Turner, Mark and Gilles Fauconnier. 1995. Conceptual integration and formal expression. *Journal of Metaphor and Symbolic Activity* 10, 183-203.

van Hoek, Karen. 1992. Paths Through Conceptual Structure: Constraints on Pronominal Anaphora. San Diego: University of California doctoral dissertation.

Zwicky, Arnold and Jerrold Sadock. 1975. Ambiguity tests and how to fail them. In John Kimball (ed.), *Syntax and Semantics,* Vol. 4, 1-36. New York: Academic Press.

The Phonology of the Lexicon: Evidence from Lexical Diffusion

JOAN L. BYBEE

University of New Mexico

In many areas of linguistics, examining the nature of diachronic changes leads to a more accurate modeling of synchronic systems.[1] Lexical diffusion—the way a sound change spreads through the lexicon—has, as yet, not been exploited as a potential source of evidence about the phonological shape of lexical representations. The present study contains evidence that sound change is both phonetically gradual and lexically gradual, and that the rate at which words undergo sound change is positively correlated with their text frequency. This correlation is found in monomorphemic words, regularly inflected words and irregularly inflected words. I argue that frequency effects in sound change may be explained by assuming that cognitive representations are impacted by every token of use.

The sound change about which new evidence will be provided here—t/d-deletion in English—has been vigorously studied by sociolinguists seeking to understand the factors controlling the variation found in this process. One of their findings is that the morphological status of the final $/t/$ or $/d/$ affects the rate of deletion. Special properties of phonological segments serving as morphemes have also been studied experimentally by psycholinguists. This paper proposes to bring together evidence from variation, experimental findings and data on text frequency to

refine a usage-based model of lexical representation and morphological organization.

The first part of this paper examines lexical diffusion in general and the
claim that frequency affects the diffusion of sound change. The evidence that
t/d-deletion is more advanced in high frequency words is presented, and a
view of phonetic variation compatible with the data is examined.

The second part of the paper addresses the morphological effects on the
variation in t/d-deletion. The morphological model of Bybee (1985, 1988)
makes certain predictions about the effect of t/d-deletion on regular verbs,
and these are tested on the data. It is found that the frequency effect demonstrated for the corpus overall is also found among regularly inflected verbs,
suggesting that at least high frequency regulars are listed lexically. A frequency effect is also found in the double-marked pasts, such as *told* and
slept. It is argued that the apparent special properties of this class are due to
the high frequency of many of its members.

1. Frequency Effects in the Lexical Diffusion of Sound Change

1.1 Lexical Diffusion

The study of lexical diffusion has primarily been directed at accounting for
irregular results of sound changes, in particular, lexical items that appear not
to have undergone a change (Wang 1969, Krishnamurti 1978). Changes that
have occurred over very long periods of time have also been the subject of
lexical diffusion studies (Krishnamurti 1978). Such changes can be said to
be taking place at the phonemic level and have led Wang and Cheng (1977)
to postulate that most sound change is lexically gradual and phonetically
abrupt.

A lexically abrupt sound change would affect all lexical items at the
same time, while one that is lexically gradual moves through the lexicon
affecting individual items or groups of items in sequence. A phonetically
gradual sound change takes place in very small increments, moving gradually through phonetic space, while a phonetically abrupt change takes place
in a single large, discrete step. If the phonological units of the lexicon are
phonemes or generative underlying representations, a sound change that affects words differentially must be phonetically abrupt, since small phonetic
increments do not exist in the structuralist or generativist lexicon. Thus the
changes reported on in Wang (1977) are changes affecting phonemes, such
as Chinese tones, final nasals, and English stress as used in diatone pairs
(*récord, recórd*).

Similarly, Labov (1981, 1994) proposes that some sound changes exhibit lexical diffusion while others are 'Neogrammarian' changes, that is, they are regular in the sense that they affect all lexical items with appropriate phonetic conditioning at the same time. The changes that exhibit lexical diffusion, according to Labov (1994: 542–43), are phonetically discrete, bringing about phonemic changes in particular words. Labov further proposes a typology of Neogrammarian vs. lexical diffusion changes: The latter, Labov proposes, are found in shortening and lengthening of segments, diphthongization of mid and low vowels, changes of place of articulation of consonants, metathesis of liquids and stops, and deletion of obstruents. Regular sound changes occur in subsystems of vowels, including vowel shifts and the diphthongization of high vowels; also regular are changes in the manner of articulation of consonants, vocalization of liquids and deletion of glides and schwa. Such changes are most often phonetically gradual and lexically regular.

Phillips (1984) does not accept Labov's claims, arguing that his dichotomy is too simplistic, as many changes affecting subsystems of vowels and the manner of articulation of consonants show evidence of lexical diffusion. Phillips implies that lexical diffusion is much more widespread than previously thought, and, based on Hooper (1976), provides a distinction between two types of lexical diffusion. In one the direction of diffusion is from the most frequent to the least frequent words, while in the other, the opposite direction of change is found. High frequency words are affected earlier by vowel and consonant reduction or assimilation processes (Fidelholz 1975, Hooper 1976, Leslau 1969). Phillips characterizes this type of change as "motivated by physiological factors, acting on surface phonetic forms" (320). Changes that affect the least frequent words first are more likely motivated by conceptual factors. These include grammatical conditioning, as in analogical leveling and diatone formation, as well as changes affecting the sequential constraints of the language.[2]

This paper concerns only the first type of change—phonetically-motivated change. Change of this type usually appears to be lexically regular once the change is complete, but evidence presented here shows that such changes affect lexical items at different rates while the change is in progress. Using t/d-deletion as the example, it will be argued that sound change can be both lexically gradual and phonetically gradual. The consequences of this finding for lexical representation is that lexical entries for words undergoing gradual change must include detail about the range of phonetic variation associated with each word.

1.2 Word Frequency in Lexical Diffusion

There exists a considerable body of evidence showing that phonetically-conditioned sound change proceeds through the lexicon, gradually working from high frequency words to low frequency words. The effects of frequency have been shown for vowel reduction and deletion in English (Fidelholz 1975, Hooper 1976), and for the raising of / a / to / o / before nasals in Old English (Phillips 1980), for various changes in Ethiopian languages (Leslau 1969), for the weakening of stops in American English and vowel change in the Cologne dialect of German (Johnson 1983), for ongoing vowel changes in San Francisco English (Moonwomon 1992), and for tensing of short *a* in Philadelphia (Labov 1994: 506–07).

Some of these changes are both lexically gradual and phonetically gradual. For instance, the schwa deletion process discussed in Hooper (1976) gradually reduces a schwa following the stressed vowel and preceding a sonorant, preferably / r / or / l /. This reduction is more advanced in higher frequency words. Thus high frequency *memory, salary, summary* and *nursery* have a more reduced penultimate syllable than low frequency *mammary, artillery, summery* and *cursory*. Of course all of these words have multiple variants in actual use, but their ranges of variation differ systematically.

No Schwa	**Syllabic [r]**	**Schwa + [r]**
every (492)	memory (91)	mammary (0)
	salary (51)	artillery (11)
	summary (21)	summery (0)
	nursery (14)	cursory (4)
evening (149)		evening (0)
(noun)		(verb + *ing*)

Table 1. Words Undergoing Reduction at Differential Rates due to Word Frequency (frequency figures from Francis and Kucera 1982)

Changes that are both lexically and phonetically gradual create a problem for traditional theories of phonemic or lexical representation: individual words with distinct ranges of variation cannot be represented by a simple set of contrastive phonological units. In the schwa-deletion example, the number of distinct lexical sets is unknown, but there must be at least three: (i) those with the schwa totally deleted, *every, evening* (noun); (ii) those in which the / r / or / l / can be syllabic or non-syllabic, *memory, salary, summary, nursery*; and (iii) those in which the schwa or syllabic resonant is always present, *mammary, artillery, cursory, evening* (verb + *ing*). These three lexical categories range over only two phonemes, since / r / and syllabic / r / are not distinguished phonemically, nor are syllabic / r / and / ´r /. This example shows that lexical items can have subphonemic detail associated with them. The fact that all three classes of words have variable pronunciations suggests that an appropriate model of the lexicon must allow for the representation of ranges of phonetic variation, and these ranges do not necessarily coincide with traditional or generative phonemes. The problem is even more severe if, as is extremely likely, there are not just three classes, but rather there is a continuum of degree of reduction, with each word exhibiting its own range of variation.[3] Moreover, the deletion of schwa and the reduction of the syllabicity of [r] are not separate processes; rather the reduction in all of these words is one continuous process.

1.3 Word Frequency and *t / d*-Deletion

The variable deletion of final / t / and / d/ in English has been well-studied in the last two decades (Labov 1972, Guy 1980, Neu 1980). The factors influencing the deletion of final / t / or / d/ are phonetic, grammatical and social:

- Phonetic: final / t / and / d/ are deleted more often if a consonant follows in the next word than if a vowel follows.

- Grammatical: final / t / and / d/ are deleted less often if they function as the regular past tense marker; they are deleted more often if they constitute the past tense suffix in words that also have a vowel change (*told, kept*).

- Social: final / t / and / d/ are deleted more often by younger people, males and members of lower social classes (Labov 1972, Neu 1980).

The data analysed for this study was generously supplied by Otto Santa Ana from his study of phonological variation in Chicano English speakers of Los Angeles (Santa Ana 1991). The speakers used in this study were all native speakers of English. The values for final / t / and / d/ were transcribed by Santa Ana from recordings made in interviews. For the present study, 2000 tokens of final / t / and / d / from forty-one speakers were used. The speakers ranged in age from 13 to 62 years; approximately half were male and half female.

No evidence of lexical diffusion or a general frequency effect has been reported for *t / d*-deletion, despite the fact that it is a well-studied example of phonological variation. However, in studies of *t / d*-deletion the words *and*, *just* and *went* are often excluded because of their high rates of deletion. These words are clear examples of lexical diffusion conditioned by high to-ken frequency, leading us to suspect a more general effect of word frequency on the diffusion of this change.

In order to test for the effects of word frequency on deletion, for each word that potentially ends in a / t / or / d / following a consonant, we re-corded the text frequency as listed in Francis and Kucera (1982). *Just, went* and *and* were excluded because of their very high frequency and high rate of deletion. All other words were divided into two groups: a high frequency and a low frequency group. The cut-off point of 35 per million was chosen, be-cause a number in this range is used in the psycholinguistic literature when frequency effects are measured. Particularly relevant to our analysis of past tense forms is the fact that Stemberger and MacWhinney (1988) report that a frequency of 35 per million divides English inflected forms in half: half the tokens of inflected forms in Francis and Kucera (1982) have a frequency greater than 35 and half have a frequency of less than 35.

Dividing the current corpus in this way, 20% of the tokens fall in the low frequency group and 80% in the high frequency group. Table 2 shows the deletion figures for the entire corpus by frequency grouping.[4]

	Deletion	Non-Deletion	% Deletion
High Frequency	898	752	54.4%
Low Frequency	137	262	34.3%

Chi-squared: 41.67, p < .001, df = 1

Table 2. Rate of *t / d*-deletion for Entire Corpus by Word Frequency

As the table shows, word frequency is a significant factor in the variation in *t / d*-deletion. It will be shown below that frequency has a general effect even when verbs are separated from nouns and adjectives. Before discussing the data on verbs and their inflections, however, let us examine the implications of phonetically and lexically gradual sound change for phonological representation.

1.4 Discussion: Phonetic Variation in Lexical Representation

Genuine lexically-determined variation cannot be represented in a variable rule, it must be represented lexically, especially if it affects all or most of the words of a particular phonological shape. Trying to build such variation into a variable rule would require repeating the contents of the lexicon in the rule.

If memory for words resembles memory for other types of sensory input, then we would not expect that words are stored with details removed, but rather that even redundant features of words contribute to the formation of a prototype structure for the phonological representation. The fact that speakers consistently produce *every*, *memory* and *mammary* with three distinct ranges of variation, means that more distinctions than those that are strictly considered phonemic exist in the lexicon.

One way of accounting for the continuous nature of such sound changes and the frequency effect they show in lexical diffusion is to assume that sound changes affect words opportunistically each time they are used. The sound change 'rules' apply in real time, so that a frequent word has more exposure to the sound change than an infrequent one. If the effects of the sound change are cycled back into the lexicon, as the speaker monitors his/her own speech and the speech of others, the lexical representations for the words gradually adjust to the new productions (Moonwomon 1992). One reason that frequent words are affected at a higher rate than infrequent ones is because they have more exposure to the pronunciation pattern. However, there are two other factors that enhance change in high frequency words when that change is reductive:[5] First, low frequency words occur less often in casual speech and thus have even less exposure to the reductive processes. Second, words repeated in the same discourse are shorter than in their first mention (Fowler and Housum 1987). Thus, given the model of sound change outlined here, words that are repeated often within a discourse, which would also be words that have a high overall frequency, undergo sound changes at a faster rate.

In the case of *t* / *d*-deletion, I am not suggesting that each word has an index of deletion probability related to its frequency. Rather, I propose that deletion takes place very gradually as the shortening of the coronal gesture and this shortening is represented lexically. (For measurements of this shortening, see Losiewicz 1992, discussed below). I also propose, following

Moonwomon, that phonological processes, such as the weakening of final / t / and / d /, apply in real time and have an effect on the words to which they apply. Thus when a word with a final coronal stop is used, that articulatory gesture is usually compressed and shortened. The output of that process is registered in memory through self-monitoring and decoding the speech of others. Thus small changes may be periodically made in the prototype representation for each word. The more a word is used, especially in contexts that are appropriate for reduction, the more reduced the word becomes. In this way, the effect of word frequency on the propagation of a change through the lexicon is explained.

Proposing that variable rules affect the lexicon is not as radical an idea as it may sound. Harris (1989) discusses the increasing 'lexical depth' of variable rules, which he regards as a natural consequence of the development of a rule. In his view, as rules develop they progress both phonetically and lexically. His examples involve phonemic change. Guy (1991a, 1991b) proposes that t / d-deletion, usually considered postlexical, applies at the deep levels of Lexical Phonology, again an indication that the variable process has penetrated the lexicon. (Below I will give evidence for representing t / d weakening in the lexical entries rather than in the lexical rules.)

The proposal that words have their own ranges of phonetic variation rather than being composed of units that belong to a (systematic) phonemic set, specifiable for each language, would seem to allow an infinite range of phonetic representations for the words of a language. Why is it that the phonetic properties of words are strictly controlled by language-specific constraints rather being infinitely variable? The reason is that what goes into the lexicon is regulated by the phonetic processes or pronunciation patterns whose function it is to automate the production of phonetic strings. The efficiency of such patterns depends upon their producing a regular and highly constrained inventory of phonetic strings. Eventually these phonological processes carry sound changes through to completion and regularize lexical representations.

Phonemes, then, do not exist in the representations of words; they are not units of lexical representation. Instead, phonemes are abstract patterns that emerge in the phonological organization of the lexicon (see Langacker this volume). To the extent that distinct phonetic units are grouped together into more abstract units, this is done on the basis of the phonetic implementation schemata, and is not a strict matter of complementary distribution, as can be seen from the examples presented so far.

1.5 Phonetic Gestures

The phonetic representations and mode of phonetic implementation that best accommodate the workings of sound change that I am trying to characterize here is gestural phonology. I am considering phonological representations to be sets of commands to the articulators and phonetic output to be a series of partially overlapping articulatory gestures (Browman and Goldstein 1990, Pagliuca and Mowrey 1987). This conception provides an explanation for the phonetic conditions that favor *t / d*-deletion, i.e. the presence of a following consonant.

Browman and Goldstein (1990) traced the articulatory gestures in the phrase *perfect memory* to see what happens to the coronal gesture in the / t / .[6] They found that the lingual gesture was present, but the preceding velar and following labial gesture overlapped the coronal one, obscuring it entirely. It would thus be perceived as deleted, even though articulatorily it is still present. This does not mean that deletion is a myth; it does mean that there is no variable rule of *t / d*-deletion. Rather there is a gradual process of shortening or reducing the lingual gesture (for which we will see evidence just below). As the gesture shortens, the likelihood that it will be overlapped and thus acoustically obscured by surrounding gestures increases. Thus in words of higher frequency, where the coronal stop is shorter, perceived deletion is more likely.

Perceived deletion leads to actual deletion, that is, loss of the coronal gesture. This loss is ongoing, but at a much slower rate than the perceived deletion. Perceived deletion leads to the restructuring of underlying forms and proceeds item by item. Actual deletion occurs because preconsonantal and prepausal environments are three times as common as prevocalic ones. If lexical representations are prototype representations of all input variations, the final coronal stop in a lexical entry will shorten and gradually move towards deletion.

This particular sound change has articulatory, perceptual and lexical dimensions. Articulatorily a gestural reduction is taking place. At the same time, the perception of the reduced consonant is masked by surrounding consonants. Lexical entries containing a final coronal stop are gradually accommodating to the changing input, and will gradually restructure, losing the stop entirely. Thus there are three sources of the surface variation: the articulatory change is gradually reducing the gesture involved; the phonetic environment conditions whether or not the gesture can be perceived, and the lexical items themselves have different degrees of reduction.

2. Morphological Effects on Sound Change and Lexical Diffusion

2.1 Past Tense of Verbs and *t/d*-Deletion

Studies of *t/d*-deletion consistently find that the final coronal stop is less likely to delete if it is the Past tense morpheme than if it is part of a monomorphemic word (Labov 1972, Guy 1980). Moreover, a consistent difference is found between the regular Past, as in *walked* and *learned*, and the Past suffix on verbs that also have a stem change, such as *kept* and *told*. This difference is consistent with an account that attributes the lower rate of deletion of Past tense *t/d* to the need to retain the information encoded in this morpheme. In the verbs with vowel change, that information is not lost. In the discussion that follows, we will see that this 'information preservation' assumption explains only part of the data.

In the data examined for the current study, it was also found that regular Past tense and Past participle forms (which were grouped together) had a lower rate of deletion than nouns and adjectives in the same frequency range. Regular *-ed* verbs in our corpus had Francis and Kucera frequencies ranging from 0 to 403 per million. The rate of deletion for all words with frequencies of 403 or less is 45.8%; the rate of deletion on *-ed* verbs is 22.6%, as shown in Table 3.

	% Deletion
All words	45.8%
-ed verbs	22.6%

Table 3. Rate of Deletion for Regular Past Tense Compared to All Other Words of Comparable Frequency (403 or less)

Guy (1991a, 1991b) offers an interpretation of *t/d*-deletion in the context of Lexical Phonology (Kiparsky 1982). Guy proposes that the variable rule of *t/d*-deletion applies at all levels of a Lexical Phonology: it applies at the base level to non-derived forms, it applies after Level 1 affixation, and again after Level 2 affixation, assuming only two levels for the purposes of his analysis. Thus monomorphemic words have three chances to undergo *t/d*-deletion; irregular Past forms, such as *kept* and *told*, have two chances—one at Level 1 after affixation occurs and again after Level 2 affixation. Regular Past tense forms are only exposed to the rule once, after Level 2 affixation. Guy proposes that the rule applies at a constant rate and that the different rates of deletion in the three categories of words is an exponent of the number of exposures the word has had to the rule.

Guy's analysis demonstrates a very interesting point: certain words are behaving as though t/d-deletion has applied to them more than once. In his analysis, this variable rule has penetrated the lexicon and is treating words differentially according to their morphological structure; words that have higher rates of deletion can be thought of as undergoing the rule repeatedly. Note, however, that Guy's hypothesis refers only to morphological structure and cannot explain the overall effect of word frequency on deletion rates.

The proposal being made here, that t/d-reduction applies in real time and has a permanent effect on the phonological shape of words in the lexicon, achieves approximately the same result. If a word already had a weakened [t] or [d] and then underwent further reduction when that word was used again, the chances that it would be perceived as deleted (preceding a consonant) would be increased. Furthermore, Guy (1991b) shows that the effect of the environment preceding the [t] or [d], which is internal to the word and thus always present, increases the rate of application of deletion in words subject to multiple applications, while the following environment does not increase the rate of application in words subject to multiple applications, because the following conditioning environment is only present in the last application of the rule, the postlexical application. The same result is predicted for the model in which rule application has a permanent effect on the lexicon, but for different reasons. The preceding environment has a stronger effect on the lexical representation because it is present each time the word is used. The following environment—a following consonant—is an 'alternating environment' and affects the lexical representation more slowly since it is not always present when the word is used (see Timberlake 1978 and Bybee 1998 for other examples of variable processes that apply less often or to a lesser extent in alternating environments).

In many ways, then, the two models make similar predictions. The difference is that the Lexical Phonology interpretation attributes differential rates of rule application to structural differences among words, while the usage-based interpretation attributes much of the differential reduction to word frequency. In the following I will show that word frequency is a significant factor in t/d-reduction, even inside of morphological classes. These facts support the usage-based account over the Lexical Phonology account, since the latter has no way of describing differential application based on word frequency. The following discussion will be situated in the model proposed in Bybee (1985, 1988), which makes certain predictions for the application of t/d-reduction to morphologically complex words.

2.2 Morphology as Lexical Organization

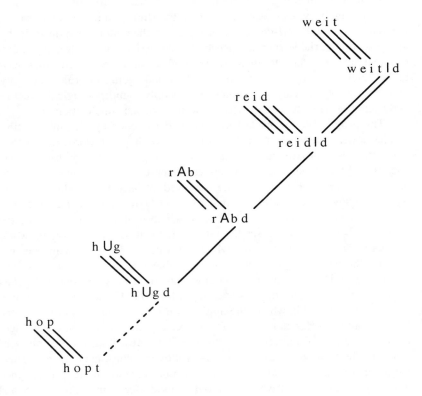

Figure 1.   Emergent Morphological Structure and the Regular Past Tense Schema

In Bybee (1985, 1988) it is proposed that the lexicon consists primarily of words, and even words that are morphologically complex may have lexical storage. It is also argued that token frequency has an effect on the way words are stored and processed, as words have varying lexical strength according to their frequency of use. Even at resting levels, high frequency words have stronger representations in memory, making them, among other things, easier to access. Morphologically complex words of high frequency are more likely to maintain their irregularities because they have a stronger representation in memory, and lower frequency words are more likely to be replaced by those formed on a regular pattern. Irregular forms are stored in the lexicon and to the extent that they form classes with other forms, patterns of similarities based on prototype structure create lexical schemas (Bybee and Moder 1983, Prasada and Pinker 1993).

Figure 1 illustrates the relevant portion of the proposed lexical network. Similarities among words are shown as lexical connections, which can be phonological or semantic. Parallel phonological and semantic connections, such as those shown in Figure 1, constitute morphological relations if they are repeated across items. A dotted line indicates similarity but not identity.

It follows from the premise that frequency of use determines representation in the lexicon, that even regular morphological formations of sufficient frequency are represented lexically. The internal structure of morphologically complex words derives from the connections made with other words. Thus the Past tense morpheme emerges from the patterns of lexical connections as a schema. Because of its high type frequency, this schema is very powerful, leading to its high productivity (Bybee 1995).

$$\ldots \text{(i) alveolar stop]}_{\text{past tense}}$$

Very low frequency verbs may not have their Past tense forms represented in memory, or they may not be represented with sufficient strength for easy retrieval. In that case, the base verb is supplied with a Past tense inflection by the general schema. This means that there are two ways of processing regular Past tense verbs—selecting them whole from the lexicon and deriving them by applying the schema to a base.

Losiewicz (1992) tested the hypothesis that high and low frequency regular verbs are processed in these two ways. She started from the finding that consonants that are parts of monomorphemic words are produced with shorter acoustic duration than those that constitute morphemes, that is, the /s/ in *lapse* is shorter than the one in *laps* (Walsh and Parker 1983). She found that the same situation holds with respect to Past tense [t] and [d], that is, in word pairs such as *swayed* and *suede* the *-ed* suffix is on average 5 msec. longer than the nonmorphemic [t] or [d]. The interpretation of this durational effect given by Walsh and Parker and by Losiewicz is that segments that are represented in the underlying form as part of the word tend to be shorter than those added in morphological processing. Losiewicz reasoned that if lexically represented consonants are shorter than added ones, and if high frequency Past tense verbs are stored as units but low frequency verbs are constructed by applying a schema to the base, then the Past tense [t] or

[d] on high frequency verbs should be shorter in acoustic duration than the same consonants on low frequency verbs.

Losiewicz constructed eight pairs of rhyming, regular Past tense verbs in which one member of the pair had a frequency of 100 per million or greater and the other had a frequency of 10 or fewer per million. Some examples are *called, mauled; covered, hovered; needed, kneaded; expected, inspected.* The stimuli verb pairs were presented in sentences which differed only in the verb. (For example, *The workers expected/inspected all the mail at noon every day.*) Each subject read only one of each pair of stimuli sentences. Subjects read the sentences into a recorder and the length of the consonants in question was measured from the waveform. The results show that on average the *-ed* suffix on low frequency verbs is 7 msec. longer than on high frequency verbs. Losiewicz concludes that high frequency multi-morphemic verbs are represented as unitary wholes in the lexicon, while low frequency multi-morphemic verbs are processed as stem + affix.

A difference in the length of the final [t] or [d] suffix varying with the frequency of the verb is predicted from the interpretation of the lexical diffusion process for t/d-reduction given above. Among verbs of sufficient frequency to have their Past tense represented lexically, we would expect that higher frequency verbs will have undergone more reduction than lower frequency verbs. Thus a frequency difference even within lexically listed verbs is predicted, in addition to the length difference found by Losiewicz. The results of the test of this hypothesis are given in the next section.

2.3 t/d-Reduction in Regular Past Tense

For the test of the effect of frequency on t/d-deletion among regular *-ed* verbs, we control the phonological environment, taking only those that favor deletion—non-prevocalic conditions. Dividing the regular verbs into two groups—those with frequencies of their *-ed* forms of 35 or fewer per million and those with frequencies over 35 per million, we find a significant effect of frequency, as shown in Table 4.

	Deletion	Non-Deletion	% Deletion
High Frequency	44	67	39.6%
Low Frequency	11	47	18.9%

Chi-squared: 5.00313, p < .05, df = 1

Table 4. The Effects of Word Frequency on t/d-deletion in Regular Past Tense Verbs (non-prevocalic only)

The results in Table 4 present strong confirmation of the hypothesis that regular verbs of higher frequency have lexical listing. If the *-ed* suffix were always added to the verb by morphological rules, there would be no reason for the length of the suffix to be affected by the token frequency of the whole unit, i.e. the Past tense verb form. The fact that the frequency of the whole unit affects the deletion rate of the suffix [t] or [d] can best be accounted for by listing the units in the lexicon and allowing gradual phonetic change to affect the lexical entries.

These data also argue against the dual processing model proposed by Pinker (1991), in which irregular forms have lexical listing, but regular ones are produced by a rule that is independent of the lexicon. In Pinker's model all regular verbs are formed in precisely the same way, and there is no way for the token frequency of the whole unit to affect the phonetic shape of the suffix.

2.4 Double-Marked Past Tense Verbs

Studies of the effects of morphology on *t/d*-deletion consistently show that double-marked Past tense forms such as *kept, found, told*, etc. have a higher rate of deletion than regular Past tense. In our data, the rate of deletion for these verbs is 42.8%. This high rate of deletion is consistent with the fact that most of these verbs have relatively high token frequency. All but two of them which occur in our corpus have frequencies over 35 per million in Francis and Kucera.

In Guy's treatment of *t/d*-deletion in Lexical Phonology, the Past tense of these verbs is formed at Level 1. After they are formed, *t/d*-deletion is available to apply to them (variably) at Level 1 and then again (variably) at Level 2. Because the variable rule has two chances to apply to these verbs, they have a higher rate of deletion than the Past tense forms derived at Level 2, which only have one chance to undergo the rule. Thus Guy's treatment claims that the different rate of deletion is due to a structural difference in the derivation of irregular and regular Past tense.

However, it is entirely possible that the different rate of deletion is due to the high frequency of these verbs and not to a structural difference between them and other verbs. If a structural difference governs the rate of deletion of these verbs, then we would expect the rate to be similar across the different lexical verbs. However, if it is frequency that conditions the rate of deletion, we would expect to find differences even among the double-marked verbs conditioned by frequency. The latter is what the data show: the higher frequency verbs of this class undergo deletion at a higher rate than the low frequency verbs, as shown in Table 5.

Total Tokens	Verb	# of Deletions	% Deletions
32	told	22	68%
9	felt	5	55%
8	left	2	25%
6	kept	4	66%
4	sent	1	25%
4	built	0	0
3	held	0	0
3	heard	0	0
2	slept	1	50%
2	lent	0	0
1	found	0	0
1	lost	0	0
1	meant	0	0

Spearman rank order correlation: p = .696
Significant at the .01 level (two-tailed or one-tailed)

Table 5. Double-marked Pasts Ordered by Frequency in our Data, with Ties Ordered by Francis and Kucera Frequency

Table 5 shows a strong effect of word frequency among the words of this class, with high frequency verbs generally showing deletion at a higher rate than low frequency verbs. The data also suggest conditioning by phonological factors: a labial stop preceding the /t/ favors deletion since the labial gesture can overlap and obscure the perception of the /t/. This explains why *kept* and *slept* have a higher rate of deletion than some of the other more frequent verbs.

The frequency effect among the words of this class cannot be accounted for in the structural account that proposes that these words are derived at Level 1 and have a higher rate of deletion because the rule has two chances to apply to them. If this account were correct, the rate of deletion for each verb would be approximately the same. I conclude, therefore, that the primary factor that accounts for the higher deletion in this class is word frequency.

2.5 Modeling

We have seen that the facts of *t / d*-deletion are consistent with the hypothesis made by the usage-based model that high frequency words are represented in the lexicon even if they are morphologically complex. The facts also support the hypothesis that sound change occurs in real time, with its effects being registered in the lexicon as small incremental changes, such that words that are used more often will undergo change at a faster rate.

With these two points now established it is possible to turn to a consideration of the question of why the Past tense suffix / t / and / d / reduce more slowly than non-suffixal / t / and / d / . The factor traditionally invoked to explain the conservatism of morphemic / t / and / d / is that the information value of the Past tense / t / and / d / is greater than that of nonmorphemic / t / and / d / . Past tense marking is often redundant; however, in cases where it is carrying some information crucial to the discourse, speakers are quite capable of slowing down their speech and adjusting junctures in such a way as to make the / t / or / d / perceptually salient. Suppression of the reduction and coarticulatory overlap will also serve to retard reduction of the phonetic substance of the lexical schema for Past tense / t / and / d / .

The data also reveal another factor that may help explain why the Past tense /t/ and /d/ reduce more slowly than nonmorphemic / t / and / d / . For some reason, regular Past tense /t/ and /d/ occur more often before a vowel than final / t / and / d / in nonverbs. For all words in the corpus ending in / t / or / d / , 22.7% occur before a vowel; of verbs ending in Past tense / t / or / d / , 40.1% occur before a vowel. Since prevocalic position is the most favorable position for / t / and / d / perceptually, their more frequent occurrence in this position would retard the reduction that is conditioned perceptually.

2.6 Theoretical Implications

Two important points for usage-based models are established by the data presented here. It has been argued that sound change, or phonetic change, affects the lexicon gradually by spreading out across lexical items from the most frequent to the least frequent, and by producing small gradual changes in the phonetic representation of lexical items. One important consequence of this view is that sound change permanently affects the lexicon, and that lexical items are not represented in an abstract phonemic notation. A second consequence is the more general point that the phonetic properties of lexical items, like their morphosyntactic and semantic properties, are affected by language use.

"Phonemes" do not exist as units; the phenomena that phonemes are intended to describe are relations of similarity among parts of the phonetic string. These relations of similarity can be captured by lexical connections and schemas just as other relations of similarity are. Complementary distribution, rather than a criterion for deciding on lexical status of a phone, is just a consequence of the fact that articulatory adjustments are conditioned by the surrounding environment. Registering such phonetic variation in the lexicon even if it is predictable provides a means for accounting for the establishment of new phonemes from distinctions that were formerly predictable, such as the [x] – [ç] distinction in German (Bybee 1994).

For most of this century, linguists have assumed the existence of units representing the phonemic status of certain segments. They have also assumed that both predictable and unpredictable phonetic variation is caused by rules acting on static underlying representations. Unaccounted for variation in phonetic strings has either been ignored (as low-level phonetic phenomena) or relegated to unexplained "inherent variation." But just as the study of details of actual language use is yielding surprising and important results in the study of morphosyntax and lexicon, the study of the phonetic details of actual language use will yield a new view of phonological phenomena.

Notes

1. The data used in this paper was generously supplied by Otto Santa Ana. I am also grateful to Valerie Daniel for inputting data, to Greg Thomson who coded and analyzed the data, and ran statistical tests on it, and to Jean Newman who provided input at various points. Thanks are also due to Janet Pierrehumbert who provided many valuable comments and suggestions on a previous version of the paper.

2. Phillips (1981) discusses the case of the diffusion of the loss of the [j] glide in words such as *tune* and *Duke* in the English of Georgia. Phillips attributes this change, which affects the least frequent words first, to a change in sequence structure conditions. I suspect, however, that it is a dialect borrowing or accommodation to the standard dialect. Words learned at the mother's knee, so to speak, would be the most conservative, while the least frequent words would be affected first.

3. Other types of representation run into the same problems. If the three classes of words were represented with different moraic structure, separate variable rules could delete the schwa and delete the mora associated with

the syllabic consonants. However, since morae are discrete units, there is a limit on the number of distinct classes that could be represented.

4. The table presents percentages for convenience. The chi-squared value was not computed on the percentages.

5. Probably all phonetic change is due to reductive mechanisms—reduction of gestures and the compression of gestures causing overlap (assimilation) (Pagliuca and Mowrey 1987); however, the surface results in terms of segments may not always seem reductive.

6. When read from a list by the same speaker, *perfect* had a released final $[t^h]$.

References

Browman, Catherine P. and Louis M. Goldstein. 1990. Tiers in articulatory phonology, with some implications for casual speech. In John Kingston and Mary E. Beckman (eds.), *Papers in Laboratory Phonology I: Between the Grammar and Physics of Speech*, 341-76. Cambridge: Cambridge University Press.

Bybee, Joan L. 1985. *Morphology: A Study of the Relation between Meaning and Form* (Typological Studies in Language 9). Amsterdam: Benjamins.

Bybee, Joan L. 1988. Morphology as lexical organization. In Michael Hammond and Michael Noonan (eds.), *Theoretical Morphology: Approaches in Modern Linguistics*, 119-41. San Diego: Academic Press.

Bybee, Joan L. 1994. A view of phonology from a cognitive and functional perspective. *Cognitive Linguistics* 5(4), 285-305.

Bybee, Joan L. 1995. Regular morphology and the lexicon. *Language and Cognitive Processes* 10(5), 425-55.

Bybee, Joan L. 1998. Lexicalization of sound change and alternating environments. In Michael Broe and Janet Pierrehumbert (eds.), *Laboratory Phonology*, Vol. 5. Cambridge: Cambridge University Press.

Bybee, Joan L. and Carol L. Moder. 1983. Morphological classes as natural categories. *Language* 59, 251-70.

Fidelholz, James. 1975. Word frequency and vowel reduction in English. *Papers from the 11th Annual Regional Meeting of the Chicago Linguistic Society*, 200-13. Chicago: CLS.

Fowler, Carol A. and Jonathan Housum. 1987. Talkers' signalling of "new" and "old" words in speech and listeners' perception and use of the distinction. *Journal of Memory and Language* 26, 489-504.

Francis, W. Nelson and Henry Kucera. 1982. *Frequency Analysis of English Usage*. Boston: Houghton Mifflin.

Guy, Gregory. 1980. Variation in the group and the individual: The case of final stop deletion. In William Labov (ed.), *Locating Language in Time and Space*, 1-36. New York: Academic Press.

Guy, Gregory. 1991a. Explanation in variable phonology: An exponential model of morphological constraints. *Language Variation and Change* 3, 1-22.

Guy, Gregory. 1991b. Contextual conditioning in variable lexical phonology. *Language Variation and Change* 3, 223-39.

Harris, John. 1989. Towards a lexical analysis of sound change in progress. *Journal of Linguistics* 25, 35-56.

Hooper, Joan B. 1976. Word frequency in lexical diffusion and the source of morphophonological change. In William Christie (ed.), *Current Progress in Historical Linguistics*, 96-105. Amsterdam: North Holland.

Hooper, Joan B. 1978. Constraints on schwa deletion in American English. In Jacek Fisiak (ed.), *Recent Developments in Historical Phonology*, 183-207. The Hague: Mouton.

Johnson, Theodore. 1983. *Phonological Free Variation, Word Frequency and Lexical Diffusion*. Seattle: University of Washington doctoral dissertation.

Kiparsky, Paul. 1982. Lexical phonology and morphology. In In-Seok Yang (ed.), *Linguistics in the Morning Calm*, 3-91. Seoul: Hanshin.

Krishnamurti, Bhadriraju. 1978. Areal and lexical diffusion of sound change: Evidence from Dravidian. *Language* 54, 1-20.

Labov, William. 1972. *Sociolinguistic Patterns*. Philadelphia: University of Pennsylvania Press.

Labov, William. 1981. Resolving the Neogrammarian controversy. *Language* 57, 267-308.

Labov, William. 1994. *Principles of Linguistic Change: Internal Factors*. Oxford: Basil Blackwell.

Leslau, Wolf. 1969. Frequency as a determinant of linguistic change in the Ethiopian languages. *Word* 25, 180-89.

Losiewicz, Beth L. 1992. *The Effect of Frequency on Linguistic Morphology*. Austin: University of Texas doctoral dissertation.

Moonwomon, Birch. 1992. The mechanism of lexical diffusion. Paper presented at the Annual Meeting of the Linguistic Society of America. Philadelphia, January, 1992.

Neu, Helene. 1980. Ranking of constraints on /t,d/ deletion in American English: A statistical analysis. In William Labov (ed.), *Locating Language in Time and Space*, 37-54. New York: Academic Press.

Pagliuca, William and Richard Mowrey. 1987. Articulatory evolution. In Anna Giacolone Ramat, Onofrio Carruba, and Giuliano Bernini (eds.), *Papers from the VIIth International Conference on Historical Linguistics*, 459-472. Amsterdam: Benjamins.

Phillips, Betty S. 1980. Old English *an ~ on*: A new appraisal. *Journal of English Linguistics* 14, 20-23.

Phillips, Betty S. 1981. Lexical diffusion and Southern *tune, duke, news*. *American Speech* 56, 72-78.

Phillips, Betty S. 1984. Word frequency and the actuation of sound change. *Language* 60, 320-42.

Pinker, Steven. 1991. Rules of language. *Science* 253, 530-35.

Prasada, Sandeep and Steven Pinker. 1993. Generalisation of regular and irregular morphological patterns. *Language and Cognitive Processes* 8, 1-51.

Santa Ana, Otto. 1991. *Phonetic Simplification Processes in English of the Barrio: A Cross-Generational Sociolinguistic Study of the Chicanos of Los Angeles*. Philadelphia: University of Pennsylvania doctoral dissertation.

Stemberger, Joseph P. and Brian MacWhinney. 1988. Are inflected forms stored in the lexicon? In Michael Hammond and Michael Noonan (eds.), *Theoretical Morphology: Approaches in Modern Linguistics*, 101-16. San Diego: Academic Press.

Timberlake, Alan. 1978. Uniform and alternating environments in phonological change. *Folia Slavica* 2, 312-28.

Walsh, Thomas and Frank Parker. 1983. The duration of morphemic and non-morphemic /s/ in English. *Journal of Phonetics* 11, 201-06.

Wang, William S.-Y. 1969. Competing changes as a cause of residue. *Language* 45, 9-25.

Wang, William S.-Y (ed.). 1977. *The Lexicon in Phonological Change*. The Hague: Mouton.

Wang, William S.-Y. and Chin-Chuan Cheng. 1977. Implementation of phonological change: The Shaungfeng Chinese case. In Wang (ed.), 86-100.

Bidirectional Processing in Language and Related Cognitive Systems

SYDNEY M. LAMB

Rice University

I gather...that the status of linguistic theories continues to be a difficult problem. In a sense the difficulty reduces to that of deciding whether the best theory is simply the most economical set of axioms from
which the language behavior can be deduced, i.e., in essence a con-
densed description. If this is true then theoretical linguistics might appear to be only a more efficient form of description. I would wish, cautiously, to make the suggestion, that perhaps a further touchstone may
be added: to what extent does the theory tie in with other, non-linguistic information, for example, the anatomical aspects of language?
In the end such bridges link a theory to the broader body of scientific
knowledge. I would personally not see much virtue in the views of
those theoreticians who feel that language...must be viewed *separately*
on the linguistic and biological levels.

Norman Geschwind (1964)

Here in Texas we like to tell Aggie jokes—about people from Texas A&M
University, who are called *Aggies*. The one that is relevant to this paper is
about a science class at Texas A&M in which each student selected a science
project to work on. One student decided to investigate what he called "the

87

toothpaste problem." Having observed, as we all do, that toothpaste comes from the tube in a flexible cylindrical shape, with the cylinder having a diameter of about one centimeter, usually broken off by users in lengths of around two centimeters, he decided to measure the length of the whole cylinder if it is not thus broken into small pieces. He carefully laid out the cylinder from a tube of toothpaste onto a long continuous stretch of paper towels and then carefully measured. I forget what the total length was, let's say 3.45 meters. Of course he observed that tubes of different sizes evidently hold cylinders of different lengths. Now came the really difficult theoretical phase of the project: To determine how they get that long cylinder into that short tube. After weeks of stewing over this problem he finally decided that, since it is quite flexible, it could be folded up and/or coiled, and then there must be a small mechanism near the output end of the tube which straightens it out just before it gets to that output unit. As the teacher was a graduate of Texas A&M, he gave the student an A.

What is the relevance of this story? As will perhaps become more clear as we proceed, some linguists who profess a cognitive interest in their work are rather like this student from Texas A&M in failing to appreciate that what comes out of the mouth as speech does not necessarily have the same form as what is/was inside that made that speech come out. We do not have to assume, and in fact it would be a mistake to assume, that we have such things as sounds in our cognitive systems, nor the analyst's symbolic representations based on speech sounds, like phonemes, morphemes, and words. Even less do we have internal rules of grammar made up of such symbols.

This paper takes the form of a series of questions ("Q1," "Q2," etc.), each of them followed by answer and/or discussion. We begin with the theme of this symposium.

1. Usage-Based Models

Q1. Why develop usage-based models?

First, we need to agree on what is meant by the term *usage*. The problem is that it has two meanings, corresponding to the two meanings of *performance*: (1) The PROCESSES by which linguistic products are produced and/or interpreted—along with related processes such as learning new vocabulary, etc.; (2) Actual PRODUCTIONS of speakers (as opposed to edited or made up ones).

In fact we should make a three-way distinction:

- LINGUISTIC EXTENSION, the set of all productions;
- LINGUISTIC PROCESSES;
- LINGUISTIC SYSTEM.

That is, we have to distinguish the linguistic productions—we may call them TEXTS even though we are talking usually or mainly about spoken productions—from the system which is capable of receiving and/or producing texts. The latter may be called the *linguistic system*. The *linguistic extension* is usage in the second sense of that term, while the *linguistic processes* constitute usage in the first sense. The term *linguistic extension* may be variously defined as the set of all possible texts of a "language" or of a "dialect" or of a speaker; or as the set of all texts in a corpus. For present purposes there is no need to make a choice among these possibilities.

The term *language* has been used for each of the three kinds of entity identified above. Which of these is the real *language*? That question is at best a terminological one, at worst a symptom of the illusion that there is such a thing as a language apart from these three entities which constitute the only realities behind that vague term. Perhaps the least confusing way to handle the terminological question is just not to use the term *language* as a technical term—since it has no real applicability other than to one of these three—using instead the three terms listed above.

Likewise, *usage-based model* is ambiguous, and the two meanings are addressed in different papers of this symposium. For this paper we are talking about usage in the sense of the linguistic processes of production and understanding.

Q1 may accordingly be rephrased: Why develop a model which is compatible with what we know about linguistic processes?

Several answers are readily forthcoming. Perhaps most important, such consideration helps to give us some assurance that we are not simply taking an excursion into fantasyland. For there are indefinitely many ways of describing the linguistic extension. Why does a linguist decide to settle on one of them? Because it is the one he learned in school? Because it uses notation like that of symbolic logic? Because it describes the linguistic extension more elegantly? More economically? Is that what makes it valid?

Here, a dichotomy of the fifties may be pertinent: GOD'S TRUTH vs. HOCUS-POCUS. The term "hocus-pocus" is not intended to be derogatory. There were many who proudly defended hocus-pocus linguistics, especially since in those days it was reprehensible to consider the minds of speakers. Hocus-pocus linguists readily admitted that what they were doing was just trying to come up with an organized description of the linguistic extension.

This being the case, we would want only to ask some of them why they were also concerned with defending one particular way of analyzing as opposed to others.

Since the mid-fifties, there has been a lot of talk of "models." I have never been comfortable with such talk in the context of hocus-pocus linguistics. If it is hocus-pocus linguistics then what is the model a model of? Not of anything real, and not even intended to be. Therefore it's not really a model of anything. It might be less misleading to quit using the term *model* in this sense; an alternative would be THEORY OF THE LINGUISTIC EXTENSION.

Linguists often seem not to appreciate the extent to which their particular way of classifying data is just one of many that could have been chosen. Let us therefore take a quick look at some different ways of classifying data of linguistic extension. We may distinguish five approaches:

(1) The building-block approach. Phonemes, morphemes, words, etc. as objects. Larger objects as composites of smaller objects.
(2) Symbols and rules. There are many varieties, seen for example in tagmemics and in the various forms of generative grammar.
(3) The approach which attempts to avoid formalism and to just list or describe "patterns." Here there are endless varieties.
(4) The network approach. It also has varieties.
(5) Mixed systems: The network with objects or symbols; the network supplemented by rules composed of symbols; for example, Halliday's *systemic networks* (Halliday 1973).

At this point it might well be emphasized that if we are only describing the linguistic extension, it is just a matter of economy or readability or convenience which of these, and which subvariety, we choose.

2. The Linguistic System

Although Q1 has not yet been answered, we turn now to the second question.

Q2. What about the "God's Truth" approach? Might there be some reality behind the linguistic extension?

If so, what might that reality be? We do not want to claim reality for some mystical entity for which no evidence exists, such as a "linguistic system" which has no location. But it is easy to identify a reality whose existence in some form will be readily acknowledged: It is the mental system of the human being. The system which is responsible for producing and understanding texts is none other than the mental information system of the speaker of the language. To adopt this view implies giving substantial recognition to individual differences, as we surely would not want to expect that any person's linguistic system is identical to that of any other person. Thus we give up on any notion of a uniform linguistic system for a speech community (even though it might be reasonable to attempt a theory of the linguistic extension for a whole community).

We have now identified two quite distinct goals, for two distinct kinds of linguistic undertaking: (1) the construction of a theory of the linguistic extension (of an individual or a community), and (2) the construction of a theory of the linguistic system (of an individual).

Q3. How can we investigate the linguistic system?

As the linguistic system is a mental system, we cannot observe it directly. But (*pace* Bloomfield, Twaddell, *et al.*), we need not be deterred on that account. The same problem does not stop particle physicists from studying subatomic particles. The answer to the question, in its simplest form, is that we investigate it by studying the linguistic extension and trying to figure out what kind of system is needed (1) to produce and to understand such material, and (2) to learn how to perform these processes. We are now approaching an answer to Q1, but the consideration of Q3 requires that we first take up Q4.

Q4. Is a theory of the linguistic extension also a theory of the linguistic system?

We need only ask this question to begin suspecting that the answer must be *no*. Is any attempt at accounting for the shape of the toothpaste that comes out of the tube as valid as any other? Don't all the forms of classifying linguistic extension tell us about the linguistic system? To see more clearly why the answer has to be *no*, let us briefly consider what kinds of things linguists look for when they are constructing theories of the linguistic extension. Such things all together may be called PATTERNS; they all involve recurrent similarities or partial similarities. We have to ask: *what are the sources of the patterns found by linguists in the linguistic extension* (cf. Lamb 1993).

For some of them, we can surely expect that the source has to be the linguistic system of the mind; for example, when we find a consistent relationship between a certain phonological form and a certain concept. This is of course the type of pattern we are interested in if we are constructing a theory of the linguistic system. In some such cases we can further deduce that the patterns evidently present in the linguistic system of the mind are there because they reflect corresponding patterns in the perceptual and conceptual and motor systems of the mind. For example, the linguistic distinction between noun phrases and verb phrases is evidently based on and developmentally derived from a corresponding distinction in perceptual systems, particularly the visual system (Lamb 1993).

Another type of pattern is exemplified by such pairs as *sane : sanity, vain : vanity, nation : national,* in which we find a consistent alternation between two vowels in alternating forms of the same morpheme. In the life of the linguist constructing a theory of the linguistic extension, it is natural to posit one of the two vowels as underlying and to derive the other from it by a rule; for it is a generally accepted practice in that analytical activity to construct rules for all possible cases of partial resemblance. But if we now ask, *what is the source of such patterns?*, we find that the explanation is diachronic, that the alternation exists in modern English as a result of the great English vowel shift of a few hundred years ago. The actual source of this pattern thus turns out to be: *Data of an earlier time as altered by diachronic linguistic change.* Linguists who construct rules based on patterns of alternation (e.g. Chomsky and Halle's *Sound Pattern of English*, 1968) are thus able to put compact phonological representations into the lexical entries of their theories of the linguistic extension of English, and they are telling us something about the history of the language. But there is no evidence that this type of pattern, with its diachronic source, reflects anything in the mental linguistic system of the contemporary speaker. It is more consistent with what we know about the brain to suppose that the modern English child learns words like *nation* and *national* as units.

Certain other patterns may be described as involving redundancy (see below for an example). This factor is not without cognitive significance, since forms which resemble other forms are easier to learn than forms with no such resemblances; and mutual resemblance can be viewed as a form of redundancy. Yet we need not assume that the mind of the ordinary person is like that of the analytical linguist, striving to eliminate all possible redundancy by constructing rules to derive redundant features (see below).

Finally, we may observe that some patterns found by the analytical linguist can be explained as resulting from the ingenuity of the linguist in finding patterns even in chaos. That such results are possible is clear from such psychological tests as the well-known ink-blot test devised by Dr. Rorschach.

The pattern whose true source is diachronic rather than cognitive deserves further discussion. We are surely under no obligation to assume that the theoretician's constructs of "underlying forms" for alternating forms resulting from changes at earlier periods of the language are somehow also constructed as cognitive realities in present-day speakers. Yet just that is sometimes assumed (with no supporting evidence). Consider, for example, the discussion on "the sounds of words that are permanently stored in the mental lexicon" in David Caplan's recent book on neurolinguistics (Caplan 1987: 208), of which the reviewer in *Language* states "we are fortunate that C's book is so fine" (Obler 1990: 383) and "Caplan has done a superb job of exposing the logic of the neurolinguistic enterprise" and that the book is "a pleasure to teach or study from" (387). But no book is perfect. Caplan observes that if *coròllary* is pronounced with emphasis on the second syllable, the first vowel is a schwa, but if *còrollary* is pronounced, with accent on the first syllable, the first vowel is an open *o*, as is the first vowel in *correlate* and *correlation*. He concludes that "it is reasonable to say that the permanent representation of the first vowel of *corollary* is an /O/ and not a schwa...." Here he has used a construct based not just on comparison of alternative forms of the same dialect but also on comparison of different dialects, those which have the form *còrollary* compared with those which use the form *coròllary*. But why should a phonological description based on historical reconstruction be attributed to the minds of contemporary speakers—especially if those who have formulated such descriptions make no claims about their being relevant to performance models? Is it not more likely that for those dialects with stress on the second syllable and schwa in the first, the entire form, schwa and all, is represented as such in the minds of their speakers, since the brain is so adept at learning details and combinations of details? And if so, there is certainly no need for any other more abstract representation to be stored in addition. (Of course, for the ordinary American dialect, in which the stress is on the first syllable, there is no need for any kind of reconstruction to put a type of *o*, open or closed according to the dialect, rather than schwa in the first syllable.)

The question of redundancy provides another instructive point of contrast between the two tasks of constructing a theory of linguistic extension and constructing a theory of the linguistic system. If the linguist adopts a goal of storing lexical forms in a maximally economical form as part of a policy of constructing a theory of linguistic extension, he might set up forms that have had all the redundancy removed and use rules to derive the redundant features from such skeletal forms. The fact that it is possible to construct a theory of linguistic extension in this way is neither justification nor evidence for assuming that somehow the mind of the ordinary speaker performs such mental acrobatics. Yet this is what is often supposed, even by some who in other respects like to have evidence to support their proposals. Thus Caplan, on the same page (208) as his discussion of *corollary*, observes that "stress contours do not have to be represented for each word, but can be derived by general rules of English phonology" and that "the nature of the syllables in a given word can be derived from the sequence of phonemes in a word on the basis of...universal constraints on syllable formation...and language-specific considerations." He then leaps from the "can be derived from" to "Therefore, neither the syllable structure nor the stress contour of a word has to be specified in its permanent mental representation in the lexicon." The mental system must then also have rules, to

> "fill in," change, and add to the phonological information at the lexical level to arrive at the superficial level

as well as an additional set of rules to

> map the superficial level of phonological representations onto an "articulatory" level of representation (ibid., p. 209).

Caplan appears to have overlooked the well-known fact that the brain is far more adept at "storing" information, including redundant information, than it is at performing calculations.

In any case, we are now ready to return to Question 3: How can we investigate the linguistic system, the mental basis for the linguistic extension? The answer is that we must consider additional types of data, beyond those used in constructing a theory of the linguistic extension. For constructing a theory of linguistic extension, the data consists of the linguistic extension, texts. This may be called the PRIMARY DATA. For a theory of the linguistic system, there are two kinds of relevant additional data:

(1) Linguistic processes—performance/usage. Here is where we return to Q1. However many things remain obscure about the mental system, one thing about it is perfectly clear: The mental system is capable of performing the linguistic processes; it is not some kind of abstract "competence" divorced from performance, but a competence to perform.[1]

(2) The biological basis of language (cf. the quotation from Geschwind at the beginning of this paper).

The point about linguistic processes, although it has been stated many times before, is important enough to be given further emphasis here, especially in view of the title of this symposium. Since we know that the linguistic system of a person's mind is capable of being put into operation for speaking and understanding, any "model" or description of language that has no plausible way of performing these processes can for that reason be ruled out as not cognitively realistic. Here then we finally have the answer to Q1.

A cognitive model of language must necessarily be a usage-based model; it must represent a competence to perform.

With respect to the biological basis of language, we may further observe that a "model" has to be a model *of something*; and that something in this case would appear to be a biological system.

In the discussion of Question 1 above, we distinguished five approaches to classifying and describing linguistic data, observing that if we are only describing the linguistic extension, it is just a matter of economy or tradition or what have you which of these, and which subvariety, we choose. These five, we may recall, are:

(1) The building-block approach (phonemes, morphemes, etc.);
(2) Symbols and rules;
(3) The approach which attempts to just list or describe "patterns;"
(4) The network approach; and
(5) Mixed systems: networks with symbols and/or rules.

We may now test these approaches in the context of the God's Truth approach as defined above. That is, we can ask whether any of these can be supposed to have (1) the ability to perform, and (2) plausible correspondence with what is known about the brain from neuroscience.

Let us start with (3). While this approach is useful and productive in the worthy activity of analyzing texts, it is of no direct help in the study of the linguistic system since, aside from not attempting to be consistent (since it eschews formal notation), it makes no pretense of describing anything other than the linguistic extension.

The building-block approach (1) would require little building blocks (of different sizes) within the mind, together with means of perceiving and manipulating them. It too should be easy for all but Aggies to reject, as it gets no support from what we know about the brain.

The system of symbols and rules (2) is akin to (1), even though it may give the appearance of greater sophistication—at least Chomsky argued (1964) that a generative grammar was more sophisticated than what he called a taxonomic grammar. But the symbols are objects, and the rules are instructions for manipulating them, and so from a cognitive point of view there does not seem to be any significant difference. In a performance interpretation, the rules would have to operate. Symbols would have to be perceived, written, replaced, moved, and otherwise manipulated, whether we write them as symbols or as objects of some other kind. Also, composites of such symbols, like "lexical entries," are just like the larger building blocks composed of smaller building blocks in the building-block approach. This type of model thus requires a central processor or internal homunculus, to carry out the operations, with its own sense organs, writing mechanism, and workspace for executing the rules. Those who propose to use rules of grammar in a cognitive context surely do not want to posit the presence of an internal homunculus; they are thus obliged to provide some realistic psychological interpretation of their rules, or else (surely more promising) to come up with an alternative to rules.

Since this point has been too long overlooked, it deserves further discussion. Such discussion could start with the Aggie joke at the beginning of this paper, but that need not be repeated. It might be helpful, though, to apply a name to the methodological infelicity in which the Aggie was indulging: INTROJECTION. It is the opposite of projection, which involves projecting things from our minds to the world outside. In introjection, a process indulged in by some model-builders, things from the outside world are *introjected* into the model being constructed. Introjection works well for some kinds of modelling: for a model of the vending machine or of the retail store—what comes out *is* what was in there. It also happens to work for the *substance* inside the tube of toothpaste, but not for its *form*. It works for a partial understanding of the factory, in that the finished product is indeed there before it is shipped to the outside of the factory. But it doesn't work so well in the case of some models that have been proposed for the linguistic system of the human mind.

To really appreciate the shortcomings of introjection as a tool in cognitive theory building, we need to go further and to appreciate that it is not only the products of the system which get introjected but derivatives of those products. Thus we have:

(1) the linguistic system (*primary*);
(2) products of the linguistic system (*secondary*);
(3) written representations of (2) (*tertiary*);
(4) symbolic writing, derived from (3), used for "rules of grammar" (*quaternary*).

Model builders who indulge in introjection are thus going beyond introjecting outputs of the system into their models; they are actually introjecting quaternary phenomena—phenomena two further steps removed from the linguistic productions.

Those who might be tempted nevertheless to find some cognitive validity in systems of rules have further problems to consider: The mind does not have little internal eyes nor other sense organs to read such symbols nor little internal pencils or other writing devices, nor little pieces of paper or other miniature media, for writing and rewriting "linguistic representations." All our sense organs are *at the external periphery of* the mind; the mind is *internal to* sense organs. If it did *contain* its own sensory devices (for interpreting symbols) and its own motor devices (for manipulating symbols), then there would have to be little homuncular perceptual structures and motor structures within these devices, and figuring *these* out would be the great neurocognitive puzzle. But since such internal devices are needed anyway, and would have to be understood for a theory of mind, why not suppose that they are the devices of the mental system itself rather than of the little homunculus that must be posited within that system if it is a rule-executor?

There are two additional problems for those who would introject rule-based approaches: Such a model requires storage space for storing the symbols and a workspace for holding representations while they are being worked on. There is no biological evidence for any such devices. Also, the rules of such models operate only in one direction, but actual people are able both to speak and to understand speech.

While those who doubt the veracity of the Aggie joke are right—I made it up—those who may find it hard to believe that investigators of language indulge in introjection as a tool in cognitive modelling may want to consider an example. A model of "the sub-components of the sound production process for words" is proposed by Caplan, drawing upon the work of others, in his book cited above (1987: 230). The model includes, among other things, "Lexical Semantic Representations," "Lexical Phonological Representations," which are inserted by "lexical insertion" into "Phrasal Structure," and "Superficial Phonological Representations," which are also inserted by "lexical insertion" into "Phrasal Structure;" but the two types of "lexical insertion" are alternatives. There is also a "Response Buffer" connected to both the "Superficial Phonological Representations" and the "Phrasal Structure." Also, going a step beyond the introjection of rules and representations at the quaternary level as indicated above, Caplan proposes the possibility that an "item" *can carry "with it an indication of its antecedent processing"* (italics mine). No evidence is presented to support the supposition that the brain has any structures to support such complex operations.

Returning now to the list of five approaches, we have ruled out the first three—object-based, symbol-based, and pattern-based—as not cognitively pertinent, although they can surely be useful in taxonomic linguistics. Likewise, the fifth, which mixes symbols and/or rules with its networks, can be disqualified on account of these symbols and/or rules. That leaves (4) the network, the only type of model yet proposed that does not encounter the difficulties discussed above. This approach has at least some immediate cognitive plausibility, as we know that the brain is a network.

3. Accessing Network Models

We are therefore ready to ask the next two questions, in accordance with the two types of pertinent additional data mentioned above: (1) linguistic processes and (2) the biological basis of language. Let us take the second of these first.

Q5. Is there a reasonable biological basis for a network model?

This question is easy to *begin* to answer, as we know that the brain *is* a network, a network of neurons. To say that, however, is not to say that *any* network model is valid. There are indefinitely many network models possible, but the brain is one specific type of network. Thus Q5 might be rephrased for application to any specific network model: is there a reasonable biological basis for *this* network model?

Some of the better-known network models (e.g. Rumelhart and McClelland 1986) have a number of features that are out of accord with what is known about the brain. In fact, their relationship to actual neural networks is so tenuous that the common practice of calling them *neural networks*, or even *artificial neural networks* (which suggests some resemblance), is rather misleading, not only to others but perhaps also to those who work with them. They have too few layers of structure; every "neuron" at each layer is connected to every "neuron" at adjacent layers; and they have a starting state with random weights of connections—equivalent to starting with random knowledge. Let us consider these points one by one:

The better-known network models have just an input layer, an output layer, and one "hidden" layer. Even the neural mechanism for the gill withdrawal reflex in the Aplysia, a simple marine snail, has two "hidden" layers (Pinel 1993: 510-12). Any complex cognitive process of humans goes through many layers within the cortex. The cortex has hierarchical structure, and the different levels of the various hierarchies, primary, secondary, and so forth, are in different cortical areas, connected by axons of pyramidal neurons. And there are *many* "hidden" layers involved in linguistic processes, not just one or two.

Likewise, it is not the case that every neuron at each level is connected to every neuron at the next higher level—far from it, as a typical level has millions of neurons, but a typical neuron has only thousands of connections to other neurons, only a fraction of one percent of the cells in its immediate vicinity and a very small fraction of one percent of those in nearby regions representing potentially neighboring levels in functional hierarchies. As James Anderson points out (1995: 304):

The usual neural network assumption of full connectivity is grievously in error. This major difference alone casts serious doubt on many attempts to apply ideas from artificial neural networks to the nervous system. If an artificial network depends critically on complete connectivity to function, and many do, it cannot be a satisfactory model of the biological nervous system.

Finally, it is a common practice of network modelers to have their networks start a learning process with random weights of connections, which then get adjusted either upward or downward after trials by a neurologically unrealistic process of "back-propagation." But random weights of connections would mean random knowledge. In the case of a child learning language, such a model would be consistent with assuming that the child starts out talking complex gibberish; but it is not so. They start out not talking at all, and when they do start talking it is with phonologically simple monosyllables (often reduplicated). In short, children do not start their lives with random knowledge; rather, they start with zero knowledge, except for that which is instinctual. Thus to be realistic as a model of processing, a network model needs to start with connections of zero or near-zero strength, and to build and strengthen connections gradually, from bottom layers up. Such a model also accords with biological evidence, as we know that infants have myelination (implying connections from one cortical region to another) only for the primary cortical areas, and it gradually spreads from there to secondary and thence to tertiary areas and beyond.

A further defect of the better-known network models has been their use in limited applications treated in isolation rather than in a natural structural context; for example, having present tense verb forms at the input layer and past tense forms at the output layer, just for the exercise of producing past tense forms upon receiving present tense forms (Rumelhart and McClelland 1986). In real life, *both* the present *and* past tense form of a verb are *receivable as input*, as alternatives connecting to the *same* structure representing the verb stem; and *either* the present *or* the past tense form can be selected for output.

Connectionist models which have been constructed without concern for biological reality might well be called HOCUS-POCUS CONNECTIONISM. Since hocus-pocus connectionism is so unrealistic and has produced such unrealistic accounts of various phenomena, many have been inclined to reject connectionism altogether, not recognizing that what they are objecting to is just one form of connectionism and that many others are possible. People on the outside of network modelling often suppose that there is only one kind of connectionism simply because that one has become widely used and known. This situation is like that which affects linguistics: Those who are not linguists often think that generative grammar is the only kind of linguistics there is. For example, some neurologists understandably would like to get information from linguistics that might be helpful in the study of aphasia, but turn only to the brand of linguistics which is best known. Neurologists who make mistakes like those of Caplan cited above are not to be condemned, but to be commended for their willingness to seek information from a related field; they have only been too trusting of the doctrines they have encountered from the only kind of linguistics they have learned about. By the same token, those who trust the doctrines of hocus-pocus connectionism, the only kind of connectionism they have heard about, have likewise been too trusting.

By now it will be evident that the type of network model being proposed here is quite unlike those discussed above. In fact, it has been arrived at from just the opposite direction from that taken by conventional network modelers, who start with simplified models of neurons and link them up in simplified ways and then attempt to apply them to the learning of complex cognitive processes.

If one were to try being more realistic about constructing a network model, taking properties of real neural networks into account as some modelers nowadays are doing (e.g. Burnod 1990), the mind soon boggles at the enormous array of possibilities. What do we do about the fact that the cortex has several different kinds of neurons with different properties? What is the functional purpose of the local arrangement of neurons into cortical columns? into the six layers of the cortex? What differential use is made of the many different neurotransmitters? Which among these many distinctions should be represented in a neural network model? Should the model try to incorporate the difference between synapses on the cell body and those on dendrites? The difference between processing within dendritic trees as opposed to that in the cell body? The different rates of speed of transmission of myelinated as opposed to unmyelinated axons, thicker vs. thinner axons? Upon choosing some arbitrary set of modelling parameters among this dazzling array of possibilities, what hope can we expect to have that those we have chosen have any resemblance to those used by the real system?

Instead of starting from the neuron, the model proposed here, the RELATIONAL NETWORK MODEL, started from language. It was built in the first place on the basis of linguistic evidence. In fact, it was constructed in its original form for purposes of a theory of the linguistic extension rather than for a cognitive model. Starting from a building-block approach, I was analyzing the relationships among units like morphemes and phonemes, using a system of network notation adapted from that of Halliday (e.g. 1973) and I discovered that if we recognize the relationships among what seemed to be various "building blocks" and identify them with a graphic notation, the result is that we find them interconnected in a network of relationships; and then we find that there is no longer any need to consider those units as having any real existence as other than locations in the network (Lamb 1971). It then became apparent that by letting activation spread through the various lines and nodes of the network according to the varying requirements of different node types, it seemed to be possible to account for the processes of speaking and understanding—although there are very complex problems to solve in working out the details of these processes. Further study of the processes has led to the need for modifications in the network model, and some still unsolved problems of processing which will no doubt lead to further amendments. The structure of the relational network is thus dictated by the requirements of accounting for linguistic data and linguistic processes. The fact that the linguistic system is a network comes as the conclusion of a process of analysis, not as a result of examining neurological evidence. Whatever resemblance relational networks have to neural networks thus comes as a happy surprise, not as structural features that were built in from the outset. We may now proceed to the next question:

Q6. Is a realistic account of processing in a network possible?

In a more specific form, we could ask about the possibility of a realistic account of processing in a relational network.

In listing some of the infelicities of well-known network models, we have already begun to consider this question. We need to distinguish several types of network processes, of which perhaps the most important is sending activation along lines of the network, from one location to others. Nodes of the network "make decisions" based on how much activation is being received, and send activation out accordingly, the strength of outgoing activation being a function of the strength of incoming activation (described more precisely below). This is the basic process involved in understanding and production of speech or writing.

The information is in the connectivity of the network. Hence no separate storage space is needed. Learning consists of building new connections, strengthening existing connections, and adjusting thresholds (see below).

Since we are talking here about a model and not directly about the brain, I prefer not to use terms like *neuron* and *axon* and the like. Instead, we may identify the main elements of a relational network in the following terms:

(1) The elements of the network are LINES and NODES, and there are different types of nodes (connections of lines to nodes, which vary in strength, might also be considered as elements of the network).

(2) At the next level of organization, we have NECTIONS, each made up of lines and nodes. The term *nection* is based on *connection* (Lamb 1994).

The nections are the modules which are connected together to form a network. Although in the development of this model the nection was arrived at on the basis of purely linguistic evidence (Lamb 1971, 1994), its major properties are like those of the neuron, highly simplified but not as much so as the "neurons" of hocus-pocus connectionism. Nevertheless, we have no evidence (beyond this resemblance) for supposing that a nection corresponds directly to a neuron; on the contrary, it is more likely that each nection corresponds roughly to a group of neurons, perhaps to a cortical column.

A diagram of a typical nection is shown as Figure 1. This one has both local and longer-distance connections, some latent, some dedicated (the difference indicated by different types of arrowhead). (This nection is shown with feed-forward connections but not the feed-backward connections needed for bidirectional processing, as discussed below.) A more delicate diagram would show many more connections and would show differing degrees of strength of connection along a gradual scale, from latent through weakly established to strongly established.

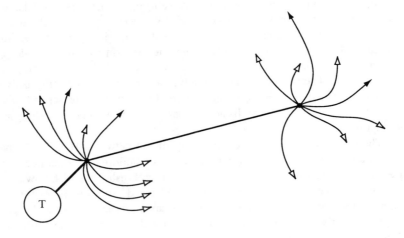

Figure 1. A Nection with Latent and Established Feed-Forward Connections

A nection can receive activation from other nections by virtue of lines connecting to it from them. It can send activation along its output lines to other nections. The amount of outgoing activation is related to the amount of incoming activation in accordance with a THRESHOLD FUNCTION. Each nection is its own processor. Indefinitely many nections can work in parallel.

The threshold function of a nection determines the amount of outgoing activation. It can be graphed as an S-shaped (sigmoid) curve, such that (1) a small amount of incoming activation (below the threshold) results in little or no outgoing activation, (2) above this threshold the level of outgoing activation rises with that of incoming activation, up to (3) a high level at which increments of incoming activation result in very little increase in outgoing activation (Figure 2).

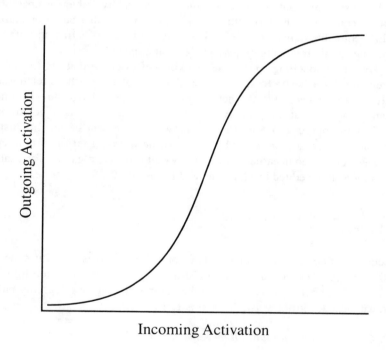

Figure 2. A Sigmoid Function

Much of the argument above in favor of the relational network approach has taken the indirect form of showing that none of the other possibilities is realistic. But there are also some more positive reasons for believing that the cognitive system is a network. For one thing, simple cognitive operations like the transmission of activation from the retina to lower levels of the visual perceptual system, from cognitive levels to muscles, etc., appear clearly to involve transmission of activation along connections of a network. Thus it is clear that at least part of the cognitive system is a network. Also, the relational network approach helps us to account for (1) unintended puns (Reich 1985); (2) slips of the tongue (Dell and Reich 1977, 1980a, 1980b); (3) Freudian slips, Freudian forgetting, and other phenomena involving association; (4) various phenomena of semantic interpretation, such as the interpretive effects of allusions to other texts like *Hamlet*, and the use of experience and of encyclopedic real-world knowledge in interpretation.

A further advantage over rule-based models is that a network allows all the linguistic information to be present at once and available for operation simultaneously (in parallel) with other portions, while also being organized in different subsystems—that is, it has different levels of structure without requiring serial processing on just one level at a time.

By briefly touching upon these two kinds of evidence that are too often disregarded by those professing to have cognitive interests—those relating to linguistic processes and to the neurological substrate of language—I do not mean to suggest that the primary data, linguistic texts, can be ignored; but it is not the purpose of this paper to show how the data of the linguistic extension can be accounted for by relational networks. That important area has been considered in earlier papers by a variety of investigators, for example in the volume edited by Copeland and Davis (1980).

4. Learning

Hocus-pocus connectionist models have prided themselves on their concern with learning—certainly a worthy concern, and not one to be taken lightly. As a relational network is a model of the end-result of a long learning process, we must accordingly ask the next question:

Q7. Can we account for how all that structure gets learned?

It seems reasonable to assume that certain properties of the network system are provided by DNA and are therefore present in the human brain as the result of a long process of "evolutionary learning." This general innate basis, that which allows a child to learn any language with rather considerable facility, might be thought of as some kind of "skeletal" system, ready for the addition of detailed connections, or it might be assumed to come with an overabundance of latent connections already present, from among which certain ones are selected for strengthening in the learning process. Depending on which of these two possibilities we choose, we could say that the system has the capacity to adapt its innate basis to the linguistic material it experiences either by building specific connections or by selecting specific connections from among those initially provided, to enable it to use a particular language. Either way, evidence from language development studies suggests that the development of the network is largely a bottom-up process, like the learning of perceptual and motor skills of other kinds.

As a methodological principle it makes sense to see how far we can get with a very simple hypothesis of how the connections get established. Accordingly we assume, as a working assumption, that the initial state of the network includes all the nections that will ever be needed and provides the potential for abundant connections among them. Based on what we know of the general abundance of redundancy and proliferation in biological systems we may assume that there will be many more nections and many more connections among them than will ever be needed for the learning a person will be able to accomplish during a long lifetime. As the information of a network is embodied in its connectivity, a major learning process ought to be, in effect, the establishment of connections. "In effect"—but in accordance with the foregoing, this effective process is accomplished as the *selection* of connections to strengthen, among the abundant collection of available potential connections. The profuse connections in the initial state, then, are very weak connections. Certain subsets of them, selected in the learning process, become strengthened. Likewise, any nection which has as yet only such weak connections to other nections, is a LATENT NECTION—not yet dedicated to any specific function. For example, by its location in the network a nection may start out in life as being available to learn some morpheme in some language, and it may or may not some day be recruited to serve for some specific morpheme in a language by virtue of getting connected to specific other nections; the means of getting connected being the selection of certain of its many available weak connections for strengthening. We thus arrive at the following simple learning hypothesis for relational networks:

Learning would thus be a process of selectively strengthening weak connections of LATENT NECTIONS—i.e., RECRUITING nections for new functions; and of effectively adding new connections to existing nections, by raising their strengths from near-zero to a higher level. The cognitive system has to be assumed to be very adept at such recruitment, for example the recruitment of high-level lexical nections for complex lexemes, both for those it has received and for those it makes up on the analogy of those it has received. After a nection has been recruited for some function, it is a DEDICATED NECTION.

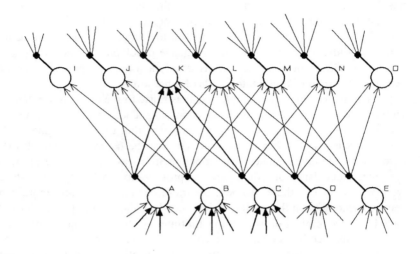

Figure 3. Illustration of General Learning Hypothesis

We may state these assumptions somewhat more formally with an abstract example, illustrated in the simplified representation in Figure 3, as a **General Learning Hypothesis**:

- **Conditions**: Connections from nections A, B, C... ("parents") to other nections I, J, K... (either local or in another area). In the initial state, such connections are very weak.
- **Process**: For example, let nection A fire while K is also receiving enough activation from other nections, say B and C, to have its initial threshold satisfied.
- **Results**: (1) The connections from A, B, and C to K are strengthened; (2) The threshold of K is raised. Such learning is increased by repeated occurrences of this process.

This process may be interpreted as follows: K has started to become dedicated to A, along with B and C, as a property able to activate it. A, B, and C represent properties or features while K represents the composite of those features. The essential process hypothesized is that any connection will get strengthened (including a dedicated connection, which can get further strengthened) if it is activated at about the same time as the node to which it is connected receives enough activation to have its threshold satisfied; and that threshold is thereupon raised.

It follows that a nection, once recruited, can thereafter have its threshold satisfied by a somewhat different set of incoming connections than those which caused it to be initially recruited. In our example, it is A, B, and C in the first instance; but with sufficient activation it might later be satisfied by activation from the combination A, B, and D. It would then have learned to respond to

A and B and (C or D) .

After further experience it will have "learned" to respond, in varying degrees, to a much more complex combination of features of varying strength. If K is a central coordinating nection (see below) for a concept or a visual image, it will normally come to represent a category rather than a single object, since it will have learned to be satisfied by a *sufficient amount* of activation, *from among* all its parent properties, as determined by its current threshold function, which is adjusted on the basis of experience.

This basic learning hypothesis covers only a small, if essential, portion of the process of learning, leaving many points untouched, including that hinted at above under *Results*: the need for repeated occurrences. But as this paper is on bidirectional processing rather than on learning, we have to move on.

5. Bidirectional Processing

In trying to account for linguistic processes we encounter an important problem that is particularly easy to overlook if one is not paying attention to the *use* of language: Linguistic processing is bidirectional; it includes both production and comprehension (the latter term is not perfect but is perhaps better than the alternatives *understanding, reception, interpretation*). Accordingly, we now turn to Question 8:

Q8. How can we account for the bidirectional processing of speech?

In the case of production, activation proceeds from perception and/or conceptual areas to the area which controls operation of the organs of speech-production; while in the receptive mode, activation proceeds from the auditory system to conceptual and/or perceptual (or motor) areas.[2]

There appear to be two possible ways of accounting for the bidirectional processing of speech in a network model:

(1) A bidirectional network, with two-way lines and nodes.
(2) Two separate (though interconnected) networks—one for reception, one for production.

The original form of relational network, which was based on purely linguistic evidence (Lamb 1971), *was* bidirectional: the lines and nodes could transmit activation in either direction. But if taken literally in this way it would fail to meet the requirement of being in harmony with what we know from biology, since we know that neurons and their fibers operate in just one direction. The nodes and lines of this type of network were considered to be abbreviations representing more complex internal structures composed of one-way lines and nodes. If a network is redrawn to show such internal structures, resulting in (approximately) a pair of networks of opposite direction, we may say that it is drawn in the NARROW NETWORK NOTATION;[3] and the original notation system for relational networks can be called the COMPACT NETWORK NOTATION.

But to say that we have two networks of opposite direction is far from the whole solution, since within it we have different ways of conceiving of (1) how the two networks are interconnected (Lamb 1994); and (2) whether or not they duplicate each other, except for direction, and if not, what differences exist.

As we can only understand the linguistic system by seeing it as interconnected with other cognitive systems, we may turn also to another question, leaving Q8 pending for the meantime.

Q9. Is bidirectional processing unique to language?

At first glance the answer might seem to be yes, since perception is supposed to work in just one direction, from the sensory input to its interpretation; while motor activation is also unidirectional, in the direction from conceptual and/or planning structures to the primary motor connections which activate muscles. The linguistic system differs in having both a perceptual (afferent) side and a motor (efferent, production) side.

But as is so often the case when considering such a complex object as the brain, things are not as simple as they seem at first glance. If you are asked to visualize a bird, you can do so (if you are like most people). What has happened in this process? If that asking was in spoken form, your receptive linguistic network sent activation, via the area for concepts of categories of objects like BIRDS, to the visual system; and the visualization of a bird consists of activating roughly the same high-level visual connections that would be activated as a result of seeing an actual bird with the eyes (cf. Farah 1988).

Moreover, if you are really visualizing a bird, it isn't just such a high-level visual nection representing the category of "birds" in the abstract, for that can't be visualized. A bird can only be visualized by visualizing various features such as its color(s), the shape of its beak, its feet, its eyes, the shape of its head, and so forth—in terms of the model (in which the visual system operates much like the receptive linguistic system, *mutatis mutandis*), activation has been sent from a conceptual nection to higher-level visual nections to mid-level visual nections, and even to lower-level visual nections, for it is at the lowest level that all the visual details are represented. This is the reverse of the order of activation that occurs in the case of input from the retina, for which the lower-level nections activate certain mid-level nections, leading to higher visual levels at which the activations of the lower levels are in effect integrated by the recognition of the object which has all those features, viz. a bird.[4] As this example illustrates, even the seemingly simplest operation in the network involves parallel activation of a large number of interconnected nections. (For more on visual imagery, see Cooper and Shepard 1984 and Kosslyn 1980.)

In sum, visualizing involves having the visual system operate in the opposite direction from that which obtains in ordinary perception. Similarly we can perform auditory and somatosensory imaging. We can form auditory images of the call of the mourning dove or the owl or the duck or what have you; we can imagine what a cat's fur feels like when we stroke its back or neck. And so forth. That is, we can get our perceptual systems to operate in the reverse of what we have been accustomed to thinking of as their normal direction of operation.

Moreover, as these examples suggest, the nections activated in such a thought process can be widely distributed. If you think about a cat, you can activate visual nections representing its appearance, auditory nections for the sound of its "meow," tactile nections representing the feeling of its fur on your fingers, the lexeme ^{L}/cat/ and the sound of its phonetic realization. What we represent in a network diagram as the nection for the concept ^{C}/cat/ (Figure 4) is thus just the central coordinating nection which can send activation to a whole family of nections, a little subnetwork of the cognitive system. What we usually think of as a concept corresponds more to that entire family, including particularly all of the details at the lowest levels, which are held together during that thought process by the higher level nections.[5]

On the other hand, it also seems to be reasonable to consider *one* of the two directions as primary. On what basis? First, activation in the primary direction probably occurs far more frequently. Second, the images we see when receiving input from the eyes are considerably more vivid than those we get when only imagining.[6] Third, we generally perform activation in the secondary direction only after we have established the necessary connections on the basis of repeated activation in the primary direction. It is not impossible to visualize things we haven't seen, but doing so is a more creative mental activity and one which most people probably perform less readily. Nevertheless, even in ordinary perception we are evidently engaged in bidirectional processing, as all the visual details (registered in low-level visual nections) remain active in our awareness even as they are being integrated at higher perceptual levels.

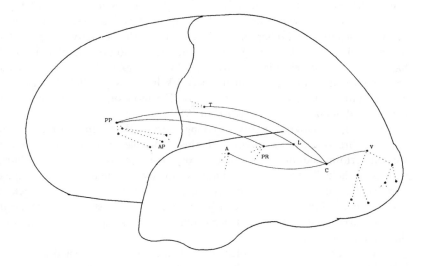

Figure 4. Major Connections of the Concept ^C/cat/

A—Auditory: recognition or auditory image of a cat's "meow"
AP—Articulatory Production: controls the articulations for *cat*
C—Conceptual: the central coordinating nection for the concept
L—Lexical: connects ^C/cat/ to its phonological expression
PP—Phonological production; PR—Phonological recognition
T—Tactile: what a cat feels like to the fingers and hand
V—Visual

Some of the cognitive subsystems relevant to this discussion are sketchily identified in Figure 5, in which lines with arrowheads at both ends are for bidirectional processing. (The direction from *lexis* to *phonological recognition* is justified by learning considerations discussed below.) In Figure 5, the dashed line indicates presence of direct connections only for high-frequency items. *Activity* covers a large area with subareas for different parts of the body; *Articulatory Production* is a specialized portion of this system. *Somatosensory Perception* includes tactile perception and detection of position and movement of parts of the body, including a subsystem for the organs of articulation, not separately shown. Nections for *Object Categories* provide cross-modal perceptual integration; those for *Abstract Categories* connect only to lexical nections and to nections for other concepts, including *Object Categories* and other types of concepts not shown.

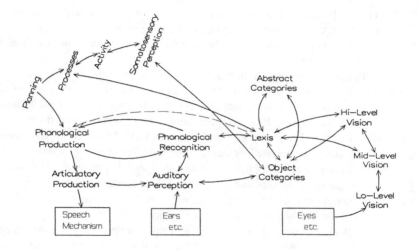

Figure 5. The Linguistic System with Related Cognitive Subsystems

On the side of motor activity, we know from neural science that here too we have bidirectional processing and that the two directions of processing are supported by two separate cortical systems (leaving aside subcortical structures), the motor (in the precentral gyrus) and the somatosensory (in the post-central gyrus), which monitors the positions and movements resulting from the motor activation.

Q10. Is bidirectional processing asymmetrical in language, as it is in perception?

In the first place, language is different in that we know that it has both a motor subsystem and a perceptual subsystem. This situation is quite different from the bidirectionality of the perceptual systems: They do not produce outputs. Thus whatever lack of symmetry may exist with respect to the linguistic system is of a different kind from that discussed above.

Having said that, we may nevertheless take note of some observations which allow us to impart some degree of primacy to the receptive side of the linguistic system:

(1) In language learning, reception generally precedes production for both lexical items and syntactic constructions.

(2) People generally have larger vocabularies for understanding than for production.

(3) Articulatory production is monitored by and thus in part controlled by auditory perception. This factor is an important part of the learning that takes place after the babbling phase of language acquisition (in which correlations between productions and their resulting sounds are learned), and it is also needed to account for the difficulty experienced by deaf people in learning how to speak.

(4) In other ways too, the receptive side controls production, as when a person recognizes that a sentence being produced is ambiguous and starts over; or when a person performs a slip of the tongue and then immediately produces the correct word.

(5) We can usually get from a word's expression to its meaning—whatever meaning we have for it—easily and directly, without searching; but we often have trouble "finding" the right word to express a concept we are trying to express or the right phrase or clause for an idea; and often we finally choose one by first trying out several possibilities till we find one that "sounds right" (some people consult a thesaurus at such times), a process which of course involves activation in the *receptive* network.

On the other side, we may observe that at the lower phonological levels, at the earliest stage of language development, the production side has primacy, in that the babbling stage appears to be driven by articulations, chosen partly on the basis of a progression from easier to more complex to produce, but partly more or less randomly; in this process the receptive side is learning what sounds result from the various articulations.

5.1 Network Structures Needed for Bidirectional Processing

Q11. How does bidirectional processing work?

As we have identified different types of bidirectional processing, we can expect more than one answer to this question. In some cases, the different directions are managed by separate subsystems. Thus, as we have observed, the subsystem for producing speech is evidently separate from (although interconnected with) that for understanding speech, as indicated in Figure 5. Likewise for writing and reading. Also, motor activity in general is in part controlled by the (separate) somatosensory system.[7]

But I don't think we want to suppose that separate subsystems are present for each of the types of perception for which imaging is possible. These cases are indicated in Figure 5 by lines with arrowheads on both ends. So the real question we are asking here concerns the cases where we would like activation to be able to go in opposite directions but without separate subsystems.

Let us leave this question simmering for a moment while we return to some unfinished business from the introduction to learning presented in Section 4 as the "General Learning Hypothesis." It was proposed that the basic learning process, which is one of strengthening connections and raising thresholds, is enhanced by repeated occurrences; but the description and accompanying Figure 3 do not specify any means for bringing about such repeated occurrences, other than (by implication) repeated occurrence of the same stimuli from outside the system. Such external stimulation is undoubtedly of great importance for learning—especially for learning variations such as other features that can also be present—but it may be reasonable to suppose that internal means for repetition are also available. Such means could be provided by sending activation (from K in Figure 3) not only to the next higher level of integration *but also back to the next lower level*. Such downward activation needs to be just strong enough to reactivate just those nections of the next lower level which are currently active, while not activating others of that level. Thus any new set of connections can get several iterations of activation, to enable them to get strengthened by a few steps in order to get established. Figure 3 may now be enhanced, resulting in Figure 6 (still a highly oversimplified diagram). For ease of reading, upward directed lines are straight and downward lines are curved.

The model needs to work in such a way that, because of gradual diminution of the strength of activation in this reinforcement cycle as iterations are repeated, the cycle becomes inactive after a few iterations, leaving its effect in strengthened connections and an elevated threshold. These strengthened connections and elevated threshold embody the learning that has taken place:

The upper-level nection (K in Figure 6) has now learned to recognize the combination of features (A, B, and C) represented by its now strengthened input connections. From now on it recognizes that combination of features as a unit—and it in turn can serve as a feature for still higher-level integration accomplished by nections at the next higher level.

As the outgoing downward lines from K (of Figure 6) have no way of knowing which of the nections of the next lower level supplied the activation leading to satisfaction of the threshold of K, they must connect to a larger set of nections of the next lower level, large enough to include those which provided the activation for K. It seems to be necessary (and not unreasonable) to assume that the downward connections from K (and from all the other higher level nections, not shown) are present from the initial state of the system, like most of the upward connections.

But if we adopt this hypothesis for learning, it provides—at no extra cost, since it was needed anyway—a simple way to account for the bidirectional processing we are concerned with. As Figure 6 illustrates for nection K, all that is needed is for the outgoing lines from nections to branch in different directions. Such a solution is considerably less costly than one which would require additional nections for the other direction.

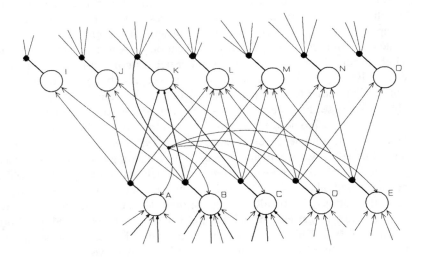

Figure 6. Enhanced Diagram of Essentials of Learning

This hypothesis of how bidirectional processing works now gives us a bonus, an explanation of the phenomenon of false attribution of properties, a consequence of the common thought pattern of thinking in categories. A person identifies an item as a member of a category and then mentally attributes to that item various properties which it doesn't actually have. Why? Because nections for those properties in that person's conceptual system are connected to the nection for the category, as a result of past experience. It takes only activation of a subset of the nections representing properties of the category to activate the nection for that category; whereupon the feed-backward activation goes to the whole set of nections representing properties of the category.

Figure 7 shows how this solution may be diagrammed for a nection representing a single conceptual category together with some of its interconnections.

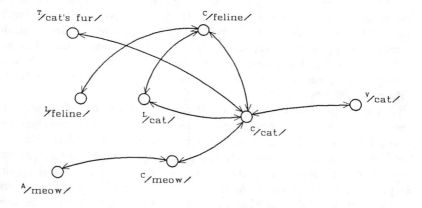

Figure 7. A Nection for the Conceptual Category CAT with a Few of its Connections to Other Nections
Areas referred to by superscript prefixes:
[A] - Auditory
[C] - Conceptual (including both concrete and abstract)
[L] - Lexical, [T] - Tactile, [V] - Visual

Q12. Is there a reasonable biological basis for this proposed answer to Q11?

This question is asked in accordance with the twin requirements given above for a reasonable cognitive model. The answer to Q11 addresses one of these requirements—it suggests a way in which the process could work. We now turn to the other, the need for neurological plausibility. It might seem at first glance that for this hypothesis of bidirectional processing to be neurologically plausible, it would be necessary that the brain have large numbers of neurons with axons branching in opposite directions and with reciprocal connections, both local and distant. But that requirement would exist only if we suppose that a nection of the model is implemented biologically as a neuron, and that is a supposition we have several reasons for rejecting, not least of which is that it would fail to provide sufficient redundancy for coping with "noise" in processing and with incidental cell damage. It seems more reasonable to suppose that a nection is implemented as a group or "bundle" of neurons. In this case, the requirement of neurological plausibility will be met if the cortex has numerous bundles of neurons such that each bundle (1) has axons branching in opposite directions and (2) has reciprocal connections to other such bundles, both local and distant.

It turns out that most pyramidal neurons (named for the shape of the cell body), the most numerous of the neuron types in the cortex, amounting to around 70% of the total (Abeles 1991: 52-53), have axons extending to the white matter (hence toward other cortical areas) where they typically branch in opposite directions (Abeles 1991, Burnod 1990, Feldman 1984)—as well as local connections to other neurons in their immediate vicinity. Their connections to other neurons are excitatory (Abeles 1991: 12, Burnod 1990: 68).

On the question of reciprocal interconnections I turn to Burnod (1990: 68-72), who proposes a neural network model based on solid neuroanatomical principles (unlike the more familiar neural network models). Burnod's model, which may be relatively compatible with the linguistically-based model of this paper, uses cortical columns as units. The cortical column typically consists of about one hundred neurons, and the "bundles" of neurons mentioned in the second preceding paragraph as implementing nections might (as a hypothesis worth investigating) be identifiable as columns of the kind used in Burnod's model.

With respect to long-distance connections, Burnod reports: "Corticocortical connections between two distant zones are reciprocal..." (p. 68). As for local connections, Burnod reports that "For each column, cortical afferences which are axons of pyramidal cells arrive from directly adjacent columns or from more distant columns..." (p. 68). A considerably more extensive account of the neuroanatomical details is provided by Feldman (1984: 161ff).

It appears, then, that we can answer our last question affirmatively.[8]

Notes

I would like to thank Ronald Langacker for his thoughtful comments on an earlier draft of this paper.

1. We might be tempted to wonder whether a "competence" that is divorced from performance should really be called *competence*, and thus also to ask whether a "competence model" is really a model of anything having cognitive reality.

2. Bidirectional processing is another problem for some rule-based approaches, since the rules operate in only one direction, and even that not realistically. The excuse that they are only intended as rules of a "competence model" is valid as long as one doesn't read too much into the term *competence* or the term *model* (cf. Note 1).

3. There have been several different proposals for analyzing the nodes of the compact network notation, most of them too half-baked to have made their way into print. Some features of a new system of narrow notation are illustrated in Figures 1, 3, and 6 of this paper.

4. This division of visual perception into three levels is arbitrary. A detailed model would have to recognize more than three, cf. Hummel and Biederman (1990). (By the way, their network model is *not* a hocus-pocus one.)

5. After presenting the first version of this paper at the symposium, I became aware that Antonio Damasio had already proposed a similar hypothesis (Damasio 1989a, 1989b, 1989c). That we both arrived at the same position independently is somewhat encouraging in that we got there from completely different starting points, he from neurology, I from linguistics.

6. The difference in vividness may be explained at least in part by the fact that in visualizing we activate only a sampling of lower level feature nections, while actually seeing something activates many nections at all levels from the retina on up.

7. Some people who have too hastily argued that Broca's Area is not used for speech production after all, since the symptoms of Broca's aphasia have been found in cases in which Broca's Area is intact, may have overlooked the fact that the symptoms of Broca's aphasia can also result

from damage to that part of the somatosensory cortex which monitors the positions and movements of the speech production organs.

8. Further evidence has been provided by Damasio (see Note 5).

References

Abeles, Moshe. 1991. *Corticonics: Neural Circuits of the Cerebral Cortex*. Cambridge: Cambridge University Press.

Anderson, James A. 1995. *An Introduction to Neural Networks*. Cambridge, MA: MIT Press.

Burnod, Yves. 1990. *An Adaptive Neural Network: The Cerebral Cortex*. Paris: Masson; London: Prentice Hall.

Caplan, David. 1987. *Neurolinguistics and Linguistic Aphasiology: An Introduction*. Cambridge: Cambridge University Press.

Chomsky, Noam. 1964. *Current Issues in Linguistic Theory*. The Hague: Mouton.

Chomsky, Noam and Morris Halle. 1968. *The Sound Pattern of English*. New York: Harper and Row.

Cooper, Lynn A. and Roger N. Shepard. 1984. Turning something over in the mind. *Scientific American* 251(6), 106-114.

Copeland, James E. and Philip W. Davis (eds.). 1980. *Papers in Cognitive-Stratificational Linguistics*. Rice University Studies 66(2).

Damasio, Antonio. 1989a. Time-locked multiregional retroactivation: A systems-level proposal for the neural substrates of recall and recognition. *Cognition* 33, 25-62.

Damasio, Antonio. 1989b. The brain binds entities and events by multiregional activation from convergence zones. *Neural Computation* 1, 123-132.

Damasio, Antonio. 1989c. Concepts in the brain. *Mind and Language* 4, 24-28.

Dell, Gary S. and Peter A. Reich. 1977. A model of slips of the tongue. *LACUS Forum* 3, 448-55. Columbia, SC: Hornbeam Press.

Dell, Gary S. and Peter A. Reich. 1980a. Slips of the tongue: The facts and a stratificational model. In Copeland and Davis (eds.).

Dell, Gary S. and Peter A. Reich. 1980b. Toward a unified model of slips of the tongue. In Victoria A. Fromkin (ed.), *Errors in Linguistic Performance: Slips of the Tongue, Ear, Pen, and Hand*, 273-286. San Francisco: Academic Press.

Farah, Martha. 1988. Is visual imagery really visual? Overlooked evidence from Neuropsychology. *Psychological Review* 95, 307-317.

Feldman, Martin L. 1984. Morphology of the neocortical pyramidal neuron. In Alan Peters and Edward G. Jones (eds.), *Cerebral Cortex*, Vol. 1, 123-200. New York: Plenum.

Geschwind, Norman. 1964. The development of the brain and the evolution of language. *Georgetown Round Table on Languages and Linguistics* 17, 155-169.

Halliday, Michael. 1973. *Explorations in the Functions of Language*. London: Edward Arnold.

Hummel, John, and Irving Biederman. 1990. *Dynamic Binding in a Neural Network for Shape Recognition*. Technical Report No. 5, Image Understanding Laboratory, Department of Psychology, University of Minnesota.

Kosslyn, Stephen M. 1980. *Image and Mind*. Cambridge, MA: Harvard University Press.

Lamb, Sydney. 1970. Linguistic and cognitive networks. In Paul Garvin (ed.), *Cognition: A Multiple View*, 195-222. New York: Spartan Books. Reprinted 1973 in Adam Makkai and David Lockwood (eds.), *Readings in Stratificational Linguistics*. University, AL: University of Alabama Press.

Lamb, Sydney. 1993. The sources of linguistic patterning. *LACUS Forum* 19, 23-44. LACUS.

Lamb, Sydney. 1994. Relational network linguistics meets neural science. *LACUS Forum* 20, 151-178. Chapel Hill, NC: LACUS.

Obler, Loraine. 1990. Review of Caplan (1987). *Language* 66, 383-388.

Pinel, John. 1993. *Biopsychology*. Boston: Allyn and Bacon.

Reich, Peter A. 1985. Unintended puns. *LACUS Forum* 11, 314-322. Columbia, SC: Hornbeam Press.

Rumelhart, David E. and James L. McClelland. 1986. *Parallel Distributed Processing*, Vol. 2, Chapter 18: On learning the past tenses of English verbs. Cambridge, MA: MIT Press.

Connectionism and Language Learning

BRIAN MAC WHINNEY
Carnegie Mellon University

1. Symbols and Connections

Linguistic behavior is governed by a rigid set of social conventions or "rules." If we wake up one morning and decide to deliberately throw all these conventions to the wind, no one would understand us. Indeed, even our best friends might think we had gone quite insane. In everyday language, we could say that we had decided to "break the rules" of English grammar. Of course, force of habit inclines us against striking off on this iconoclastic course. Having spent so many years of our lives cooperatively following "the rules," it is easier to continue to follow them than to wander off into new territory. This view of linguistic rules as social conventions and habits is grounded firmly on everyday experience and common sense. I think it is a view that virtually everyone accepts.

During the 60s and 70s, scientists took this common sense idea of a linguistic rule and reworked it into a basic principle underlying artificial intelligence (AI), Chomskyan theoretical linguistics, and cognitive psychology. By viewing the brain as a computer, they began to think of the mind as a system for transforming symbolic strings according to well-specified rules. The vision of human language as a system of formal rules was an important ingredient underlying two decades of work in linguistics and cognitive science. This work led to the emergence of complex and impressive systems of rules and symbols based on what I have called the "Big Mean Rules" (MacWhinney 1994) and the "Big Mean Flowcharts."

In recent years, the biological and epistemological underpinnings of these great symbolic systems have become increasingly shaky and vulnerable. Two basic observational problems faced by all of these analyses are the fact that no developmental psychologist ever observed a child learning a rule and that no neuroscientist ever traced the neural substrate of either a rule or a symbol. Similarly, attempts in the 1970s to demonstrate the psychological reality of rules in adults (Fodor, Bever, and Garrett 1974; Jaeger 1984; Linell 1979; Ohala 1974a; Ohala 1974b; Ohala 1974c; Trammell 1978) yielded uniformly disappointing results. Of course, one could argue that the fact that no one has ever seen the top quark should not prevent us from constructing theories that rely on the reality of this subatomic particle. But analogies of this type are misleading. In fact, carefully controlled experiments with huge collectors of heavy water sunk deep in caves have provided solid tangible evidence for the reality of even this most elusive of physical entities. No such solid evidence has ever been provided for either linguistic rules or linguistic symbols.

Given these doubts and empirical failures, it made sense for researchers to begin to explore alternatives to symbols and rules. In the late 80s, work in connectionist modeling (Rumelhart and McClelland 1986a) began to challenge the necessity of linguistic rules and categories, focusing attention instead on models based on simple, observable cues and connections between these cues. These new models correct a fundamental, fatal flaw inherent to symbolic models: the problem of excessive descriptive power.

The great power of AI systems derives from the computational architecture of the Von Neumann serial computer and the application of this architecture to human cognition by Simon, Newell, and their followers (Klahr and Kotovsky 1991; Newell and Simon 1972). This architecture provided unlimited symbol passing, full generativity, and unlimited scalability based on the system of data paths, memory addresses, and processing cycles that could be formalized in the logic of production systems. A modeler could take a few symbols, concatenate them into rules and, magically, the computer could conjure up a working model of mental processing. These models were at the same time both too powerful and too weak. They were too powerful in that they allowed one to model the learning of things that could never in reality be learned. At the same time, they were too weak in that they failed to generalize properly across language types and patterns. Moreover, attempts to identify a uniquely correct model without adding further constraints were shown to be impossible in principle (Anderson 1978). Neural nets (Grossberg 1987; Hopfield 1982; Kohonen 1982) limit this descriptive power by imposing two stringent limitations on computational models: a prohibition against **symbol passing** and an insistence on **self-organization**.

Neural networks require that the computations involved in the models echo the connectionist architecture of the brain. The basic constraint involved here is the prohibition against symbol passing. Neuroscience has shown that the brain cannot use memory addresses to bind variables; there is no neural mechanism that can assign an absolute "address" to a particular neuron (Squire 1987). Neurons do not send Morse code, symbols do not run down synapses, and brain waves do not pass phrase structures. Unlike the computer, the brain has no general scheme for register assignment, data pathing, or memory addressing. Moreover, the individual components of the neural system do not have the reliability of the electrical components of a standard digital computer (von Neumann 1956). In general, the brain provides no obvious support for the symbol passing architecture that provides the power underlying the von Neumann machine. Instead, computation in the brain appears to rely ultimately on the formation of redundant connections between individual neurons.

By itself, the requirement that computation be performed locally without symbol passing or homunculi is not enough to fully constrain descriptive power. One could still hand-wire a connectionist system to perform a specific function or to model a particular behavior. By detailed weight setting and the use of gating and polling neurons, virtually any function can be wired into a neural net (Hertz, Krogh and Palmer 1991). An early example of a fully hand-wired connectionist architecture was Lamb's Stratificational Grammar (Lamb 1966). More recently, we have seen hand-wired connectionist models in areas such as speech errors (Dell 1986; MacWhinney and Anderson 1986; Stemberger 1985), ambiguity resolution (Cottrell 1985), and lexical activation (Marslen-Wilson 1987). The "implementational" approach to hand-wiring spares the modeler the tedium of hand-wiring by running the wiring procedure off symbolic templates. For example, Touretzky (1990) has shown that there are techniques for bottling the full power of a LISP-based production system architecture into a neural net. These demonstrations are important because they show how difficult it is to control excessive modelling power. However, they tell us little about how language is implemented in the brain.

In order fully to constrain descriptive power, modelers must match the constraint against symbol passing with the requirement that networks be **self-organizing**. This is to say, that models cannot be hand-wired and the connections between units must be developed on the basis of automatic learning procedures. It is this property of neural nets that makes them particularly interesting to the developmental psychologist and which also poses the greatest challenge to detailed modeling work. When the prohibition against symbol passing is combined with the demand for self-organization, the class of potential models of language learning becomes extremely limited. In fact, there is currently no detailed model of language acquisition that can satisfy these two criteria. Is this evidence that the criteria are too strict? I think not. Rather it is evidence that we can use these criteria to constrain our search for a truly plausible model of language acquisition. More importantly, it appears that those models which come closest to satisfying these criteria are also the same models that display further interesting and important properties, such as category leakage (McClelland and Kawamoto 1986), graceful degradation (Harley and MacAndrew 1992; Hinton and Shallice 1991; Marchman 1992), and property emergence (MacWhinney, Leinbach, Taraban, and McDonald 1989).

When these twin constraints are taken seriously, along with the standard conditions that must be imposed on any formal model (MacWhinney 1978b), building successful models becomes a tough job. When we add a third constraint—the need to demonstrate scalability—building powerful connectionist models becomes a nearly impossible task. Some modelers try to make headway against these odds by ignoring the scalability constraint and confronting only the first two constraints. This leads them to building models of very small pieces of the language acquisition puzzle. For example, some networks are constrained to well-defined topics such as the acquisition of the English past tense (Cottrell and Plunkett 1991) or German gender (MacWhinney et al. 1989). Other models have focused on small slices across larger problems such as question answering (St. John 1992) or word recognition (McClelland and Elman 1986). Some of these toy models may use only a few dozen sentences or a few dozen words. When one attempts to add additional words or sentences to these models, their performance often begins to degenerate. These problems with inadequate scalability are particularly serious in the study of language acquisition, since the move from a vocabulary of 500 words to a vocabulary of 700 words is a smooth accretional transition for the language-learning child. If connectionist models are to provide serious alternatives to symbolic models, it is crucial that they directly address each of these three issues: scalability, symbol passing, and self-organization. Any attempt to ignore one of these constraints detracts from the impact of the connectionist enterprise.

2. Grand Pretensions, Modest Reality

Like the symbolic paradigm before it, the connectionist paradigm seeks to provide a general model of human cognition. Because it has staked out such a wide territory, connectionism is committed to providing an account of all of the core issues in language acquisition, including grammatical development, lexical learning, phonological development, second language learning, and the processing of language by the brain. Despite these grand pretensions, the reality of connectionist modeling is more sober and modest. In fact, much of the work to date has focused on the learning of narrow aspects of inflectional morphology in languages like English and German. While limited, work in this area has taught us a great deal. This paper sketches out the achievements of connectionist models in this well-researched area and then examines how we can move from these preliminary achievements to a fuller, more explanatory, unified approach to all of the core issues facing language acquisition theory.

Let us begin by reviewing some recent connectionist models of the learning of inflectional morphology. The first study of this topic was a model of English past tense marking presented by Rumelhart and McClelland (1987; 1986b). A more fully elaborated version of this model was developed by MacWhinney and Leinbach (1991). The task of these models was to convert the stem of an English verb into another inflected form, such as the past tense. For example, given a stem such as *eat*, the model could produce *eats*, *eating*, *ate*, or *eaten*.

Like all connectionist models, this model based its performance on the development of the weights on the connections between a large collection of "units." The pattern of inputs and the connections between units was designed to implement the pattern of an autosegmental grid that has been developed in phonological theory (Goldsmith 1976; Nespor and Vogel 1986). The idea is that each vowel or consonant sound is a bundle of features that sits inside a slot within the framework or grid of the syllable. Words, in turn, are formed from combinations of syllables in a metrical grid.

The MacWhinney-Leinbach model used 12 consonantal slots and 6 vowel slots and allowed for words of up to three syllables. The segments of the stem were filled into this grid in right-justified fashion (MacWhinney 1993), as in this example for the word *bet* :

CCC VV CCC VV CC<u>b</u> V<u>E</u> CC<u>t</u>

A further syllable was reserved for the suffix in the output. Each of the slots was in turn composed of a group of feature units. Since each of these feature units was bound to its particular slot, we can think of each unit as a slot/ feature unit. For example, the first filled consonantal slot in the representation for *bet* had active units for the labial, consonantal, and voiced features required for the sound /b/. Each of the consonantal slots had ten units and each of the vowel slots had eight units, for a total of 168 sound units per word. The architecture of the network had the shape shown in Figure 1.

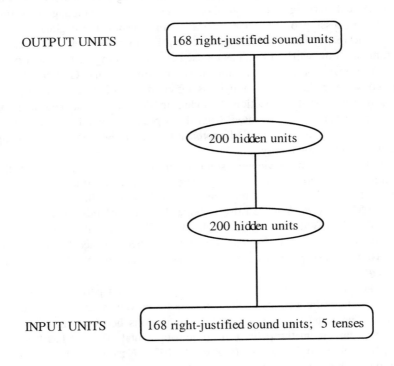

OUTPUT UNITS   168 right-justified sound units

200 hidden units

200 hidden units

INPUT UNITS   168 right-justified sound units; 5 tenses

Figure 1. Architecture of the MacWhinney-Leinbach Past-Tense Network

The complete training corpus used 6949 different verb forms, derived from the 2161 highest frequency verbs in English (Francis and Kucera 1982). Of these 2161 verbs, 118 were irregulars and 2043 were regulars. The frequency with which a given form was included in the training epochs was determined by its frequency in the Francis and Kucera (1982) word frequency list. The highest frequency verbs were included most often. Learning in the model was controlled by the back-propagation algorithm (Rumelhart, Hinton and Williams 1986).

The network did an excellent job learning its input corpus, producing the correct output forms for 97% of the forms. At the end of 24,000 epochs of training, the only forms that it was still missing were low-frequency irregulars such as *bled* or *underwent*. Generalization testing showed that most new verbs were produced in the regular past, but that a few forms were treated as irregulars. Additional generalization testing is reported in MacWhinney (1993) and Ling and Marinov (1993).

English is a relatively poor language, at least in regard to its system of inflectional morphology. It has virtually no marking of case or gender. Nouns have only a single basic suffix for plurality and virtually the same suffix for the possessive. Although there are a few irregular past tense verbs, even the system of verbal morphology is fairly simple. Fortunately, we do not have to look far afield for a more challenging problem. Even a closely related language like German presents us with a far richer system of inflectional morphology. So rich, indeed, that Mark Twain (1935[1880]) once complained that:

> a person who has not studied German can form no idea of what a perplexing language it is.... Every noun has a gender, and there is no sense or system in the distribution; so the gender of each must be learned separately and by heart. There is no other way. To do this, one has to have a memory like a memorandum book. In German, a young lady has no sex, while a turnip has. Think what overwrought reverence that shows for the turnip, and what callous disrespect for the girl.

Any English speaker who has studied German, be it in the context of the classroom or in the country itself, has probably reached a very similar conclusion.

The vagaries of German gender are compounded by the fact that written German still clings to a system of case-marking only slightly simpler than that found in Classical Latin. For example, the definite article is declined through all four cases and all three genders in the singular and across all four cases with gender neutralized in the plural. The result of these various obligatory markings is the paradigm for the definite article in Table 1.

	Masc.	Fem.	Neut.	Plural
Nom.	der	die	das	die
Gen.	des	der	des	der
Dat.	dem	der	dem	der
Acc.	den	die	das	die

Table 1. The German Definite Article Paradigm

This paradigm is rife with homonymy. Only six distinct forms of the definite article occur in the 16 cells in the paradigm. This means that many of the forms cover several meanings. For example, the article *der* can mean either 'masculine singular nominative,' 'feminine singular genitive,' 'feminine singular dative,' or 'plural genitive.'

In order to select the correct form of the definite article, the language learner has to know three things about the noun—its case, its number, and its gender. Number is the easiest category, since it bears a fairly straightforward relation to real-world properties. Case is somewhat more abstract, but it can generally be figured out through a combination of cues from the verb, related prepositions, and some word order patterns. However, there is little in the external situation that can help the child figure out the gender of a noun (Maratsos and Chalkley 1980). It is possible that the noun's gender could be simply memorized or even inferred on the basis of its use within the paradigm. For example, knowing that the novel noun *Gann* is treated as *den Gann* in the accusative, the child can infer that it takes the form *der Gann* in the nominative. However, recent work by Köpcke and Zubin (Köpcke 1982; Köpcke 1988; Köpcke and Zubin 1983; Köpcke and Zubin 1996; Köpcke and Zubin 1984; Zubin and Köpcke 1981; Zubin and Köpcke 1986) has shown that Mark Twain's view of gender as arbitrary and unpredictable is incomplete and partially incorrect.

In fact, Köpcke and Zubin have shown that there are dozens of phonological cues that can be used to predict the gender of a German noun. For example, almost all nouns ending in *-e* are feminine, as in *die Sonne, die Ente,* and *die Tante*. Almost all nouns beginning with *dr-, tr-,* and *kn-* are masculine, as in *der Knecht, der Trieb,* and *der Drang*. There are dozens of other cues like these. In addition to these purely phonological cues, there are derivational endings such as *-chen, -lein, -ett, -tum, -ei,* and so on, each of which reliably specifies a particular gender.

MacWhinney, Leinbach, Taraban, and McDonald (1989) constructed a series of models of the acquisition of German gender. The first model dedicated a series of nodes to the cues enumerated by Köpcke and Zubin, along with a series of nodes for case and number cues. The second model made no explicit coding of the Köpcke-Zubin cues, instead simply encoding the phonological form of the base in the manner of the MacWhinney-Leinbach model for English. Much to our surprise, the network with no hand-coding of features outperformed the hand-crafted network in terms of both learning and generalization. These results provide nice support for the view of connectionist networks as providing emergent self-organizing characterizations of linguistic systems. Similar results for hand-wired vs. emergent solutions are reported by Daelemans, Gillis, and Durieux (1994) for the learning of Dutch stress by a connectionist network.

The architecture of the successful non-handcrafted German simulation had the form in Figure 2. The input to the network was a pattern across 143 phonological units representing the noun stem and 11 phonological units representing suffixes attached to the noun. In addition, there were 5 semantic units representing inherent gender and 17 cues that provided a distributed pattern of surface structure information helpful in determining the case for the noun. However, the actual identity of the case was not given. This network was trained with 2000 German nouns from all cells in the paradigm. It learned the training set completely. When tested with 200 new nouns, the system was able to guess the gender of the new words with 70% accuracy. This compares with a level of 80% accuracy that could be expected from a native German speaker (Köpcke 1982).

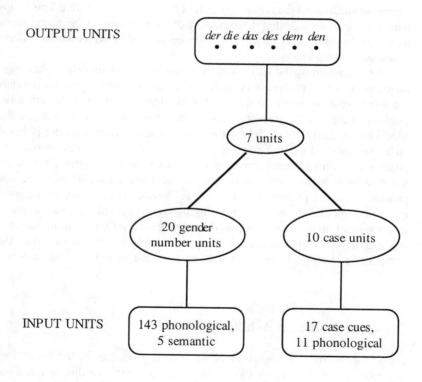

Figure 2. Network Architecture for German Stress

The model also succeeded in capturing a variety of important developmental phenomena. Like the children studied by MacWhinney (1978a) and Mills (1986), the model showed early acquisition of the nominative and delayed acquisition of the genitive. These acquisitional order effects are undoubtedly due to the fact that the frequencies of the four cases in the training corpus were based on their actual distribution in German corpora. Also, like German children, the model made good use of reliable cues to gender such as final -e or some of the derivational markers. Like children, the model was able to use the paradigm to infer word class. For example, given the accusative form *den Bauer*, the model could produce the genitive singular form *des Bauers*. Native speakers can do this on the basis of only one exposure to the word and the model displays similar behavior. Like children, the model frequently omitted the article. This occurred when the output units did not reach threshold. Finally, the model demonstrated the same tendency toward overgeneralization of the feminine gender often found in children. This is apparently due to the fact that the similarity of the feminine to the plural lends it enough frequency and paradigmatic support to tend to overcome the effects of the other two genders.

When evaluating the success of these connectionist models of language acquisition, it is important to consider the extent to which symbolic models are able to address similar problems. For the learning of English verb morphology, Ling (1994) presents a model that performs about as well as the MacWhinney-Leinbach model for English. Although Ling's model is based on a conventional symbol passing architecture, it uses an input-driven induction algorithm, thereby avoiding problems with hand-wiring. However, the detailed feature combinations constructed by Ling's pattern associator provide no clear representation of rules and would probably not be accepted as a full symbolic model by many linguists and psycholinguists. Nonetheless, the head-on comparison of models conducted by Ling is quite interesting and further connectionist work by Bullinaria (1997) shows that the competitive testing of symbolic and connectionist models can be quite instructive.

3. Lexical Items: An Achilles Heel?

Despite their basic successes, there are several properties of the MacWhinney models that should give us serious cause for worry. In this sense, these weaknesses are actually more instructive than their successes. These weaknesses play a parallel role in both the model for English and the model for German.

3.1 Problem 1: Homophony

Because these models convert from phonology to phonology without using discrete representations for lexical items, they both run into serious problems with homophonous forms. Consider what happens to the three homophones of the word *ring* in English. We can say *the maid wrung out the clothes, the soldiers ringed the city,* or *the choirboy rang the bell.* These three different words all have the same sound /rêN/ in the present, but each takes a different form in the past.

A similar problem arises in German. The stem *Bund* can be either *der Bund* or *das Bund*, depending on whether it is an 'alliance' or a 'bundle or sheaf of wheat.' And the stem *Band* can be either *der Band* or *das Band* depending on whether it means a 'volume of a book' or a 'rubber band.' The problem here is that, in order to control this variation, one needs to distinguish the meanings of the two homophonous lexical items involved. If the network has no concept of "lexical item" this is difficult to do. These problems also affect the formation of the plural. For example, the singular form *das Wort* has two plural forms *die Wörter* (several isolated words) and *die Worte* (connected words or speech).

3.2 Problem 2: Compounds

A parallel problem crops up in the formation of the past tense of compound words. The English training set included several compounds based on irregular verbs such as *undergo, rethink,* and *undo.* The fact that the past tense of *undergo* is *underwent* depends on the fact that *undergo* is a variant of the stem *go.* When the compound itself is high enough in frequency, the network can learn to treat it as an irregular. However, the network had a hard time learning the past tense of low frequency irregular compounds. At the end of training, the model was still not producing *underwent* correctly, even though it had learned *went* early in training. It is clear that the model was not able to use its learning about *go ~ went* to facilitate learning of the far less frequent form *undergo ~ underwent.*

A similar problem emerged in the learning of the gender of compounds in German. The model quickly learned that *Mutter* ('mother') was feminine, because the noun was so frequent. However, there is a competing tendency to treat words with final *-er* as masculine. And this tendency led the model to treat the less frequent form *Grossmutter* ('grandmother') as masculine, although it is clearly a variant of *Mutter* and should be feminine.

3.3 Problem 3: Derivational Status

The model was also not capable of utilizing information regarding the derivational status of lexical items. As Kim, Pinker, Prince, and Prasada (1990) have noted, the past tense forms of denominal verbs are uniformly regular. For example, the word *ring* can be used as a verb in a sentence such as *the groom ringed her finger* and we would never say *the groom rung her finger*. However, as we noted earlier, the network of the MacWhinney-Leinbach simulation cannot use the derivational status of the verb *ring* to make this distinction.

German provides even clearer examples of the importance of derivational status. All German nouns that derive from verbs are masculine. For example, the noun *der Schlag* ('blow'; 'cream') derives from the verb *schlagen* ('to hit'). However, there is no motivated way of indicating this in the model. In general, the model includes no independent way of representing morphological relationships between words. Thus, no distinction is made between true phonological cues such as final /e/ or initial /kn/ and derivational markers such as *-chen* or *-ett*. This leads to some very obvious confusions. For example, masculines such as *der Nacken* ('neck') and *der Hafen* ('harbor') end in phonological /en/, whereas neuters such as *das Wissen* ('knowledge') and *das Lernen* ('learning') end in the derivational suffix *-en*. Confusion of these two suffixes leads to inability to correctly predict gender for new nouns ending in /en/.

3.4 Problem 4: Early Irregulars

A well-known child language phenomenon is the u-shaped learning curve for irregular verbs in English. For a verb such as *go*, children may begin with *went*, then show some occasional usage of *goed*, and finally settle in on correct usage with *went*. During the period of oscillation between *goed* and *went*, it is usually *went* that predominates. However, not all irregular verbs show this pattern and not all overregularizations enter at the same time. The MacWhinney-Leinbach model showed the oscillation between *goed* and *went* terminating in correct usage, but it did not show early use of *went*. The reason for the failure of the model to produce early *went* is that the network is configured to construct the past tense as a variation on the phonological form of the present tense. A more accurate model would allow direct learning of *went* as a rote form. But the capacity to learn rote associations between sound and meaning involves the capacity to learn lexical items and this means that we will need a connectionist architecture specifically designed for this type of learning.

3.5 The Core Problem

These four weaknesses we have discussed can be linked to a single core problem: the absence of any way of representing lexical items. Because these models have no lexical items, they are forced to rely on sound features as the only way to determine inflectional morphology. Of course, it would be a mistake to imagine that the sound form of words has no impact on inflection and derivation. In fact, it seems that what really happens during both production and comprehension is that both the sound and meaning of stems and affixes are available in parallel, although the time course of their activation may vary (Kawamoto 1993).

One way of addressing this problem is to mix both sound features and meaning features without providing any explicit representation of lexical items. Attempts to achieve lexical access without lexical representations have been partially effective in models of reading (Kawamoto 1993; Plaut and McClelland 1993) and spelling (Seidenberg and McClelland 1989). Models of reading and spelling can avoid lexical representations, because orthographic-phonological correspondences typically make little reference to lexical items. However, these models run into more serious problems (Cottrell and Plunkett 1991; Hoeffner 1992), when dealing with language learning and word production. Models of the Hoeffner type display this problem most clearly. They learn to associate sound to meaning and store these associations in a distributed pattern in the hidden units. This approach works well enough until the model is given more than about 700 forms. At this point, the large pool of hidden units is so fully invested in distinguishing phonological and semantic subtypes and their associations that there is simply no room for new words. Adding more hidden units doesn't solve this problem, since all the interconnections must be computed and eventually the learning algorithm will bog down. It would appear that what we are seeing here is the soft underbelly of connectionism—its inability to represent Islands of Stability in the middle of a Sea of Chaos. Perhaps the problem of learning to represent lexical items is the Achilles' heel of connectionism.

4. A Solution to the Lexical Learning Problem

4.1 Lexicalist Connectionism

Given the seriousness of these problems and the extent to which they have limited the full effectiveness of connectionist models for English and German, we decided to explore alternatives to fully distributed representations. The core assumption in our new approach is that the lexical item serves a central controlling and stabilizing role in language learning and processing. We can refer to this revised approach as **lexicalist connectionism**. Predecessors to lexicalist connectionist models can be found in localist connectionist models of the type developed by Dell (1986) and Stemberger (1985), where a central role is given to the lexical item. However, because of their localist node-based architecture, these models were forced to rely on hand-wiring.

In order to model lexical learning without hand-wiring, we turned to the self-organizing feature map (SOFM) framework of Kohonen (1982) and Miikkulainen (1990; Mikkulainen and Dyer 1991). In this framework, word learning is viewed as the association of a large number of phonological features to a large number of semantic features. These many features constitute a high-dimensional space. However, the association of these many dimensions can be compressed onto a 2-D feature map in which nearby vectors in the input space are mapped onto nearby units in the 2-D map. The two dimensions of the visible representation do not have any direct relation to features in the input data set; rather they preserve the topological relations inherent in the high-dimensional space.

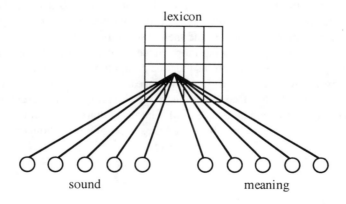

Figure 3. Mapping Lexical Items as Sound-Meaning Associations

Schematically, one can think of the map as a 2-D compression that associates sound and meaning in the way suggested by Figure 3. Learning involves the strengthening of weights between particular inputs and units on the map. This can be done in strict accord with established biological principles of lateral inhibition and the redistribution of syntactic resources (Kohonen 1982) using a computationally efficient algorithm that is faithful to these biological principles (Miikkulainen 1990).

Using this algorithm, we found that a network with 10,000 nodes can learn up to 6000 lexical associations with an error rate of less than 1%. In this implementation, we used four floating-point numbers to represent sound and four additional floating-point numbers to represent meaning. The shape of these eight numbers for each item was generated randomly. At the beginning of learning, the first input vector of eight numbers would lead by chance to somewhat stronger activation on one of the 10,000 cells. This one slightly more active cell would then inhibit the activation of its competitors. Once it has won this particular competition, its activation would be negatively damped to prevent it from winning for all of the items. Then, on the next trial, another cell would win in the competition for the next lexical item. This process would repeat until all 6000 items had developed some "specialist" cell in the feature map. During this process, the dynamics of self-organization would ensure that items that shared features would end up in similar regions of the feature map.

One way of following the development of the feature map is to track the average radius of the individual items. After learning the first 700 words, the average radius of each word was 70 cells; after 3000 words, the radius was 8; after 5000 words the radius was 3; and after 6000 words the radius was only 1.5 cells. Clearly, there is not much room for new lexical items in a feature map with 10,000 cells that has already learned 6000 items. However, there is good reason to think that the enormous number of cells in the human brain means that the size of the initial feature map is not an important limiting constraint on the learning of the lexicon by real children.

4.2 Using Maps for Retrieval

In order to permit full use of the lexicon in processing, we next proceed to supplement the basic SOFM architecture with additional connections. We have done this by simultaneously building up three identical parallel feature maps: the sound map, the meaning map, and the association map. Figure 4 illustrates the relations of these three maps. In this figure, a particular location on the association map relates a location on the sound map to a location on the meaning map.

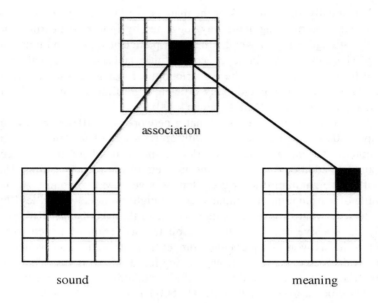

Figure 4. The Development of Bidirectional Sound-Meaning Associations

During training, the sound and meaning maps are given full input patterns. Each then comes to take on its own pattern of internal organization. Although these patterns emerge as quite similar, they are not constrained externally to be identical. Once patterns are established on the two basic maps, we start a period of Hebbian learning. When a particular sound and a particular meaning are active on the two lower maps, we then reinforce the most highly active unit on the association map. This unit then becomes the effective center of the lexical item. Once this initial association is formed, we can use this device as an auto-associator. We can then turn on a sound and retrieve the corresponding meaning by activating the correct associator unit. This models lexical comprehension. We can also turn on a meaning and retrieve the corresponding sound. This models lexical production.

5. Using Lexical Representations

This implementation allows us to put aside our earlier worries regarding lexical learning as an Achilles' Heel for connectionist models of language learning. We now have structures that function like lexical items and which developed in a fully self-organizing way without external intervention or corrective training. We cannot manipulate these items with standard symbol passing techniques, but additional input can develop their connections to other processes. In this section, I will discuss some of ways in which we can use these representations to make further progress in connectionist models of language acquisition.

5.1 Learning Inflectional Morphology

The first crucial application of this new modeling effort has been to the acquisition of inflectional morphology. Our initial goal was to see if the model could learn to inflect verbs for the English past tense. The network is first given the set of input forms used in the MacWhinney-Leinbach simulations for English. Each phonological input is paired with a randomly generated, but consistent, semantic representation. Included in the semantic representation are features that consistently represent the meanings signaled by English verb inflections: present, past, perfect, progressive, and third singular. During this lexical training, the network learns inflected items such as *went* and *gone*, as well as regularly inflected items such as *goes*, *going*, *jumped*, and *runs*. The network also acquires a large number of bare-stem verbs such as *go*, *run*, and *jump*.

Before this training is completed, we introduce a few generalization trials. These trials take verbs that have been learned as bare-stems, but not yet as inflected forms. For example, the network already knows *jump*, but has not yet learned *jumped*. At this point, the network engages in the process of **masking** (Burgess 1995; Burgess and Hitch 1992; Carpenter, Grossberg and Reynolds 1991; Cohen and Grossberg 1987; Grossberg 1987) which leads to the temporary suppression of *jump* and the isolation of *-ed* as the not-yet-recognized form. Masking is a general process that is used to suppress the status of any phonological string that has been recognized. In this particular case, masking leads to the isolation of the part that the child already knows from the residue. In other words, isolation is a result of the operation of the process of masking. The suffix is then learned as a new lexical item that associates *-ed* with the meaning of the past tense. In the terms of MacWhinney (1978a), learning involves associating the "unexpressed" meaning of the past tense with the "uncomprehended" sound string *-ed*.

Learning of the other inflectional suffixes proceeds in a similar way. When the system is asked to produce the past tense of a new verb, masking is used in reverse. For example, the past tense of *jump* is produced by (1) activating *jump*, (2) masking the semantics and phonology of *jump*, (3) reactivating the network with 'past,' and (4) retrieving *-ed*. The output phonology of *jump* and the *-ed* suffix is then available for read-out from the articulatory buffer and the child can produce *jumped*.

This approach to the problem of learning the English past tense solves a number of problems faced by earlier non-lexical models. First, the model succeeds in capturing both rote lexicalization and combinatorial lexicalization within a single connectionist model. Rote forms are picked up directly on the feature map. Combinatorial forms are created by the isolation of the suffix through masking and the use of masking in production. Second, the model no longer faces the earlier problems that stemmed from a lack of lexical items. Homophony is not a problem, because the meanings of the homophones of /rêN/ are now representationally distinct. The model can locate *go* inside *undergo* and *Mutter* inside *Grossmutter* because it now has lexical items and can use masking. In German, derivational suffixes like *-chen* can be used as cues to gender because these suffixes now have their own representational status. Finally, the model no longer has any problem with the early acquisition of irregulars such as *went*. Since the learning is grounded now on lexical items, these high-frequency forms are some of the first forms learned.

This model relies on three crucial processing mechanisms. The first mechanism is the self-organizing competitive learning incorporated in the feature map. The second mechanism uses Hebbian learning to develop a central associative map for lexical comprehension and production. The third mechanism is the masking process which works to extract inflections.

5.2 The Logical Problem

The ability to produce *went* by rote and **goed* by combination within the same lexical feature map also allows us to begin work on a general solution to the so-called "logical problem of language acquisition" (Baker and McCarthy 1981; Gleitman 1990; Gleitman, Newport and Gleitman 1984; Morgan and Travis 1989; Pinker 1984; Pinker 1989; Wexler and Culicover 1980). In the case of the competition between *went* and **goed*, we expect *went* to become solidified over time because of its repeated occurrence in the input. The form **goed*, on the other hand, is supported only by the presence of the combinational *-ed* form. Figure 5 illustrates this competition:

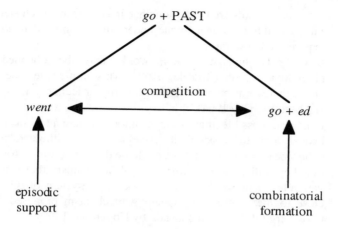

Figure 5. Competition between Episodic and Combinatorial Knowledge

This particular competition is an example of what Baker and McCarthy (1981) call a "benign exception to the logical problem." It is benign because everyone will agree that there is only one way to say 'goed' and that is *went*. However, in other cases, people will argue that there is no obvious way to "correct" a given error by using an obviously related form. Such cases would be considered "non-benign." Later (Section 5.4), we will examine some non-benign cases.

5.3 Masking and Buffering

The masking mechanism underlies not only inflectional extraction, but also syntactic processing more generally. In order to process sentences, we need to have some process that deactivates each lexical item immediately after it is activated. The trace of this masked item must then be stored provisionally in some separate form apart from the main lexicon. The simplest way to do this is to activate a second copy of the original item (Burgess and Hitch 1992). This could be done by creating a complete secondary copy of the primary lexicon. However, even this complete duplication of the lexicon would only guarantee memory for two words at a time. A more flexible system would convert the initial lexical representations to some other pattern. There have been several suggestions regarding the nature of this short-term verbal memory.

1. As soon as words are linked together into conceptual clusters, they can be used to activate a unique underlying meaning that no longer requires verbal storage.

2. Before this linkage occurs, words may be obtained in a phonological loop (Baddeley 1986). This immediate rehearsal requires that words be present in a primarily articulatory form (Gupta and MacWhinney 1994).

3. It is also possible that some additional mechanism operates on lexical items to encode their serial occurrence without reference to either meaning or sound. This could be done in terms of some additional episodic, possibly hippocampal, mechanism that stores activation levels of words prior to masking. A system of this type is close to the Competitive Queuing mechanism proposed first by Grossberg (1978) and then again by Houghton (1990).

Further experimental work will be needed to understand more closely which of these three mechanisms is involved at which point in the storage of short term verbal memories. What is important for our current simulations is only the fact that there is evidence that neural mechanisms are available to support masking in the lexicon (Gupta and MacWhinney 1997).

5.4 Argument Frame Extraction

Earlier versions of the Competition Model (MacWhinney 1988) presented a system for the control of syntax through lexical argument (or "valency" or "dependency") relations. From a connectionist viewpoint, the masking process is what triggers the acquisition of argument relations. To illustrate this process, consider an example in which the child already knows the words *Mommy* and *Daddy*, but does not know the word *like*. Given this state of lexical knowledge, the sentence *Daddy likes Mommy* would be represented in this way:

d æ d i		l aI k s		m a m i
Daddy		unknown		Mommy

For the first and last phonological stretches, there are lexical items that match. These strings and the semantics they represent are masked. The unknown stretch is not masked and therefore stimulates lexical learning of the new word *likes*. The core of the learning for *likes* is the association of the sound /laIk/ to the meaning 'like.' In addition to this association, the central association feature map now constructs links not only to sound and meaning, but also to argument relations. The initial argument frame for the word *likes* is [[arg1, preposed, *Daddy*][arg2, postposed, *Mommy*]]. Further exposures to sentences such as *Daddy likes pancakes* or *Billy likes turtles* will soon generalize the dependency frame for *likes* to [[arg1, preposed, HUMAN][arg2, postposed, OBJECT]].

The implementation of the acquisition of argument frames follows the logic developed by Gupta and MacWhinney (1992) for the acquisition of German declensional marking. That model used a SOFM for the extraction of cooccurrence patterns between articles and nouns. Using these patterns, the full shape of the German declensional pattern emerged inside the SOFM. Nodes in the map took on the role of associating particular constellations of case and number marking on the article with one of the three grammatical genders of German. This system was then linked to a back-propagation system that responded to additional phonological cues to gender. The general shape of this type of model is given in Figure 6 which includes the basic components of Figure 4 along with additional maps for argument structures and articulatory control.

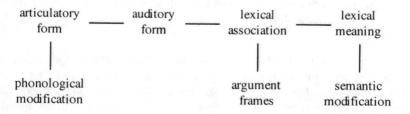

Figure 6. A Connectionist Account of the Shape of Linguistic Representations

The argument frame feature map is intended to capture a few basic grammatical categories which will then be related to particular lexical items. However, these argument frames will also activate patterns in the meaning and auditory form feature maps. The feature map is designed to include two basic effects. One is the activation of the correct argument frame for a specific lexical item. The other is the activation of argument frames for semantically related groups of words or lexical "gangs." Words that have similar meanings will tend to activate similar argument structures.

Lexical gang effects help us address some remaining aspects of the "logical problem of language acquisition." Bowerman (1988) cites overgeneralization errors such as **I poured the tub with water*, **I unsqueezed the ball*, and **I recommended him a soup* as potential evidence for the logical problem. However, recovery from these errors can be viewed as similar to recovery from errors such as *goed*. Figure 7 illustrates the situation.

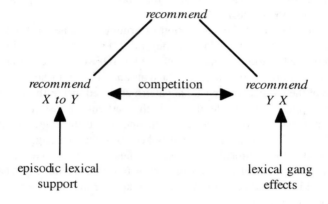

Figure 7. Competition between Lexical Argument Frames and Lexical Gang Effects

The Competition Model (MacWhinney 1988) treated the argument structures for inflectional morphemes as similar to the structures for verbs and prepositions. For the English past tense, the masking and extraction of the phonological form /t/ from the verb *jumped* produces a frame specifically linked to the sound and meaning of *jump*. Over time, the meaning of [arg1] of the past tense morpheme becomes generalized to any verb and the sound becomes generalized so that the /t/ and /d/ forms of the morpheme require stem-final non-dentals (voiceless and voiced, respectively) and vowels, whereas the /Id/ form requires a final dental consonant.

5.5 Modification Systems

In addition to the basic maps for lexical associations and argument frames, Figure 6 has systems for phonological and semantic modification. Phonological modification operates to enforce general phonological patterns when words are linked together. Semantic modification works to adapt meanings when words are linked together. Often this linkage is predictable and obvious. However, sometimes words are placed together even at the expense of standard argument frames. Because connectionist systems are constraint-satisfaction systems, rather than rule systems, they can deal with partial violations in the combinations of words. Consider a combination like *another sand*. Typically, the word *another* requires a count noun and *sand* is a mass noun. However, when the listener is confronted with this particular combination, it is still possible to retrieve an interpretation by treating *sand* as a count noun. This can be done by thinking of bags of sand, types of sand, alternative meanings of the word *sand*, or even the act of applying sandpaper to something. MacWhinney (1989) talks about these semantic extension effects in terms of a process of "pushy polysemy."

5.6 Sentence Compilation

Currently, our actual implementation of argument frame effects has focused on the use of a simple recurrent network, rather than feature maps. The task we have selected is the acquisition of English and Dutch as both first and second languages. Figure 8 illustrates the shape of the model we have used:

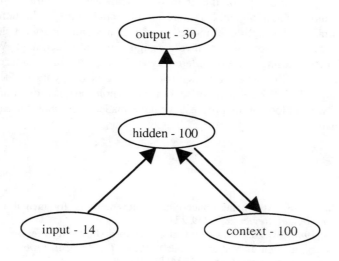

Figure 8. *Network Architecture for Acquisition of English and Dutch*

The input to the model is a corpus of sentences from the language illustrating the major syntactic frames, including relative clauses, imperatives, and various word order types. For each word, the input cues include animacy, number, part-of-speech, and case-marking for pronouns.

This model learns the input corpus in a few runs. We then test it using the experimental agrammatical sentences used in Competition Model studies by McDonald (1987; 1989) and Kilborn and Cooreman (1987) for Dutch, and Bates, McNew, MacWhinney, Devescovi, and Smith (1982) for English. Overall, the match of the model to the experimental data was excellent.

6. Limitations and Prospects

This modeling work with connectionist nets has advanced to the point where it can compete on an equal footing with the more powerful rule-based symbolic models. These networks minimize hand-wiring and maximize self-organization. Because of this, they are attractive to developmental psychologists. They also avoid reliance on hardware address and symbol passing. And it is this that makes them attractive to cognitive neuroscientists. But they are still incomplete in many ways. In our modeling of language learning, we have made good progress in the areas of lexical learning, inflectional morphology, and role assignment. But there is still much work to be done. We need to link up the high-level modeling of role assignment to detailed aspects of lexical processing and local role assignment and attachment. We need to model the learning of more different types of inflectional structures. And we need to deal in greater detail with lexical effects on syntax. There may still be an Achilles' Heel that will doom this whole process to failure. But, for now, we can look at the progress we have made as grounds for cautious optimism.

References

Anderson, John. 1978. Arguments concerning representations for mental imagery. *Psychological Review* 85, 249-277.

Baddeley, Alan. 1986. *Working Memory.* Oxford: Oxford University Press.

Baker, Charles L. and John J. McCarthy (eds.). 1981. *The Logical Problem of Language Acquisition.* Cambridge, MA: MIT Press.

Bates, Elizabeth, Sandra McNew, Brian MacWhinney, Antonella Devescovi, and Stan Smith. 1982. Functional constraints on sentence processing: A cross-linguistic study. *Cognition* 11, 245-299.

Bowerman, Melissa. 1988. The "no negative evidence" problem. In John Hawkins (ed.), *Explaining Language Universals*, 73-101. London: Blackwell.

Bullinaria, John A. 1997. Modelling reading, spelling and past tense learning with artificial neural networks. *Brain and Language* 59, 236-66.

Burgess, Neil. 1995. A solvable connectionist model of immediate recall of ordered lists. In Gerald Tesauro, David Touretzky, and Joshua Alspector (eds.), *Neural Information Processing Systems* 7. San Mateo, CA: Morgan Kaufmann.

Burgess, Neil and Graham Hitch. 1992. Toward a network model of the articulatory loop. *Journal of Memory and Language* 31, 429-460.

Carpenter, Gail, Stephen Grossberg, and John Reynolds. 1991. ARTMAP: Supervised real-time learning and classification of nonstationary data by a self-organizing neural network. *Neural Networks* 4, 565-588.

Cohen, Michael and Stephen Grossberg. 1987. Masking fields: A massively parallel neural architecture for learning, recognizing, and predicting multiple groupings of patterned data. *Applied Optics* 26, 1866-1891.

Cottrell, Garrison. 1985. *A Connectionist Approach to Word Sense Disambiguation.* Rochester, NY: University of Rochester.

Cottrell, Garrison and Kim Plunkett. 1991. Learning the past tense in a recurrent network: Acquiring the mapping from meaning to sounds. *Proceedings of the Thirteenth Annual Conference of the Cognitive Science Society*, 328-33. Hillsdale, NJ: Lawrence Erlbaum.

Daelemanns, Walter, Steven Gillis, and Gert Durieux. 1994. The acquisition of stress: A data-oriented approach. *Computational Linguistics* 20, 421-51.

Dell, Gary. 1986. A spreading-activation theory of retrieval in sentence production. *Psychological Review* 93, 283-321.

Fodor, Jerry A., Thomas G. Bever, and Merrill F. Garrett. 1974. *The Psychology of Language: An Introduction to Psycholinguistics and Generative Grammar.* New York: McGraw-Hill.

Francis, W. Nelson and Henry Kucera. 1982. *Frequency Analysis of English Usage: Lexicon and Grammar.* Boston: Houghton Mifflin.

Gleitman, Lila. 1990. The structural sources of verb meanings. *Language Acquisition* 1(1), 3-55.

Gleitman, Lila R., Elissa L. Newport, and Henry Gleitman. 1984. The current status of the motherese hypothesis. *Journal of Child Language* 11, 43-79.

Goldsmith, John. 1976. An overview of autosegmental phonology. *Linguistic Analysis* 2, 23-68.

Grossberg, Stephen. 1978. A theory of human memory: Self-organization and performance of sensory-motor codes, maps, and plans. *Progress in Theoretical Biology*, 5, 233-374.

Grossberg, Stephen. 1987. Competitive learning: From interactive activation to adaptive resonance. *Cognitive Science* 11, 23-63.

Gupta, Prahlad and Brian MacWhinney. 1992. Integrating category acquisition with inflectional marking: A model of the German nominal system. *Proceedings of the Fourteenth Annual Conference of the Cognitive Science Society*, 253-8. Hillsdale, NJ: Lawrence Erlbaum.

Gupta, Prahlad and Brian MacWhinney. 1994. Is the articulatory loop articulatory or auditory? Re-examining the effects of concurrent articulation on immediate serial recall. *Journal of Memory and Language* 33, 63-88.

Gupta, Prahlad and Brian MacWhinney. 1997. Vocabulary acquisition and verbal short-term memory: Computational and neural bases. *Brain and Language* 59, 267-333.

Harley, Trevor, and Siobhian MacAndrew. 1992. Modelling paraphasias in normal and aphasic speech. *Proceedings of the Fourteenth Annual Conference of the Cognitive Science Society*, 378-83. Hillsdale, NJ: Lawrence Erlbaum.

Hertz, John, Anders Krogh, and Richard Palmer. 1991. *Introduction to the Theory of Neural Computation.* New York: Addison-Wesley.

Hinton, Geoffrey and Tim Shallice. 1991. Lesioning an attractor network: Investigations of acquired dyslexia. *Psychological Review* 98(1), 74-95.

Hoeffner, James. 1992. Are rules a thing of the past? The acquisition of verbal morphology by an attractor network. *Proceedings of the Fourteenth Annual Conference of the Cognitive Science Society*, 861-6. Hillsdale, NJ: Lawrence Erlbaum.

Hopfield, John J. 1982. Neural networks and physical systems with emergent collective computational abilities. *Proceedings of the National Academy of Sciences* 79, 2554-2558.

Houghton, George. 1990. The problem of serial order: A neural network model of sequence learning and recall. In Robert Dale, Christopher Mellish, and Michael Zock (eds.), *Current Research in Natural Language Generation*, 287-319. London: Academic Press.

Jaeger, Jeri J. 1984. Assessing the psychological status of the vowel shift rule. *Journal of Psycholinguistic Research* 13(1), 13-36.

Kawamoto, Alan. 1993. Non-linear dynamics in the resolution of lexical ambiguity: A parallel distributed processing account. *Journal of Memory and Language* 32, 474-516.

Kilborn, Kerry and Ann Cooreman. 1987. Sentence interpretation strategies in adult Dutch-English bilinguals. *Applied Psycholinguistics* 8, 415-431.

Kim, John, Steven Pinker, Alan Prince, and Sandeep Prasada. 1990. Why no mere mortal has ever flown out to center field. *Cognitive Science* 15, 173-218.

Klahr, David and Kenneth Kotovsky. 1991. *Complex Information Processing: The Impact of Herbert A. Simon.* Hillsdale, NJ: Lawrence Erlbaum.

Kohonen, Teuvo. 1982. Self-organized formation of topologically correct feature maps. *Biological Cybernetics* 43, 59-69.

Köpcke, Klaus-Michael. 1982. *Untersuchungen zum Genussystem der deutschen Gegenwartssprache.* Tübingen: Niemeyer.

Köpcke, Klaus-Michael. 1988. Schemas in German plural formation. *Lingua* 74, 303-335.

Köpcke, Klaus-Michael and David Zubin. 1983. Die kognitive Organisation der Genuszuweisung zu den einsilbigen Nomen der deutschen Gegenwartssprache. *Zeitschrift für germanistische Linguistik* 11, 166-182.

Köpcke, Klaus-Michael and David Zubin. 1996. Prinzipien für die Genuszuweisung im Deutschen. In Ewald Lang and Gisela Zifonun (eds.), *Deutsch - typologisch*, 473-91. Berlin: Walter de Gruyter.

Köpcke, Klaus-Michael and David Zubin. 1984. Sechs Prinzipien fur die Genuszuweisung im Deutschen: ein Beitrag zur natürlichen Klassifikation. *Linguistische Berichte* 93, 26-50.

Lamb, Sydney. 1966. *Outline of Stratificational Grammar.* Washington: Georgetown University Press.

Linell, Per. 1979. *Psychological Reality in Phonology: A Theoretical Study.* Cambridge: Cambridge University Press.

Ling, Charles. 1994. Learning the past tense of English verbs: The symbolic pattern associator vs. connectionist models. *Journal of Artificial Intelligence Research* 1, 209-229.

Ling, Charles and Marin Marinov. 1993. Answering the connectionist challenge. *Cognition* 49, 267-290.

MacWhinney, Brian. 1978a. The acquisition of morphophonology. *Monographs of the Society for Research in Child Development* 43(1), 1-122.

MacWhinney, Brian. 1978b. Conditions on acquisitional models. *Proceedings of the 1978 Annual Conference*, 421-427. New York: Association for Computing Machinery.

MacWhinney, Brian. 1988. Competition and teachability. In Richard Schiefelbusch and Mabel Rice (eds.), *The Teachability of Language*, 63-104. New York: Cambridge University Press.

MacWhinney, Brian. 1989. Competition and lexical categorization. In Roberta Corrigan, Fred Eckman, and Michael Noonan (eds.), *Linguistic Categorization*, 195-241. New York: Benjamins.

MacWhinney, Brian. 1993. Connections and symbols: Closing the gap. *Cognition* 49, 291-296.

MacWhinney, Brian. 1994. The dinosaurs and the ring. In Roberta Corrigan, Susan Lima, and Gregory Iverson (eds.), *The Reality of Linguistic Rules*, 283-320. Amsterdam: John Benjamins.

MacWhinney, Brian and John Anderson. 1986. The acquisition of grammar. In Irwin Gopnik and Myrna Gopnik (eds.), *From Models to Modules*, 3-25. Norwood, N.J.: Ablex.

MacWhinney, Brian and Jared Leinbach. 1991. Implementations are not conceptualizations: Revising the verb learning model. *Cognition* 29, 121-157.

MacWhinney, Brian, Jared Leinbach, Roman Taraban, and Janet L. McDonald. 1989. Language learning: Cues or rules? *Journal of Memory and Language* 28, 255-277.

Maratsos, Michael and Mary Chalkley. 1980. The internal language of children's syntax: The ontogenesis and representation of syntactic categories. In Keith Nelson (ed.), *Children's Language*, Vol. 2, 127-214. New York: Gardner.

Marchman, Virginia. 1992. Constraint on plasticity in a connectionist model of the English past tense. *Journal of Cognitive Neuroscience* 5, 215-234.

Marslen-Wilson, William D. 1987. Functional parallelism in spoken word-recognition. *Cognition* 25, 71-102.

McClelland, James and Jeffrey Elman. 1986. Interactive processes in speech perception: The TRACE model. In James McClelland and David Rumelhart (eds.), *Parallel Distributed Processing*, Vol. 2, 58-121. Cambridge, MA: MIT Press.

McClelland, James and Alan Kawamoto. 1986. Mechanisms of sentence processing: Assigning roles to constituents. In James McClelland and David Rumelhart (eds.), *Parallel Distributed Processing*, Vol. 2, 272-326. Cambridge, MA: MIT Press.

McDonald, Janet L. 1987. Sentence interpretation in bilingual speakers of English and Dutch. *Applied Psycholinguistics* 8, 379-414.

McDonald, Janet L. 1989. The acquisition of cue-category mappings. In Brian MacWhinney and Elizabeth Bates (eds.), *The Crosslinguistic Study of Language Processing*, 375-396. New York: Cambridge University Press.

Miikkulainen, Risto. 1990. A distributed feature map model of the lexicon. *Proceedings of the 12th Annual Conference of the Cognitive Science Society*, 447-54. Hillsdale, NJ: Lawrence Erlbaum.

Miikkulainen, Risto and Michael Dyer. 1991. Natural language processing with modular neural networks and distributed lexicon. *Cognitive Science* 15, 343-399.

Mills, Anne E. 1986. *The Acquisition of Gender: A Study of English and German.* Berlin: Springer-Verlag.

Morgan, James and Lisa Travis. 1989. Limits on negative information in language input. *Journal of Child Language* 16, 531-552.

Nespor, Marina and Irene Vogel. 1986. *Prosodic Phonology*. Dordrecht: Foris.

Newell, Allen and Herbert Simon. 1972. *Human Problem Solving*. Englewood Cliffs, N.J.: Prentice-Hall.

Ohala, John. 1974a. Phonetic explanation in phonology. *Papers from the Parasession on Natural Phonology*, 257-274. Chicago: CLS.

Ohala, John J. 1974b. Experimental historical phonology. In John M. Anderson and Charles Jones (eds.), *Historical Linguistics*, Vol. 2, 353-89. New York: American Elsevier.

Ohala, Manjari. 1974c. The abstractness controversy: Experimental input from Hindi. *Language* 50, 225-235.

Pinker, Steven. 1984. *Language Learnability and Language Development*. Cambridge, MA: Harvard University Press.

Pinker, Steven. 1989. *Learnability and Cognition: The Acquisition of Argument Structure*. Cambridge, MA: MIT Press.

Plaut, David and James McClelland. 1993. Generalization with componential attractors: Word and nonword reading in an attractor network. *Proceedings of the Fifteenth Annual Conference of the Cognitive Science Society*, 824-9. Hillsdale, NJ: Lawrence Erlbaum.

Rumelhart, David, Geoffrey Hinton, and Ronald Williams. 1986. Learning internal representations by error propagation. In David Rumelhart and James McClelland (eds.), *Parallel Distributed Processing*, Vol. 1, 318-62. Cambridge, MA: MIT Press.

Rumelhart, David and James McClelland. 1986a. *Parallel Distributed Processing*, Vol. 1. Cambridge, MA: MIT Press.

Rumelhart, David E. and James L. McClelland. 1986b. On learning the past tense of English verbs. In James L. McClelland and David E. Rumelhart (eds.), *Parallel Distributed Processing*, Vol. 2, 216-71. Cambridge, MA: MIT Press.

Rumelhart, David and James McClelland. 1987. Learning the past tenses of English verbs: Implicit rules or parallel distributed processes? In Brian MacWhinney (ed.), *Mechanisms of Language Acquisition*, 195-248. Hillsdale, N.J.: Lawrence Erlbaum.

Seidenberg, Mark and James McClelland. 1989. A distributed, developmental model of word recognition and naming. *Psychological Review* 96, 523-568.

Squire, Larry. 1987. *Memory and Brain*. New York: Oxford University Press.

St. John, Mark. 1992. The story gestalt: A model of knowledge-intensive processes in text comprehension. *Cognitive Science* 16, 271-306.

Stemberger, Joseph. 1985. *The Lexicon in a Model of Language Production.* New York: Garland.

Touretzky, David. 1990. BoltzCONS: Dynamic symbol structures in a connectionist network. *Artificial Intelligence* 46, 5-46.

Trammell, Robert. 1978. The psychological reality of underlying forms and rules for stress. *Journal of Psycholinguistic Research* 7, 79-94.

Twain, Mark. 1935. The awful German language. *The Family Mark Twain.* New York: Harper and Brothers. [From *A Tramp Abroad,* originally published 1880.]

von Neumann, John. 1956. Probabilistic logics and the synthesis of reliable organisms from unreliable components. In Claude Shannon and John McCarthy (eds.), *Automata Studies,* 43-98. Princeton, NJ: Princeton University Press.

Wexler, Kenneth and Peter Culicover. 1980. *Formal Principles of Language Acquisition.* Cambridge, Mass.: MIT Press.

Zubin, David and Klaus-Michael Köpcke. 1981. Gender: A less than arbitrary grammatical category. *Papers from the Seventeenth Regional Meeting of the Chicago Linguistic Society,* 439-449. Chicago: CLS.

Zubin, David A. and Klaus-Michael Köpcke. 1986. Gender and folk taxonomy: The indexical relation between grammatical and lexical categorization. In Colette Craig (ed.), *Noun Classes and Categorization,* 139-180. Amsterdam: John Benjamins.

The Effect of the Interlocutor on Episodic Recall: An Experimental Study

CONNIE DICKINSON AND T. GIVÓN

University of Oregon

1. The Continuum of Methodology

1.1 The Two Senses of "Usage-based"

Much like Syd Lamb in his comments at the symposium, we have been struck by the two extreme senses of "usage based" employed there. At one extreme one finds the largely theoretical sense of **user-based models**, with descriptions that claim to stand for actual mental operations. At the other extreme one finds the largely methodological sense of **usage-produced data**, with descriptions that purport to have been built strictly off the empirical input of actual communication. As is often the case with extreme reduction, this one too engenders two kinds of one-legged animals. On the one hand, we have theoretical models that are highly cognitive in their aspirations, but are curiously detached from the kind of usage data that should drive a self-proclaimed user model—the data of on-line language production and comprehension, as well as of attention, memory and retrieval. On the other hand, we have descriptions that fairly wallow in the textual data-base, while remaining largely indifferent to the cognitive entity that is responsible for the data-base—the mind that produces and interprets the text.

As is often the case with extreme reduction, we need to keep reminding ourselves that only a two-legged animal can walk, and that the missing leg is indeed missed, and for good reasons. To paraphrase Immanuel Kant, "theory without methodology is blind, and methodology without theory is empty." Less than surprising then, the split leaves some of us squarely in the muddled middle, since both senses of "usage-based" seem to us absolutely indispensable. That is, if we are to avoid the now-familiar pitfalls of the two reductionist schools of Amerian structuralism—the Chomskyites with their use-less theories, and the Bloomfieldians with their mind-less data.

A reminiscent split between two reductive extremes can also be seen in the work on conversation. But before going into that, a few words about the natural history of linguistic methodology.

1.2 The Problem of Access and the Limits of Intuition

Our traditional descriptive method, however intuitive, has always rested on unimpeachable empirical foundations. To determine the semantic correlates of a form, you hold all variables constant but one. You then manipulate that one variable, and record the semantic effect of the manipulation. As a simple-minded illustration of this method, consider the elicitation of Swahili verb paradigms:

(1) a. *Manipulating variable* **a** *(subject pronoun)*:

   ni-limuona = '**I** saw him/her'
   ku-limuona = '**you** saw him/her'
   a-limuona   = '**s/he** saw him/her'

   b. *Manipulating variable* **b** *(tense-aspect)*:

   ni-**li**-muona = 'I **saw** him/her'
   ni-**na**-muona = 'I **see** him/her'
   ni-**ta**-muona = 'I **will see** him/her'
   ni-**me**-muona = 'I **have seen** him/her'

   c. *Manipulating variable* **c** *(object pronoun)*:

   a-li-**ni**-ona = 's/he saw **me**'
   a-li-**ku**-ona = 's/he saw **you**'
   a-li-**mu**-ona = 's/he saw **him/her**'
   a-li-**ki**-ona = 's/he saw **it**'

   d. *Manipulating variable* **d** *(verb stem)*:

   a-li-ki-**ona** = 's/he **saw** it'
   a-li-ki-**piga** = 's/he **hit** it'
   a-li-ki-**amba** = 's/he **said** it'

   e. *Manipulating variable* **e** *(transitivity)*:

a-li-ki-on-**a**	's/he saw it'
a-li-mu-on-**ea**	's/he saw it for him/her'
ki-li-on-**ewa**	'it was seen'
ki-li-on-**eka**	'it was visible'
a-li-mu-on-**esh**	's/he showed him/her'
wa-li-on-**ana**	'they saw each other'

Our manipulations have yielded rich data concerning the various form-meaning associations along the verb-inflectional paradigm. But the validity of our results rests upon the two related assumptions:

(a) The meaning of the manipulated forms is accessible to conscious reflection.
(b) All speakers will respond uniformly.

Another kind of functionalist methodology, the quantified distributional study of grammar in text, is designed to take over precisely where assumption (a) is weak, and assumption (b) thus becomes untenable. One of the most striking facts that all grammarians—be they Aristotle, Bopp, Jespersen, Bloomfield, Tesnière, Harris, Halliday or Chomsky—could not but notice is that roughly the same informational contents can be packaged into a wide array of different syntactic clausal structures. That is:

(2) a. Marla saw Henry.
   b. **Marla** didn't **see Henry.**
   c. Go **see Henry!**
   d. Who **saw Henry?**
   e. Did **Marla see Henry?**

(3) a. Marla saw Henry.
   b. She **saw Henry.**
   c. **Marla saw** him.
   d. **Henry** was **seen** (by **Marla**).
   e. The woman who **saw Henry** was **Marla.**
   f. The man **Marla saw** (was **Henry**).
   g. We told **Marla** to **see Henry.**
   h. We suspected that **Marla saw Henry.**
   i. We suspected **Marla** of **seeing Henry.**
   j. As for **Henry, Marla saw** him.
   k. Having **seen Henry,** (**Marla** left).
   l. After **Marla saw Henry**...

Harris' (1957) early transformational observations hinged on noting these **co-occurrences** of meaningful units. That is, all the clauses in (2) and (3) seem to more or less involve the same agent/subject, patient/object and verb, and thus in a sense "refer to the same event." The variation in syntactic structure in (2)/(3)—with lexical variables held constant—must surely map onto a parallel variation in meaning.

So far, the analytic task seems to parallel the verb-paradigm manipulations in (1). And indeed, in the case of negation (2b) and non-declarative speech-acts (2c, d, e), the functional correlates of structural variation seem obvious and accessible.[1] However, both the speakers' and the linguist's intuitions about the functional correlates of syntactic structure are much harder to nail down with any degree of cross-subject reliability in the case of the manipulations in (3)—pronouns (3b, c), passives (3d), relative clauses (3e, f), verb complements (3g, h), raising to object (3i), Left-dislocation (3j), adverbial clauses (3k, l). Our **propositional semantic** intuition about agents, patients and verbs seems both accessible and replicable. But our **discourse-pragmatic** intuition about the communicative function of grammar turns out to be rather fickle. And that is where the quantified distributional method steps in to fill the gap.

1.3 On Defining "Communicative Function"

In attempting to understand how the same information-bearing clause mutates through so many different syntactic structures, our natural instinct is to look for different **communicative uses** that co-occur systematically with different structures. But in order to accomplish this in a responsible way—given the manifest limits of our intuition—functionalists must find some means of observing the use of grammar in its natural habitat—in natural communication.[2]

Suppose we then go and observe ongoing communication and record it for future analysis on tape or paper. We have got a text now, but how do we identify "communicative functions" in it? This question, a subversive silent partner of the working text linguist, has given rise to two radical responses, both of which contrived to bypass the question. One radical bypass is that of **functional intuitionism**, as seen in the Praguean notion of "communicative dynamism" or the Hallidayan "theme." The other radical bypass is that of **naive iconism**, the practice of conferring functional-sounding labels on all grammatical structures.[3]

However important these two extreme approaches have been in the process of discovering the functional correlates of grammar, they both turn out to bog down in methodological circularity. The inaccessibility of communicative function to conscious reflection eventually compels the intuitionist to fall back on structure as a means of discovering function. The Pragueans' automatic equation of "fronted clausal position" with "theme" is a glaring case in point. At the other extreme, naive iconism is susceptible to the same circularity. Structures are seldom 100% iconic; but even if they were, in the absence of a structure-independent definition of "function," iconism decays into tautology.

The only viable alternative to both extreme bypasses is to define communicative functions independently of both structure and intuition. The fundamental justification for such a procedure is essentially logical:[4]

(4) *Correlation vs. tautology*:
If two entities A and B are said to correlate, then neither can partake in the other's definition; otherwise stating that they 'correlate' is stating a tautology.

This alternative requires careful examination of grammar in real language texts—an approach that might be termed the "grammar-in-text" approach.

1.4 "Discourse Context" as a Heuristic

For the grammar-in-text linguist, the task of defining communicative function independently of both structure and intuition boils down to roughly the following procedure:

(5) a. Define, independently of both structure and intuition, a set of **discourse contexts**.
b. Study the **distribution** of the various grammatical structures in—or their **association** with—these discourse contexts.
c. When significant correlations are observed, seek explanatory hypotheses about why the correlations are the way they are.
d. Argue—in a principled, theory-guided fashion—that the observable discourse contexts indeed correspond to some unobservable **communicative functions**.

The Achilles heel of procedure (5) is of course step (5d), the *sine qua non* link in the chain of scientific reasoning, whose absence sooner or later yields devastating consequences. This link rests on vital theoretical connections to other empirical domains, as well as on further theoretical reasoning about the text-distribution facts. This is where the linguist's grammar-in-text distributional study links up with relevant theories of face-to-face interaction, information processing and mental representation; that is, with the social, cognitive and neurological underpinnings of language.

The distributional study of grammar in text can also be viewed from a methodological perspective, that of linguistics as a would-be empirical science. From this perspective, any pairing between a particular grammatical structure and a proposed communicative function is only a **hypothesis** to be tested inductively. Like most hypotheses in a complex domain, suggested form-function associations cannot be tested directly. Rather, what one tests is their deduced **logical consequences**.

In both the functional intuitionist and naive iconist approaches to communicative function, the question of testing is routinely bypassed. What is true of one observed instance of a grammatical construction, in or out of text, must presumably be true of all other (yet unobserved) instances of the same construction. As in the case of Chomsky's idealized "competence," the question of **population variation, sampling** and **induction** is moot.

For the grammar-in-text linguist, population variation, sampling and induction are harder to ignore. Hypotheses may indeed be reached by diverse routes—intuition, analogy, common sense, divine guidance. Regardless of their sources, hypothesis formation is probably best viewed in the context of Hanson's (1958) schema of **abductive reasoning** (following Peirce 1934: 134):

(6) *Hypothesis about the communicative function of syntactic structures*:
   a. **Puzzling facts**: Various facts about the behavior of syntactic structures a and b do not make sense given our current theoretical perspective.
   b. **Hypothesis**: But if structure a turned out to have the communicative function x, and structure b the communicative function y, their behavior would now make perfect sense.
   c. **Abduction**: Therefore hypothesis (6b) must be the case, and our current theoretical perspective must be expanded to incorporate (6b) as an integral part.

Since communicative functions X and Y are unobservable mental entities, one must now deduce some **logical consequences** of X and Y that can be observed directly. In this case, one argues for a stable association between the invisible X and Y and two observable discourse contexts P and Q:

(7) *Deduced logical consequences of hypothesis (6b):*
   Unimpeachable theoretical grounds compel us to assume that communicative functions X and Y must be strongly associated with discourse contexts P and Q, respectively.

The exact strength of the predicted association (7) must for the moment remain open. At the very least, the association must be a **one-way conditional** association, that is:

(8) If context P, then function X (but not necessarily vice versa); if context Q, then function Y (but not necessarily vice versa).

A **bi-conditional** association would be more desirable on theoretical grounds,[5] but is probably unrealistic at this juncture, given the strong heuristic residue in prediction (7).

It is only the deduced logical consequences of hypothesis (6b)—prediction (7)—that can now be tested inductively, following the standard **falsificatory testing** procedure (Popper 1959):

(9) *Falsificatory testing of the association between syntactic structures A and B and discourse contexts P and Q, respectively*:
    a. **Sampling**: Collect all instances of structures A and B and discourse contexts P and Q in a large enough body of text.[6]
    b. **Descriptive statistics**: Express the distribution of structures A and B in contexts P and Q as percentages of their total populations.
    c. **Observing correlations**: Decide whether the numerical distributions match prediction (7).
    d. **Inferential statistics**: Apply statistical tests to the observed distributions to see whether the correlations are not simply due to random fluctuation in sampling.

Our testing procedure of course is not a guarantee that the tested prediction (7) is verified, but, at best, that the results of testing are compatible with the tested hypothesis; i.e. that for the moment we have **failed to falsify** one deductive consequence of our original hypothesis (6).[7]

Nor does repeated failure to falsify (7) guarantee that the original hypothesis (6b) is non-trivial, theoretically interesting, or central to the investigation at hand. Such guarantees, such as they are, must come first from the initial process of hypothesis formation. That is, they must come from the complex chain of—first abductive, then deductive—theoretical reasoning that associated visible structures A and B with putative, invisible functions X and Y (6), and then associated the invisible functions X and Y with the visible discourse contexts P and Q (7). But when proper theoretical reasoning has driven the formulation of hypotheses and deduction of their testable consequences, then the text-distributional study of the communicative function of grammar can be, at least in principle, a viable empirical undertaking.[8]

However useful the text-distribution method has proven to be, under certain conditions—and given more ambitious theoretical goals—it too is destined to reach its natural limits. Whereby one must let go of it and reach out for other methods, ones that manipulate much more directly and explicitly the relevant cognitive variables that are responsible for language production and comprehension. In other words, one moves on, unavoidably, to a controlled experimental methodology.

2. Memory and Conversation: Background

2.1 Interactional and Cognitive Approaches

During communication, speakers/hearers are engaged simultaneously in a great number of tasks; most prominent among them are the management of **cooperative interaction** between the (two or more) interlocutors, and the processing of **coherent information flow**. Although intuitively it seems reasonable that the two tasks are not totally divorced from each other, the methodological approaches that emerged earlier on in discourse studies have often tended to split the study of these two aspects of human communication. The first approach, conversational analysis, has focused almost entirely on the study of face-to-face communication, and within it primarily on the organization of the **turn-taking** system and the linguistic and paralinguistic cues used to regulate it (see e.g. Sacks, Schegloff and Jefferson 1974; Goodwin 1982; *inter alia*). The second approach, focusing primarily on information flow and the role of grammatical cues in regulating it, has concentrated almost entirely on the study of monologuic discourse (e.g. Chafe 1979, 1980, 1987, 1994; Givón 1979b, 1983, 1985, 1988, 1992, 1994; Du Bois 1987; Tomlin 1985, 1987a, 1987b, 1991; *inter alia*).

One would be remiss not to observe that an integrated approach to the study of discourse has been around for just as long, most prominently among researchers of early child language acquisition (Ervin-Tripp 1970, 1976; Dore 1973; Keenan 1975, 1977; Ochs and Schieffelin 1976; Scollon 1976; Guo 1992; *inter alia*). This approach has focused from the very start on the social nature of early child communication, where information flow itself is highly collaborative. More recently this approach has been extended to face-to-face communication among adults, where collaboration between interlocutors has been shown to play an important role in building a coherent communication (e.g. Clark and Wilkes-Gibbs 1986; Clark and Schaefer 1987; Goodwin 1988, 1995a, 1995b; Wilkes-Gibbs 1986, 1995; Wilkes-Gibbs and Clark 1992; Anderson 1995; *inter alia*). What these studies suggested to us is that to quite an extent the dichotomy between discourse as interaction and discourse as information flow is an artificial one, reflecting accidents of history and methodology, as well as perhaps pre-existing philosophical or ideological differences.

In parallel with the initial dichotomy between interactional and information-flow studies, the two extreme methodological paradigms have also diverged, often implicitly, in their approach to and dependence on **cognitive models** of language processing. The conversational analysis paradigm has tended to de-emphasize cognitive models, focusing on the **situated social context** of face-to-face communication. Such an emphasis is often characterized by the assertion that "it is all in the social situation." Information-flow research, on the other hand, has tended to express its generalization in frameworks increasingly couched in cognitive terms (e.g. van Dijk and Kintsch 1983; Chafe 1987, 1994; Anderson, Garrod and Sanford 1983; Givón 1992, 1994; Tomlin 1991; Gernsbacher 1990; *inter alia*). But cognitively-oriented studies have tended to ignore the interactional aspects of discourse, and thus the seminal position of face-to-face communication in shaping human language and its supporting cognitive and neural mechanisms.

There is something both unnecessary and undesirable about this degree of separation between the two sub-fields of discourse studies. To begin with, the episodic memory system that is most relevant to making coherent multi-clausal (or multi-turn) communication possible is the very same cognitive system that must support both interactive and monologuic communication. The attentional sub-systems deployed in both types of communication are presumably the same. And the short-term memory systems that are used in both types of communication are prerequisite to episodic storage in both, and are no doubt the very same. What is more, the attentional and memory systems that are involved in face-to-face communication process, simultaneously, the interactional and informational aspects of communication. Finally, the social-situational aspect of face-to-face communication is not an objective, external entity. Much like other kinds of information available to the organism, the speech situation must be selectively extracted from the "objective" situation, and converted into a running mental representation. And it is only this **on-going cognitive model** of the speech situation that is actually relevant to the process of face-to-face communication. Fundamentally, then, the dichotomy between "situational" vs. "cognitive" is no doubt somewhat of a false dichotomy.

2.2 Episodic Memory and Working Memory

Our paper receives its ontology from an interest in the potential integration—as against separation—of the mental representation of the speech situation and episodic information. Before outlining our goals and methodology, it would be useful thus to survey what we assume is known about the memory systems associated with discourse production and comprehension.

Following the literature, one has to assume that the early episodic memory system, the one based in the medial-temporal hippocampus and related cortical structures, is the system that represents the episodic information *during* both visual information acquisition and verbal communication (Squire 1987; Squire and Zola-Morgan 1991; Mishkin 1978; Mishkin et al. 1984; Mishkin and Petri 1984; *inter alia*). This system is not modality-specific, so that **both verbal and visual** information find their way into the same processing and representation system.

Information entering early episodic memory probably passes via some modality-specific **working memory** "buffer" of limited capacity and/or short duration. These buffers have been viewed by some as rehearsal loops that keep alive an "echoic," perceptual representation of short input segments, before further processing converts them into more durable "cognitive" representation (Baddeley 1986; Squire 1987; Gathercole and Baddeley 1993; Carpenter and Just 1988; Gernsbacher 1985; *inter alia*). But others view working memory as a more elaborate device where considerable analysis, inference, and processing may take place, and where attention, both modality-specific and global/conscious, is an essential, perhaps the most essential, component (Bower and Morrow 1990; Just and Carpenter 1992; Posner, in personal communication). And a recent review even attributes longer duration to this cognitive capacity (Ericsson and Kintsch 1995).

Some of the salient characteristics of the hippocampus-based episodic memory system are, briefly (following Squire and Zola-Morgan 1991; *inter alia*):

(a) It is extremely malleable and involves further processing and reprocessing and reorganization of stored information (Loftus 1980).

(b) It is a limited-capacity processor in which storage-space and processing activity compete.

(c) It is emptied periodically and thus remains available for the processing of in-coming new information.

(d) It is thus a crucial intermediary between the more modality-specific immediate recall buffers ('loops;' Baddeley 1986) and longer-term episodic storage, most likely in the frontal or pre-frontal neo-cortex.

(e) Impairment in episodic recall due to hippocampus lesions is dissociated from both procedural and lexical-semantic knowledge.

(f) Hippocampus lesions do not impair the recall of old, long-established episodic knowledge, presumably because of the latter's different (frontal-cortical) localization.

(g) Surface grammatical information that is preserved in some perceptual form in working memory does not survive into episodic representation. Put another way, grammatical clues are stripped from the episodic representation of speech (Gernsbacher 1985).

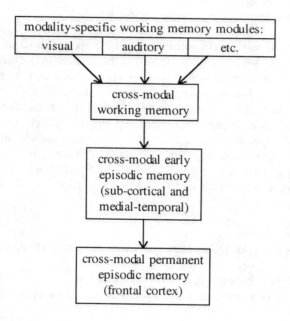

Figure 1. Relationship between Modality-Specific Immediate Recall and Cross-Modal Early Episodic Memory (integrated from Baddeley 1986; Squire and Zola-Morgan 1991)

A schematic representation of the relationship between working memory and episodic memory is given in Figure 1.

2.3 Mental Representation of the Speech Situation

The existence of an ongoing mental representation of the current speech situation must be assumed if one is to explain even the most rudimentary facts of the grammar of **deictic expression**, where the meaning of definite ("accessible") referents is dependent on their spatial position relative to the speaker's (and sometimes the hearer's).

(10) **Pronouns**:   I, you, we, y'all
      Demonstratives: this, that
      Locative deictics: here, there, yon
      Temporal deictics: now, then
      Deictic verbs: go, come, bring, take

Since the putative mental model must represent the speech situation at the very time of speech, and since in conversation the speaker may change constantly, the mental representation of the *current* speech situation may not necessarily be preserved in longer-term episodic memory. In a way then, the mental model of the current speech situation has some of the characteristics of **shorter-term working memory**—a necessary but not sufficient condition for episodic storage. Still, some representation of *past* speech situations must be preserved in longer-term episodic memory under some conditions, in precise association with other facets of "contents." Such an assumption is necessary in order to account for our interpretations of communications such as:

(11) So then he told **me**:
"I want **you** to take **this** chair right **now** and put it **there** next to you."
Boy, **I** tell **you**, he's got the nerve! So **I** told him:
"**That** chair is **yours**, so **I** don't see why **you**'d want it **here** next to **me**."

People often recall, and later report with direct quotes, precisely such details of conversations. And without indexing the propositional contents inside the quotes to the shifting speaker ('he,' 'I'), the interpretation of *I, me, you, your, here, there, this, that* becomes impossible. One must conclude that in addition to maintaining a **running mental model** of the *current* speech situations, listeners or readers can also construct—and preserve in longer-term memory—a representation of *past* (or otherwise remote or reported) speech situations.

If a running mental model of the current speech situation does exist, can it be identified with short-term working memory? And does the same one-way association—necessary but not sufficient—hold between the running model and the long-term model of the speech-situation as the one holding between working memory and episodic memory, respectively? These questions, and indeed the possible existence of a running mental representation of the speech situation, have received scant attention in the cognitive literature. But these issues are of vital concern for a cognitively-oriented approach to the study of conversation.

The research questions that we are interested in concern the exact nature of the relation between the running mental model of the speech situation and episodic memory; the extent to which information from one is integrated into the other; and the communicative—and ultimately cognitive—conditions that affect such integration.

2.4 Mental Representation of the Hearer's Beliefs and Intentions

The speech situation and who is talking to who is only one small aspect of the interactional information that must be represented in speaker's mind. An even larger issue concerns the representation of the interlocutor **belief and intentional states** at the time of communication. For example, the conventional use of speech-acts (cf. Grice 1975) is inconceivable without assuming that speakers carry a running mental model of hearers' belief and intentional states. Likewise, the entire grammar of referential coherence, tense-aspect, negation, modality and evidentiality, foregrounding and backgrounding, presupposition and assertion, etc. would be utterly nonsensical without assuming the existence of such mental representations in the speaker's mind (see Chafe 1994; Givón 1994; *inter alia*). The curious fiction that some forms of human discourse are *not* hearer-oriented is just that, fiction. As Morti Gernsbacher (in personal communication) has suggested, the production of written or monologuic text simply anticipates the intended audience's epistemic and intentional states; and this anticipation shifts and is updated constantly during monologuic discourse production. In a very real sense then, narrative text has never been anything but an impoverished and feedback-deprived dialoguic endeavor.

2.5 Goals of the Research Project

Our current study is but an early foray into a series of related areas, characterized initially by the question: Are the interactional and informational aspects of an ongoing communication—whether monologuic or dialoguic—processed and stored separately in episodic memory? Or conversely, is there an integrated system that is responsible for both aspects of communication?

That the question may not have a simple, clean answer is quite likely. Evidence from conversational analysis (cf. Goodwin 1982, 1988, 1984; *inter alia*) suggests that many informational aspects, particularly relevance, topicality, or thematicity, are negotiated during communication. But the study of conversation also reveals that conversations can be either highly cooperative or extremely non-cooperative, and that non-cooperative conversations in a way resemble two parallel monologues. In cognitive terms, this may suggest that the mental representation of the communicative transaction in episodic memory could be of two extreme types. A cooperative interlocutor may create an *integrated* mental representation of the interactional and informational aspects of the communication. A non-cooperative interlocutor, on the other hand, may either ignore interactional clues, or may represent them separately, without integration into a unified episodic representation.

The present study is an attempt to gradually probe the effect of the interlocutor's contribution to the interaction on the speaker's episodic model of both the informational and the interactional aspects of communication. In the first five experiments, reported here, an information baseline is set up (Control Conditions I, II, and III), then the effects of two types of intervention by an interlocutor are assessed (Conditions IV and V). Two more conditions that aim at assessing the degree of integration of interactional information with episodic information are in the process of being investigated. The results we report here should be thus considered the first step in a complex, long-term study.

3. Methodology

3.1 Overall Design

Five experimental conditions were created in the phase of the study reported here. The first three (I, II, III) serve as controls for all subsequent conditions, creating a base-level of episodic recall to which all subsequent conditions are then compared. The last two conditions (IV, V) assess the effect of two types of face-to-face interaction, taking place between episodic input and its recall, on subsequent episodic recall. In all conditions, subjects viewed the same short video film. The viewing was followed by various interventions, following which the subjects were asked to verbally recall the events of the film. Their verbal recollections, as well as the verbal interaction preceding it in Conditions IV and V, were recorded and transcribed. This section deals with the methodology common to all five experimental conditions. Procedures specific to the individual conditions will be discussed in subsequent sections.

3.2 Text Elicitation

A short, 6.25 minute-long video was used. This video had been developed previously for use in another experimental project (Givón 1991). The following is a brief summary of the story:

Synopsis of the Chicken Story

A man walks toward a tree, leans his farming implements on it and goes on to chop wood with an axe. A woman appears and walks to him. After some conversation, she takes the wood, moves aside and collects some more wood, then carries it all away. The man quits his chopping, collects his tools and walks off toward a grove. The scene shifts to the woman coming around a small shed. She unloads her wood, lights a fire, fetches water from a barrel and sets a pot of water to boil. She disappears behind the shed and comes back carrying a chicken. She tries to slaughter it with a knife, but clumsily bungles the job and the chicken escapes. After some perfunctory chasing, the woman goes back to the house, brings out some bread and cheese, makes a sandwich, wraps it up and leaves with it. The scene shifts to the man hoeing in the field. The woman arrives and offers him the package. They sit down, the man unwraps the food, rejects it, throws it back at the woman, then chases her around the tree with his hoe. (Givón 1991: 143-144)

The Chicken Story film does not have a prototypical western plot-line or structure. The subjects cannot rely on western cultural norms to understand, contextualize, and infer meaning. The actors spoke Swahili and thus the subjects could not understand the language and received no overt language input. The video was also designed to present many simple, active and transitive events. The camera changes location twice, resulting in three basic locales—or episodes—for the action. The camera, for the most part, simply follows the movements of the characters.

3.3 Subjects

The subjects were sixty University of Oregon undergraduates who were offered extra credit in an introductory linguistics course in exchange for their participation. All spoke English as their native language and were accustomed to watching videos.

3.4 Computing a Baseline Control for Recalled Information

In order to have a standard for comparing the subjects' recollection of the video, it was necessary to create a baseline control for the "information contents" of the elicitation film. Most studies of text rely on the experimenter's intuitive judgments as to what is the "gist"—most salient, important, indispensable—information in an elicitation text. In this study we create the information baseline from subjects' own on-line descriptions of the film during viewing. Under this on-line condition (I), ten subjects watched the film and were instructed to describe the events as they watched them. Their on-line verbal descriptions were tape-recorded and transcribed. All event clauses mentioned by at least *seven out of ten* subjects were included in the baseline. This cutoff point—7 and above—was determined by computing the mean (4) and standard deviation (3) of the number of subjects that mentioned those clauses. We thus included in the baseline all clauses above one standard deviation from the mean. Although this cutoff point is somewhat arbitrary, the measure pulls in the clausal events most likely to be noticed by all subjects. A total of fifty-eight baseline clauses were identified (see Appendix).

3.5 Semantic Considerations

The problem of deciding what constitutes "the same event" (or "the same state") in the subjects' on-line verbal descriptions is far from trivial. The detailed grammatical form of the event-clause was not taken into consideration. Thus, relative clauses, adverbial clauses and independent clauses were considered on a par. In examples (12) below, the underlined verbs were considered to indicate separate event-clauses.

> (12) a. *REL-clause followed by main clause*:
>   a man **carrying** tools **walked** over to some trees
>   b. *Main clause followed by ADV-clause*:
>   he **picked up** the axe **to chop** some wood

c. *Main clause followed by REL-clause*:
   she **walked** over to the man who was **hoeing** the ground
d. *Main clause followed by REL-clause*:
   a woman **came** over **wearing** a white blouse and a peach
   skirt

Verbal complement clauses pose somewhat of a problem. We found no perception, utterance, cognition or manipulation verb complements in our transcripts. But aspectual and modality-verb complements were common. Such complements share their temporal, spatial and subject-NP reference with the main clauses. They also tend to be highly integrated syntactically with their main clause (Givón 1990: ch. 13). We decided, then, to consider such verbs and their complements as single clauses, as in:

(13) *Aspectual and modality verbs and their complements:*
   a. she **started to make** a fire
   b. she **tried to cut off** its head
   c. she **began breaking** branches
   d. he **started chasing** her around

How does one determine when two different verbs in the transcripts of two different subjects refer to the same event in the film? Most verbs in our transcripts depict physical motion and/or physical manipulation of objects. We divided verbs initially into four sub-groups: simple transitive, motion, stative, and complement-taking verbs. Deciding whether two (or more) verbs referred to the same event was based first on the verbs falling into the same general category; second on whether their arguments referred to the same participants (entities); and third on the identity of the case-roles of the participants (Fillmore 1968; Givón 1984: ch. 4).

Motion verbs presented somewhat of a problem in that some are syntactically transitive (*enter, leave, approach*); some have ablative or allative directional senses (*come, go*). Others incorporate manner into their meaning (*walk, run*). Because the directional sense of some motion verbs depends on the perspective taken by the speaker, and is not necessarily part of the event itself, we ignored subtle differences resulting from variation in perspective. Both transitive and manner-incorporating motion verbs were counted as simple motion verbs that require a locative argument. For example, clauses (14a-d)) below were be counted as representing the same event, while clauses (15a-c) were not. *Approach* (14c) is syntactically a transitive verb, but was considered as encoding the same event as the other verbs in (14), since it has the same locative argument (*the fireplace*). *Carry* in (15c), on the other hand, does not encode the same event as clauses (14a, b) because it has an additional argument (*the wood*).

(14)   *'Same event' judgment:*
    a. she **came** back over to the fireplace
    b. she **went** back over to the fireplace
    c. she **approached** the fireplace
    d. she **walked** over to the fireplace

(15)   *'Different event' judgment:*
    a. she **came** back over to the fireplace
    b. she **walked** quickly
    c. she **carried** the wood over to the fireplace

Our procedures sometimes led to the exclusion of verbs which intuitively seem to encode the same events. However, such stringent requirements allow for consistency based on our three criteria:

(a)   **Verb class**: motion, transitive, complement-taking, stative

(b)   **Reference to same entities**: 'man,' 'woman,' 'chicken,' 'pot,' 'fire,' 'woods,' 'axe,' 'wood,' 'matches,' etc.

(c)   **Type and number of semantic arguments**: agent, patient, locative, dative, beneficiary, instrumental, manner, etc.

Self-referring interjections by the speaker such as *I think, then I saw, I thought* were not counted. Given our criteria, we found very few cases where inclusion or exclusion was problematic. Some of the variations in the choice of verbs to represent baseline clauses can be found in the Appendix.

3.6 General Experimental Procedures

All subjects watched the film on a large overhead video projection screen. They were told that after viewing they would be asked to recount, with as much detail as possible, what happened in the film. Directly after viewing, they were asked to perform various intervening tasks (see Sections 4, 5, and 6 below). After viewing, all subjects were then asked to describe what they remembered of the film, starting at the beginning and proceeding in order. They were explicitly enjoined from adding personal evaluations or comments, but asked to merely "tell us what happened" from beginning to end, with as much detail as possible. Their narrations were recorded and transcribed. Their correspondence to the information baseline (Appendix) was then computed by the criteria described above.

3.7 Control Conditions I, II, and III

The first three experimental conditions, used as controls for the final two conditions, involved three different variants of obtaining a base-level of recall performance:

CONDITION I: on-line verbalization during viewing;
                 a distractor task between viewing and recall

CONDITION II: no on-line verbalization during viewing;
                 no time delay between viewing and recall

CONDITION III: no on-line verbalization during viewing;
                 a distractor task between viewing and recall

The choice of each control condition was motivated by specific considerations. It has been reported in a previous study (Givón 1991) that the on-line descriptions of the film were on the average twice as long and more detailed than the post-viewing recalled descriptions. We chose Condition I to assess whether previous verbalization during viewing affects the amount or fidelity of recalled information.

Since the hippocampus-based episodic memory system depends on time for consolidation (Squire 1987; Squire and Zola-Morgan 1991), we wanted to make sure that it was the effect of conversational intervention (Conditions IV and V), rather than the effect of time delay *per se*, which was responsible for any differences in recall following conversational intervention. Conditions II and III were chosen to provide a control on the independent effect of time delay, by contrasting them with each other.

In choosing an intervening distractor task for Conditions I and III, we followed Baddeley's (1992) observation that tasks which differ greatly from each other, functionally or cognitively, produce fewer interference effects. We thus chose as distractor task a verbal arithmetic manipulation (see below).

4. Conditions I, II and III

4.1 Procedures

4.1.1 Condition I

In Condition I, ten subjects were asked to verbally describe the video as they watched it. They were encouraged to keep talking and to report only what they saw happening on the screen rather than indulge in evaluation or reflections. Their on-line description was tape-recorded. Directly following the film presentation, the subjects performed a distractor task, counting backwards from 400 by threes for four minutes. They were then asked to recall the video. Subjects were discouraged from evaluation and asked to simply tell what happened in the video, starting at the beginning and continuing sequentially to the end.

The recorded on-line description was transcribed and used to create the baseline of salient events. The recall description was transcribed and compared with the baseline. The procedures outlined in Section 3.5 above were used to determine which clauses in the recall matched those in the baseline. The total number of clauses produced by each subject was also computed.

4.1.2 Conditions II and III

In Condition II ten subjects watched the film in silence, and then immediately produced their verbal recall. Their descriptions were tape-recorded, transcribed and compared with the baseline. The total number of clauses for each subject was also recorded.

In Condition III ten subjects watched the film in silence, then performed for 4 minutes the same distractor task as in Condition I (see above). They then gave their verbal recollections of the film, and those were recorded, transcribed and analyzed in the same manner as in Conditions I and II.

4.2 Results

The narration produced by each subject was recorded, transcribed, and then compared with the baseline produced by the subjects in Condition I (see Appendix). As noted earlier, this baseline consisted of 58 clauses mentioned on-line by at least 7 of the subjects of Condition I. The total number of clauses produced in the recalled description were also counted for each subject. Means and standard deviations for each condition were calculated. The results pertaining to baseline events recalled in Conditions I, II, and III are given in Table 1 below.

Condition	# of Subjects	Mean # Baseline Clauses Recalled	Std. Deviation
I	10	38.1	6.59
II	10	37.4	4.99
III	10	36.1	5.36

Table 1. Mean Number and Standard Deviations for Number of Baseline Clauses Recalled

The results reported in Table 1 were subjected to a one-way ANOVA analysis. No significant difference was found between the three conditions ($F(2, 27) = 0.32, p < .7302$). Neither on-line verbalization (Condition I) nor time delay and distractor task (Condition III) produced any significant effect on the number of baseline events recalled. This is particularly surprising in that the subjects in Condition I created the baseline; yet their recall of baseline events did not differ significantly from that of the subjects in Conditions II and III.

It is of interest to see whether some differences between the three conditions may exist but somehow are not captured by the baseline measure. To assess this possibility, we also recorded the total number of clauses produced by the subjects under each condition. Means and standard deviations were then computed for each condition; the results are given in Table 2 below.

Condition	# of Subjects	Mean # Clauses Produced	Std. Deviation
I	10	107.1	19.1
II	10	99.0	38.76
III	10	96.2	23.95

Table 2. Means and Standard Deviation for the Total Number of Clauses Produced

These results were also subjected to a one-way ANOVA. No significant difference was found between the three conditions ($F(2, 27) = 0.39, p < 0.6817$). However, the standard deviation in Condition II is quite large

(38.76) due to a single subject who produced 200 clauses. Subjects in Condition I, while more consistent (their standard deviation was smaller), produced on the average only slightly more clauses than those in Conditions II and III.

4.3 Further Analysis

As noted above, we found no statistically significant differences between the three conditions in terms of the number of baseline clauses or the total number of clauses produced. But we wondered to what extent the subjects in Condition I matched the verbal material they themselves produced on-line. Did their general pattern of recall differ significantly from the subjects in the other two conditions? To evaluate this, we compared the number of Condition-I subjects who mentioned a specific baseline clause in the on-line task with the number of those who mentioned that clause in the recalled text. The baseline itself was made out of the clauses mentioned by seven or more subjects in the on-line description in Condition I. So each one of the 58 baseline clauses has a specific value of how many subjects mention it—7, 8, 9 or 10. And a clause that was mentioned by x number of subjects in the on-line task might be mentioned by either more or fewer subjects in the recall task (see Appendix).

We now examined the percent distribution of clauses in the recall task that were mentioned more often, less often, or the same number of times as in the baseline, for all three conditions (in terms of the numbers of subjects mentioning them). Our initial assumption was that most of the clauses would be mentioned less often in the recall task than in the baseline, given memory decay. But did subjects in Condition I mention any of the clauses more often in their recalled text than in the baseline? If this were the case, it would suggest that perhaps they were not relying in their recall primarily on their previous verbalization. This conclusion would be true especially if the proportions of more-mentioned, less-mentioned, and same-number-mentioned in Condition I differed from Conditions II and III. The results of this analysis are given in Table 3 below.

Condition	Clauses Mentioned More Often		Clauses Mentioned Less Often		Clauses Mentioned Same #		Total	
	#	%	#	%	#	%	#	%
I	11	18.97	36	62.06	11	18.97	58	100.0
II	12	20.69	37	63.79	9	15.52	58	100.0
III	13	22.42	36	62.06	9	15.52	58	100.0

Table 3. Proportions of Clauses Mentioned More, Less and the Same Number of Times as in the Baseline

These results were subjected to a one-way ANOVA analysis. No significant differences were found between the conditions ($F(2, 173) = 0.03$, $p < 0.9733$). It appears that the resources which subjects in all three conditions were drawing upon in the recall task were similar, and that on-line verbalization (Condition I) did not help the subjects in their subsequent recall task. Nearly 19% of the clauses recalled in Condition I were mentioned by more subjects in recall than in the on-line production. So apparently some subjects recalled clauses that did not appear in their on-line verbalization.

4.4 Interim Discussion: Conditions I, II, and III

Both in terms of the number of recalled baseline events and the total number of narrated events, we found no significant differences between the three conditions. Condition I revealed no advantage of on-line verbalization during viewing. Several past studies (Paivio 1969; Yuille and Paivio 1967; Schnorr and Atkinson 1969) have reported the advantage of visual imagery when added to verbal rehearsal; but the converse does not appear to hold in our study.

We found no significant difference between Conditions II and III. The distractor task with its associated time delay produced no effect on either the number of baseline clauses recalled (Table 1) or the total number of clauses produced (Table 2). The lack of effect of the distractor task on recall was perhaps to be expected. Recent work on memory indicates that different types of tasks and different modalities used to perform them may draw on different cognitive resources (Baddeley 1992). The results presented so far allow us to conclude that whatever differences we find between the interactive conditions IV and V and the three control conditions must be due to the effect of the intervening conversational interaction itself, rather than to the presence of an on-line verbalization, the time delay, or the distractor task.

5. Condition IV

5.1 General Considerations

The purpose of Condition IV was to study the effect on recall of contradictory information. Many previous studies have shown that new information presented to a subject between observation time and recall time can alter or supplement the recall of previously acquired information (Loftus 1975, 1980; Loftus et al. 1978). However, Loftus (1980) found that there are limits, in terms of plausibility, on the type of misinformation that is likely to be integrated. If the misinformation is presented first and blatantly contradicts a clearly perceived feature of an important object in an event, subjects tend to reject the misinformation, and further, tend to be more resistant to other, more subtle, forms of misinformation. However, if more subtle misinformation is presented first, and the more blatantly contradictory misinformation is presented later, the subtle misinformation is still likely to be incorporated into the subjects' recall, even when the subsequently-presented more blatant misinformation is rejected.

Loftus' work suggests that new information is not automatically integrated. Subjects can compare the new information with their initial mental representation and either accept (and integrate) or reject it. Pre-existing information that is less central to the event or episode is more easily modified than information about more central features, presumably because central features receive stronger—more distinct, durable or retrievable—memory representation.

In this study, we were not so much interested in whether *specific* pieces of misinformation would or would not be integrated into the recall of the video, but rather in the overall effect of contradictory information on recall. Our hypothesis regarding Condition IV was that the effort needed to make sense of contradictory information and either reject or integrate it into a pre-existing memory representation of the film would result in fewer event-clauses recalled.

5.2 Procedures

Each of the ten subjects was asked to watch the film with another "student." They were told that they would later be asked to discuss the video with that "student," and would then be asked to recall the film. The "student" was actually a volunteer posing as a student. After viewing the video, this volunteer discussed the video with the subject. The volunteer encouraged the subject to be aggressive and produce most of the discussion. During the discussion, the volunteer provided contradictory information about four events in the film:

(16) *Contradictory information supplied by volunteer:*
1. The woman was initially chopping wood
2. The chicken was killed
3. The woman brought the man water as well as food
4. The man became angry when the woman spilled the water

In the film, the man, not the woman, is initially chopping wood; the chicken escapes; the woman does not bring water; and she does not spill the non-existent water. The first two false bits of information can be considered "blatantly" contradictory. The wood-chopping scene is fairly long and detailed; and the chicken obviously did escape. The final two bits are somewhat more "subtle" and plausible. The woman did fetch some water, although she did not take it to the man. And the man did become angry in the final scene, although not because the woman spilled the water.

The volunteer did not attempt to push the bits of contradictory information on the subjects, but simply presented them as her version of the story. If the subject objected, the volunteer simply stated that that's what she thought happened, and then moved on to the next topic. We did not expect the subjects to "swallow" the distortions. We simply wanted to see the effect of contradictory information on their overall episodic recall.

As in the first three conditions, the subjects were asked to describe what happened in the video from beginning to end, avoiding evaluative comments. The narrations were recorded, transcribed and analyzed via the same protocol as in Conditions I, II, and III.

5.3 Results

The mean number and standard deviation of baseline clauses recalled under Condition IV is given in Table 4 below, together with those of control conditions I, II, and III.

Condition	# of Subjects	Mean # Baseline Clauses Recalled	Std. Deviation
I	10	38.1	6.59
II	10	37.4	4.99
III	10	36.1	5.36
IV	10	**29.9**	5.34

Table 4. Mean Number and Standard Deviation for Recalled Baseline Events (4 conditions)

A clear difference appears between the number of baseline events recalled in Condition IV and those recalled in the control conditions I, II, and III. These results were subjected to a one-way ANOVA analysis. A significant difference was found between Condition IV and Conditions I, II, and III ($F (3, 39) = 4.46$, $p < 0.0092$). Subjects in Condition IV recalled approximately 20% fewer of the baseline clauses than did the subjects in the control conditions.

We were again interested in comparing the total number of clauses produced, and here again a clear difference emerged between Condition IV and the three control conditions. The results are given in Table 5 below.

Condition	# of Subjects	Mean # Clauses Produced	Std. Deviation
I	10	107.1	19.1
II	10	99.0	38.76
III	10	96.2	23.95
IV	10	**60.1**	17.88

Table 5. Mean and Standard Deviation for the Total Number of Clauses Produced

The results were subjected to a one-way ANOVA analysis, revealing a significant difference between Condition IV and the three control conditions ($F (3, 36) = 6.23$, $p < 0.0016$). Subjects in Condition IV produced on the average 40% fewer clauses in their recalled narration than those in the control conditions. However, the number of baseline events recalled in Condition IV (29.9, Table 4) is approximately half that of the mean number of clauses produced (60.1, Table 5). In other words, half of the clauses recalled by the subjects in Condition IV were baseline clauses. In contrast, in the three control conditions only about 37% of the recalled clauses were baseline clauses. To express this difference more explicitly, we took the average number of baseline clauses recalled in each condition and divided it by the average total number of clauses produced. The results of this computation are given in Table 6 below.

Condition	# of Subjects	Mean % of Baseline Out of Total # of Clauses	Std. Deviation
I	10	35.57	6.09
II	10	37.78	7.79
III	10	37.53	7.86
IV	10	49.75	7.56

Table 6. Percent of Baseline Clauses Recalled out of Total Number of Clauses Recalled

These results were subjected to a one-way ANOVA analysis. A significant difference was found between Conditions I, II, and III and Condition IV (F (3, 36) = 8.83, $p < 0.0002$). Condition I had the *lowest* ratio, 35.57%; while Condition IV had the highest, 49.75%. As one may recall, the subjects in Condition I created the baseline. Yet baseline clauses constituted a smaller number of their total production. What appears to have happened is that while the subjects in Condition IV recalled less, what they did recall are the more salient baseline events. In contrast, subjects in Condition I, who recalled more baseline clauses, also produced a proportionately larger body of "elaborative," non-baseline events. Such clauses depict events that are perhaps less central and thus less salient, as compared to the baseline events.

In sum, the deliberately-planted misinformation indeed creates an uncertainty and reduced recall. But the impact of this uncertainty hits unevenly—more in the elaborative portion of recalled information than in the baseline of "core" information. By comparison, on-line verbalization (Condition I) did not significantly affect the recall of baseline events, but rather stimulated the production of more elaborative, "non-core" descriptions.

5.4 Cross-Subject Individual Variation

We next turn to analyzing the output of individual subjects in Condition IV. Six of the ten subjects produced less than thirty of the baseline clauses. Only two out of the thirty subjects in the other three conditions produced less than thirty baseline clauses. We decided to evaluate the subjects of Condition IV according to how strongly the misinformation was represented in their recall of the baseline events. To do this, we scored the effect on each subject of the four false bits of information. If the subject reproduced the inaccuracy, he was given a score of 1. That is, if the subject stated that the woman killed the chicken he would receive a score of 1 for that bit of false information. If the subject stated that the woman killed the chicken but expressed some uncertainty, i.e. added statements or adverbs expressing doubt such as "I thought," "maybe," or "it seemed like," the subject was given a score of 0.5. If the subject reproduced an accurate report, i.e. "the woman didn't kill the chicken" or "the chicken got away," they received a score of 0. Finally, if they reproduced an accurate report but it was coded with uncertainty, i.e. "I didn't think she killed it, but maybe she did," they again received a score of 0.5. The coding system is reproduced in (17) below.

(17) *Scoring schema:*
    a. accurate report with no uncertainty   = 0
    b. accurate report with uncertainty   = 0.5
    c. inaccurate report with uncertainty   = 0.5
    d. inaccurate report with no uncertainty   = 1.0

A sample of this scoring is given in (18) below.

(18) *Examples of scoring:*

    It looks like she's about to cut its head off, but
    it got free and ran away   = 0

    She doesn't succeed in killing it   = 0

    I guess she had a jug of water, although I don't
    remember really   = 0.5

But she's just gonna take care of it [the chicken]
then and there and, I guess I didn't think that
she did   = 0.5

...and then the lady was chopping wood...and
then...the man was chopping wood with an ax   = 1.0

She spilt over the bucket of water   = 1.0

An overall score of 4 would indicate that a subject accepted all four false bits without uncertainty. A score of 0 indicates that they rejected all four false bits without uncertainty. The results of this analysis are given in Table 7 below, where the reaction to false information is placed, for each subject, against the number of baseline clauses recalled in Condition IV.

Subject	Degree of Acceptance of False Claim	# of Baseline Clauses Recalled by Each Subject
1	3.5	22
5	2.0	24
6	0.5	27
3	0.0	28
4	0.0	29
7	0.0	29
8	0.0	31
2	0.0	34
10	0.0	35
9	0.0	40

Table 7. Degree of Acceptance of False Claims Compared to Number of Baseline Clauses Recalled

A Pearson Correlation Test addressed the relationship between the number of baseline clauses recalled in Condition IV ($M = 29.9$) and degree of acceptance of false information ($M = 0.6$). The correlation turns out to be statistically significant, $r(8) = -0.71047$, indicating that these two variables are inversely related. However, only three of the subjects expressed doubt or "swallowed" the false statements. Subject #1 reproduced all but one of the false claims. This subject stated that the woman was chopping wood first, she brought the man water, and she spilled the water, but expressed doubt as to whether the chicken was killed or not. This subject produced the lowest number of baseline clauses. Subject #5 expressed doubt concerning all four of the false statements, and Subject #6 expressed doubt as to whether the woman brought the man water.

Subjects #9 and #10 produced the largest number of recalled baseline clauses. These two subjects also expressed a large degree of doubt about the false information given by the volunteer. Both asked the volunteer if she had seen the same movie they had. Both strongly rejected the volunteer's misinformation during the conversation. The number of clauses produced by these two subjects is similar to the average number of clauses produced in the three control conditions.

5.5 Interim Discussion of Condition IV

Loftus (1975, 1980) has reported the effect of misinformation on subjects' later recall of events. However, her studies assessed the effect of misinformation on specific details. Our results seem to indicate that false claims can have a global depressing effect on the number of event-clauses recalled. The more the subject accepts the misinformation, it seems, the fewer events are recalled; and the loss seems to target more specifically elaborative detail over baseline events.

One may wish to argue that the causal chain may have been the reverse: The subjects who accepted the false information did so *because* their memory representation was weaker to begin with. However, there is a statistically significant difference between subjects in this condition and those in the other three conditions. It may be that, by sheer chance, the subject group in this condition included more subjects with poorer memory capacity. But the consistency of recall of baseline events among the thirty subjects in the three control conditions makes this possibility unlikely.

6. Condition V

6.1 General Considerations

In the next experiment, we tried to create a more natural conversational situation. We were interested in the effect on episodic memory of trying to explain the events of the video to someone who had not seen the film. In the three control conditions, subjects were told to recall the film events in sequence. Likewise in Condition IV, the volunteer and the subject were told to discuss the film in sequential order. In the intervening task in Condition V, however, between viewing and recalling, the subjects were required to answer questions about the film from another person who had not seen it. The subjects thus had to **make thematic sense** of the events while recalling them to the other person. Their recall during the interaction may be out of linear order, but their aim is nevertheless to make the story coherent to a person who had not seen the film.

We expected that such an intervening task would demand, and thus result in, a more elaborate mental representation of the story in the mind of the narrator, and a higher-level understanding, as compared to the more simple control tasks of sequential recall. The task facing the subjects under Condition V presumably demanded of the subjects a more precise identification of referents, locations and other more local details.[9]

After the intervening conversation, both subjects were instructed to individually narrate the events of the film. The narration from the subjects who did *not* watch the film was not analyzed in this study.

6.2 Procedures

Twenty subjects participated in this condition, ten who watched the film, ten who didn't. After viewing, each subject who watched the film was paired with one who didn't. The subject who had not seen the film was instructed to ask questions about it. Both subjects were told that they would have to narrate the story later.

Subjects who watched the film were told that they would be asked questions about it by a person who had not seen it. They were told not to elaborate, but to simply answer all questions. These subjects had a hard time following this instruction and often volunteered information about events when not asked to. After approximately four minutes of verbal interaction, both subjects were asked to immediately recall the story, starting at the beginning and providing as much detail as possible.

The conversations between the subjects as well as the subsequent individual narrations were recorded and transcribed. The conversations and the narrations by subjects who did see the film were compared to the baseline. The total number of event-clauses produced was also counted.

6.3 Results

The mean number of baseline clauses recalled by the subjects who saw the film, as well as the standard deviations, are given in Table 8 below, where they are compared with the results of the preceding four conditions.

Condition	# of Subjects	Mean # Baseline Clauses Recalled	Std. Deviation
I	10	38.1	6.59
II	10	37.4	4.99
III	10	36.1	5.36
IV	10	29.9	5.34
V	10	**29.1**	**9.43**

Table 8. Mean Numbers and Standard Deviations for Recalled Baseline Clauses (5 conditions)

Much like in Condition IV, the total number of baseline clauses recalled in Condition V was lower than that of the three control conditions. But what stands out in particular was the large cross-subject variation in Condition V. Subjects in this condition produced both the largest (46) and the smallest (17) number of baseline clauses. Seven subjects produced fewer than thirty clauses, two produced over forty, and only one produced a number close to the mean of the three control conditions (33). The standard deviation for Condition V tells the story, being almost twice that of the other four conditions. We will return to this point in Section 6.4 below.

The results given in Table 8 were subjected to a one-way ANOVA analysis, comparing the mean number of baseline clauses recalled for all five conditions. A significant difference was found between conditions ($F (4, 45) = 4.28$, $p < 0.0051$). A Duncan's Multiple Range Test indicated that the means for Conditions I (38.1), II (37.4), and III (36.1) were significantly larger than the means for Conditions IV (29.9) and V (29.1). But the differences between the means of Conditions I (38.1), II (37.4), and III (36.1) were not significant. The means of Conditions IV (29.9) and V (29.1) did not differ significantly from one another either.

The total number of clauses produced was also counted and compared with the other four conditions. The results are given in Table 9 below.

Condition	# of Subjects	Mean # Clauses Produced	Std. Deviation
I	10	107.1	19.10
II	10	99.0	38.76
III	10	96.2	23.95
IV	10	60.1	17.88
V	10	73.0	**25.65**

Table 9. Means and Standard Deviations for the Total Number of Clauses Produced (5 conditions)

The subjects in Condition V produced more clauses than in Condition IV, but still fewer than in the three control conditions.

These results were subjected to a one-way ANOVA analysis, comparing the mean number of total clauses produced for all five conditions. A significant difference was found between some of the conditions (F (4, 45), $p < 0.0009$). A Duncan's Multiple Range Test indicated that the means for Conditions I (107.1), II (99.0) and III (96.2) did not differ significantly. The means for Conditions IV (60.1) and V (73.0) also did not differ significantly between them. But the means of the three control conditions I (107.1), II (99.0) and III (96.2), when taken together, are significantly larger than the means of Conditions IV (60.1) and V (73.0). When the means of Conditions III (96.2) and V (73.0) are compared separately, however, the difference between them is not significant.

The statistical analysis thus identifies three groups whose members differ significantly across groups but not within groups:

(a) Conditions I, II, and III
(b) Conditions IV and V
(c) Conditions III and V

As with Condition IV, we also computed the ratios of baseline clauses recalled over the total number of clauses produced. The results are given in Table 10 below.

Condition	# of Subjects	Mean % of Baseline Out of Total # of Clauses	Std. Deviation
I	10	35.57	6.09
II	10	37.78	7.79
III	10	37.53	7.86
IV	10	**49.75**	7.56
V	10	39.86	**11.30**

Table 10. Percentage of Baseline Clauses Recalled out of Total Number of Clauses Produced (5 conditions)

Condition V had only a slightly higher ratio of baseline clauses over total clauses than the three control conditions, while Condition IV had a clearly higher ratio.

These results were also subjected to a one-way ANOVA analysis, comparing the percent of baseline clauses out of the total clauses across all five conditions. The difference between conditions was significant (F (4, 45), $p <$ 0.0008). A Duncan's Multiple Range Test indicated that the mean of Condition IV (49.75) was significantly higher than the means for Conditions I (35.57), II (37.78), III (37.53) and V (39.86).

Although subjects in Condition V recalled almost the same number of baseline events as those in Condition IV, the ratio of baseline events to total number of events produced in this condition resembled more the ratio in the three control conditions. Also, Condition V did not differ significantly from Condition III in terms of total number of clauses produced; although it did differ significantly in that respect from Conditions I and II.

6.4 Analysis of Individual Variation

The large cross-subject variability in the number of baseline clauses recalled in Condition V begs for further exploration. In an attempt to account for this large variation, we counted the number of questions asked by the respective subjects who did not see the film, as well as the number of baseline events mentioned during the conversation between the two subjects. The results are given in Table 11 below.

Subject	# of Baseline Events Recalled	# of Baseline Events Mentioned in Conversation	# of Questions Asked during Conversation
1	17	8	15
2	21	16	47
3	24	12	23
4	24	18	51
5	26	7	21
6	27	26	13
7	29	6	37
8	33	24	18
9	44	35	90
10	46	34	66

Table 11. Number of Baseline Clauses Recalled by Each Subject Compared with the Number of Baseline Clauses Mentioned during Conversation and Number of Questions Asked during Conversation (Condition V)

A correlation was found between the number of questions asked during the conversation and the number of baseline events recalled later by the responding subject (who saw the film). There was also a correlation between the number of baseline events mentioned during the conversation and the number of baseline clauses recalled later by the subject who saw the film.

The results in Table 11 were subjected to a Pearson Correlation Test, addressing the relationship between number of baseline clauses mentioned during the conversation ($M = 18.6$) and number of baseline clauses later recalled by the viewing subject ($M = 29.1$). A significant positive correlation between the two variables was revealed ($r(8) = 0.80113, p < 0.0053$).

A Pearson Correlation Test was also applied to the relationship between the number of questions asked during the conversation ($M = 38.1$) and number of baseline clauses recalled later by the viewing subject ($M = 29.1$). A significant positive correlation between these two variables was also found ($r(8) = 0.69133, p < 0.0268$).

A Pearson Correlation Test also revealed a statistically significant correlation between the number of questions asked during the conversation ($M = 38.1$) and the number of baseline clauses mentioned during the conversation ($M = 18.6$), ($r(8) = 0.61354, p < 0.0592$).

6.5 Interim Discussion

The results of Condition V indicate that the conversation which intervened between the viewing and recalled narration strongly affected recall. The wide cross-subject variation in Condition V turns out to be directly related to specific features of the conversation. The more baseline clauses were mentioned during the intervening conversation, the more baseline clauses were recalled during subsequent narration. Conversely, a paucity of mentioned baseline clauses during the conversation yielded a corresponding paucity in their subsequent recall. This effect is not due to the mere presence or absence of previous verbal encoding of events, since in Condition I subjects produced an on-line verbalization during viewing and before recalling. And the comparison of Condition I to Conditions II and III showed that previous verbalization did *not* affect later recall. On the other hand, the verbalization of events during the intervening conversation in Condition V significantly enhances later recall. It thus appears that verbally rehashing baseline events during a *conversation*—i.e. *interactive* rather than monologuic verbalization—is what enhanced later recall.

The number of questions asked during the interaction also affected the number of baseline clauses recalled later. This correlation was somewhat weaker than the one between number of baseline clauses mentioned in conversation and later baseline recall. The content of these questions was apparently a factor. While the number of questions asked correlated significantly with the number of baseline clauses produced during the interaction, the questions did not always pertain to baseline events. Thus, for example, one subject who recalled only 21 baseline clauses later on was asked 47 questions during the conversation. But during their conversation, only 16 baseline clauses were mentioned. And further, 32 of the 47 questions, viz. 68%, concerned details which were not part of the baseline (the weather, the ages of the actors, what clothes they were wearing, etc.). Thus, it appears that both the number and content of the questions affect recall.

One may wish to argue that Condition V differs from Condition I in that it provides the opportunity for additional rehearsal. But so does Condition IV, where the intervening verbalization did not enhance recall, presumably due to the presence of contradictory information. Thus, neither previous verbalization (Condition I) nor previous rehearsal (Condition IV) enhanced recall. The results of Condition V clearly suggest that it was the *quality* of verbal interaction itself that was responsible for the effect. When a **cooperative interaction** was not achieved, i.e. when the conversation did not produce many **coherent questions** and **relevant responses**, subsequent episodic recall of the film suffered. In Condition IV, episodic recall suffered due to the presence of non-cooperative misinformation. But when the interaction was more cooperative, with many pertinent questions and answers and no contradictory information, i.e. in instances of Condition V, recall benefitted.

7. Tentative Conclusions

7.1 Conversational Cooperation and Episodic Recall

We have shown that interposing conversational interaction between the presentation of episodic information and its subsequent recall has two possible effects on the recalled information. When the interlocutor is uncooperative and introduces misleading, contradictory information (Condition IV), the amount of episodic information recalled later goes down. On the other hand, when the verbal interaction is cooperative, involving a greater number of coherent questions and responses (Condition V), the amount of episodic information recalled later goes up. This effect goes beyond the effect of mere prior verbalization (I), and probably reflects the salutary effect of the need to reorganize the information **more coherently** during **cooperative interaction**. The quality of the intervening verbal interaction (Condition V) during the consolidation of episodic information, rather than the mere quantity of rehearsed verbalization (Conditions I and IV), appears to make the real difference.

7.2 Integration of Episodic and Situational Memory

The five experimental conditions we report here, taken together, can be considered as controls for a series of ongoing and future experiments. Thus far, we have only measured the effect of various interactional conditions on the recall of *episodic* information. But as noted in Section 2, there are good grounds for suspecting that at least some *interactional* information must be integrated into episodic memory. The conditions under which the two types of information processed during conversation, episodic and interactional, interact and are either integrated or not integrated in episodic memory, remain our current preoccupation. The two conditions we are trying to test now are:

> **CONDITION VI**: Two subjects who saw the same Chicken Story film are told to tell each other in detail about the film, after being told that they saw *similar but not identical* films. Their recall of *their conversation* is then solicited and recorded.

CONDITION VII: Two subjects who saw two different movies (one of them the Chicken Story) are told to tell each other in detail about the film they saw; both were told they saw the *same* film. Their recall of *their conversation* is likewise solicited and recorded; but only the data from the subjects who saw the Chicken Story film are analyzed.

We are interested, first, in the relative balance in the recorded recall of the conversation between recall of interactional detail vs. recall of episodic information about the Chicken Story. Second, we are interested in the degree to which the interactional and episodic information is integrated into a coherent unified representation. And third and perhaps most crucial, we are interested in the way specific features of the conversation—cooperative (Condition VI) vs. non-cooperative (Condition VII) interaction, explicit agreement or contradiction, etc.—affect various aspects of the subjects' recall of both the interactional and episodic information.

Notes

1. Even here, the limits of the linguist's intuition are already obvious in the case of negation (2b), where the pragmatics of the negative speech-act had been totally obscured by its logic (Givón 1979a: ch. 3).

2. We will take it for granted that 'text' can be either written or spoken, and either conversational ('collaborative') or non-conversational.

3. See Dik (1978) and Foley and van Valin (1984), *inter alia*.

4. In spite of their obvious pitfalls when practiced exclusively, both functional intuitionism and structural iconism retain legitimate—indeed, important—roles in the process of hypothesis formation. Intuition is the wellspring of hypothesis formation (Hanson 1958). And the iconism of grammar probably hovers around 80%–90% (see further below).

5. The theoretical grounds involve the assumption that the association must be strong enough *both* ways in order to be part of both speech perception (form to meaning) and speech production (meaning to form).

6. The size of the text is determined by the frequency of the A, B and P, Q in the text and amount of variation found in their respective associa-

tions. There is no way of determining this in advance. One may consider an arbitrarily-chosen length of text as a *pilot* study, to be augmented if necessary by additional text.

7. Like all hypotheses, our original hypothesis (6) no doubt has multiple logical consequences, and testing all of them is potentially an endless task:

    > ...The game of science is, in principle, without end. He who decides one day that scientific statements do not call for any further test, and that they can be regarded as finally verified, retires from the game... (Popper 1959: 53).

8. The process of theoretical reasoning and repeated testing eventually must extend into experimental psycholinguistic work, since "communicative function" must eventually decompose into mental operations that are performed in the mind/brain of the speech producer or comprehender.

9. This demand was not present to such an extent in Condition IV, where both the interlocutors had watched the film together.

Appendix

Baseline Clauses and Number of Subjects Recalling Each.
(Number of subjects producing clauses in baseline given in parentheses.)

		Conditions					
		I	II	III	IV	V	Total
1.	There's a man/guy (7)	5	7	5	4	3	24
2.	a man/guy/he walking (7)	7	10	6	6	6	35
3.	person/he carrying tools/shovels/ax (8)	6	7	8	4	7	32
4.	he's wearing a white T-shirt and white shorts (7)	0	5	4	1	5	15
5.	he's putting/setting/leaning them/shovels + prep. (7)	8	8	10	8	7	41
6.	he takes/picks up/has an ax/hatchet (7)	9	8	10	4	5	36
7.	he's walking/going + prep. (8)	9	8	7	2	4	30

8. he chops/cuts/hits/breaks wood/kindling/it/bran-ches/sticks (10)	10	10	10	9	10	49
9. someone else/a person/a wo-man/she coming/walking + prep. (8)	9	10	10	10	10	49
10. they're talking (7)	6	3	4	4	2	19
11. she's asking/wondering/ques-tions/ something/what (7)	3	6	6	3	7	25
12. he speaks/talks/responds/an-swers (7)	3	2	2	0	2	9
13. she's taking/picking up/col-lecting/grabbing/gathering wood/kindling/sticks (10)	9	10	8	9	7	43
14. she's walking/wandering + loc. (9)	7	10	8	9	5	39
15. she puts/sets/lays wood/pie-ces/sticks/kindling + loc. (8)	1	1	3	2	0	7
16. she's getting/picking up/col-lecting/grabbing/gathering/ taking them/kindling/fire-wood/shrubs/sticks (9)	6	7	4	3	4	24
17. she breaks/cuts/snaps bran-ches/twigs/shrubs/ones/pieces/ sticks/them (9)	7	8	9	9	5	38
18. she picks/grabs/gathers the bundle/stuff/pile/sticks/bran-ches/them (8)	5	5	8	6	4	28
19. she walks/goes/wanders + loc.	4	3	5	4	5	21
20. man/guy walks/goes/wanders + loc. (8)	2	4	4	1	2	13
21. he picks up/takes/gets/ grabs/gathers tools/them (10)	2	8	4	1	3	18
22. he's walking/wandering + loc. (9)	1	8	4	2	4	19
23. she/the woman comes/walks/goes + loc. (10)	8	9	7	3	6	33
24. she holds/carries/brings/takes the wood/sticks/bundle/kind-ling/branches (9)	3	2	1	0	3	9

25. she sets/puts/drops sticks/it/ wood/them/bundle/bunch + loc. (10)	7	5	7	2	3	24
26. she walks/wanders/goes + loc. (7)	2	1	2	0	0	5
27. she picks up something (7)	4	2	2	2	1	11
28. she starts/makes/builds/lights a fire (10)	10	10	10	10	9	49
29. she puts/adds them/kindling/ sticks/pieces/wood/ branches/shrubs/twigs + prep. (10)	8	3	3	1	2	17
30. she picks up/takes/grabs/gets a pot/pail/bowl/bucket (9)	9	7	8	8	6	38
31. she walks/goes/wanders + loc. (8)	7	10	9	8	5	39
32. she's putting/pouring/getting/tipping water/liquid + prep. (9)	9	10	9	8	7	43
33. she's walking/coming + loc. (8)	5	6	2	3	4	20
34. she sets/puts pan/pail/it/pot on the fire/block (8)	10	9	9	9	6	43
35. she adds/puts leaves/wood/ them/shrubs/fuel + prep. (7)	3	1	2	1	1	8
36. she walks/goes back/to/towards outhouse/shed (10)	10	9	7	10	8	44
37. she's carrying/getting/has something (7)	7	9	8	8	10	42
38. she walks back to/toward the fire (7)	2	5	2	4	3	16
39. it is/looks like a chicken/animal (9)	5	1	2	1	0	9
40. she has/picks up/grabs a knife (7)	10	6	8	6	3	33
41. she's slaughtering/killing/sacrificing/decapitating/cutting the chicken/chicken's head (10)	9	10	10	9	10	48
42. the rooster/chicken/it gets/ runs away (10)	10	8	8	9	9	44
43. she forgets/gives up it/the chase (8)	7	6	9	6	5	33

44. she goes/walks back to/to-wards the shed/building/shack (8)	10	10	10	10	9	49
45. she takes/grabs/carries/pulls out something (7)	10	10	10	10	7	47
46. she walks/comes back to/to-ward the fire (7)	5	5	3	5	6	24
47. she unwraps/takes out/opens/unfolds it/something/package (8)	8	4	6	5	4	27
48. she picks up/grabs/has/gets the knife (7)	4	2	2	0	1	9
49. she cuts/slices it/the food/something/them/pieces (10)	9	10	9	7	8	43
50. she puts something/every-thing/it in/into bag/cloth/wrapping/sack/bundle (8)	4	2	0	2	1	9
51. she rolls/rewraps/wraps it/the cloth/all/everything up (10)	8	8	8	8	6	38
52. she walks/goes back + loc. (7)	9	4	5	7	7	32
53. he/the man is turning/wack-ing/hitting/hoeing the earth/ground/garden (8)	9	4	9	5	4	31
54. the woman enters/comes/walks + loc. (8)	8	5	4	2	2	21
55. she calls/talks/speaks (7)	6	4	4	2	3	19
56. she gives/hands him the pack-age/bundle/food (7)	9	8	7	7	6	37
57. he is angry/mad/disgusted/pissed/upset/not happy/not pleased (9)	3	7	9	3	6	28
58. he's chasing/running after her (10)	10	10	10	10	10	50

References

Anderson, Anne. 1995. Negotiating coherence in dialogue. In Gernsbacher and Givón (eds.), 1-40.

Anderson, Anne, Simon Garrod, and Anthony Sanford. 1983. The accessibility of pronominal antecedents as a function of episodic shift in narrative text. *Quarterly Journal of Experimental Psychology* 35A, 427-440.

Baddeley, Alan. 1986. *Working Memory*. Oxford: Oxford University Press.

Baddeley, Alan. 1992. Working memory: The interface between memory and cognition. *Journal of Cognitive Neuroscience* 4(3), 281–288.

Bower, Gordon and Daniel Morrow. 1990. Mental models in narrative comprehension. *Science* 247, 44-48.

Carpenter, Patricia A. and Marcel A. Just. 1988. The role of working memory in language comprehension. In David Klahr and Kenneth Kotovsky (eds.), *Complex Information Processing: The Impact of Herbert Simon*, 31-68. Hillsdale, NJ: Erlbaum.

Chafe, Wallace. 1979. The flow of thought and the flow of language. In Givón (ed.), 159-182.

Chafe, Wallace (ed.). 1980. *The Pear Stories: Cognitive, Cultural and Linguistic Aspects of Narrative Production*. Norwood, NJ: Ablex.

Chafe, Wallace. 1987. Cognitive constraints on information flow. In Tomlin (ed.), 21-51.

Chafe, Wallace. 1994. *Discourse, Consciousness and Time: The Flow and Displacement of Conscious Experience in Speaking and Writing*. Chicago: University of Chicago.

Clark, Herbert and Edward F. Schaefer. 1987. Collaborating on contributions to conversations. *Language and Cognitive Processes* 2, 19-41.

Clark, Herbert and Deanna Wilkes-Gibbs. 1986. Referring as a collaborative process. *Cognition* 22, 1-39.

Dik, Simon. 1978. *Functional Grammar*. Amsterdam: North Holland.

Dore, John. 1973. *The Development of Speech Acts*. New York: City University of New York doctoral dissertation.

Du Bois, John. 1987. The discourse basis of ergativity. *Language* 63, 805-855.

Ericsson, K. Anders and Walter Kintsch. 1995. Long-term working memory. *Psychological Review*, 102(2), 211-245.

Ervin-Tripp, Susan. 1970. Discourse agreement: How children answer questions. In John Hayes (ed.), *Cognition and the Development of Language*, 79-108. New York: Wiley.

Ervin-Tripp, Susan. 1976. Some features of early child-adult dialogues. *Language and Society* 7, 357-373.

Fillmore, Charles. 1968. The case for case. In Emmon Bach and Robert T. Harms (eds.), *Universals of Linguistic Theory*, 1-88. New York: Holt.

Foley, William and Robert van Valin. 1984. *Functional Syntax and Universal Grammar*. Cambridge: Cambridge University Press.

Gathercole, Susan E. and Alan D. Baddeley. 1993. *Working Memory and Language*. Hillsdale, NJ: Erlbaum.

Gernsbacher, Morton A. 1985. Surface information loss in comprehension. *Cognitive Psychology* 17, 324-363.

Gernsbacher, Morton A. 1990. *Language Comprehension as Structure Building*. Hillsdale, NJ: Erlbaum.

Gernsbacher, Morton A. and T. Givón (eds.). 1995. *Coherence in Spontaneous Text* (Typological Studies in Language 31). Amsterdam: Benjamins.

Givón, T. 1979a. *On Understanding Grammar*. New York: Academic Press.

Givón, T. (ed.). 1979b. *Discourse and Syntax* (Syntax and Semantics 12). New York: Academic Press.

Givón, T. (ed.). 1983. *Topic Continuity in Discourse: A Quantitative Text-Based Study* (Typological Studies in Language 3). Amsterdam: Benjamins.

Givón, T. 1984. *Syntax: A Functional-Typological Introduction*, Vol. 1. Amsterdam: Benjamins.

Givón, T. (ed.). 1985. *Quantified Studies in Discourse, Text* 5(1/2), 1-145.

Givón, T. 1988. The pragmatics of word-order: Predictability, importance and attention. In Michael Hammond, Edith Moravcsik, and Jessica Wirth (eds.), *Studies in Syntactic Typology* (Typological Studies in Language 17), 243-284. Amsterdam: Benjamins.

Givón, T. 1990. *Syntax: A Functional-Typological Introduction*, Vol. 2. Amsterdam: Benjamins.

Givón, T. 1991. Some substantive issues concerning verb serialization: Grammatical vs. cognitive packaging. In Claire Lefebvre (ed.), *Serial Verbs: Grammatical, Comparative, and Cognitive Approaches*, 137-184. Amsterdam: Benjamins.

Givón, T. 1992. The grammar of referential coherence as mental processing instructions. *Linguistics* 30, 5-55.

Givón, T. 1994. Coherence in text, coherence in mind. *Pragmatics and Cognition* 1(2), 171-227.

Goodwin, Charles. 1982. *Conversational Organization*. New York: Academic Press.

Goodwin, Charles. 1988. Embedded context. Paper read at the AAA Annual Meeting. Phoenix, Arizona, November 1988.

Goodwin, Charles. 1995a. Sentence construction within interaction. In Uta Quasthoff (ed.), *Aspects of Oral Communication*, 198-219. Berlin: Walter de Gruyter.

Goodwin, Charles. 1995b. The negotiation of coherence within conversation. In Gernsbacher and Givón (eds.), 117-137.

Grice, H. Paul. 1975. Logic and conversation. In Peter Cole and Jerry Morgan (eds.), *Speech Acts* (Syntax and Semantics 3), 41-58. New York: Academic Press.

Guo, Jiansheng. 1995. The interactional basis of the Mandarin modal *neng* 'can.' In Joan Bybee and Suzanne Fleischmann (eds.), *Modality in Grammar and Discourse*, 205-238. Amsterdam: Benjamins.

Hanson, Norwood R. 1958. *Patterns of Discovery*. Cambridge: Cambridge University Press.

Harris, Zellig. 1957. Co-occurrence and transformation in linguistic structure. *Language* 33, 283-340.

Just, Marcel A. and Patricia A. Carpenter. 1992. A capacity theory of comprehension: Individual differences in working memory. *Psychological Review* 99(1), 122-148.

Keenan, Elinor Ochs. 1975. Again and again: The pragmatics of imitation in child language. *Pragmatics Microfiche*.

Keenan, Elinor Ochs. 1977. Making it last: Uses of repetition in children's discourse. In Susan Ervin-Tripp and Claudia Mitchell-Kernan (eds.), *Child Discourse*, 125-138. New York: Academic Press.

Loftus, Elizabeth F. 1975. Leading questions and the eyewitness report. *Cognitive Psychology* 7, 560–572.

Loftus, Elizabeth F. 1980. *Eyewitness Testimony*. Cambridge: Cambridge University Press.

Loftus, Elizabeth F., David G. Miller, and Helen J. Burns. 1978. Semantic integration of verbal information into a visual memory. *Journal of Experimental Psychology: Human Learning and Memory* 4, 19–31.

Mishkin, Mortimer. 1978. Memory in monkeys severely impaired by combined but not by separate removal of amygdala and hippocampus. *Nature* 273, 297-298.

Mishkin, Mortimer, Barbara Malamut, and Jocelyne Bechevalier. 1984. Memories and habits: Two neural systems. In Gary Lynch and James L. McGaugh (eds.), *Neurobiology of Learning and Memory*, 65-77. New York: Guilford.

Mishkin, Mortimer and Herbert L. Petri. 1984. Memories and habits: Some implications for the analysis of learning and retention. In Nelson Butters and Larry R. Squire (eds.), *Neuropsychology of Memory*, 287-296. New York: Guilford.

Ochs, Elinor and Bambi B. Schieffelin (eds.). 1979. *Developmental Pragmatics*. New York: Academic Press.

Paivio, Allan. 1969. Mental imagery in associative learning and memory. *Psychological Review* 76, 241–263.

Paivio, Allan. 1971. *Imagery and Verbal Processes*. New York: Holt.

Peirce, Charles. 1934. *Pragmatism and Pragmaticism*. Cambridge, MA: Harvard University Press.

Popper, Karl. 1959. *The Logic of Scientific Discovery* [2nd ed., 1968]. New York: Harper and Row.

Sacks, Harvey, Emanuel Schegloff, and Gail Jefferson. 1974. A simplest systematics for the organization of turn-taking for conversation. *Language* 50, 696-735.

Schnorr, John A. and Richard C. Atkinson. 1969. Repetition versus imagery instructions in the short- and long-term retention of paired associates. *Psychonomic Science* 15, 183–184.

Scollon, Ronald. 1976. *Conversations with a One-Year-Old Child*. Honolulu: University of Hawaii Press.

Squire, Larry R. 1987. *Memory and Brain*. Oxford: Oxford University Press.

Squire, Larry R. 1991. Declarative and non-declarative memory: Multiple brain systems supporting learning and memory. *Journal of Cognitive Neuroscience* 4(3), 222–241.

Squire, Larry R. 1992. Memory and the hippocampus: A synthesis from findings with rats, monkeys, and humans. *Psychological Review* 99(2), 195–221.

Squire, Larry R. and Stuart Zola-Morgan. 1991. The medial-temporal lobe memory system. *Science* 253, 1380-1385.

Tomlin, Russell. 1985. Foreground-background information and the syntax of subordination. In Givón (ed.), 85-122.

Tomlin, Russell. 1987a. Linguistic reflections of cognitive events. In Tomlin (ed.), 455-479.

Tomlin, Russell (ed.). 1987b. *Coherence and Grounding in Discourse* (Typological Studies in Language 11). Amsterdam: Benjamins.

Tomlin, Russell. 1991. Focal attention, voice and word-order: An experimental cross-linguistic study. *Technical Report 91–10*. Eugene, OR: Institute of

Cognitive and Decision Sciences, University of Oregon. [Revised version appeared 1995 in Pamela Downing and Michael Noonan (eds.), *Word Order in Discourse*, 521-558. Amsterdam: John Benjamins.]

van Dijk, Teun and Walter Kintsch. 1983. *Strategies of Discourse Comprehension*. New York: Academic Press.

Wilkes-Gibbs, Deanna 1986. *Collaborative Processes of Language Use in Conversation*. Stanford, CA: Stanford University doctoral dissertation.

Wilkes-Gibbs, Deanna. 1995. Coherence in collaboration: Some examples from conversation. In Gernsbacher and Givón (eds.), 239-267.

Wilkes-Gibbs, Deanna and Herbert Clark. 1992. Coordinating beliefs in conversation. *Journal of Memory and Language* 31, 183-194.

Yuille, John C. and Allan Paivio. 1967. Latency of imaginal and verbal mediators as a function of stimulus and response concreteness-imagery. *Journal of Experimental Psychology* 75, 540–544.

The Development of Person Agreement Markers: From Pronouns to Higher Accessibility Markers

MIRA ARIEL

Tel-Aviv University

1. From Free Pronouns to Verbal Agreement: Introduction

Grammatical items often begin their linguistic life as regular lexical items (Meillet 1912). Grammaticization is said to have occurred when the position of such lexemes (or even phrases) becomes fixed, their meaning is generalized/bleached, their domain of applicability enlarged, significantly raising their frequency, their form modified (usually phonetically reduced), and their occurrence made obligatory, even when informationally redundant (see Bybee et al. 1994). Bybee (1985: 38) described the process, saying that "frequent items are gradually reduced both phonologically and semantically, and are simultaneously gradually fused, again both phonologically and semantically, with lexical matter contiguous in the syntactic string." High frequency is then a prerequisite for grammaticization (see also Hopper and Traugott 1993). A similar process of grammaticization may also turn less grammatical items into more grammatical ones. This is what happens to pronouns when they gradually become bound inflections.[1]

Graduality is characteristic of grammaticization. Full forms first reduce (usually as a result of de-stressing) and become dependent and cliticized, and only then do they become (obligatory) bound morphemes, sometimes merging with other morphemes to such an extent that they become "portmanteau" morphemes (see Heine and Reh 1984, Bybee et al. 1990, Croft 1990, Hopper 1991). The old, alternative forms may continue to be used alongside the innovative forms. Bybee (1985), however, added to the characterization of such historical changes that this fusion is not merely the result of frequent phonological adjacency, but is, rather, dependent on the coherent relation between the fusing elements. The more relevant the items are to each other, the more likely they are to fuse. Person agreement, argued Bybee, is not the best candidate for morphological fusion (as opposed to aspect, for example). But she did find that 56% of the languages in her sample had person inflections on the verbs nonetheless. I will suggest that this "surprising" fact results from an independently motivated though unrelated function, namely the tendency for highly accessible referents to be linguistically coded by highly reduced forms. In other words, agreement markers are seen as the diachronic outcome of speakers' synchronic preference for reduced pronouns, forms which well match the high degree of accessibility usually associated with the speaker and the addressee.[2]

Indeed, typologists are in agreement that most verbal inflections are developments of free pronouns (See Greenberg 1966, Dixon 1979, Lehmann 1987, Hopper and Traugott 1993). Givón (1976: 180) believes that "verb agreement paradigms *always* arise from anaphoric pronoun paradigms" (original emphasis). Comrie (1978, 1981) agrees with Givón in general, and offers as example the Mongolian languages, currently undergoing this very change. Givón (1971) had originally argued for such a development with respect to Bantu languages. Moscati et al. (1969) in effect show this for many verbal forms in all Semitic languages (and see Gesenius-Kautzsch-Cowley 1910, who explicitly make this claim). Steele (1977) discusses the cliticization of pronouns to verbs in a few Uto-Aztecan languages, and Mithun (1991) describes the development of bound pronouns in other North American languages. Haiman (1991) argues for such a development for Northern Italian dialects. Bosch (1983), who incorporates this insight into his synchronic theory about pronoun uses, cites 18th and 19th century grammarians who held this view too (Brugmann and Delbrück 1911, Windisch 1869, Horne Tooke 1798/1968, Bopp 1816, Miklosich 1868 and Grimm 1812). Later we can cite Meillet (1912), Jespersen (1924/1965) and Bally (1932). Dixon (1980) argues the same point for Australian languages, suggesting a gradual development of pronouns into agreement clitics/ inflection. Helmbrecht (1995a) mentions Tabasaran, Batsbi and Udi (all East-Caucasian languages). Even American Sign Language, as described by Newport and Meier (1985), seems to inflect for agreement in a manner which is unmistakably pronominal in origin. Such an origin explains not only the formal affinity between free and bound pronouns, but also why universally, inflections do not mark more distinctions than free pronouns, and sometimes less (see Barlow 1992).[3]

The development of pronouns into inflections can take place at different times for different persons/numbers etc., and each stage in the pronoun-agreement development constitutes a potentially stable, functional system (see Mithun 1991). This graduality explains why there is disagreement in the field as to the status of verbal person markers. Although formal grammarians tend to view agreement as a morphosyntactic sentential phenomenon involving the copying of some features from one argument onto a second "agreeing" source, thereby denying agreement any referential or anaphoric function, agreement markers are often referential and/or anaphoric (see Ariel 1990, 1991, Helmbrecht 1995a, and especially Barlow 1992 for persuasive arguments regarding the discoursal, rather than purely formal nature of agreement). In fact, as Anderson (1985) claims, it is no easy matter to determine which are inflectional agreement markers and which are clitics attached to the verb. This is so because they often exhibit the properties of both bound affixes and independent words (see Haiman 1991 for clitics). Intermediate status is characteristic of change in progress (see Steele 1977 re Mono, for example, though, as Mithun p.c. notes, pronominal affixes can persist over thousands of years). In fact, Bybee et al. (1994) argue that the original semantic meaning of a grammaticized morpheme lingers on, or at least traces of it do (see also Hopper 1991), which would account for the referential power of even fully grammaticized person agreement markers which had developed out of independent pronouns (as opposed to other sources). Dixon (1979), Jelinek (1984), Anderson and Keenan (1985), Ariel (1985, 1990), Mithun (1986a, 1991), Du Bois (1987a,b), Van Valin (1987), Anderson (1988) and Barlow (1992) assume that at least some verbal person markers are nominal and/or referential arguments. Moravcsik (1987) and Haiman (1991) see them as mere agreement features copied into the verb. Jespersen (1922, 1924/1965) even considers them superfluous, counter-logical markers.

I suggest these opposing views actually reflect the analysts' observations of the two opposite ends of the historical process which may (but need not) turn fully referential pronouns (free lexemes) into pure "agreeing" inflections (bound morphemes). In fact, for the most part, it is various intermediate stages which are found, best leading to intermediate and variable statuses assigned to such markers (see Doron 1987, Fassi Fehri 1987, Gilligan 1987 and Haiman 1991, where a few tests are implemented). I therefore agree with Zipf (1935: 246-9) and Croft (1990: 232) that pronouns and inflections form a continuum from independent words to complete fusion, although for specific paradigms/languages the case may be quite unequivocal. Similarly, but not necessarily in exact tandem with this formal continuum, person agreement markers manifest anything between full referentiality and no referentiality. But this scale is not so different from what can be observed in full NPs. Du Bois (1980, Ms.) suggests that even full NPs with determiners exhibit different degrees of referentiality, with the less referential NPs often being absorbed under a predominantly verbal concept, in a verb-object conflation.

The changes from full pronouns to bound, inflectional markers, like many other morphological formations, are unidirectional, but still the changes to the verbal forms are sometimes cyclical, repeating themselves in "re-grammaticization" processes (Dixon 1994: 182-5, see Kemmer 1993 for syntagmatic versus systemic change). As Givón (1976: 172) said, "Agreement systems meet their predictable demise via phonological attrition much like other bound affixes." And then, there can be re-generation of the very same system, gradually leading to new bound affixes (see Watkins 1962, Wartburg 1969: 238 and Steele 1977). I will argue below that in colloquial Hebrew, future tense verbal forms may now be undergoing such a renewal, with pronouns obligatorily cooccurring with the verbal forms, even though future verbs are inflected for person (number and gender).

Given that universally, agreement markers tend to develop from pronouns, the first question to be addressed is why and how agreement markers develop out of free pronouns. I will mainly discuss two potential explanations: NP detachment (2.1) and Accessibility Theory (2.2). I will suggest that both historical paths are plausible, and that synchronic distributional restrictions may testify to one or the other alternative in specific cases (2.3). I will then address another question pertaining to this grammaticization process: the motivation for the consistent pattern of agreement marking found, according to which it is mostly first/second persons which are overtly marked on the verb, whereas third person is not. The two questions are obviously related, and a good explanation for the process should also motivate the resulting marking pattern. My argument will be that Accessibility Theory can resolve both questions in a unified way (3.1). Briefly, I will argue that only first and second person referents are consistently very highly accessible, and hence only they merit a grammaticization process of reduction which ultimately results in the obligatory coding of first/second persons by highly accessible markers (the agreement morphemes). Third person referents are not consistently highly accessible, and hence lower accessibility markers (pronouns, full NPs) are more suitable for coding them. 3.2 adduces empirical evidence for the accessibility account.

In 4 I consider other potential explanations for the prevalent marking pattern. I will discuss typological markedness (4.1), as well as Bybee's frequency-driven morphologization (4.2). I will argue against using these theories to explain the predominant person verbal agreement pattern by relying on textual distributions (in 4.3 and 4.4 respectively). The current grammaticization process of verbal person agreement in Hebrew future tense serves as a test case for the competing theories discussed. I argue that only Accessibility Theory can account for this new development (5). I then examine the possibility of extending the accessibility account provided for the nominative verbal agreement pattern to the ergative verbal agreement pattern of Mayan in 6. I conclude that both patterns show sensitivity to the degree of accessibility associated with the relevant argument.

In 7, I mention cases where third person verbal agreement is marked. I argue that such attested cases only form counter-examples to the typological markedness account, but not to Accessibility Theory. I also specify what would count as a true counter-example to the accessibility account. No such cases have been reported in the literature to the best of my knowledge. I conclude with reinterpreting the predominant pattern to be overt marking for first/second persons versus no agreement for third persons (8). No agreement is distinguished from zero agreement, and hence, although typological markedness cannot account for the predominant verbal agreement pattern, it is not after all challenged by those cases where 3rd person verbs are overtly marked.

2. The Mechanism Responsible for the Pronoun —> Bound Agreement Change

If one accepts that many person inflections develop out of pronouns, then one needs to argue that prior to the creation of inflection, an overt pronoun cooccurred with the verb. Once it was there, a cliticization process could plausibly be argued for. Most researchers have been interested in explaining the surprising fact that some languages at some point started inserting a superfluous pronoun into certain clauses, although it was not called for grammatically (2.1). While some agreement systems may have indeed developed in such seemingly double-subject clauses, I would like to argue that person markings on verbs mainly arise in single subject sentences, the subjects of which are free pronouns. I would then have to account for the superfluous NP subject, rather than pronoun, later inserted into the clause (2.2).

2.1 A Superfluous Pronoun Appears: Sentential Rhythm and NP Detachment

Whereas the change from full pronominal forms to bound inflections (1b to c) seems unproblematic, resulting from phonological processes, the syntactic change involved in the insertion of a superfluous pronoun (the change from 1a to b) has been seen as the main problem to be accounted for. That is, why some languages manifest(ed) a double marking of the subject (or absolutive), at least for a period, or alternatively, why a perfectly grammatical zero-subject sentence starts containing an overt pronoun:

(1) a. NP/zero # V —>[4]
     b. NP/zero # Pronoun # V —>
     c. NP/zero # clitic+V/V$_{[+inflection]}$

One path of change argues that pronoun insertion is brought about for sentence rhythm. Paul (1880/1995), Jespersen (1924/1965), Vendryes (1925/1952), Bally (1932), Wartburg (1962), Lambrecht (1980, 1981) and Auger (1993, 1994) consider French to have evolved a verbal person marking system out of the nominative pronouns, the accusative pronouns (*moi, toi*, etc.) now substituting for the nominative ones. Old French, argues Wartburg (1962,) was a verb-second language. When the first word of the sentence was unstressed (e.g., *que*), and hence did not quite count as a first element, the nominative pronouns were added for the rhythm of the sentence. Hence, for Wartburg the change schematically looks as in 2 (see also Kuen 1957, who refers to Thurneysen 1892, and Harris 1978):

(2) a. Zero # Verb$_{[+inflection]}$
   b. Unstressed word # *je/tu*... # Verb$_{[inflection\ disappearing]}$
   c. (NP) # *je/tu*...$_{[pronoun\ reduced\ to\ prefixal\ conjugation]}$ + Verb

Haiman (1991) argues for a similar, and even more advanced, development in Northern Italian dialects, which, due to Germanic influence, adopted a V/2 constraint. This primarily affected inverted constructions, and especially second person verbal forms, a fact which leads Haiman to hypothesize that the addition of the "superfluous" pronoun initially occurred in interrogatives, where second person references are most natural. Indeed, in some related Romantsch dialects (Sumeiran, Puter and Vallader), bound verbal person markers are still restricted to inverted word order.

Givón (1976) proposes a different motivation for inserting the seemingly superfluous pronoun-later-turned-affix into the sentence. Agreement is seen as originally a topic marker rather than as a subject marker. It develops in left and right dislocated NP constructions, where topics are overtly mentioned twice, once in full NP form and once in pronominal form, as in:

(3) a. Maya$_i$, she$_i$ kissed me.
   b. She$_i$ kissed me, Maya$_i$

Since the topic representations in such sentences are obviously prominent, such syntactic constructions are naturally used in contexts where a shift from the current topic to a new one is proposed by the speaker. The connection of verbal agreement to topicality can further account for the fact that agreement is most common for subjects, but less so for objects, more so for definite NPs (see Givón 1976 on Swahili direct objects) and for animate NPs (see Moravcsik 1978, Comrie 1981). A frequent usage of such constructions then leads to a reanalysis of the marked construction as unmarked, and thus as no longer specifically restricted functionally (see also Bosch 1983). At the very end of the process, the anaphoric relation between the full NP topic and the pronoun may be reanalyzed as a grammatical relation of subject-predicate. Concomitant with this development, phonological changes are expected, such as de-stressing, cliticization and even fusion. Thus, what started as a superfluous pronoun, inserted in order to highlight a topic, may end up as an agreement marker.

Givón's analysis is claimed to account for a variety of languages: non-standard French (as above), Bantu languages, as well as English and French-based Pidgins and Creoles. Fassi Fehri (1987) has claimed a similar origin for agreement in Arabic. Lambrecht (1980) is a study of topic marking in non-standard French, which indeed testifies to the correlation between the frequency of topic shifting sentences with the use of cliticized/bound pronouns. This is also how I interpret Nadasdi's (1995) findings that subjects that are [+definite] and [+specific] (i.e., more plausibly topics) are likely to cooccur with clitics 3.5 times more often than subjects that are [-definite] and [-specific]. Indeed, as befits a grammatical change, it is gradual, so that even in the 1980s Lambrecht claims that the "autonomous" personal pronouns (*moi, toi* etc.) as well as the full NPs in such constructions do not function as full-fledged grammatical subjects.

2.2. A Superfluous NP Subject Appears: Accessibility and Inflection

In effect in line with Sanford and Garrod (1981), Givón (1983) and Chafe (1987), I have argued (Ariel 1985, 1988, 1990, 1991, 1996) that when reference to mental entities is made, the speaker chooses her referring expression according to how she assesses the accessibility of the specific entity for her addressee at the current stage of the discourse. The higher the mental accessibility, the higher the accessibility marker chosen. Accessibility markers are specialized for a variety of degrees of accessibility, and non-arbitrarily so. Lower accessibility markers are more informative (calculated according to amount of lexical material), more rigid (i.e., identify a mental entity relatively uniquely) and less attenuated (lengthier or accented, regardless of informativeness). Higher accessibility markers are on the whole less informative, less rigid and more attenuated (regardless of informativeness). Such a form-function correlation seems only reasonable, given that mental entities currently not highly accessible are better retrieved by supplying more information, for the addressee has to choose among very many mental entities he stores in his long-term memory. Highly accessible entities, on the other hand, cannot be numerous, because we can only keep a very limited number of mental entities highly accessible at any given moment.

However, there are indications that accessible information is de-accentuated, even pronounced less intelligibly as an unambiguous signal that the information concerned is Given rather than New.[5] In other words, it is not only that the speaker invests more energy in coding New information, because it is harder to process. She also intentionally aims at reducing the form expressing accessible information, since it is a useful linguistic cue for the addressee to search for an already available entity. Now, the form-function correlation between accessibility markers and degree of mental accessibility is not perfectly transparent, but the following scale of accessibility markers is quite representative of many languages (though not all languages have all the options listed, see Ariel (1990) for discussion of accessibility and universality). The differences in the degrees of accessibility coded by (any) full NPs, free pronouns, bound pronouns, agreement and true zeroes prove to be crucial in the development of verbal person agreement markers:

(4) *The accessibility marking scale.*
zero < reflexives < poor agreement markers < rich agreement markers < reduced/cliticized pronouns < unstressed pronouns < stressed pronouns < stressed pronouns + gesture < proximal demonstrative (+NP) < distal demonstrative (+NP) < proximal demonstrative (+NP) + modifier < distal demonstrative (+NP) + modifier < first name < last name < short definite description < long definite description < full name < full name + modifier.

I have focused on two types of considerations taken into account by the speaker when assessing the degree of accessibility associated with specific mental entities in the addressee's memory (although other factors are no doubt involved): entity salience and unity. The former criterion refers to the degree of salience of the potential antecedent (linguistic or non-linguistic); the latter refers to the strength of the connection between the referring expression/accessibility marker and the potential antecedent. The Unity criterion is mainly relevant for anaphoric references, and pertains to the distance and the degree of cohesion between the units (e.g., clauses) containing the two expressions. It is the first criterion, antecedent salience, which will ultimately prove crucial for the formation of agreement inflections. All things being equal, the entities mentioned on the left in 5 are more salient than the ones on their right:

(5) *Antecedent salience*
  a. Speaker > addressee > nonparticipant (third person)
  b. High physical salience > low physical salience
  c. Topic > nontopic
  d. Grammatical subject > nonsubject
  e. Human > animate > inanimate
  f. Repeated references > few previous references > first mention
  g. No intervening/competing referents > many intervening/ competing referents

It is agreed upon that inflections which developed out of pronouns must have derived from attenuated pronouns. All we need add via Accessibility Theory is that this reduction is not merely the result of phonological processes characteristic of fast speech pronunciations of frequently mentioned items, but is also the result of speakers' intention to mark some referents as extremely accessible, even more accessible than regular pronoun antecedents are. The following examples from Hebrew, where the speaker oscillates between full pronouns and reduced pronouns, show how sensitive speakers are to properly marking degrees of accessibility of referents for their addressees.[6] (6) exemplifies how the already repeatedly established discourse topic (the press, previously referred to by stressed and destressed *they*) is either referred to by a full pronoun (*hem*) or by a cliticized one (*h*), depending on the degree of cohesion between the clause containing the anaphoric expression and the previous clause containing a coreferring expression ('but' and 'another thing' signal a shift from current discourse unit, thereby lowering the accessibility of the discourse entity 'the press' and encouraging full pronominal forms—see originally Li and Thompson 1979):

(6) i. ... **h** [=hem] + mociim   et   ze   kaxa...
           They   publish acc.   this like-this...

   ii. aval **hem** madgishim... **h**   notnim kama...
         But   they   emphasize...   they   give   some...

iii.	od	davar she+	**hem**	asu...
	Another	thing that	they	did...

(7) exemplifies how first, when a new entity is introduced into the discourse it is referred to by a proper name (Nubar), whereas the current topic is coded by a pronoun (Cameron, referred to by stressed and unstressed pronouns). However, once both discourse entities become highly accessible (both antecedents being close by and repeatedly referred to), the discourse topic is coded by a reduced pronoun (h), while the not quite as accessible entity is referred to by a full pronoun (hu):

(7) Preceding discourse (translated): Cameron$_i$... HE$_i$... he$_i$ talked to Nubar$_j$... Nubar$_j$ said... Nubar$_j$ was still...

h$_i$ [=hu]	pashut	diber	ito$_j$...	**hu$_j$**	xashav...
He	simply	talked	with-him	He	thought...

So, if the reduction (of some occurrences) of pronouns into cliticized, and later into bound morphemes is motivated by the wish to conform to the form-function convention correlating degree of mental accessibility with type of referring expression/accessibility marker, the structure of (8b), which may contain an overt NP subject, is the final link in a change initiated in structures such as a.i through a.iii:

(8) a.　i.　Pronoun # Verb

　　　ii.　Cliticized Pronoun+Verb

　　　iii.　zero # $V_{[+inflection]}$

　　b.　　NP/Pronoun/zero # $V_{[+inflection]}$

The problematic link for Accessibility Theory is the change from 8aiii to b. In the most extreme case, the addition of a superficially redundant slot for a subject results from a (gradual) reanalysis of the person marker as merely an obligatory agreement feature on the verb, in some cases (such as Hebrew future tense), as simply nonexistent (i.e., reinterpreted as a part of the verbal form).[7] Such reanalysis depends on a high degree of fusion between the person marker and the verb, a fusion which discourages (but does not preclude) perceiving the reduced pronoun as referential. A final potential development may eliminate the referential power of agreeing verbs, which may bring about a ban against zero subjects, so that overt subjects are required, rather than optional. But I suggest that full NPs start occurring alongside person inflections in such constructions even before the referential power of agreement is eliminated (if at all), because at least in some situations, the degree of accessibility associated with the referent is not deemed high enough to merit reference by agreement only (as opposed to a free or even bound pronoun). The more fused the former pronoun is (even if still referential), the higher the degree of accessibility it marks, and hence, the more restricted the contexts for its use are to very high accessibility.

Note that speakers cannot even treat the mental representations corresponding to themselves as highly accessible at all times, as is seen in the following examples from Hebrew (both translations from an Alice Walker story), where the speaker refers to herself by zero or by pronoun (both marked bold), depending on the criterion of Unity (relation to a previous mention). Note that all past tense inflections contain a first person agreement marker:

(9) ze   haya   davar shel ma bexax   bishvil   yalda   o
    It   was   nothing   for   (a) girl or

    isha   le+heanes.   ani acmi   neenasti,   kshe
    (a)woman to get raped   I   myself was raped-1st.sg, when

    Ø hayiti   bat-shtem-esre.   Ima   af paam lo   yadaa, u-
    [I] was-1st.sg twelve-years-old. Mama never (not)   knew, and

    Ø meolam lo   siparti   le- ish.   (Noga 1985).
    [I] never (not) told-1st.sg (to) anybody.

(10) Hu   pashut   himshix   le-nasot le-alec   oti   la-cet
     He   just   kept   trying   to make   me   (to)go

     ito,   ve-lifamim,   mi-tox   herged, ani xoshevet,
     with-him,   and sometimes, out of   habit,   I   guess-fem sg,

     Ø   halaxti   ito.   gufi   asa   ma   she-
     [I] went-1st.sg with-him.   My-body   did   what   (that) [it]

shulam she-yaase.   ve-   ima   meta. ve-   **ani**
was-being-paid to do. And   Mother died And   I

haragti   et   buba.
killed-1st.sg acc.   Bubba (*Noga* 1985).

While in both examples the speaker is the continuing discourse topic and
the mother is an intervening local topic, in (10) the return to the speaker as
the discourse topic comes after a much less cohesive clause (the mother's
death). Hence the choice of an overt first person pronoun in (10) but zero
pronoun in (9).

As noted above, Bybee (1985) argued that it is surprising that although
persons are not so crucially relevant to the events depicted by verbs, 56% of
the languages she examined marked persons on their verbs. It seems that
person marking is more prevalent than tense marking (50% of the languages), though not more than tense and aspect taken together. According to
Accessibility Theory, the motivation behind verbal person markers is not
the same as that behind tense and aspect marking. It is possibly accidental
that persons are marked on verbs. The motivation is based on high referent
accessibility plus phonological processes, encouraging reduced forms to be
bound to free forms. Indeed, although most languages cliticize their pronouns to verbs (Dixon 1979), some attach them to something other than the
verb: e.g., a few Pama-Nyungan languages, according to Mithun (1986b). In
Ngiyambaa, the bound clitics are attached to the first sentential constitu-
ent—see Dixon (1980). In Serbian/Croatian, clitic pronouns occupy second
sentence position, in some Iranian languages cliticized pronouns attach to
various sentential elements (Croft 1990, p.c.), and in my Hebrew data, innovative reduced pronouns were not always adjacent to the verb (see (7)
above). In other words, reduction, as well as cliticization, is independent of
the creation of an inflectional paradigm, although it is a necessary pre-
condition for it.

The next step which must be satisfied for a specifically verbal inflectional paradigm to develop is for the verb and the controlling argument to be
adjacent (so they can fuse). This can be due to the prototypical subject (or
absolutive) verb ordering, or to the special position allocated for clitics (see
the mechanism of verbal attraction, as discussed by Heine and Reh 1984 and

Lambrecht 1994). That verbal agreement typically develops for core arguments (subjects, objects; agents, patients; ergatives, absolutives) may in fact result from the fact that such core arguments tend to be adjacent to their verb.

2.3. Accessibility Theory versus NP Detachment

Logically speaking, it is hard to decide what mechanism better explains the development of person agreement. All the theories in 2.1 and 2.2 adequately motivate the occurrence of the pronoun which later develops into an agreement marker. In fact, however, I think that the three theories account for different kinds of change mechanisms, all of which may well have occurred, but in different languages. In order to see that different mechanisms are involved, we need to see that the stages of development are at least to some extent different, and/or that synchronic restrictions point to different diachronic sources. For example, those dialects mentioned by Haiman 1991 as showing agreement only in inverted constructions clearly attest to the source of inflection development there (interrogatives). I would here like to concentrate on the differences between Accessibility Theory and NP detachment as explanations for the development of inflectional paradigms.

Note that if person verbal markers develop out of free, referential pronouns, rather than copied arguments (the accessibility explanation versus the NP detachment explanation), it is to be expected that such bound pronouns bear a referential function. Speakers should then be reluctant, at the initial stages at least, to refer to the subject entity twice (by an overt subject as well as by a person marker—see Steele 1977 for a similar argument). In those languages where there is some restriction on the cooccurrence of inflection and overt subjects, it is more plausible to assume a change via accessibility, since it can naturally account for why such restrictions exist. On the NP detachment analysis, such a general ban on overt subjects would be highly surprising, since lexical NPs and pronouns referring to them cooccur in Left and Right-dislocated sentences.

Under an NP detachment diachronic development, a more appropriate synchronic restriction would be one where agreement is prohibited for non-topical NPs. If agreement develops in topic-shifting constructions (Left and Right-dislocated sentences), it would only be natural that NPs unsuitable for coding topics should never initially trigger the insertion of the pronoun which later serves as the basis for the cliticization process. Next, where agreement marks all three persons, third person in particular, NP detachment constructions are again the likely source. This derives from the fact that NP detachments are prevalent for third person NPs.[8] Where inflections only mark first/second persons, Accessibility Theory provides the more plausible account. Accessibility Theory predicts that non-participants (third persons) are not as extremely accessible as the speaker and addressee (see (5) above), and do not merit a reduction in coding as do the speaker and addressee. Hence, third persons are predicted to not often be coded by bound pronominal forms (see the discussion in 3.1 below).

We proceed now to examine some synchronic restrictions pointing to either NP detachment or to accessibility historical paths of change. The Colloquial French data (Lambrecht 1980, 1981) point to an NP detachment source. Third person verbs are marked, and verbs of quantified NPs (unsuitable topics) tend not to carry agreement. But my data for the initiation of a new future person inflection in Hebrew (see section 5 below) shows that left and right dislocated NPs are not necessarily involved in the initiation of the new inflectional paradigm. NP dislocations were extremely rare in my data, and none of the innovative reduced pronouns in future tense occurred in NP dislocated constructions. These new future forms are better motivated by Accessibility Theory (see section 5).

According to Accessibility Theory, although the final stage of inflection formation regularly allows full NPs functioning as the subjects of the inflected verbs, in the intermediate stages (which may last quite long), such cooccurrences may be prohibited, since the agreement marker is still perceived as a full-fledged referring expression. A few examples for such restrictions follow, corroborating my hypothesis that accessibility considerations motivate the development of verbal agreement.

According to McCloskey and Hale (1984), in Irish, some but not all person-number combinations have inflected forms. But those which do, require zero subjects, disallowing overt NP subjects. So-called analytic forms (non-inflected verbs) require overt pronouns (or full NPs) as subjects. Moreover, as predicted by Accessibility Theory, synthetic forms (inflected) are typically first or first/second person. Analytic forms are typically third persons. When both analytic+pronoun and synthetic+zero forms are allowed (in specific Connacht dialects), it is restricted to third person. A similar case is Gavião (Andean Equatorial). It too does not use pronominal prefixes when overt NPs occur (Dixon 1994: 47). Chamorro (based on Doron 1987) reflects a later stage, where full NPs are allowed to cooccur with inflected verbs, but pronouns are not. In other words, it seems that inflections have grammaticized and become obligatory, but pronouns are still seen as marking too similar a degree of accessibility to agreement markers, and are thus prohibited. The same holds for Swahili (see Dixon 1979, Corbett 1991: 110-11) and Biblical Hebrew (see Gesenius-Kautzsch-Cowley 1910), where personal pronouns occur only when they are emphatic. In two special present tense paradigms found in Hebrew, which are grammatical borrowings from Aramaic, and hence entered Hebrew relatively late (see Ariel 1998), inflected forms cannot cooccur with overt subjects for the most part (*ani xoshvatni 'I think-first person').

In Ngiyambaa (and in fact in most Australian languages, see Dixon 1980) a sentence can include either a free pronoun or a bound clitic, but not both.[9] In general, those Australian languages which did not develop bound clitics commonly use free pronouns, whereas those that have developed them hardly ever use pronouns. In Venetian and Padovano Italian, third person verbal markers may be missing when a full NP occurs as subject. In some Romantsch dialects preverbal tonic pronouns are in complementary distribution with bound atonic pronouns (see Haiman 1991, who relies on others). Pemon (Cariban) also exhibits a complementary distribution between full NPs, pronouns and pronominal affixes (Jose R. Alvarez p.c.). Allen (1995) claims the same pattern for Inuktitut (an Eskimo-Aleut language): Overt first/second person pronouns occur only for extreme emphasis.

Hebrew allows zero with verbs inflected for person, but does not force it. In other words, both full NPs and pronouns can cooccur with inflected verbs. However, where verbs are not inflected for person (as in present tense) an overt subject is (almost) always required (similar to a typical non zero-subject language such as English). Moreover, as argued in Ariel (1990), although Modern Colloquial Hebrew does not absolutely ban the cooccurrence of overt subjects with inflected verbs (first and second person past and future tenses), past tense verbs are routinely accompanied by zero subjects and not by overt pronouns (82.5% in natural conversation, 89.2% in written discourse). Similar findings hold for the future tense in written (but not conversational) Hebrew: 76.5% of future inflected verbs in my data had no overt subject (for data sources see Ariel 1990). In other words, although grammatically acceptable, sentences containing person-marked verbs overwhelmingly tend not to have overt subject pronouns, which means that there is at least a discoursal if not grammatical complementary distribution between verbal person markers and overt pronouns (though not with full NPs).

Hebrew is quite typical in this respect (Gilligan 1987: 164-5 also mentions São Tomé Creole, Pashto and Ecuadorian Quechua). In fact, all so-called pro-drop phenomena were initially linked to rich person inflection (Taraldsen 1980, Rizzi 1982, Chomsky 1982, Gilligan 1987, Comrie 1988, and see Jespersen 1937, Benveniste 1971 and Givón 1976 for earlier suggestions in this spirit). Gilligan (1987), a cross-linguistic study of 100 languages, found that 93% allow zero subjects. Of these, 81.7% (76 languages) have inflected verbs, and only 18.3% (17 languages) allow zero subjects without person marking. Only two languages show agreement but no zero subjects.

Such facts point to an accessibility source for the development of inflection, since only Accessibility Theory, which treats agreement markers as referential (in varying degrees), can motivate the restrictions on the cooccurrence of pronouns and agreement markers. However, I wish to emphasize that different inflectional paradigms may result from differently motivated mechanisms. Specifically, NP detachments lead to (overt) third person agreement primarily, and Accessibility Theory motivates (overt) first/second person agreement primarily. The latter, however, is the universally predominant inflectional pattern.

3. The Accessibility Account for the Prevalent Person Agreement Pattern

3.1. The Speaker, the Present and the Concealed One: Prototypical Accessibility Differences between First/Second and Third Person Referents

It is a well-known fact that overt verbal inflections are more common for first and second persons than for third person. In fact, Benveniste (1971) claimed that the Indo-European person inflections for all three persons is the exception (see also Givón 1976), and that third person agreement should be seen as having developed for symmetry only. He mentions Turkish, and American Indian and Semitic languages as languages marking first and second persons on verbs but not third persons. (See also Huehnergard 1987,

Moscati et al. 1969, Haiman 1985, Mithun 1986b, 1988, 1989, 1991, Dixon 1979, Munro 1974, Croft 1987, Helmbrecht 1995a, Du Bois 1987a). In a statistical study, Bybee (1985) found that whereas 54% of the languages which manifested agreement did not mark third person on the verb, only 14% did not mark first person.

Even if they exist, third person agreement markers may have distinctive marking and change patterns from first/second persons. Moravcsik (1978) mentions the Athapascan languages, where different tones apply to first/second versus third person. Foley and Van Valin (1984) note that whereas first and second person verbal affixes are prefixes in Plains Cree (Algonquian), third person verbal markers are suffixal. Mithun (1991) argues that historically, not all inflections arise uniformly: "Among persons, first and second person pronouns often become bound before third" (102). Synchronically they may then occupy different positions within the verb (e.g., prefixes versus suffixes), number may be marked differently and/or earlier for first/second persons than for third person, third person may be inflected only for non-specifics, or it may not be marked at all. In fact, as argued by Watkins (1962) for Celtic languages and by Bybee (1985) for Modern Provençal dialects, even when languages do have third person verbal inflections, these sometimes tend to be reanalyzed as part of the stem or another morphological marking (the preterite in the latter case), at least synchronically. It seems that there is pressure to view third person verbs as not including a person marker, even if they originally did.

Now, a possible explanation for the difference in inflectional patterns for first/second persons and for third persons is the general asymmetry between the three persons, conceptually, and in the way they are coded in the languages of the world. Benveniste (1971), and following him generative grammarians, distinguished between first and second person pronouns on the one hand, which they classified as deictic, and third person pronouns on the other hand, which were considered anaphoric (see also Bergsträsser 1928/1983, Chafe 1976, and Anderson and Keenan 1985). Indeed, the Hebrew grammarians' terms for the three persons are quite telling in this respect: first person is the 'speaker,' second person is the one 'present' and third person is the 'concealed' one. The same difference can explain why first/second person reflexives can (marginally) refer extra-linguistically, even in languages where third person reflexives require a linguistic (c-commanding) antecedent (a difference first noted by Ross 1970). In fact, many of the world's languages do not even have forms that are strictly speaking third person personal pronouns. Instead, they use the general demonstrative pronoun for such references (Steele 1977, Greenberg 1978, Dixon 1980, Comrie 1981, Mithun 1989, 1991, Allen 1995). Helmbrecht (1995b) mentions Lak in this connection, and Udi (where in fact the third person verbal marker has developed out of a demonstrative pronoun). Split ergativity systems often distinguish between first/second persons and third persons (Dixon 1979, DeLancey 1981). These differences are clearly related to the different discourse roles played by the three persons, with the first and the second referring to actual participants in the speech event, and the third specifically marked as not participating in the discourse (see Hockett 1966, Benveniste 1971, Silverstein 1976 and Lyons 1977, inter alia). As Lyons (1977: 638-9) says: "That there is a fundamental, and ineradicable, difference between first-person and second-person pronouns, on the one hand, and third-person pronouns, on the other, is a point that cannot be emphasized too strongly."

More recently, researchers have preferred to analyze the differences between the two speech act participants and the non-participant third person in terms of the higher salience/referentiality/animacy of the former. Such researchers were trying to define scales of NP prominence of various sorts, distinguishing between definite and indefinite NPs, subjects and objects, animates and inanimates, etc., in order to account for case marking, for example. In such frameworks, a person hierarchy emerged, since first and second persons are more prominent in that they are more likely to form the topic of the sentence (Silverstein 1976, Kuno 1976, Givón 1976, Hawkinson and Hyman 1976, Dixon 1979, 1980, Comrie 1981, 1986, and Mallinson and Blake 1982, as cited in Jelinek 1984). It is also easier to empathize with the speaker, then with the addressee, and last with a third party, argued Kuno (1976). Givón (1971) noted that whereas both speech act participants are human, third person referents are not necessarily so. They may very well be inanimate.

Following Du Bois (1987b), I suggest that the animacy scales are in this case equivalent to the accessibility scale, and that it is accessibility considerations which provide an adequate account for the prevalent agreement marking, distinguishing between first/second and third persons.

3.2. Empirical Evidence for the Accessibility Account

Let us review some empirical evidence for the very high accessibility coding of first/second person references, as opposed to third person references. Harel (1992) is a collection of taped and published long phone conversations between acquaintances in Hebrew. If we concentrate on the high accessibility pronoun/zero subjects in Harel (1992), we can see how often third person referents are considered accessible enough so as to merit such high accessibility markers. According to Accessibility Theory, it is very high accessibility cases which induce bound person morphemes. Table (1) shows how infrequent third person highly accessible referents are in the data (third persons constitute 22.8% of all referents), as compared with the frequent references to first/second persons by high accessibility markers:[10]

1st Person	2nd Person	3rd Person	Total
367 = 51.3%	255 = 35.7%	93 = 13%	715 = 100%

Table 1. Zero/Pronominal Subjects in Harel (1992)

To see how much more often first and second person referents are taken as **extremely** accessible, compare the percentage of zero subjects each of the three persons contributes in this text:

1st Person	2nd Person	3rd Person	Total
65 = 31.55%	125 = 60.7%	16 = 7.7%	206 = 100%

Table 2. Zero Subjects in Harel (1992)

Note that for Accessibility Theory, it is not really inter-person frequency comparisons that matter. It is the frequency of high accessibility coding per person which is crucial. In other words, we expect many of the first/second person referents, but few of the third person referents, to be extremely accessible, regardless of their absolute frequencies in discourse. Let us now look at a Hebrew single topic journalistic narrative (Levy 1995), where third person references are by far the most frequent (81% of all references). As predicted by Accessibility Theory, it is full NPs that form the majority of third person references: 71.5% (153 instances). Table 3 lists the frequency of zero-subject choices for each of the three persons in Levy (1995), and again there is a gap between first/second persons and third person. Clearly, a much higher proportion of first/second person referents are coded by the highest accessibility marker:

1st Person	2nd Person	3rd Person
14 = 35.9%	9 = 81.8%	29 = 13.5%

Table 3. Zero Subjects in Levy (1995) (percentages calculated out of total numbers of occurrences per person)

Next, consider the data from Lotan (1990), a Hebrew face-to-face conversation. Table 4 presents the data for pronoun and zero (calculated together) for the 3 persons. Even though there are twice as many more third person subjects (100) than first and second person subjects (47 each), the latter's proportions among high accessibility markers is much higher (2.35 times more) than that of third person subjects.

1st Person	2nd Person	3rd Person	Total
47 = 41.2%	47 = 41.2%	20 = 17.5%	114 = 100%

Table 4. Zero/Pronoun Subjects in Lotan (1990)

Concentrating on zeroes versus pronouns only (by ignoring full NPs), we still see a preference for first/second persons to be coded by zeroes more often than third persons. Table 5 presents the actual numbers found Note that whereas for first/second persons these percentages are also the percentages of zeroes out of the total number of references, this is not so for third persons, which are also referred to by full NPs. The percentage of references to third persons by zero out of the total number of references is 4%.

1st Person	2nd Person	3rd Person
19 = 40.4%	20 = 42.5%	4 = 25%

Table 5. Zero Subjects in Lotan (1990) (percentages calculated out of numbers of high accessibility occurrences per person)

These different zero-subject ratios for first/second versus third persons repeat themselves. In interviews and short stories rendered into written Hebrew (*Noga* pieces analyzed in Ariel 1990), third person referents are 3.5 times more likely to be coded by pronouns than by zeroes (counts here do not include lexical NPs). First person referents, on the other hand, are 1.4 more times likely to appear as zeroes than as pronouns. Second person referents are intermediate (1.9 times more pronouns than zeroes). Table 6 presents the relevant data:

	1st Person	2nd Person	3rd Person
Zero	168 = 57.7%	13 = 35%	38 = 22%
Pronoun	123 = 42.3%	24 = 65%	135 = 78%
Total	291 = 100%	37 = 100%	173 = 100%

Table 6. Zero versus Pronoun Choices in Interviews and Short Stories in Hebrew (analyzed in Ariel 1990)

Colloquial Hebrew contains many more overt pronouns than written Hebrew. Although the recording of a conversation between intimates showed that pronouns are now more prevalent for all persons, the person differences are still consistent: first person subjects were 2.45 as likely to occur as pronouns as in zero form. For second person referents the ratio was 1.7 in favor of pronouns, and for third person referents the ratio was 12 times in favor of pronouns (and we should also note that in addition, third persons were often referred to by full NPs, which the first two persons were not).

Third person referents are by default of rather low accessibility. They are not automatically extremely accessible as the speaker and the addressee are. Hence, they require special circumstances to merit pronominal or zero reference. One such special case is being the discourse topic. Indeed, in Ariel

(1990) I showed that of the meager 4.5% of third person pronouns (relatively high accessibility markers) referring to antecedents mentioned in a previous, rather than a current paragraph (low accessibility in terms of distance), 92% referred to the global discourse topic of the text. Topicality, then, renders an entity highly accessible. However, even if we concentrate on the one continuing discourse topic in Levy (1995), which constituted 36.5% of all third person references and over two thirds of the zero/pronoun choices for third persons, the percentage of high accessibility marking is not as high as might be expected: Almost half of the references to the discourse topic employed full NPs. Table 7 lists third person expressions referring to the one human discourse topic in Levy (1995):

Full NP	Pronoun	Zero	Total
31 = 45.6%	17 = 25%	20 = 29.4%	68 = 100%

Table 7. Third Person References to the Global Discourse Topic (Levy 1995)

These discourse data are echoed by similar observations re third versus first/second person references in other languages. Jelinek and Demers (1994), who discuss languages of the Northwest coast of North America, observe—just like Mithun (1991)—that although third persons are usually zero-marked on the verbs, third persons are not really zero-marked in discourse: "The 3sg. deictic element has important discourse uses. It appears frequently in narratives to mark continuity of reference and sequential action across clauses" (715). Furthermore, a set of demonstrative particles that are neither arguments nor predicates serve to mark a contrastive reference. These are limited to third persons, and appear as adjuncts, thus "compensating" for the zero marked verb. Malotki (1982) argues that while Hopi has no person inflection, it has only first and second person pronouns. The third person counterpart is a demonstrative pronoun. Similarly, Allen (1995) found an asymmetry between first/second person zero subjects and third person zero subjects in Inuktitut. Even in agent role, where referents are most often Given (and hence, an overt NP occurred only in 1% of the cases overall), third person arguments were overt rather than zero in 41% of the cases (though third person subjects were relatively marginal). What is constant in all these findings is that third persons are consistently coded by relatively lower accessibility markers. The actual differences in coding do vary (deictic/demonstrative particles vs. pronouns/agreement; demonstrative vs. personal pronouns; overt vs. zero subjects), but the overall principle remains, linking the less accessible third person references with relatively lower accessibility marking.

The difference in degree of accessibility between first/second and third person referents explains why in many languages there is a difference in zero-subject options according to persons, allowing first and second person zeroes much more freely. Such a distinction is predicted by Accessibility Theory, since the speaker and the addressee, who are prototypically more accessible than third person referents, should be referred to by using higher, less informative forms of accessibility markers. Zeroes are obviously the least informative forms. Such differences among the persons have been noted for Finnish, for example.[11] Andrews (1993) finds that in South-Western Otomí, whereas first and second person prefixes and suffixes (more attenuated forms) on predicative nominals distinguish dual and plural, pronouns (less attenuated forms) must be used for third person referents. Cohen (1995) notes this for spoken Latin (as reflected in Plautus' *Psudolus*). Grammarians have assumed that English does not allow zero subjects, but many have argued against this accepted wisdom (as witnessed by a vibrant e-mail testimony to that effect on The Linguist list in February 1993). In any case, it is quite clear that although English zero subjects are limited to main clauses, and although initial auxiliaries tend to be omitted as well, zeroes are quite severely restricted to first and second persons (e.g. *don't know/picked him up, did you?*). Philips and Reynolds (1987), who examined prospective jurors' responses, found that subject deletion "occurs far more often with first-person singular pronouns" (77). The prospective jurors simply did not use second person subjects, but although they did refer to third persons, they did not use zero subjects there. However, *you* as subject was frequently dropped in judges' courtroom language use (Philips 1984).

Ixil (a Mayan language) also tends to use zeroes for first and second persons, but not for third persons.[12] In fact, the common zero references for second persons in imperatives (see Sadock and Zwicky 1985, Gilligan 1987) can also be cited in favor of the thesis connecting zeroes and salience. According to Accessibility Theory, the referent in this case is predictable, given the nature of the action depicted by the verb (a plausible action to be requested or demanded from an addressee) and the salience of the addressee

(Thrashner 1974). In other words, the identity of first and second person referents (but not third person referents) can often be deduced much more easily. They should then be coded by higher accessibility markers—zero versus overt pronouns in the cases mentioned here.[13] I suggest that a similar though less extreme coding difference between first/second and third person referents is reference by a full pronoun (for third persons) versus reference by an agreement marker (for first/second persons). The more reduced forms are invariably reserved for the more highly accessible referents.

The general finding is then that first and second person referents are consistently highly accessible, but third person referents are only extremely accessible when they happen to be the continuing discourse topic(s). Even so, many other third person entities are mentioned in the same discourses, causing great variability in degree of accessibility for third person referents. Thus, there is nearly a 100% correlation between first/second person and extremely high accessibility. Not only do first person markers (pronominal, agreement or zero) refer to the speaker (at least partially for plural references), these references are also made to the discourse topic in many cases (in Levy 1995, 31—79.5%—out of the 39 first person uses refer to the discourse topic, although the writer-narrator is not the discourse topic). On the average, only 25.7%-50.9% (depending on the text) of third person subject referents are perceived to be highly salient (as judged by zero/pronoun choices). This means that whereas the degree of accessibility associated with third persons varies greatly within and across texts, this is not so with respect to first/second person references. **Extremely** high accessibility, the relevant factor for the accessibility account, remains constant for first and second persons across **all** texts.

4. Alternative Accounts for the Person Agreement Pattern

Even though I have presented evidence that accessibility theory can indeed account for the prevalent verbal person agreement favoring overt marking for first/second persons and zero marking for third persons, we should examine other theories which can potentially account for these data: a typological markedness account (4.1), and a frequency-driven morphologization account (4.3). Based on textual counts, I will argue against each of them (4.2, 4.4 respectively). I should stress, however, that I am only arguing against these theories as accounting for the prevalent marking differential. Not only are these theories functional in other linguistic changes, they can actually motivate other, marginal person verbal agreement patterns (see Ariel 1998, and see also Section 8 below).

4.1. Typological Markedness: Third Person Verbs are Unmarked, First/Second Person Verbs are Marked

A possible explanation for the universal finding that third person verbs are commonly marked by zero, as opposed to the overt person markers signalling first and second persons, can be offered on the basis of markedness distinctions between the persons. An explanation relying on markedness was the explanation adopted by most researchers (see Greenberg 1966, Kurylowicz 1968, Givón 1976, Moravcsik 1978, 1987, Dixon 1979, Bybee 1985, 1988, Lapointe 1987), and is the one presented in typological textbooks (e.g., Croft 1990, Mathews 1991, Hopper and Traugott 1993). As Bybee (1985: 135) put it: "Zero marking... tends to occur on the most frequent and less conceptually marked items." In fact, the non-markedness of third persons is mostly seen to derive from their high frequency in texts. Such theories assume that "grammars code best what speakers do most" (Du Bois 1985: 363). Since frequently used forms tend to be short, third person references and/or third person verbal forms, assumed to be the most frequent, should be shortest, and often zeroes. This explanation is particularly suitable for those who argue for an NP detachment source for agreement development, since they cannot otherwise motivate why it is first/second persons which are marked whereas third person is zero marked, when it is precisely third person which commonly occurs in NP detachment constructions.

Note that typological markedness cannot itself motivate the recurrent pattern of zero marking for third person verbal agreement (as "virgin zeroes"). It needs to rely on another hypothesis which would explain why a language should develop any inflectional paradigm where persons are marked on verbs in the first place. A possible reason is that verbs need to be related to subjects (minimally), and agreement signals the grammatical relation of predicate-argument. Now, there is, of course, no reason why predicate-argument relations need to be overtly specified for first/second persons, but not for third persons. If such a marking is functional, it is equally functional for all persons. The predication marking function of agreement seems to better motivate inflectional paradigms where **all** three persons are marked on the verb (at least originally—see Ariel 1998). The typological markedness account, then, has to posit not only predicate-argument marking of all persons, but also a later stage in which a reduction of only the third person marker occurs (so-called non virgin zeroes, see Croft 1990), as a result of the relative high frequency of third person verbal forms.

Note, however, that inflections do not always show a marking that is only sensitive to persons, but rather to the specific gender and number within the person, distinguishing between 'you-masculine-singular,' 'you feminine singular,' 'you masculine plural,' 'you feminine-plural'. If so, then typological markedness would have to assume that each variant of third person verbs (including 'they-feminine' where available, for example) is more frequent than each first/second person verbal forms. The relevant data for this is presented in 4.4 (see (15) and Table 14), which makes it clear that at least some third person verbal forms are not at all frequent (e.g., third person feminine-singular). In 4.2 I will ignore this problem, and assume that the pre-agreement stage includes only three basic pronouns, each specialized for one person, perhaps with additional morphemes for gender and number (similar to the pronominal Chinese system). I will then argue that a serious problem for typological markedness is that not all frequency counts show third person verbal forms to be the most frequent verbal forms in discourse (4.2). I will therefore conclude that typological markedness is not necessarily responsible for the prototypical agreement paradigm.

4.2. Empirical Evidence against Typological Markedness: Inconsistent Frequency Counts

"Zero marking... tends to occur on the most frequent and less conceptually marked items" (Bybee 1985: 135). Greenberg (1966) had originally argued for a frequency-markedness correlation, with Zipf's (1935) law motivating this correlation "economically" (and see also Haiman 1983). Indeed, previous frequency studies found a difference in the frequency of occurrence of first, second and third person verbal forms. Bybee (1985) quotes Juilland and Chang-Rodríguez' (1964) findings for written Spanish and Rodríguez Bou's (1952) findings for spoken Spanish. Between 41% and 51% of all verbs (depending on the specific tense and genre) are third person singular, between 22%-31% are first person singular, and only between 4% and 16% are second person singular. Philips and Reynolds (1987) also state that third and first person verbs are the most common in their data (prospective jurors answering lawyers' questions). Such data corroborate the typological marking claim, even though they cannot really explain the close affinity between first and second person marking, when in terms of frequency, first and third persons are much more similar to each other.

Let us now check a few more texts. What I found was that different genres show different person ratios (although one would need to examine larger quantities of text in order to establish a secure correlation between genre and relative person frequencies). In Levy (1995), the narrative about a single human topic, the findings are even more extreme than those for Spanish. There are 4.75 times as many third person verbs as first and second person taken together, as shown in Table 8:

	No. of occurrences	% of occurrence
1st person:	39	14.8%
2nd person:	11	4.2%
3rd person:	214	81%
Total:	264	100%

Table 8. Frequency of Verbs According to Person in Levy (1995)

Third person verbs seem to be the most common ones, then, motivating the shortness of the verbal forms for third persons. The markedness scale predicted from such findings (if obtained on a larger scale) is presented in (11), and it perfectly fits the prevalent person agreement marking pattern (scales here and hereafter are proportional to the percentages of occurrence in the cited texts):

```
                         3rd        1st         2nd
(11) Least marked  <---------------------------------> Most marked
```

The next text I examined, Morris (1994), is a collection of slightly edited American English personal stories. Unlike the third person narrative, here first and third person verbs are equally frequent:

	No. of occurrences	% of occurrence
1st person:	224	45.6%
2nd person:	45	9.2%
3rd person:	222	45.2
Total:	491	100%

Table 9. Frequency of Verbs According to Person in Morris (1994)

Note that such findings (if obtained on a larger scale) would predict the following marking scale, which is different from the scale resulting from the previous text:

```
                    1st/3rd                2nd
(12) Least marked  <----------------------------------> Most marked
```

It predicts that inflection in second person should be most frequent, while there should be no person inflections for both first and third person. This is obviously not true. Alternatively, if zero marking is assigned to only one category, which is at least as frequent as the next one, zero marking should have been assigned to **either** first **or** third person verbal forms. This would imply that on the basis of such texts, first and third person zero marking would have been equally prevalent in the languages of the world. This is definitely not the case. Of course, the data as such do not contradict typological markedness, because the thesis is formulated in its weak version, namely that the least formally marked form is of greater or equal frequency as a more marked form. But they certainly do not lend it substantial support.

A third discourse, the face-to-face Hebrew conversation (Lotan 1990), shows no difference in the frequency of first, second and third person verbal forms (the differences here are not statistically significant):

	No.	Percentage
1st Person	47	32.4%
2nd Person	45	31.0%
3rd Person	53	36.5%
Total	145	99.9%

Table 10. Frequency of Verbs According to Persons in Lotan (1990)

According to these conversational data (if obtained on a larger scale), either all or none of the persons should have been zero marked on the verb. Again, due to the weak formulation of the typological markedness thesis, these findings do not constitute a counter-example to typological markedness, but they predict that person verbal markings/zeroes would be equally distributed among the three persons in the languages of the world. This is obviously false.

A fourth source I checked for the distribution of the three persons reveals a fourth pattern. Table 11 presents the number of verbs for each of the persons used in children's free conversations among themselves (on three separate occasions, February 2, 7, 9 1996, children's ages 7:5, 7:3, 5:8 and 5:6). The data is limited to all and only future tense verbs (exclusive of those used as imperatives), since it was conducted for a specific purpose (see section 5 below):

1st Person	2nd Person	3rd Person	Total
51 = 56.7%	11 = 12.2%	28 = 31.1%	90 = 100%

Table 11. Frequency of Future Tense Verbs According to Person in Children's Hebrew Conversations

Such findings (if obtained on a larger scale) would correlate with the following markedness scale, which does constitute a counter-example to the predictions made by typological markedness (see scale 11 above). It predicts that if only one person is zero marked on the verb, it would be first person:

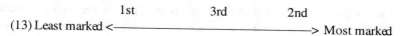

                            1st   3rd   2nd
    (13) Least marked <————————————————————————————> Most marked

A fifth text I studied was Harel (1992). The findings are presented in Table 12:

	No. of occurrences	% of occurrences
1st person:	370	45.7
2nd person:	255	31.5
3rd person:	185	22.8
Total:	810	100.0

Table 12. Frequency of Verbs According to Person in Harel (1992)

The formal markedness predicted from such relative frequencies (if obtained on a larger scale) is the symmetric scale in (14) (note that second person is 1.4 times more frequent than third person, and first person is 1.45 times more frequent than second person):

                            1st   2nd   3rd
    (14) Least marked <————————————————————————————> Most marked

This too is an unequivocal counter-example for typological markedness re verbal agreement. It predicts zero first person marking as opposed to overt marking for second and third persons, a pattern which is not attested, as far as I know.

The findings presented in Tables 8-12 have quite inconsistent results for the typological markedness explanations. Levy (1995) seems to support the non-markedness of third person verbal forms, since these are the most frequent verbal forms there. Morris (1994) and Lotan (1990) are consistent with it only because typological markedness is formulated in its weak version. The children's data and Harel (1992) clearly refute the assumption that third person verbal forms are unmarked in terms of verb form frequency.

Du Bois (1987b), who notes that genres differ significantly in the functional pressures they impose on the speaker (he specifically mentions narratives versus conversations and first versus third person narratives), concludes that for argument structure, it is narratives which are the better source for teasing out discourse strategies used for smooth information flow. Greenberg (1966: 45) notes that narratives would have many more third person references, and suggests conversations for the study of person. The following quote from Croft (1990: 87) emphasizes the need to consider oral data for markedness research:

> Generally, one attempts to use the "unmarked" text style, that is conversation or oral narrative, rather than written genres. One reason for doing this is that studies... have indicated that the textual frequencies for certain "marked" categories increase in formal written styles, and hence, they are not such reliable indicators of correlations between text frequency and other markedness criteria. (Actually, what this really indicates is that there is a correlation between informal, oral style and some, if not all, unmarked categories).

Milroy (1992: 5) in effect agrees with Croft, especially regarding the appropriate source for analyzing linguistic change:

> it is in spoken, rather than in written, language that we are able to detect structural and phonetic changes in their early stages.

Milroy (1992) emphasizes that conversational data specifically is superior to other oral genres, if linguistic change is the object of inquiry:

> it is typically in the day-to-day situational context of speaker interaction that structural changes take place, and it is in these contexts that they have to be investigated (Milroy 1992: 32).

In conversation, Milroy argues, speakers do not mind so much if a linguistic change they are making causes some vagueness or ambiguity. They know that their messages contain many redundancies anyway, their addressees can rely on freely available contextual cues, and they can always stop them and ask for some clarification. This is particularly relevant for the change at hand, which reduces forms (pronouns) and makes them more opaque.

Hence, it seems that Harel (1992), Lotan (1990) and the children's data are the appropriate texts for examining linguistic change. These conversational data do not support the typological markedness proposal. But then, the Spanish findings for spoken discourse were quite different, and supportive of the typological markedness proposal. I therefore suggest we draw the conclusion that texts drastically vary in the frequency of their verbal forms according to person. (Note that the number of patterns of distribution equals the number of sources I checked). Thus, while I do not wish to argue that first/second person are always more frequent than third persons, I think that the findings in 4.2 argue against assuming that all in all third person is by far the most frequent person in verbs. If third person cannot be shown to be consistently the most frequent verbal form, the typological marking account fails, since it crucially relies on third person verbal forms being the most frequent ones in change-initiating discourses.

4.3 Frequency-driven Morphologization

For typological markedness we have concentrated on third persons **verbal** forms. However, we can try and account for the differential verbal markings by focussing on the overt **first/second** person **markings**. Instead of explaining the zero marking on third person verbal forms, one can motivate the overt markings on first and second persons (see Bybee et al. 1990), i.e., the fusion of first and second person pronouns, but not third person pronouns, with verbal forms. It is only reasonable that "... in order for a gram to fuse with a stem it must occur contiguous to the stem with sufficient frequency and be in the same phonological phrase or intonation unit as the stem" (Bybee et al. 1990: 29, and see Givón 1971). This resembles the accessibility account. But note that the accessibility account is oblivious to whether first/second person pronoun-verb pairs are less, equally or more frequent than third person-verb pairs. All it relies upon is that the proportion of referents of extremely high accessibility is higher for first/second person than for third person referents. For the frequency-driven morphologization account, pronoun-verb pairs are directly compared across the three persons, and the most frequent one(s) are expected to encourage inflection formation.

For the frequency-driven morphologization account to work, all we need assume is a high frequency of first/second person **pronoun**-verb adjacent cooccurrences, as opposed to a low frequency of third person pronoun-verb cooccurrences. In other words, one can claim that regardless of whether third person verbal forms in general are or are not the most frequent, when it comes to pronominal references, perhaps first/second persons predominate, and hence the tendency to reduce first/second person pronouns to agreement markers (see Croft 1990: 80). Indeed, I think such an assumption can perhaps explain why certain Hebrew cognition verbs have an agreement marker only for first person in present tense, although Hebrew present tense does not usually have any person agreement (see Ariel 1998). For the predominant agreement pattern, the explanation could argue roughly as follows (William Croft p.c.): Accessibility considerations explain why the prototypically less accessible third person referents are mostly referred to by overt NPs, whereas the consistently highly accessible first/second person referents are referred to by pronouns. The rest takes place automatically, due to the high frequency of the cooccurrence of first/second person pronouns with verbs, as opposed to a relatively lower counterpart cooccurrence for third person pronouns.

4.4 Empirical Evidence against Frequency-driven Morphologization: Inconsistent Frequencies of First/Second versus Third Person Pronoun-Verb Cooccurrences

The frequency-driven morphologization explanation is based on direct and absolute inter-person frequency comparisons. It is the high frequency of the cooccurrence of subject pronouns next to verbs which should govern the formation of overt agreement markers. Thus, absolute numbers of references to highly accessible antecedents should be compared (because they are the ones which would be coded by pronouns in the pre-agreement stage). Since my data come from Hebrew and English, subject pronouns will be the high accessibility markers counted for English, and both pronouns and zeroes will be counted for Hebrew. Once we compare these ratios, however, it is again not clear why it is third person verbs which are consistently unmarked for person. In other words, it is not invariably the case that first/second subject pronouns (and zeroes) outnumber third person subject pronouns (and zeroes).

For instance, in Harel (1992) (the Hebrew phone conversations between acquaintances), there are 3.95 times as many first person and 2.75 second person zero/pronoun subject references as there are third person zero/pronoun references (for actual data see Tables 1, 2). Such findings seem to support the frequency-driven morphologization hypothesis regarding the creation of agreement markers for first/second persons. However, in Levy (1995) (the Hebrew narrative), there are more third person high accessibility references adjacent to verbs (1.4 times more than first person, 5 times more than second person). This would predict third/first overt marking versus zero marking for second person. Yet another pattern emerges from the children's data of future tense. There are over 4 times as many first person zero/pronouns as there are second and third person zero/pronouns. While these findings may indeed motivate first person agreement marking, there is an equal number of second (10) and third (9) person zero/pronouns. These two should then be predicted to be zero marked. Needless to say, none of these predictions are borne out.

Similar numbers characterize the ratio of subject pronominal references in the Hebrew interviews and short stories presented in Table 6 above and in the English personal narrative (Morris 1994). In the interviews and short stories, there is hardly a difference between third and first person pronoun-verb combinations (1.09 times more third person), but there is a large gap between these two and second person pronoun-verb combinations (5.1 times more first persons, 5.6 times more third persons). This means that according to the Hebrew interviews and short stories, as well as Levy (1995), it should have been first and third person pronouns which should have cliticized onto the verbs in a zero-subject language. But a language without zero subjects (where I count both zeroes and pronouns) is the more plausible origin for agreement creation. Counting this way, although there are more first than third person zero/pronoun references in the short stories and interviews (1.7 times more—see the data in Table 6), the gap between third and second person zero/pronoun references is significantly larger (4.7 times more third person zero/pronouns). Hence, again one would expect first and third person pronouns to have developed into agreement markers rather than first and second person references.

In Morris (1994) there are almost 2 first person subject pronouns per one third person subject pronoun, but about 2.7 third person subject pronouns per one second person subject pronoun. Similarly, in Huebner's (1983) data on the acquisition of the English pronominal system by an adult (as a second language), while there are 1.66 more first than third person pronouns (as expected), there are twice as many third person pronouns as there are second person pronouns (an unexpected finding). Agreement should have then developed for both first and third persons, not for first and second persons (the gap between which is 5.3 in Morris, 3.33 in Huebner). The data for Huebner (1983)(mostly narratives, some dialogues) are presented in Table 13:

1st Person	2nd Person	3rd Person	Total
1777 = 52.6%	533 = 15.8%	1070 = 31.6%	3380 = 100%

Table 13. Frequency of Subject Pronouns According to Person in Huebner (1983)

I have not analyzed the data on persons according to number and gender in the data presented so far. But this is relevant for languages where each agreement marker corresponds to a specific free pronoun, as is the case in Hebrew. I believe it sheds light on other languages as well. Note that the second person feminine verbal forms are not just the masculine forms + some feminine gender marker, although this is the common Hebrew pattern elsewhere. Rather, they are directly derived from the free feminine pronoun (*at* –> *t, aten* –> *ten* 'you-fem-sg/pl,' just like the masculine forms are: *ata* –> *ta, atem* –> *tem* 'you-masc-sg/pl'). There is no way to derive the feminine forms here from the masculine ones, for the regular Hebrew feminine markers added are *a, at*, or *et* (and never *a* deletion, as in the singular form here, or *m* –> *n*, as in the plural forms). In other words, I believe that collapsing verbal or pronominal forms into three groups (the three persons) distorts the picture, where plural and feminine references are of quite low frequencies. If fusion results from adjacency, then we should consider actual adjacent forms, rather than the abstract category "person." And actual adjacent forms are different within the same person category (cf. *he, she, it*).

Looking at Morris (1994), it would seem that an English-style language developing inflection would need to skip a few positions if it were to develop the common first/second person agreement pattern:

(15) I: 197 > they: 50 > he: 45 > you: 42 > we: 24 > it: 14 > she: 3.

It is the first, fourth and fifth positions on the frequency scale above which routinely develop person agreement markers on verbs. They are not, however, the most common pronouns. Third person *they* and *he* are more frequent than *you* and *we*.[14]

Table 14 presents the frequency of subject pronouns and zeroes according to person, gender and number in Levy (1995) and Harel (1992):

Levy (1995)		Harel (1992)	
	Least frequent		
Y-fm-sg/Y-fm-pl/Y-ms-pl	0	**Y-fm-sg/Y-fm-pl**/They-fm	0
She/They-fem	2	She	9
Y-msc-sg/**They-ms**	11	Y-pl-ms	21
I	15	We	26
We	24	**They-ms**	27
He	45	**He**	67
Y-ms-sg	234	I	341
	Most frequent		

Table 14. Frequency of Zero/Pronouns in Levy (1995) and Harel (1992) (Y = 'you,' persons in bold = out of their "proper" place in the frequency hierarchy).

If we assume that agreement markers arise simply because of high cooccurrence frequencies of specific subject pronouns, but not others, with verbs, then it is not at all clear why feminine agreement ever arises. Note that all feminine subjects are invariably in the least frequent categories, often with no occurrences at all. Ignoring Levy (1995), where the most common subject is 'he' with 'we' following, consider the conversational data from Harel (1992), which initially seemed to constitute a more reasonable source for the unmarked inflectional paradigms according to the frequency-driven morphologization proposal. Note that agreement indeed develops for 'I' and 'you-msc-sg,' which top the list, but it then ignores the more frequent 'he' and 'they-msc,' and develops for 'we' and 'you-pl-msc'. It then hops over 'she,' but does develop for 'you-sg-fem' and 'you-pl-fem,' skipping 'they-fem,' which shares their very low frequency. In Huebner's (1983) data, whereas 'I' is the most frequent pronoun, 'he' is equally frequent as 'you'. 'They' is twice as frequent as 'we,' which in turn is only slightly more frequent than 'she' (1.16 times more).

A frequency count for Latin pronouns is quoted in Greenberg (1966: 35). Whereas 'I' and 'you-sg' are indeed by far the most common pronouns, third person singular *is* is about 5 times more frequent than 'we,' and 7.65 times more frequent than 'you-pl'. Nonetheless, as we know, agreement tends to develop for 'we' and 'you-pl' much more often. In the data from Spanish quoted by Bybee (1985) (and mentioned above), second person plural forms do not occur at all in the spoken data, nor in the preterite of the written data. They constitute 1% of present indicatives in the written data. In the Lorge magazine English pronoun count quoted in Greenberg (1966: 35-6), *he* and *it* each considerably outnumber *we* (2.75 and 2.9 times more respectively).

Finally, note that although it is only common-sensical that typological marking and frequency-driven morphologization should complement each other, the findings in 4.2 and 4.4 have quite the opposite results for the two kinds of explanations (regarding virgin and non-virgin zeroes). Levy (1995) seems to support the **non**-markedness of third person verbal forms (only if genders and numbers are calculated together), since they are the most frequent verbal forms. It nonetheless manifests a frequent third person **pronoun**-verb cooccurrence, which would support the grammaticization of third rather than first/second person agreement marking through frequent adjacency of pronouns and verbs. Thus, based on Levy (1995), one theory predicts zero third person marking, while the other predicts overt third person marking. The data from Harel (1992), on the other hand, argue against the assumption that third person verbal forms are unmarked in terms of verb form frequency (they should therefore be marked morphologically), but it is nonetheless somewhat compatible with assuming that agreement arises simply due to the frequent cooccurrence of certain but not other pronouns (first/second versus third person) with verbal forms (third person verbs should then be zero marked).

Thus, it seems that accounting for the differential verbal markings by contrasting first/second with third person **pronouns** (the frequency-driven morphologization account) fares no better than accounting for it by counting first/second versus third person **verbs** (the typological markedness account). Each of the accounts seems to gain support from some textual counts, but is refuted by others. The Accessibility Theory account is the only one which is supported by **all** the textual counts. This is so because Accessibility Theory argues that verbal person inflections (deriving from free pronouns) develop in response to form-function coding considerations encouraging an appropriate fit between highly accessible referents and highly uninformative, non-rigid, and short forms (cliticized pronouns, agreement markers and zeroes—see Ariel 1985 and onwards for evidence supporting this claim). Reduction (possibly followed by cliticization and fusion) of pronouns should occur only when referents are extremely accessible. We have seen typical examples of this general phenomenon in 2.2 above (and see Ariel 1990, 1991, 1996 for many more examples), and specifically for first/second versus third person referents in 3.1 above.

Accessibility Theory can then provide an adequate explanation for the common differences in person verbal markings: first and second person referents are more accessible than third person referents (other things being equal). Hence, in some languages, first/second person references are codable by pronouns, whereas third persons are coded by demonstrative pronouns only (lower accessibility markers); in many languages zero subjects are freer for first/second persons; and in yet others, pronouns referring to first/second persons are more prone to undergo a process of de-stressing and reduction, which may later lead to cliticization and finally fusion with the verb, a state we identify as full-fledged agreement. I suggest that the grammaticization process initiated for the speech act participants is prevalent because they are **consistently** of high salience, rather than consistently high frequency. Third person referents are extremely salient only when they are the continuing discourse topic (but see Table 7 above). On other occasions they are quite inaccessible, certainly in comparison to the speaker and the addressee. There is thus no consistently high degree of accessibility associated with third person references.

5. Hebrew Future Tense Person Inflections: A Test Case

Note that Accessibility Theory, NP detachment and typological markedness all present plausible explanations for the person verbal inflectional paradigms found in many of the world's languages (especially if we ignore frequency problems). They actually complement each other in principle, since whereas typological markedness motivates zero markings for third person verbs, Accessibility Theory motivates overt marking for first/second person verbs. Moreover, both theories are independently well-motivated, accounting for a wide range of data in addition to verbal person inflection patterns. Perhaps we can assume that both of them are sometimes at work in tandem, converging on encouraging overt versus reduced/zero markings (Givón 1991 explicitly makes this assumption). The reason for this is that both seem to call for the use of reduced/zero forms for the same linguistic codings: often enough the most frequent forms are also the highest accessibility markers (e.g., the current discourse topic is both frequently referred to and is routinely coded by high accessibility markers).

However, we cannot say that the two theories always work in tandem. I have already shown one reason for this, namely that high **frequency** (of high accessibility)—the typological markedness criterion—is distinct from **consistency** (of high accessibility)—the accessibility criterion. These two criteria do not always overlap, and it is the latter which determines which pronouns develop into person markers. Here I will argue that accessibility theory can motivate the creation of Hebrew future verbal agreement when typological markedness cannot be said to operate for another reason: Neither NP detachment nor predicate-argument relation marking, which must be presupposed prior to the application of typological markedness, can be said to be involved in this grammaticization process.

I have proposed (Ariel 1990) that new cliticized pronouns are now emerging in Colloquial Hebrew future tense. First note that as predicted by Accessibility Theory, prior to the inflection formation stage, the zero subject option should diminish. This is crucial, since it assures that overt pronouns, rather than zeroes, be used as subjects. This is clearly true for Hebrew future tense. In my intimate conversation data, whereas most of the past tense first/second person references were coded by zero (82.5%) there were no future tense zero subjects. Data from children's conversations (see Table 11 above) show that zero subjects occurred with future tense verbs mainly in frozen expressions and impersonals. Out of the remaining 62 optional zero/pronoun choices, zero was chosen only in 7 cases (11.3%). Such numbers are the opposite of the zero/pronoun pattern in past tense mentioned above, and attest to the vanishing referentiality of the future agreement markers. Indeed, native speakers, asked to quickly translate from English to Hebrew clauses such as: *I/you/he went/go/will go* (out of context) provided overt pronouns for all third persons, and crucially, they did the same for first and second persons in future (and present) tenses.[15] But for the first/second person past tense, they offered zero subjects. In other words, future tense first/second person agreement markers are not taken as referential forms, unlike the counterpart past tense forms (hence the independent pronouns supplied by the translators).

Accessibility Theory then predicts that first and second person pronouns will be reduced in pronunciation, due to the very high degree of accessibility consistently associated with their referents. Table 15 shows the frequency of occurrence for reduced pronouns (e.g., *an* or *ni* for *ani* 'I') in the different persons and tenses. Clearly, the great majority of first and second person future verbs occur with cliticized pronouns, although this is not the case for present and past, nor for third person future.

	Past	**Present**	**Future**
1st person	1 = 3.2%	15 = 26.8%	10 = 76.9%
2nd person[16]	0	3 = 20%	1 = 100%
third person	1 = 5%	3 = 10.7%	0

Table 15. Percentages of Reduced Pronouns out of the Total Use of Pronouns in the 3 Tenses According to Person (full NPs not included) (intimate conversation—see Note 6)

Past tense inflections are still perceived as transparent (the person agreement marker is clearly identified as a separate unit, which is, moreover, formally similar to the independent pronoun—see Table (16)). It is conceived as referential for first and second persons, so zero subjects can be freely used with it. Future tense person agreement inflections are not transparent (the verbal forms are "portmanteau" forms) and hardly felt as referential anymore. A quick look at Table 16 shows how past first/second person agreement markers still resemble free pronouns, whereas third person verbs do not contain an element resembling the third person pronominal form (singular first person was no doubt analogized to second person agreement). This is the prototypical agreement pattern.

Now, compare past and future agreement markers. The latter are not as transparently related to free pronouns, although the pronoun consonant is there for all 2nd person forms and for plural first person.[17] Again, no such traces are discernible for inflected verbs used for third persons. According to Accessibility Theory, since first/second person future forms are no longer transparent, they are not perceived as containing referring pronominals (they have undergone a desemanticization of their referential force). Overt pronouns must then be used. I propose that a new verbal paradigm is now emerging for future tense (see the numbers for reduced pronouns in Table

Person	Pst:Root +	Prs infl	Indep. Pron.	Future
1st	safar +	ti	ani	?espor/yispor
2nd f	safar +	t	at	t+isper+i
2nd m	safar +	ta	ata	t+ispor
3rd f	safra +	Ø	hi	t+ispor
3rd m	safar +	Ø	hu	(y)+ispor
1st pl	safar +	nu	anu/anaxnu	n+ispor
2nd pl f	s(a)far +	ten/m	aten/m	t+ispor+na
2nd pl m	s(a)far +	tem	atem	t+isper+u
3rd pl f	safru +	Ø	hen/m	t+ispor+na
3rd pl m	safru +	Ø	hem	(y)isper+u

Table 16. Past and Future Inflections in Comparison to Free Pronouns (shown with verb root 'count')

15), and again, since third persons are not consistently highly accessible, but first and second person referents are, it is only first/second persons which trigger consistent pronoun reduction, followed by cliticization. This cliticization may very well eventually lead to the creation of obligatory person markers. The missing steps are the freezing of one form of reduced pronoun (i.e., either *an* or *ni* for *ani*, 'I'), and the obligatory adjacency of the subject pronoun to the future verb.

What is interesting about this new paradigm is that it is evolving even though the marking of the predicate-argument relation is still successfully performed by the original verbal agreement. Thus, whereas the pronominal traces of the verbal agreement markers are quite opaque in future inflections, since the verbal forms themselves are "portmanteau" forms, they quite unequivocally mark the different persons (similar to third person singular *s* in English). Hence, whereas the predicate-argument function is served by the existing system, reference tracking has become difficult due to the diminishing referential power of the agreement. It is this problem, then, that encourages the new verbal agreement formation. The new paradigm cannot also be motivated by the wish to code third person verbal forms by the least marked forms (the creation of non-virgin zeroes according to typological markedness), since they already are the basic and least marked verbal forms. Last, this development is unrelated to NP detachments, which were rare in general, and did not at all occur for future tense in my data. The development of a new inflectional paradigm from independent pronouns then attests to speakers' wish to reduce the forms referring to first/second persons regardless of the potential usefulness of marking predicate-argument grammatical relations and/or abiding by the typological markedness principle.

6. Nominative and Ergative Verbal Person Agreement

This paper is concerned with nominative verbal person agreement patterns. However, if verbal agreement is sensitive to the degree of accessibility associated with the nominative argument in accusative languages, it should equally be sensitive to the degree of accessibility associated with ergatives in ergative languages. Indeed, the accessibility account proposed here is partly paralleled in an account of ergative agreement marking proposed by Du Bois (1987a,b). Briefly, Du Bois (1987a) argues that (third person) absolutives are not marked on verbs, because these are commonly introduced by lexical forms. Overt pronominal affixes are then superfluous. This is comparable to the accessibility approach, in that both approaches examine verbal agreement in terms of its role in **reference** to entities. Note that Du Bois analyses a phenomenon which was mostly seen as functional for disambiguating argument roles—ergative marking—and shows its **verbal** marking to be primarily a reference tracking system. I also argue that nominative verbal agreement functions for the most part as a reference tracking system. In this view, nominative, as well as ergative verbal agreement markers, are primarily referential expressions, rather than pointers as to predicate-argument relations (see also Dixon 1979, Croft 1990: 105). Both analyses argue that Givenness/accessibility is responsible for verbal agreement, rather than markedness considerations. This follows from the referential function attributed to verbal agreement.

Note that Dixon (1979: 79, 1994), who does emphasize the differences between verbal and nominal case marking, is puzzled by the fact that in nominal case marking the (conceptually) unmarked case (nominative for accusative languages, absolutive for ergative languages) is often zero marked on nouns, as it should be, but quite the same (conceptually) unmarked cases are consistently overtly marked on verbs (agreement is often overt for nominatives, as well as for first/second person absolutives). If we assume different paths of development for nominal and verbal markers (which is supported by the different forms assumed as the historical sources for these markers—see Dixon (1994: 185-206)), it is not surprising that verbal agreement patterns differently from nominal case marking in terms of markedness. They serve different functions. In verbal agreement, the indexing of case (whether accusative or ergative) is merely a by-product of the agreement. It is on a par with person, gender and number, namely a feature guiding the addressee as to the intended referent. But in nominal case marking, the indexing of case is itself the primary function.

Du Bois' (1985) notion of competing motivations is very relevant for agreement marking (again, whether ergative or accusative). If verbal agreement is the result of grammaticization of very high accessibility marking, then we expect overt marking (highly attenuated referring expressions) for highly accessible discourse entities. Now, just as I have concentrated on consistent accessibility differences between the persons, Du Bois discusses consistent Givenness differences between agents (ergatives) on the one hand, and intransitive subjects and accusatives (absolutives) on the other hand. Since ergatives consistently refer to Given (actually, highly accessible) discourse entities, we expect them to be overtly marked on the verb, since such markers code referents of consistently high accessibility. The same applies to nominatives in accusative languages (though to a lesser extent, because nominatives include intransitive subjects as well). Since absolutives do NOT consistently refer to highly accessible entities, no verbal marking is expected. Similarly, since third persons (in general) do not consistently refer to highly accessible entities, third person coding is not expected to (often) grammaticize as verbal inflection. First/second coding is.

There are, then, generalizations about the correlations between Givenness/accessibility and case on the one hand, and between accessibility and person on the other. However, ergatives, nominatives and absolutives must take all persons. Hence, converging, as well as conflicting motivations, are bound to present themselves. Indeed they do. Third person absolutives are expected to be non-overtly marked by both the case and the person criteria (both third person and absolutive case do not correlate with Givenness/high accessibility). Indeed they are not (in Mayan). First/second person ergatives are predicted to encourage overt verbal marking by both criteria (since both agents and speech act participants are expected to be highly accessible). Indeed they are (in Mayan).

Theoretically, third person ergatives show a clash between the person and the case predictions (low accessibility for person, high accessibility for case), but statistical findings (Du Bois 1987b) show that in effect they are mostly Given. They are accordingly marked in Mayan. Two other person/case combinations potentially motivate competing marking patterns: first/second person absolutives and third person nominatives. The former belong in a case not characteristic of Given entities, but they themselves are clearly and consistently highly accessible, despite that role. They are indeed marked in Mayan. The latter belong to a case role that more often than not is Given (nominative), but they themselves are not consistently highly accessible, as we have seen in the counts above. Hence, the lack of uniformity in verbal marking according to persons. In Mayan languages (see Du Bois 1987a) and in Yawa (Papuan, see Dixon 1994: 76), at least, whereas third person absolutive is zero marked on the verb, first/second persons are overtly marked. In Choctaw-Chickasaw (2 close dialects, Muskogean—see Dixon 1994: 37-8, based on others), agents, patients and datives are marked on the verb (intransitives being assigned to any one of these roles), and again, first/second persons are overtly marked in all roles, although third person is not. Thus, the patient role, which is expected to represent non-Given entities for the most part, is nevertheless overtly marked on the verb for first/second persons, because first/second persons are consistently highly accessible. The same applies to third person nominatives in many languages, which are zero-marked rather than overtly (see Section 3 above).

Thus, the verbal marking for third person ergatives (and nominatives) and for first/second absolutives is potentially influenced by two competing motivations: Case role calls for one type of accessibility marking (low for absolutives, high for nominatives), and person calls for the opposite type of accessibility marking (high for first/second persons, low for third persons). This is why first/second person absolutives may "diverge" from the non-marking of absolutives, and why third person nominatives may "diverge" from the overt marking characteristic of nominatives. Looked at this way, the inconsistent marking for persons in both nominative and ergative verbal agreement systems is only apparent, and can be motivated in exactly the same way, namely by reference to form-function correlations between referring expressions and consistent high degrees of accessibility of certain discourse entities.

7. Counter-examples to Typological Marking and to Accessibility Theory

Table 17 sums up the differences in what the relevant data is according to Accessibility Theory, frequency-driven morphologization and typological markedness. It will help us see which data forms a counter-example to each theory.

	Typological Markedness	Frequency-driven Morphologization	Accessibility Theory
What person is reduced/zero?	3rd person	1st/2nd person	1st/2nd person
What form is compared for frequency?	verbal forms	nominative pronouns in pre-agreement stage	Reduced nominative pronouns in pre-agreement stage
How is frequency calculated?	Absolute numbers compared across the 3 persons	Absolute numbers, compared across the 3 persons	Proportional numbers per person, compared across the 3 persons

Table 17. Relevant Data for Typological Markedness, Frequency-driven Morphologization and Accessibility Theory regarding Verbal Person Agreement

In the end, then, it seems that the controversy hinges on what linguistic elements are considered paradigmatic alternatives (or "what to count"—see Croft 1990: 87-8). I am claiming that the relevant paradigmatic alternatives in this case are often (though not always) referring expressions, rather than verbal forms. Moreover, the relevant counts are mostly intra-person counts, rather than inter-person ones (at least not directly so). I believe that this is why Accessibility Theory can explain linguistic marking patterns which constitute counter-examples to other theories.

English third person singular simple present tense is the only person to be marked on the verb. Greenberg (1966: 44) further notes that first person is zero-marked in Dutch, while third person has an overt person marker. These are counter-examples to a theory which argues that third person verbal forms are unmarked. However, they do not necessarily form counter-examples to Accessibility Theory, because what is compared under Accessibility Theory is the linguistic code or codes (in cases of double-marking) used to specify the **entity** involved, and not the verb (alone). Hence, in English we would compare a, b and c below, and indeed find that precisely because of the overt marking on the verb, third person references are signalled by more lexical information than first/second persons:[18]

(16) a. **I** (verb)+**zero**
    b. **You** (verb)+**zero**
    c. **S/he/it** (verb)+**s**

In other words, unlike typological markedness, Accessibility Theory does not determine that third person **verbs** absolutely be zero-marked/least marked. It only has predictions for nominal markers (wherever they may be), and it predicts that if and when grammaticized, third person referents (verbal person agreement included) will be consistently coded by relatively lower accessibility markers than first/second person referents (i.e., longer, more informative forms). More patterns are then compatible with Accessibility Theory, among them (1) in Table 18 below, where no person agreement occurs on any verb, (2), the prevalent agreement pattern, where only first and second persons show verbal agreement, and (3), where only third person verbal agreement occurs. Of course, there can be many other sub-patterns, but we will make do with these. What patterns 1-3 in Table 18 have in common is that third person **referents** are invariably coded by lower accessibility marking than first/second person, be it overt subject vs. zero subject (in 1), pronoun/lexical NP vs. agreement (in 2), or overt agreement vs. zero agreement (in 3).

Note that whereas (1) and (2) are consistent with both Accessibility Theory and typological markedness, (3), where the third person verb is more marked than the first/second person verb, is only consistent with Accessibility Theory. In addition to the English and Dutch counter-examples mentioned above, in Modenese Italian, third person present tense shows more marking than first and second persons (according to Gilligan 1987). In Nez Perce too only third person verbs are marked (see Mithun 1996). According to Mithun, third person referents are first introduced overtly, and then followed by zero subjects but nonetheless referred to pronominally on the verb. First and second persons are routinely referred to by zero subjects, and their verbs are zero-marked. Hence, first/second persons are coded by a higher accessibility marker (zero vs. bound pronominals in this case).

Genuine counter-examples for Accessibility Theory would be patterns obligatorily requiring lower accessibility marking for first/second person referents than for third person referents. Thus, if there were languages which allowed zero subjects for third person referents, but not for first/second person referents (4 below) or alternatively, if in a language with free zero subjects, only first/second person verbal agreements occurred (5), then typological markedness would constitute a better account, for these are not counter-examples for it, although they are for Accessibility Theory, since in each of these cases first/second persons are coded by lower accessibility markers than third persons (overt vs. zero subject, overt vs. zero verbal agreement). As far as I know, whereas there are languages (albeit very few) which manifest pattern (3), there are none which pattern as in (4) or (5). This is surprising under a typological markedness account.

		1st Person	2nd Person	3rd Person
1.	Ref Exp	zero	zero	overt
	V Agr	zero	zero	zero
2.	Ref Exp	zero	zero	overt
	V Agr	overt	overt	zero
3.	Ref Exp	zero	zero	zero
	V Agr	zero	zero	overt
4.	Ref Exp	overt	overt	zero
	V Agr	zero	zero	zero
5.	Ref Exp	zero	zero	zero
	V Agr	overt	overt	zero

Table 18. Five Types of Agreement (Ref Exp = Referring expression, V Agr = Verbal agreement)

Moreover, recall that (a) typological markedness requires an additional mechanism to explain the initial creation of agreement (be it NP detachment, predicate-argument marking or Accessibility Theory), while Accessibility Theory does not; (b) typological markedness cannot explain why zero subjects are more prevalent for first/second persons than for third persons, while Accessibility Theory simultaneously motivates the prevalent verbal agreement marking as well this and as many other distributional and grammatical restrictions. Crucially, (c) typological markedness relies on an assumption that third person verbal forms are the most frequent in discourse, but we have seen that they are not necessarily so. Accessibility Theory relies on the assumption that first/second person referents are consistently highly accessible, and we have seen evidence that this is a consistent finding across text types.

8. Conclusions: Distinguishing Between Zero Agreement and Absence of Agreement

Is zero always a marker of nonmarkedness? It often is, as in singular (most often zero-marked) versus plural (often overtly marked) forms. Thus, when a formal distinction is required between two forms, it is indeed the less frequent form which will normally be formally marked. But zero is not always the unmarked member of the paradigm (Dressler 1987: 14). For example, whereas Chinese zero/pronoun choices indeed show zero to be the unmarked member (in terms of frequency—there are more zeroes than pronouns according to Li and Thompson 1979), English zeroes (unmarked formally) are extremely marked nonetheless, in that they are heavily restricted in their distribution, as compared with overt pronouns. This appears to be a paradox.

However, according to Accessibility Theory, there is no zero third person agreement in fact (and see also Mithun 1986b). No inflection is not the same as zero inflection. Inflection simply never arose for third person (and if it did, it would tend to disappear or be reanalyzed). Hence, the (formally) unmarked, basic verbal form associated with third persons is the one **used** for third persons, just **because** it has **no** person marking. So-called third person verbs are unmarked because no functional pressure (that is, an accessibility-based form-function correlation) motivated such a marking. As Croft (1990: 158-9) argues:

The final criteria for markedness are typological frequency and typological distribution (dominance). The typological-frequency criterion is relatively simple to account for: **if a grammatical semantic category is very infrequent, it simply will not be expressed as a distinct grammatical category in many languages** (emphasis added).

In other words, I am suggesting with Mithun (1991) that third person verbal markers are not useful enough to merit grammaticization, because third person referents are not consistently highly accessible, whereas first and second person marking is often grammaticized, because of the consistent high accessibility associated with their referents (and see Bátori 1982 for a similar analysis for Hungarian).

Although theorists of markedness have debated which markedness criteria should be used (see Cairns 1986 and Odlin 1986), how consistent the results of various markedness criteria should be, what grammatical components are amenable to a markedness analysis (see the various articles in Eckman, Moravcsik and Wirth 1986), the terms considered members of a contrast set seem to be trivially taken as a given (but see Croft 1990: 87-88). While this may often be justified, I suggest that the opposition taken for granted here (**verbs** used for third persons versus verbs used for first/second persons) is not always the relevant one for natural language coding. It is only relevant when predicate-argument relations are to be marked, but often enough this is not what speakers choose to mark, at least not initially. Instead, we should measure the form coding the **referent** separately from the form coding the verb, even if they are in specific instances merged. Looked at this way, verbal forms are now equally long and complex for all the persons, of course. Common ways of referring to the various persons, on the other hand, are not:

(17) 1st person: inflection
2nd person: inflection
3rd person: pronoun/demonstrative/full NP.

In other words, the verbal form used for third person is indeed the least marked form, but at least originally, it is the unmarked **basic verbal form**, used for all persons, and not only for third persons. It is not specific for third persons, even though it often seems to be used solely for them. And the reason it seems to be dedicated to third person is that bound pronouns tend to merge with this basic verbal form only or mostly for first/second persons. I therefore endorse Mithun (1986b) and Croft's (1990: 271) distinction between zero-marked verb agreement and absence of agreement. I believe that Benveniste (1971: 197-8) in effect held this very position too. The third person "only presents the invariable inherent in every form of the conjugation... the 'third person' is not a 'person'; it is really the verbal form whose function is to express the *non-person*."

Once we assume that so-called third person verbal forms are not actually zero-marked, because they do not really form part of a contrast pair with first/second person verbal forms, the data presented above as counterexamples for typological markedness (English, Dutch, Nez Perce) are no longer relevant, since in the absence of an opposition between forms (verbs, in this case), typological markedness (between verbal forms) is simply inapplicable.

Summing up, I have argued that for the most part, it is not verbal forms alone (typological markedness) and not absolute numbers for pronoun-verb cooccurrences (frequency-driven morphologization) for the three persons which should be compared. We should compare verbal forms alone only if overt subjects are equally present or absent (zero) for the three persons. Since third persons are normally coded by overt subjects, but first/second persons are often coded by zero subjects accompanied by overt verbal agreement, we should actually compare the coding for the subject AND the verb taken together. We then see that in fact, it is first/second persons that are less marked formally, because what for third person is coded syntactically (a subject-verb combination) is coded morphologically for first/second persons (verb+person agreement, see Croft (1990: 80) for syntactic versus morphological marking). But combinations of first/second person subjects with verbs are not necessarily the most frequent ones! Hence, it must be the ratio of very high accessibility references **per person** which is crucial for this marking. Thus, even if third person verbs are more frequent, and even if third person pronoun-verb cooccurrences are sometimes more frequent, what determines the finding that first/second, rather than third person pronouns become person agreement markers is not their frequency, but rather, the proportion of very high accessibility references that each performs. These textual frequencies are consistently close to 100% for first/second references, whereas they are between 26%-51% for third person references (see 3.2 above).

Accessibility Theory, then, offers a specific application of the frequency-driven morphologization hypothesis. Indeed, once we apply frequency counts to categories and comparisons defined by Accessibility Theory, the usual assumptions about grammaticization processes involving adjacent forms apply: Highly frequent adjacent forms tend to fuse together. But in this case, it is **intra**-person very high accessibility frequency comparisons, rather than **inter**-person straight frequency comparisons which determine which pronouns will grammaticize into agreement markers.

Notes

I would like to thank Joan Bybee, Bernard Comrie, Shlomo Izre'el, Suzanne Kemmer and Marianne Mithun for very helpful comments on previous drafts of this paper, and Gila Batori for statistical analyses. I am deeply indebted to William Croft for criticizing me harshly, proposing to me alternative explanations, and patiently responding to all my valid and invalid counter-arguments. I am convinced that our lengthy correspondence and discussions over this topic greatly improved the quality of my argumentation. Last, I am most grateful to Sandra Thompson, who patiently and meticulously read the paper, made very many insightful comments, and forced me to clarify numerous points which had been quite obscure before. I hope this version reflects how much I appreciated her comments.

1. However, bound pronominal inflections may have other origins of course, e.g., plurals (see Comrie 1981), unspecified reference markers and a cislocative 'hither' (see Mithun 1996, Janssen to appear), participles and auxiliaries (see Bybee et al. 1990, Helmbrecht 1995a).

2. In fact, speakers may reduce pronouns for centuries without turning them into inflections, as in English *you*, which is often actually pronounced *ya*, and *I* ([ay]) as [schwa].

3. In French, for example, pronouns distinguish between masculine and feminine but verb clitics do not, but see Moravcsik (1978) and Perkins (1992) for a few counter-examples.

4. The relative ordering of the NP and the verb is not crucial.

5. See Chafe (1970, 1976, 1987), and Yule (1981) on Givenness and attenuation, Fowler and Housum (1987) on the usefulness to the addressee of reducing old words, Terken and Nooteboom (1988) for the effect of accentuation on the processing of Given and New information, and Gurman-Bard (1995) on degree of intelligibility of words referring to New versus Given information.

6. These examples are taken from an intimate, face-to-face conversation, recorded on January 8, 1987.

7. Indeed, inflection is often obligatory once the person marker is bound —see Croft (1990: 273) for such a universal. Mithun (1991, p.c.) has argued virtually in the same spirit. Givón (1976, 1983) and Lehmann (1987) argue similarly that the same discourse need for anaphoric references motivates both pronominal references and agreement markings. Agreement is the syntacticization of identification by using only a partial description for the entity intended. However, unlike Mithun and me, they do not assume that this process first occurs when the overt NP is missing.

8. Presumably, on the NP detachment theory, first/second person agreement markers develop by analogy to third person agreement, since, as I am reminded by Sandra Thompson p.c. there is hardly any use for first/second persons in NP detachment constructions (cf. *I, I will do it).

9. Dixon indeed goes on to link the diachronic origin of these bound clitics in free pronouns to this synchronic complementary distribution.

10. Some first and second person subjects also included lexical NPs (e.g., 'all of us') and were here excluded too.

11. As reported by Maria Vikuna on an e-mail message on The Linguist list (2.17.1993).

12. As testified to by Glenn Ayres in an e-mail message to The Linguist list, 2.23.1993.

13. Note that first and second person pronouns are sometimes quite long (e.g., Biblical Hebrew *anoxi* 'I,' Modern Hebrew *anaxnu* 'we,' Ngiyambaa *barrazga*, 'you-sg,' the Japanese long varieties for 'I,' i.e., two syllables and up). Third person pronouns, on the other hand, when they exist, are not so lengthy. This seems surprising under Accessibility Theory, since first/second persons refer to more accessible entities. I tentatively suggest that in addition to rich agreement, the length of pronouns is crucially linked to zero-subject options in the language. Thus, in English, which is not at all a free zero-subject language, first/second person pronouns must be quite short. In a zero-subject language such as Hebrew, first and second person pronouns may (but need not) be longer than third person pronouns, because the former are used when the degree of accessibility associated with their referents is relatively lower.

14. In a search conducted for me by John Du Bois of 30 Corpus of Spoken American English transcripts totalling 146,410 words, the following frequency of occurrence can be established for subject pronouns:

    i. I: 4112 > they: 1306 > he: 1264 > we: 1113 > she: 598

    This scale, which is similar though not identical to the one in 15 above, does not include second person *you* (3320) nor third person *it* (2848), since these two forms are undistinguished for grammatical role. The count is also rough since first/second more than third person references are realized by zeroes, not here counted.

    Note, first, the large gap between *I* and *we* (both first person), second, the large gap between *he/they* and *she* (all third person), and last, the resemblance between the frequency of *they*, *he* and *we* (third and first persons). Recall, however, that languages develop verbal person agreement for *we* (and *I*), but not for *they* or *he*.

15. I thank Ehud R. Toledano and the students in my pragmatics class (Fall 1995) for providing these translations for me.

16. Imperative forms were here ignored, whether in the prescribed normative or in the non-normative (future) form.

17. Thus, 'you-fem-sg' was originally *anti* and later *atti*. However, it has long become *at* (due to phonological loss) and so the *i* vowel in *t+ishber+i* 'you-fem-sg-will break' is now opaque. The same goes for

'you-pl msc,' now *atem*, but formerly *atum*, which motivates the *u* in *t+ishber+u*, and 'you/they-fem-pl,' now *aten/hen*, but formerly *atenna/henna*, which motivate the *na* in *t+ishbor+na*, 'you/they-fem-pl-will break' (see Gesenius - Kautzsch - Cowley 1910).

18. And since Dutch, too, is a non zero-subject language (according to Gilligan 1987), the coding of first person is performed by a pronoun, whereas third person requires both a pronoun (or a lexical NP) and the overt verbal marker. Hence Dutch too is not a counter-example for Accessibility Theory.

References

Allen, Shanley. 1995. Null subjects and null objects in early Inuktitut. Paper presented at the ellipsis workshop in the Functional Approaches to Grammar conference. Albuquerque, New Mexico, 7.25.1995.

Anderson, Stephen R. 1985. Inflectional morphology. In Shopen (ed.), Vol. III, 150-201.

Anderson, Stephen R. 1988. Inflection. In Hammond and Noonan (eds.), 23-43.

Anderson, Stephen R. and Edward L. Keenan. 1985. Deixis. In Shopen (ed.), Vol. II, 259-308.

Andrews, Henrietta. 1993. The function of verb prefixes in South-Western Otomí. Arlington: Summer Institute of Linguistics and University of Texas at Arlington.

Ariel, Mira. 1985. *Givenness Marking*. Tel-Aviv University doctoral thesis.

Ariel, Mira. 1988. Referring and accessibility. *Journal of Linguistics* 24(5), 65-87.

Ariel, Mira. 1990. *Accessing NP Antecedents*. (Croom Helm Linguistics Series.) London: Routledge.

Ariel, Mira. 1991. The function of accessibility in a theory of grammar. *Journal of Pragmatics* 16(4), 141-161.

Ariel, Mira. 1996. Referring expressions and the +/- coreference distinction. In Thorstein Fretheim and Jeanette Gundel (eds.), *Reference and Referent Accessibility*, 13-35. Amsterdam: John Benjamins.

Ariel, Mira. 1998. Three grammaticalization paths for the development of person verbal agreement in Hebrew. In Jean-Pierre Koenig (ed.), *Discourse and Cognition: Bridging the Gap*. Stanford: CSLI.

Auger, Julie. 1993. More evidence for verbal agreement marking in Colloquial French. In William J. Ashby, Marianne Mithun, Giorgio Perissinotto, and Eduardo Raposo (eds.), *Linguistic Perspectives on the Romance Languages*, 177-98. Amsterdam: John Benjamins.

Auger, Julie. 1994. Pronominal clitics in Quebec Colloquial French: A morphological analysis. Doctoral dissertation, University of Pennsylvania (IRCS report 94-29).

Auger, Julie. 1995. Les clitiques pronominaux en Français parle informel: Une approche morphologique. *Revue Quebecoise de Linguistique* 24(1), 21-60.

Bally, Charles. 1932/1965. *Linguistique Générale et Linguistique Française*. Bern: A. Francke Verlag.

Barlow, Michael. 1992. *A Situated Theory of Agreement*. (Outstanding Dissertations in Linguistics.) New York: Garland.

Barlow, Michael and Charles A. Ferguson (eds.). 1987. *Agreement in Natural Language*. Stanford: CSLI.

Bátori, István. 1982. On verb deixis in Hungarian. In Weissenborn and Klein (eds.), 155-65.

Benveniste, Emile. 1971. *Problems in General Linguistics*. Translated by Mary Elizabeth Meek. Coral Gables, Florida: University of Miami Press.

Bergsträsser, Gotthelf. 1928/1983. *Introduction to the Semitic Languages*. Translated with notes and bibliography and an appendix on the scripts by Peter T. Daniels. Winona Lake, Indiana: Eisenbrauns.

Bopp, Franz. 1816. *Über das Conjugationssystem der Sanskritsprache*. Frankfurt am Main: Andreäischen.

Borer, Hagit. 1983. *Parametric Syntax*. Dordrecht: Foris.

Borer, Hagit. 1986. I-subjects. *Linguistic Inquiry* 17(3), 375-416.

Bosch, Peter. 1983. *Agreement and Anaphora*. London: Academic Press.

Brugmann, Karl and Berthold Delbrück. 1911. *Grundriss der Vergleichenden Grammatik der Indogermanischen Sprachen* (Vol. 2, revised edition 1911, 1916; Vol. 3, 1893). Strassburg: Trübner.

Bybee, Joan L. 1985. *Morphology*. Amsterdam: John Benjamins.

Bybee, Joan L. 1988. Morphology as lexical organization. In Hammond and Noonan (eds.), 119-41.

Bybee, Joan L. 1994. The grammaticalization of zero: Asymmetries in tense and aspect systems. In William Pagliuca (ed.), *Perspectives on Grammaticalization*, 235-54. Amsterdam: Benjamins.

Bybee, Joan L., William Pagliuca and Revere Perkins. 1990. On the asymmetries in the affixation of grammatical material. In William Croft, Keith Denning and Suzanne Kemmer (eds.), *Studies in Typology and Diachrony*, 1-42. Amsterdam: John Benjamins.

Bybee, Joan L., Revere Perkins and William Pagliuca. 1994. *The Evolution of Grammar*. Chicago: University of Chicago Press.

Cairns, Charles E. 1986. Word structure, markedness, and applied linguistics. In Eckman et al. (eds.), 13-38.

Chafe, Wallace L. 1970. *Meaning and the Structure of Language*. Chicago: University of Chicago Press.

Chafe, Wallace L. 1976. Givenness, contrastiveness, definiteness, subjects, topics, and point of view. In Li (ed.), 25-57.

Chafe, Wallace L. 1987. Cognitive constraints on information flow. In Russell Tomlin (ed.), *Coherence and Grounding in Discourse*, 21-51. Amsterdam: John Benjamins.

Chafe, Wallace L. and Chao, Wynn. 1986. Indefinite NPs and the interpretation of discourse-based null elements. In Eckman et al. (eds.), 65-84.

Chomsky, Noam. 1982. *Some Concepts and Consequences of the Theory of Government and Binding*. Cambridge, MA: MIT Press.

Cohen, Even-Grey. 1995. Accessibility markers in Latin and an assessment of the criteria determining them. Seminar paper, Tel-Aviv University.

Comrie, Bernard. 1978. LSA Summer Institute class notes.

Comrie, Bernard. 1981. *Language Universals and Linguistic Typology*. Oxford: Blackwell.

Comrie, Bernard. 1986. Markedness, grammar, people, and the world. In Eckman et al. (eds.), 85-106.

Comrie, Bernard. 1988. Linguistic typology. In Newmeyer, Frederick J. (ed.), *Linguistics: The Cambridge Survey*. Vol. I, 447-61. Cambridge: Cambridge University Press.

Corbett, Greville. 1991. *Gender*. Cambridge: Cambridge University Press.

Croft, William. 1987. Agreement vs. case marking and direct objects. In Barlow and Ferguson (eds.), 159-79.

Croft, William. 1990. *Typology and Universals*. Cambridge: Cambridge University Press.

DeLancey, Scott. 1981. An interpretation of split ergativity and related patterns. *Language* 57(3), 626-57.

de Saussure, Ferdinand. 1959. *Course in General Linguistics*. Translated into English by Wade Baskin. New York: Philosophical Library.

Dixon, R. M. W. 1979. Ergativity. *Language* 55(1), 59-138.

Dixon, R. M. W. 1980. *The Languages of Australia*. Cambridge: Cambridge University Press.

Doron, Edit. 1987. On the complementarity of subject and subject-verb agreement. In Barlow and Ferguson (eds.), 201-18.

Dressler, Wolfgang. 1987. Introduction. In Dressler (ed.), 3-22.

Dressler, Wolfgang (ed.). 1987. *Leitmotifs in Natural Morphology*. Amsterdam: John Benjamins.

Du Bois, John W. 1980. Beyond definiteness: The trace of identity in discourse. In Wallace Chafe (ed.), *The Pear Stories,* Vol III. Roy Freedle (ed.), *Advances in Discourse Processes*, 203-74. Norwood: Ablex.

Du Bois, John W. 1985. Competing motivations. In John Haiman (ed.), *Iconicity in Syntax*. 343-65. Amsterdam: John Benjamins.

Du Bois, John W. 1987a. Absolutive zero: Paradigm adaptivity in Sacapultec. *Lingua* 71(1-4), 203-22.

Du Bois, John W. 1987b. The discourse basis of ergativity. *Language* (63)4, 805-55.

Du Bois, John W. Ms. Reference and identification.

Eckman, Fred R., Edith A. Moravcsik and Jessica R. Wirth (eds.). 1986. *Markedness*. New York: Plenum.

Even-Shoshan, Abraham. 1982. *Ha-Milon Hechadash*. [A Hebrew dictionary.] Jerusalem: Kiryat-Sefer.

Fassi Fehri, Abdelkader. 1987. Agreement in Arabic, binding and coherence. In Barlow and Ferguson (eds.), 107-58.

Foley, William A. and Robert D. Van Valin Jr. 1984. *Functional Syntax and Universal Grammar*. Cambridge: Cambridge University Press.

Foley, William A. and Robert D. Van Valin Jr. 1985. Information packaging in the clause. In Shopen (ed.), Vol. 1, 282-364.

Fowler, Carol A. and Jonathan Housum. 1987. Talkers' signaling of "New" and "Old" words in speech and listeners' perception and use of the distinction. *Journal of Memory and Language* 26, 489-504.

Gesenius, W. - E. Kautzsch - A.E. Cowley. 1910. *Gesenius' Hebrew Grammar*. As edited and enlarged by Emil Kautzsch. Translated from German by G.W. Collins. Translation revised by Arthur Ernest Cowley. Oxford: The Clarendon Press.

Gilligan, Gary M. 1987. *A Cross-linguistic Approach to the Pro-drop Parameter*. Doctoral dissertation, University of Southern California.

Givón, Talmy. 1971. Historical syntax and synchronic morphology. *CLS* 7, 394-415. Chicago: CLS.

Givón, Talmy. 1976. Topic, pronoun, and grammatical agreement. In Li (ed.), 149-88.

Givón, Talmy (ed.). 1983. *Topic Continuity in Discourse: A Quantitative Cross-Language Study*. Amsterdam: John Benjamins.

Givón, Talmy. 1991. Markedness in grammar: Distributional, communicative and cognitive correlates of syntactic structure. *Studies in Language* 15(2), 335-70.

Givón, Talmy. 1993. *English Grammar: A Function-based Introduction*, Vol. I. Amsterdam: John Benjamins.

Greenberg, Joseph H. 1966. *Language Universals, with Special Reference to Feature Hierarchies* (Janua Linguarum series minor 59). The Hague: Mouton.

Greenberg, Joseph H. 1978. How does a language acquire gender markers? In Greenberg (ed.), Vol. III, *Word Structure*, 47-82. Stanford: Stanford University Press.

Greenberg, Joseph H. (ed.). 1978. *Universals of Human Language*. Stanford: Stanford University Press.

Grimm, Jacob. 1812. Article in *Hallesche Allgemeine Zeitung*, 7 February 1812, Sp. 258f.

Gundel, Jeanette K., Kathleen Houlihan and Gerald Sanders. 1986. Markedness and distribution in phonology and syntax. In Eckman et al. (eds.), 107-38.

Gundel, Jeanette K., Kathleen Houlihan and Gerald Sanders. 1988. On the functions of marked and unmarked terms. In Michael Hammond, Edith A. Moravcsik and Jessica R. Wirth (eds.), *Studies in Syntactic Typology*, 285-301. Amsterdam: John Benjamins.

Gurman-Bard, Ellen. 1995. The control of intelligibility in dialogue: The messy, the sticky, and the oyster-catcher's egg. Presented at Haifa university, April 4, 1995.

Haiman, John. 1983. Iconic and economic motivation. *Language* 59(4), 781-819.

Haiman, John. 1985. *Natural Syntax*. Cambridge: Cambridge University Press.

Haiman, John. 1991. From V/2 to subject clitics: Evidence from Northern Italian. In Traugott and Heine (eds.), Vol. 2, 135-57.

Hammond, Michael and Michael Noonan (eds.). 1988. *Theoretical Morphology*. San Diego: Academic Press.

Harel, Zvi. 1992. Yossi, believe me as you never believed me before. *The Haaretz Supplement*, November 13, 1992, 20-25.

Harris, Martin. 1978. *The Evolution of French Syntax: A Comparative Approach*. London: Longman.

Hawkinson, A. and Larry Hyman. 1975. Hierarchies of natural topic in Shona. *Studies in African Linguistics* 5, 147-70.

Heine, Bernd and Mechthild Reh. 1984. *Grammaticalization and Reanalysis in African Languages*. Hamburg: Helmut Buske Verlag.

Helmbrecht, Johannes. 1995a. The syntax of personal agreement in East-Caucasian languages. Ms.

Helmbrecht, Johannes. 1995b. The typology of 1st person marking and its cognitive background. Ms.

Hockett, Charles F. 1966. What Algonquian is really like. *International Journal of American Linguistics* 32, 59-73.

Hopper, Paul J. 1991. On the principles of grammaticization. In Traugott and Heine (eds.), Vol. 1, 17-35.

Hopper, Paul J. and Elizabeth Closs Traugott. 1993. *Grammaticalization*. Cambridge: Cambridge University Press.

Horn, Lawrence. 1984. Toward a new taxonomy for pragmatic inference: Q-based and R-based implicature. In Deborah Schiffrin (ed.), *Meaning, Form and Use in Context: Linguistic Applications*, 11-42. Washington, DC: Georgetown University Press.

Horne Tooke, John. 1798/1968. *Diversions of Purley* (2 vols). London: Scholar Press.

Huebner, Thom. 1983. *A Longitudinal Analysis of the Acquisition of English*. Ann Arbor: Karoma.

Huehnergard, John. 1987. "Stative," predicative form, pseudo-verb. *Journal of Near Eastern Studies* 47(3) 215-32.

Janssen, Theo A. J. M. To appear. Deixis and reference. In Geert Booij, Christian Lehmann and Joachim Mugdan (eds.), *Morphology: A Handbook on Inflection and Word Formation*. Berlin: Mouton de Gruyter.

Jelinek, Eloise. 1984. Empty categories, case and configurationality. *Natural Language and Linguistic Theory* 2(1), 39-76.

Jelinek, Eloise and Richard A. Demers. 1994. Predicate and pronominal arguments in Straits Salish. *Language* 70(4), 697-736.

Jespersen, Otto. 1922. *Language, its Nature, Development and Origin*. London: George Allen & Unwin.

Jespersen, Otto. 1924/1965. *The Philosophy of Grammar*. New York: W. Norton & Company.

Jespersen, Otto. 1937/1984. *Analytic Syntax*. Chicago: University of Chicago Press.

Juilland, Alphonse and E. Chang-Rodríguez. 1964. *Frequency Dictionary of Spanish Words*. The Hague: Mouton.

Kemmer, Suzanne. 1993. *The Middle Voice*. (Typological Studies in Language 23.) Amsterdam: John Benjamins.

Kuen, Heinz. 1957. Die Gewohnheit der mehrfachen Bezeichnung des Subjekts in der Romania und die Gründe ihres Aufkommens. In Günter Reichenkron et al.

(eds.), *Syntactica und Stilistica: Festschrift für Ernst Gamillscheg zum 70. Geburtstag.* Tübingen: Niemeyer.

Kuno, Susumo. 1976. Subject, theme, and the speaker's empathy—A reexamination of relativization phenomena. In Li (ed.), 417-44.

Kurylowicz, Jerzy. 1968. The notion of morpho(pho)neme. In Winfred P. Lehmann and Yakov Malkiel (eds.), *Directions for Historical Linguistics*, 65-81. Austin: University of Texas Press.

Lambrecht, Knud. 1980. Topic, French style: Remarks about a basic sentence type of Modern Non-Standard French. *BLS* 6, 337-60. Berkeley: BLS.

Lambrecht, Knud. 1981. *Topic, Antitopic and Verb-agreement in Non-standard French.* Pragmatics and Beyond Vol. II: 8. Amsterdam: John Benjamins.

Lambrecht, Knud. 1994. *Information Structure and Sentence Form.* Cambridge: Cambridge University Press.

Lapointe, Steven G. 1987. Toward a unified theory of agreement. In Barlow and Ferguson (eds.), 67-87.

Lehmann, Christian. 1987. On the function of agreement. In Barlow and Ferguson (eds.), 55-65.

Levy, Gideon. 1995. That I should have to defend Arafat? *The Haaretz Supplement.* February 17, 1995, 14-16.

Li, Charles N. (ed.). 1976. *Subject and Topic.* New York: Academic Press.

Li, Charles N. and Sandra A Thompson. 1979. Third-person pronouns and zero anaphora in Chinese discourse. In Talmy Givón (ed.), *Syntax and Semantics 12: Discourse and Syntax*, 311-35. New York: Academic Press.

Lyons, John. 1977. *Semantics.* Vols. 1 and 2. Cambridge: Cambridge University Press.

Malotki, Eckehart. 1982. Hopi person deixis. In Weissenborn and Klein (eds.), 223-52.

Mathews, Peter H. 1991. *Morphology.* Cambridge: Cambridge University Press.

McCloskey, James and Kenneth Hale. 1984. On the syntax of person-number inflection in Modern Irish. *Natural Language and Linguistic Theory* 1(4), 487-533.

Meillet, Antoine. 1912. L'évolution des formes grammaticales. Reprinted in Meillet 1958, *Linguistique Historique et Linguistique Générale.* Paris: Champion.

Miklosich, Franz. 1868. *Vergleichende Grammatik der Slavischen Sprachen.* Reprinted, Heidelberg, 1926 (Wien: Braunmüller).

Milroy, James. 1992. *Linguistic Variation and Change.* Oxford: Blackwell.

Mithun, Marianne. 1986a. Disagreement: The case of pronominal affixes and nouns. In Deborah Tannen and James E. Alatis (eds.), *Language and Linguis-*

tics: The Interdependence of Theory, Data, and Application. Proceedings of GURT 1985, 50-66. Washington, DC: Georgetown University Press.

Mithun, Marianne. 1986b. When zero isn't there. *BLS* 12, 195-211. Berkeley: BLS.

Mithun, Marianne. 1988. Lexical categories and the evolution of number marking. In Hammond and Noonan (eds.), 211-34.

Mithun, Marianne. 1989. Historical linguistics and linguistic theory: Reducing the arbitrary and constraining explanation. *BLS* 15, 391-488. Berkeley: BLS.

Mithun, Marianne. 1991. The development of bound pronominal paradigms. In Winfred P. Lehmann and Helen-Jo Jakusz Hewitt (eds.), *Language Typology 1988: Typological Models in Reconstruction*, 85-104. Amsterdam: John Benjamins.

Mithun, Marianne. 1996. New directions in referentiality. In Barbara Fox (ed.), *Studies in Anaphora*, 413-35. Amsterdam: John Benjamins.

Moravcsik, Edith A. 1978. Agreement. In Greenberg (ed.), Vol. IV, 331-374.

Moravcsik, Edith A. 1987. Agreement and markedness. In Barlow and Ferguson (eds.), 89-106.

Morris, Celia. 1994. *Bearing Witness: Sexual Harassment and Beyond —Everywoman's Story*, 36-38; 38-43. Boston: Little, Brown and Company.

Moscati, Sabatino, Anton Spitaler, Edward Ullendorff and Wolfram von Soden. 1969. *An Introduction to the Comparative Grammar of the Semitic Languages*. Wiesbaden: Otto Harrassowitz.

Munro, Pamela. 1974. *Topics in Mojave Syntax*. Doctoral dissertation, University of California, San Diego.

Nadasdi, Terry. 1995. Subject NP doubling, matching, and minority French. *Language Variation and Change* 7(1), 1-14.

Newmeyer, Frederick J. 1991. Iconicity and generative grammar. *Language* 68(4), 756-796.

Newport, Elissa L. and Richard P. Meier. 1985. The acquisition of American Sign Language. In Slobin (ed.), Vol I. 881-938.

Odlin, Terence. 1986. Markedness and the zero-derived denominal verb in English: Synchronic, diachronic, and acquisition correlates. In Eckman et al. (eds.), 155-68.

Paul, Hermann. 1886/1995. *Prinzipien der Sprachgeschichte*. London: Routledge.

Perkins, Revere D. 1992. *Deixis, Grammar, and Culture*. Amsterdam: John Benjamins.

Philips, Susan U. 1984. Contextual variation in courtroom language use: Noun phrases referring to crime. *International Journal of the Sociology of Language* 49, 29-50.

Philips, Susan U. and Anne Reynolds. 1987. The interaction of variable syntax and discourse structure in women's and men's speech. In Susan U. Philips, Susan Steele and Christine Tanz (eds.), *Language, Gender, and Sex in Comparative Perspective*, 71-94. Cambridge: Cambridge University Press.

Reinhart, Tanya. 1981. Pragmatics and linguistics: An analysis of sentence topics. *Philosophica* 27(1): *Special Issue on Pragmatic Theory*, 53-94.

Rizzi, Luigi. 1982. Negation, *wh*-movement and the null subject parameter. In Luigi Rizzi (ed.), *Issues in Italian Syntax*, 117-84. Dordrecht: Foris.

Rodríguez Bou, Ismael. 1952. *Recuento de Vocabulario Español*, Vol III. Rio Piedras: University of Puerto Rico.

Ross, John Robert. 1970. On declarative sentences. In Roderick A. Jacobs and Peter S. Rosenbaum (eds.), *Readings in English Transformational Grammar*, 222-272. Waltham, Mass.: Ginn and Company.

Sadock, Jerrold M. and Arnold M. Zwicky. 1985. Speech act distinctions in syntax. In Shopen (ed.), Vol. I, 155-96.

Sanford, Anthony J. and Simon C. Garrod. 1981. *Understanding Written Languages*. Chichester: John Wiley and Sons.

Shopen, Timothy (ed.). 1985. *Language Typology and Syntactic Description*. Vol. I: *Clause Structure* and Vol III: *Grammatical Categories and the Lexicon*. Cambridge: Cambridge University Press.

Silverstein, Michael. 1976. Hierarchy of features and ergativity. In R. M. W. Dixon (ed.), *Grammatical Categories in Australian Languages*, 112-71. Canberra: Australian Institute of Aboriginal Studies.

Slobin, Dan I. 1973. Cognitive prerequisites for the development of grammar. In Charles A. Ferguson and Dan I. Slobin (eds.), *Studies of Child Language Development*, 175-208. New York: Holt, Rinehart and Winston.

Slobin, Dan I. (ed.). 1985. *The Crosslinguistic Study of Language Acquisition*. Vols. 1 and 2. Hillsdale, N.J.: Erlbaum.

Slobin, Dan I. (ed.). 1992. *The Crosslinguistic Study of Language Acquisition*. Vol. 3. Hillsdale, N.J.: Erlbaum.

Steele, Susan. 1977. Clisis and diachrony. In Charles N. Li (ed.), *Mechanisms of Syntactic Change*, 539-79. Austin: University of Texas Press.

Tanz, Christine. 1980. *Studies in the Acquisition of Deictic Terms*. Cambridge: Cambridge University Press.

Taraldsen, Knut T. 1980. *On the Nominative Island Condition, Vacuous Application, and the That-trace Filter.* Indiana: Indiana University Linguistics Club.

Terken, J. and S. G. Nooteboom. 1988. Opposite effects of accentuation and deaccentuation on verification latencies for Given and New information. *Language and Cognitive Processes* 2(3/4), 145-63.

Thrashner, Randolph H. Jr. 1974. *Shouldn't Ignore These Things: A Study of Conversational Deletion.* Doctoral dissertation, University of Michigan, Ann Arbor.

Thurneysen, Rudolf. 1892. Zur Stellung des Verbums im Altfranzösischen. *Zeitschrift für Romanische Philologie* 16.

Traugott, Elizabeth and Bernd Heine (eds.). 1991. *Approaches to Grammaticalization*, Vols. 1-2. Amsterdam: John Benjamins.

Van Valin, Robert D. Jr. 1987. Case marking and the structure of the Lakhota clause. In Johanna Nichols and Anthony Woodbury (eds.), *Grammar Inside and Outside the Clause*, 363-413. Cambridge: Cambridge University Press.

Vendryes, Joseph. 1925/1952. *Language: A Linguistic Introduction to History.* Translated by Paul Radin. London: Routledge & Kegan Paul.

Wartburg, Walther V. 1969. *Problems and Methods in Linguistics.* Translated into English by Joyce M. H. Reid. Oxford: Blackwell.

Watkins, Calvert. 1962. *Indo-European Origins of the Celtic Verb.* Dublin: Dublin Institute for Advanced Studies.

Weissenborn, Jürgen and Wolfgang Klein (eds.). 1982. *Here and There: Cross-Linguistic Studies on Deixis and Demonstration.* Amsterdam: John Benjamins.

Windisch, Ernst. 1869. Untersuchungen über Ursprung des Relativpronomens in den Indogermanischen Sprachen. In Georg Curtius (ed.), *Studien zur Griechichischen und Lateinischen Grammatik*, Vol 2. Leipzig: Hirzel.

Wright, Joseph. 1905/1968. *The English Dialect Grammar.* London: Oxford at the Clarendon Press.

Yule, George. 1981. New, current and displaced entity reference. *Lingua* 55, 41-52.

Zipf, George Kingsley. 1935. *The Psychobiology of Language: An Introduction to Dynamic Philology.* Cambridge, Mass: MIT Press.

Interpreting Usage: Construing the History of Dutch Causal Verbs

ARIE VERHAGEN
University of Leiden

1. Introduction

There is a famous epistolary novel in Dutch literature, *Sara Burgerhart*, written by Betje Wolff and Aagje Deken and first published in 1782, that is still being read not only in university by students of literary history but also in literature classes at schools (or at least some of them). It is possible for present day readers to understand most of the text without special training, even though several features of the language used are recognizably different from modern usage. One of these features is the use of *doen* as a causal verb. An example from this text is:

(1) *Ja, ik heb u genoeg gezegd, om u te **doen** weten, dat ik u bemin...*
     'Yes, I have said enough to you in order to make [lit.: do] you
     know that I love you'

Modern users of the language experience this use of *doen* as somehow strange; they would not use it in this context themselves, but rather prefer *laten*. But they have no problem in interpreting the sentence; specifically, they immediately understand that *doen* is used as a causal verb here. So for readers at the turn of the 21st century, there is simultaneously something familiar and something strange in the language of the 18th century novel, in this respect: it is sufficiently familiar to allow understanding to proceed, but the motivation for use of (in this case) *doen* is not transparent. It is this somewhat paradoxical situation that constitutes the topic of this paper, both analytically and methodologically.

The occurrence of *doen* in older texts frequently gives rise to such experiences of strangeness without understanding being impossible. Speakers of Modern Standard Dutch therefore often remark that *doen* tends to sound 'old-fashioned' in contexts like (1). Such an intuition is usually couched in terms of a contrast between minimal pairs. Upon encountering a case like (1), one says: "I would prefer *laten* over *doen* here," thereby constructing a minimal pair. At least one Dutch historical linguist (Duinhoven 1994) took this intuitive preference for *laten* over *doen* as the essential observation to be explained by an analysis of the history of *doen* and *laten*, and thus proposed a theory that analyzes it as the result of an *actual* historical process of *doen* being replaced as a causal verb by *laten*.

However, regardless of the details of this proposal, it should be kept in mind that minimal pairs are hardly ever encountered in actual language use, and that one therefore runs the risk of projecting present-day intuitions onto the historical developments. This is not to say that such intuitions are simply misguided; they are not, and it is a valid question how they might be explained. But in this paper I will try to show that an analysis that is explicitly based on an investigation of actual usage events, rather than intuition alone, is not only superior in empirical scope, but also theoretically more interesting, as it enables us to take dynamic relationships between meaning and context into account (in this case, as we shall see, mainly *cultural* context, but also narrative conventions), and thus to be explicit about the relationship between linguistic knowledge, such as knowledge of the meaning of the words *doen* and *laten*, and other kinds of knowledge.

2. The Semantics and Pragmatics of *doen* and *laten*: An Overview

The verbs *doen* (cognate of English *do*) and *laten* (cognate of *let*) have been in use as causal verbs since the oldest records of Dutch (early Middle Ages). Both take bare infinitival complements (without the infinitival marker *te*). At present, *laten* is much more frequent than *doen*, but (contrary to the suggestion in Duinhoven 1994), *doen* is definitely not generally obsolete; rather, there are particular types of contexts in which it is just the 'right' word to use. In fact, *doen* and *laten* exhibit a particular distribution relating to different types of causation. It is useful to see what the pattern of usage is and how it can be analyzed, before addressing the issue how the use of the verbs may actually have changed.

Consider the following two examples with *laten*:

(2) *De agent **liet** hen passeren.*
     'The officer let them pass.'

(3) *De sergeant **liet** ons door de modder kruipen.*
     'The sergeant had/made [lit.: let] us crawl through the mud.'

Note that the interpretation of *laten* ranges from permissive causation, as in (2), to coercive causation, which is the most natural reading for (3).[1] (See Talmy 1988, Kemmer and Verhagen 1994: 120, and specifically for Dutch, Verhagen and Kemmer 1997: 66-69, for arguments that permission is in fact a subtype of the general conceptual category of causation.) Other cases may be intermediate or neutral in this respect, such as:

(4) *Zij **liet** de agent haar rijbewijs zien.*
     'She showed [lit.: let see] the officer her driver's license.'

Some typical examples of causal *doen* are:

(5) *De stralende zon **doet** de temperatuur oplopen.*
     'The bright sun makes [lit.: does] the temperature rise.'

(6) *CDA **doet** problemen 'paars' even vergeten* (newspaper headline)
'The Christian Democratic Party makes [lit.: does] [one/people] briefly forget the problems of the purple coalition [i.e.: the coalition of liberals and social democrats]'

In Verhagen and Kemmer (1997), it is argued that the difference between the two verbs in Modern Dutch can be well understood in terms of Talmy's (1988) theory of **force dynamics**. Croft (1991: 167) gives the following graphical 'summary' of Talmy's ideas:

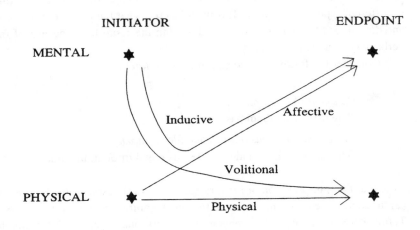

Figure 1. Asymmetries in Causation Type

Figure 1 captures the fact that people tend to distinguish different types of causation, depending on whether the situation they are talking about is conceived of as taking place in the physical or in the mental realm ('naive dualism'). Causal relations in the physical world are conceived of as *direct*: They are governed by natural laws, and in an important sense inevitable (given the initiating force, there is no way that the result can be avoided). Causal relations in the mental world, on the other hand, are conceived of as *indirect*: The initiating forces are intentions, and they cannot produce the intended result completely on their own. In order to get another mind to change its cognitive state, one has to make a 'detour' via the physical world (there is no telepathy, hence the strongly bent top line in Figure 1). Moreover, at the endpoint of the causal relationship, the target-mind has its own somewhat autonomous contribution to make to the entire causal event; the force produced by the initiator is not in itself sufficient for producing the effect. Verhagen and Kemmer argue that it is precisely this distinction that underlies the difference in usage of *doen* and *laten*: By means of *doen* the event is categorized as one of "direct causation," while *laten* categorizes an event as one of "indirect causation," in the sense that some other force than the initiator's is more directly involved in producing the result.

So (2), (3), and (4) are all examples, despite the differences, of indirect causation; in particular, they are of the inducive type in Figure 1, i.e. events that in one way or another involve communication, with intentions on the part of the initiating person, and recognition on the part of the endpoint-person.[2] No such 'higher' mental states and processes are involved in instances of direct causation, which are marked by *doen*. Example (5), being a case of physical causation, provides a straightforward illustration. Example (6), taken from a newspaper headline, is especially interesting in that it does *not* mean that the Christian Democratic Party intentionally communicates to everybody that they should forget certain problems, despite the fact that a political party, i.e. a human institution, is easily conceived of as capable of intentionally performing activities. Rather, this sentence evokes the idea of the chaos within the Christian Democratic Party after their defeat in the latest elections had aroused so much interest that it automatically caused everybody to forget these problems. In other words: although the CDA, as a human institution, may well communicate messages to others, it is not depicted in that way in this type of event, marked with *doen*.[3]

3. Some Problems for a Diachronic Analysis

The fact that *doen* and *laten* differ semantically in the modern language does not, of course, in itself exclude the possibility that the use of *doen* is gradually decreasing over the centuries, as Duinhoven (1994) has suggested (cf. Section 1). And in fact, some general results of text counts seem to confirm this idea. A corpus was collected consisting of a relatively large number of instances of both *doen* and *laten* from the 18th, 19th, and 20th centuries, from similar kinds of texts; Table 1 gives the general *doen/laten* ratios in each of these three centuries. From these data, it is obvious that the relative frequency of *doen* has diminished over time.[4]

Century	doen	laten
18th	1.22	1.00
19th	1.03	1.00
20th	0.72	1.00

Table 1. Ratio of doen/laten over 3 Centuries
(frequency of laten in each century = 1.00)

However, some problems arise as soon as we look at some more details. The first complication becomes apparent when we consider not the
ratios per century but the absolute frequencies in the same amount of text.
Consider Table 2.[5]

Century	doen	laten
18th	89	73
19th	70	68
20th	44	61

Table 2. Absolute Numbers of doen/laten in Same Amount of Text

What this table shows is that the frequency of *doen* does indeed decrease
over the years, but the frequency of *laten* does not *in*crease. If the latter were
replacing the former, it seems we would have to expect such an increase.

The second problem with the idea of *doen* becoming obsolete is that it
predicts the decline of *doen* to be general, the idea being that *doen* would
gradually become less suited to marking relationships of cause and effect (cf.
Duinhoven 1994). But when we distinguish between different types of text
in our corpus, there appear to be considerable differences, as a comparison of
Tables 3 and 4 shows.

Century	doen	laten
18th	1.08	1.00
19th	1.00	1.00
20th	0.80	0.98

Table 3. Ratio of doen/laten over 3 Centuries in Fiction
(frequency of laten in 18th century = 1.00)

Century	*doen*	*laten*
18th	1.73	1.00
19th	0.92	0.36
20th	0.16	0.60

Table 4. Ratio of *doen/laten* over 3 Centuries in Non-Fiction (frequency of *laten* in 18th century = 1.00)

There is a very striking difference here: While the use of *doen* in non-fiction texts diminishes dramatically between the 18th and the 20th centuries (according to Table 4 as much as 90%, in these data), the decrease in fictional texts is relatively minor (according to Table 3 about 25%). It appears then that different text types show different developments. Rather than a uniform, constant decrease of *doen* in the language in general, there seems to be a variable development. This phenomenon of diachronic variability, i.e. variability, through time, of the variation across context types, is especially relevant in view of the variation in the use of *doen* and *laten* that can be observed synchronically in the modern language. In a corpus of Modern Dutch,[6] the *doen/laten*-ratio varies considerably over different genres, from .10 in weekly magazines, through .66 in popular science books and articles, to as much as 1.62 in the subcorpus of 'officialese' described in Renkema (1981). The latter subcorpus is actually the only one in which *doen* outnumbers *laten* (I will return to this point below).

In view of these observations, it seems plausible that the historical change, whatever its precise nature, will have affected different genres differently; it would be a change in a pattern of variation, which a straightforward one-factor analysis will probably not be able to account for.

Finally, this idea of diachronically 'variable variation' is confirmed by the fact that *doen* has not simply withdrawn from combinations with specific lexical items. Often, both *doen* and *laten* occur with a given verb in earlier periods as well as the present; but the proportion of *doen* and *laten* instances has shifted. For example, we as Dutch speakers have the intuition that we would rather have *laten* than *doen* in (1), but the combination *laten weten* is not absent from the 18th century material, as exemplified in (7):

(7) *...en dewijl hij geen' tijd zou hebben, om een uurtje of anderhalf voor mij te vaceren, bad ik hem, naa de Synode...mij zulks te* **laaten** *weten*...(Van Goens 1776-1777)

'...and since he would not have time to take my place for an hour or an hour and a half, I requested him...to let me know [inform me] after the Synode...'

In fact, the combination *doen weten* is still in use today; witness such examples as (8). Note that this case has actually been produced, and that here we don't have the intuition that *doen* should be replaced by *laten*. I give the full context, because it will turn out to be useful for understanding the use of *doen* here.

(8) *Het zweet brak hem uit. Hij rees omzichtig van zijn stoel. De barones reeg hem aan het harpoentje van haar ogen. Hij glimlachte geruststellend en begaf zich naar de gangdeur. In de hal liep hij naar de enige deur, die hij stellig van binnen zou mogen afsluiten. Met een zucht* **deed** *hij de buitenwereld weten dat het kleine vertrek bezet was, en hij zonk op de bril om na te denken.*

'He started to sweat. He cautiously rose from his chair. The baroness harpooned him with her eyes. He smiled reassuringly and went to the passage door. In the hall, he walked to the only door of which he was confident that he could lock it from the inside. With a sigh he made [lit.: did] the outside world know that the small room was occupied, and sat down on the seat in order to think.'

So the picture is rather complicated; empirically it comprises a number of observations of synchronic variation and apparent changes in the use of causal verbs, as well as a number of intuitions about actual instances: With many cases from older texts, present-day readers have an experience of strangeness and one of recognition simultaneously. Now, a good analysis should provide a resolution of this paradox, and it is in that sense that intuitions, viz. those of contemporary as well as later interpreters of instances of use, form part of the empirical basis for an explanatory account. To us as modern speakers of the language, certain aspects of the older texts are not fully understandable, and we want a good analysis to improve our understanding. I will now present an analysis that satisfies this criterion.

4.   Animacy and Authority

4.1 In Modern Standard Dutch

Recall the claim in Section 2 that *laten* marks indirect causation, and *doen* direct causation. Given the rather strict relation between (in)directness and the 'naive dualism' of Figure 1, there should be a clear correlation between the use of *doen* and *laten* and animacy. With *laten* we should find more animate causers than with *doen*. Consider Table 5, which contains some figures from Verhagen and Kemmer (1997).

	laten (n = 444)	*doen* (n = 130)
Causer animate	99%	42%
Causer inanimate	1%	58%

χ^2= 268.25, df=1, p<<0.001

Table 5. Distribution of Animate Causers in Causatives with Explicit Causees in the Eindhoven Corpus (±1970)

The table gives the distribution of animacy in causative constructions in Modern Dutch that have an explicit causee. The correlation of *laten* with animacy of the causer is clear,[7] as well as a correlation of *doen* with inanimacy of the causer. However, the latter correlation is weaker: 42% animate causers with *doen* is a considerable portion. Verhagen and Kemmer (1997) discuss several special cases in this set. One type consists of those instances where the description itself refers to an animate being, but its animacy is not relevant in the event (as in *Hij deed me aan mijn moeder denken*, which means 'He reminded me of my mother,' and refers to some observable characteristics or behavior of the subject; see also the discussion of (6) above). Example (8), as the context shows, denotes the sliding of the latch of the bathroom door, and the causee is not an actual human being, so that there is no actual communication, which is emphasized by the use of *doen* (cf. Verhagen and Kemmer 1997 for further discussion). In the present context, some very interesting cases are those where the causer is God, as in (9), or where it is the government, as in (10):

(9) *Zij smeekte Jezus, haar de goede weg te **doen** bewandelen.*
'She begged Jesus to make [lit.: do] her walk in the right path.'

(10) *De regering stelt zich voor deze herstructurering gefaseerd te **doen** plaatsvinden.*
'The government intends to have [lit.: do] this reorganization take place in stages.'

The interesting thing about (9) is that the woman in question is not requesting Jesus to communicate with her, but rather to intervene in her mind directly (divine beings probably belonging to the small set of animate beings that can, in some cultures, be conceptualized as capable of influencing minds directly). In other words, the writer is categorizing the event here as in some sense involving direct causation, and this has the effect that the event is beyond the control of anyone else but Jesus.

Something very similar is going on in (10). In actual fact it is hard to believe that the reorganization will take place independently of the cooperation of many other people besides those in government. Still, the government is presenting the situation in precisely this way (this sentence was produced by a member of government in a message to the Dutch parliament). Again, the result of the event is presented as inevitable given the government's intentions, as beyond the control of anyone but the government (just as a physical result is conceived of as inevitable given the appropriate physical cause). So the use of *doen* is clearly motivated. Especially in the latter type of cases, we see that authority of the causer can provide motivation for the use of *doen*: activity from any other participant than the causer is essentially irrelevant for producing the result, so the causal event may be categorized as direct. This provides us with an immediate and plausible explanation for the fact mentioned above that in the Eindhoven Corpus of Modern Dutch, the only subcorpus in which *doen* outnumbers *laten* is the one containing 'officialese,' i.e. texts from government officials and politicians in The Hague (Renkema 1981).

What this analysis first of all shows is that in order to explain actual usage of the same linguistic expressions in different contexts, we have to take into account how the simple, abstract models invoked by such words (here, *doen* and *laten*) are embedded in more complex, concrete models of personal and social relationships, religion, etc. Not all of this can be simply *predicted* from the abstract models invoked by the words; a model such as Talmy's, even though it provides a valid generalization over many cases, does not entail how it is to be applied to any particular situation. Usage always involves specific speakers/writers, hearers/readers, at a specific time, in specific contexts; and since these influence production and understanding, facts of production and understanding do not in themselves relate immediately and unambiguously to the abstract models invoked by the words.

We would therefore say that a usage-based model will rather naturally take the form of some sort of constraint-satisfaction model. From the perspective of language production, in the cases just discussed animacy of the causer is an inhibitive factor for the use of *doen*, but authority or divinity may be activating factors for *doen*. Other factors of the context may also come into play, in particular the evaluation of the relevant aspects of the situation by the speaker. In some situations then, 'authority' may be stronger than 'animacy,' resulting in *doen* being used.[8] From an interpretive perspective, the use of *doen* is itself a constraint on the interpretation of the utterance, and may contribute, together with other factors, to an interpretation of the causer as inanimate in one case, or to the result being presented as inevitable in another. Thus a linguistic expression may have a constant 'weight,' i.e. a constant contribution to make to the communicative event, while the ultimate interpretation is always dependent on some sort of weighted sum of *all* constraints in the event. A single communicative event therefore never really provides conclusive evidence for the nature of what is contributed by one of its elements. This is precisely the reason why investigation of a diversity of actual usage events is important for this kind of theoretical position. In other words: A usage-based view should comprise a theoretical position as well as a methodology that 'fits' it.

4.2 Over the Last Three Centuries

Given the above view of the way the actual use of linguistic elements may relate in complex ways to contextual factors, a specific hypothesis on the historical development of *doen* and *laten* suggests itself: If it is true that features such as 'authority,' 'communication,' and 'inevitability' may provide motivation for the use of the causal verbs, then perhaps it is these factors of which the weight has changed over time, thus providing a (partial) explanation for the observed changes in usage. Specifically, the relative weights of 'authority' (favoring *doen*) and 'communication' (favoring *laten*) may have been different in the past, possibly in a way that could help explain the observed decrease of *doen*. Since these factors are particularly relevant in the case of events with animate causers, we should start by looking at details of any changes in the frequency of causers with *doen*.. Table 6 summarizes the relevant primary frequency data for the texts collected:

	18th	**19th**	**20th**
Causer animate	57%	47%	20%
Causer inanimate	40%	52%	80%
Indeterminate (absent)	3%	1%	

$\chi^2 = 26.44$, df=4, p<<0.001

Table 6. Animacy of Causers with *doen* over 3 Centuries
(n = 75 for each century)

It is clear from the table that there is a general tendency: The proportion of animate causers with *doen* has decreased quite dramatically. Whereas animate causers occurred with 57% of the *doen*-cases in this corpus in the 18th century, this becomes a minority of 47% in the 19th century, and a still smaller minority of 20% in the 20th. Now, of the factors mentioned above, the most plausible one to have changed much over the last three centuries is that of authority: We already know from all kinds of sources that 200 years ago, authority was a much more important determinant of social and personal relationships, or at least of their evaluation, than it is today. It is not difficult to find examples in 18th century texts like the following:

(11) *ik heb Tante...zo wel eens **doen** zien, dat haar manier van doen zeer dikwyls verbaast verre afweek van hare wyze van zeggen.* (Wolff and Deken 1782)
'I showed [lit.: did see] Aunt every so often...that what she did frequently differed amazingly from what she said'

(12) *...en ik [=Sophia Willis] poogde myn kinderen te **doen** begrypen, dat zy óók genoeg zouden hebben, indien zy hun begeerten vroeg leerden beteugelen.* (Wolff and Deken 1782)

'...and I tried to make [lit.: do] my children understand that they would also be satisfied if they learned to control their desires early.'

(13)   ...*dog dat Sijn Hoogheydt nogtans in dese wel gedaan hadde, omme alvorens sijn opstel aan de Raidpensionaris te **doen** zien.* (Van Hardenbroek 1782)[9]

'...but that His Highness had nevertheless done well in this case, in first showing [lit.: to do see] his document to the Counsellor.'

In (11) there is a relationship of authority (at least) because the *I* has been appointed executor of a last will that imposes certain obligations on the *Aunt*; (12) is a case of a parent-children relation, and in (13) the causer is a king, and the causee a counsellor. Such causers will be termed **institutional authorities**: persons for whom it is clear in the immediate context that they have some authority by virtue of a specific institutional role such as being a sovereign, a military official of high rank, or an expert with respect to the process involved, like a doctor in the case of medical treatment. By counting such cases, we may get some indication whether the decrease in the relative frequency of animate causers with *doen* may be attributed to a decrease in the importance of authority as a factor in categorizing causal events.

Now in order to get a good picture of possible developments in actual usage, we have to look, not so much at percentages of uses in each century, but rather at the figures for animacy and authority in equal amounts of text: It is only by looking at absolute frequencies that we can see if the factor considered may also explain (part of) the *general* decrease of the use of *doen* that has been observed.

The results are summarized in Table 7 below. Column 1 gives the numbers of animate causers, column 2 the numbers of these that are also institutional authorities, and column 3 gives the numbers of inanimate causers.[10]

	Animate Causers	Authorities	Inanimate Causers
18th century			
doen	54	40	35
laten	68	23	5
19th century			
doen	33	9	37
laten	54	15	4
20th century			
doen	10	4	34
laten	53	6	8

Table 7. Animacy and Authority over 3 Centuries, in Equal Amounts of Text

Clearly, the most striking tendency to be noted here is that the frequency of institutional authorities as causers decreases drastically over the three centuries *in general*, independently of the choice of causal verb. Secondly, this tendency appears to have a special effect on the frequency of *doen* but not that of *laten*. This can be explained on the assumption that 'authority' is a (positive) motivating factor for *doen*, but not (a positive or negative one) for *laten*. So it seems that the diminishing role of authority in the texts is a major factor in the decrease of *doen*, and one that is also part of a general cultural development: Authority has become a far less important aspect of our models of interpersonal relations (if not of these relations themselves). Due to the importance of authority in interpersonal relationships in the 18th century, situations caused by humans which invited the inference that the outcome depended only on the causer were common; due to changes in the cultural view of personal relationships, such inferences have apparently become much more unusual.

Another notable conclusion to be drawn from these data is that there has been no *general* decrease in the use of *doen*, but only in specific combinations. There is clearly an asymmetry between the categories in Table 7: The use of *doen* with inanimate causers is strikingly stable over the three centuries (the top rows for each century in column 3), contrary to its use with animate causers (column 1). The latter component, in fact, seems to be fully responsible for the observed overall decrease of the use of *doen*. Therefore, any purported explanation of the change in terms of *doen* becoming gradually less suitable for expressing causation has a very serious problem here. What appears to have happened is mainly that it is far less normal now than in the 18th century to depict a situation of communication between people as involving so much authority on the part of the causer that the result could be regarded as inevitable. In fact, as the table shows, the role of the feature 'authority' in the texts has diminished overall, and the decrease in the frequency of *doen* simply parallels this.[11]

Now this explanation presupposes that in a general sense, the function of *doen* has not changed. When we conceive of the conceptual content of a linguistic element as a network of senses—prototypes and extensions, and schemas generalizing over these—in the sense of Langacker (1988), then we can say that the most general schema of *doen* has not changed. *Doen* still has 'directness of causation' as its conceptual content, and this captures the fact that it is produced less often with animates now than it used to be, given apparent and in fact well-known changes in our cultural values concerning authority, if not in the actual role of authority in society. On the other hand, a change may be claimed for some more specific levels in the network, where it is connected to cognitive models like those of interpersonal relationships, God, and perhaps others like these. As far as one wants to call it a change in the language, it is actually indistinguishable from the change in the culture.[12]

This situation is strongly reminiscent of the characterization of cultural knowledge by D'Andrade (1987). D'Andrade points out that there are hierarchical relationships between cognitive models in a culture; the "folk model of the mind" (laying out what kinds of mental states and processes there are, how they are caused, what is intentional and what is not, etc.) is an abstract model that enters into a number of other more complex and more specific models of activities like buying and selling. Now to know a culture is not just to know a relatively large number of its essential models; it is to know a network of hierarchically related models, and especially to know the models that enter into many other models in that culture (D'Andrade 1987:112). Knowledge of the meaning of *doen* appears to be just another example of this situation, so that changes in certain specific parts of the network of models with which *doen* is connected, do not necessarily change the general abstract content of this meaning.

So the kind of evidence that I have presented, which can only be produced by investigating actual usage, is very powerful in that it has a specific *theoretical* implication: Accounting for actual usage requires a view of cognitive models of different degrees of abstractness as hierarchically related and strongly interacting. Knowing the language in the sense of being able to use it properly includes knowing these more specific models too, and is therefore inextricably intertwined with knowing the culture.

5. Interpreting Usage on a Micro-Level

The force of the specific argument just presented largely rests on the parallelism for the case of *doen* in the columns of animacy (1) and authority (2) in Table 7, and the asymmetry between these two and the column of inanimacy (3). The argument would be strongly reinforced if the analysis also provides the conceptual instruments to make sense of particular cases that are not directly accounted for in terms of the correlation that the table presents. In this section, I would like to present two examples of this kind.

5.1 Gender

The first special case is related to the fact that in order to assign a causer to the category 'authority' for Table 7, it was required, as indicated in Section 4.2, that there was independent evidence for this status in the text—that is how "institutional authority" was defined. But authority might also be relevant in other ways than these. In particular, difference in gender was not used as an indication of authority in the relationship. However, we know that in the 18th century there was a tremendous asymmetry in gender roles and a corresponding difference in balance of authority and power. More specifically, a major moral point of the famous novel *Sara Burgerhart*, which is the source of a large part of the 18th century data collected, is precisely that the proper relationship between man and wife is one of authority (not unambiguously so, for in certain areas wives were considered experts, but the general pattern is clear enough). This raises the question of which causal verbs were used in the description of communication between men and women. There are not that many instances in my data,[13] but the distribution is nevertheless striking.

Let us consider some examples: (14) and (15) have male causers and female causees, and they have *doen*; in (16) and (17) causers and causees are of the same sex, and these have *laten*.

(14) *Ja, ik heb u genoeg gezegd, om u te **doen** weten, dat ik u be-min...*

'Yes, I have said enough to you in order to make [lit.: do] you know that I love you...' [causer male, causee female]

(15) *Gy* [=Jacob Brunier] *voldeed uw zeven Dames; gy kon om snuif en tandpoeders denken...en ons tevens in uw nieuwe denkbeelden **doen** delen.* (Wolff and Deken 1782)

'You satisfied your seven Ladies; you were able to think of snuff and tooth powders...and also have us share your new ideas.' [causer male, causee female]

(16) *...en dewijl hij geen' tijd zou hebben, om een uurtje of anderhalf voor mij te vaceren, bad ik hem, naa de Synode...mij zulks te **laaten** weten...*

'...and since he would not have time to take my place for an hour or an hour and a half, I requested him...to let me know [inform me] after the Synod...' [causer and causee both male]

(17) *...ik* [=Sara] *was dus zeer in verzoeking om aan Letjes naaister, Madame Montmartin, zo half en half te **laten** merken, dat ik in het laatste geval was...*

'...I was thus very much tempted to more or less let Letje's dressmaker, Mrs. Montmartin, notice that I was in this kind of situation...' [causer and causee both female]

The distribution in the whole set of 14 cases is shown in Table 8:

	doen ($n = 8$)	*laten* ($n = 6$)
Female Causer		
Female Causee	0	3
Male Causee	1	0
Male Causer		
Female Causee	6	0
Male Causee	1	3

Table 8. Gender and Causatives in the 18th Century

All six cases of *laten* involve same-gender communication. On the other hand, in six out of eight cases of *doen* a male communicates something to a female. So even though the number of instances is not very large, the pattern is very suggestive: apparently males 'made' (or 'had') females know things, whereas both males and females among themselves 'let' each other know things.

Only one instance shows the reverse pattern; example (18) has a female causer and a male causee:

(18) *Indien er iets mocht voorvallen, 't geen u nodig schynt my te doen weten, zo verzoek ik u ernstig om my met uwe brieven te veréeren.*

'If ever something might happen that seems to you necessary to tell [lit.: do know] me, I sincerely request you to honor me with your letters.'

In fact, however, even this case can be seen to support the analysis. Notice that the clause with the causal event is embedded under *request*. And the requester is male, the 'requestee' is female. Thus it is the male who himself puts the female in a position of authority, so to speak, and there is abundant evidence in the text, including this sentence ('sincerely request,' 'honor me'), that this particular man is eager to show a lot of respect towards this particular woman. In other words, the use of *doen* here is very polite, just as the use of a formal form of address by a superior towards a subordinate is polite.

5.2 Subjectivity

The second special case I would like to consider is the discrepancy between fiction and non-fiction noted in Section 3. As Tables 3 and 4 showed, the frequency of *doen* decreased much more in non-fiction than in fiction. The figures are extracted and represented in Table 9.

Century	Fiction	Non-fiction
18th	1.08	1.73
20th	0.80	0.16

Table 9. From Tables 3-4: Ratios of *doen* (relative to *laten*) in 18th vs. 20th Century

In fiction, the relative frequency of *doen* (taking the frequency of *laten* in the 18th century as 1.00) went from 1.08 to .80; in non-fiction it went from 1.73 to .16. In terms of the types of causation proposed by Talmy (as depicted in Figure 1), we know from Section 4.2 that the use of *doen* with inducive causation, i.e. with animate causers, decreased drastically. Consequently, the natural question to ask is whether there could be a reason for a difference between fiction and non-fiction in the domain of affective causation, i.e. causation with an inanimate cause and a mental effect.

Consider what a conceptualizer, reader or writer, or whoever is construing the description of the event, knows when s/he reports such a type of causation: The conceptualizer is effectively reporting from the causee's mind. Saying something of the type 'Such and such *made* X *realize* so and so,' creates an internal, personalized perspective for one particular character. So this type of causation can be reported by narrators who have the power to look inside a character's head. Some typical examples from the 20th century texts in the data are the following:

(19) *Eerst waren het angst en pijn die hem huilen **deden**...*
'At first it was fear and pain that made [lit.: did] him cry...'

(20) *...zij [=zijn herinneringen] kwamen hem 's avonds gezelschap houden en **deden** hem lachen of somber voor zich uit staren.*
'...they [=his memories] came at night to keep him company and made [lit.: did] him laugh, or gloomily stare in front of him.'

(21) *Een poort naar niets en voor niemand, in geen enkel opzicht geschikt haar een gevoel van triomf te bezorgen, of te **doen** denken dat hij alleen voor haar gebouwd was.*
'A gate to nothing and for nobody, in no way fit for giving her a feeling of triumph, or for making [lit.: doing] her think that it had been built just for her.'

Such sentences are recognizably narrative. Besides the internal perspective created by the (affective) causal predicates, they contain expressions denoting subjective experiences, such as *angst* ("fear"), *herinneringen* ("memories"), *somber* ("gloomily"), *gevoel bezorgen* ("give a feeling"). But even without such additional indications of subjectivity, causative sentences of this type do not fit in a purely objective report; for example, consider (22), taken from a newspaper article on a Labor Party congress:

(22) *Een blik op de voorste rij, waar zijn voorgangers gezeten waren,*
      deed *de nieuwe PvdA-voorzitter beseffen dat hij het niet gemak-*
      kelijk zou krijgen.
      'A glance at the first row, where his predecessors were seated,
      made [lit.: did] the new Labor Party president realize that his job
      was not going to be easy.'

When reading this, we immediately know that we are not on the front
page of the newspaper, where the 'hard facts' of the news are presented, but
in a story providing background to a more objective report given elsewhere.
In such background 'human-interest' stories, personal involvement is allow-
able. It seems clear that the chance of this type of causation occurring is
larger in fiction than in non-fiction. We furthermore know that this kind of
subjectivity (a character's subjectivity, rather than speaker's subjectivity, cf.
Sanders 1994:24-5), though definitely not a modern invention, has become
very prominent in literary narrative especially since the rise of the modern
novel.

Now consider Table 10; it gives figures indicating the numbers (in
terms of the normalized frequencies of Tables 3-4) of *doen* that entail an internal perspective (as indicated by an experiential complement verb).

	doen	Internal Perspective
Fiction		
18th century	1.08	.26 (24%)
20th century	0.80	.37 (46%)
Non-fiction		
18th century	1.73	.14 (8%)
20th century	0.16	.04 (24%)

Table 10. Frequency of *doen* with Internal Perspective

We see another asymmetry here: In terms of percentages, *doen* with implied internal perspective is increasing both in fiction and in non-fiction, but
much more so in fiction, and, more importantly, it is only in the fiction
part of this corpus that the actual number of this kind of events increases. In
these data, almost half of the *doen*-instances in modern fiction are accounted

for by this specific type of affective causation. The claim seems justified, then, that the increase of subjective internal perspectives in modern literary fiction is at least partly responsible for the fact that in this type of text, the frequency of causal *doen* has not diminished to the same extent as in other text types; in narratives the decrease of *doen* with animate causers is partly compensated, as it were, by an increase of *doen* with an implied personal perspective. Again, it becomes evident that an account of actual usage must take into account specific details of the conceptual network connected to a linguistic element.

6. Conclusions

Theoretically and descriptively, the first conclusion is, of course, that in a *general* sense the meaning of *doen* in Dutch has not changed essentially over the last 300 years (and probably not even over a longer period; cf. Note 1). What has changed are cultural conceptions of the role of authority and gender in causal events, and also cultural practices of (subjective) narration. By the same token, however, it has become clear that the use of the word is connected in particular ways to other cognitive models; in a usage-based network conception of the meaning of *doen*, this implies that details of the network did change over time (and consequently, if we equate the meaning with the entire network, the meaning of the word itself has changed). Knowing how to use the word (a criterion for knowing its meaning) and knowing how to behave in one's culture turn out to be indistinguishable notions.

Methodologically, one important point to note is that a theoretical conclusion of this type is in fact strongly dependent on investigation of a variety of actual usage events, including their contexts. Acceptability, useful as it may be, could not have provided the evidence that is the basis for this insight into these relations between knowledge of language and knowledge of culture, including the historical relations.

Finally, we have in fact resolved the paradox noted at the end of Section 3, where it was noted that we, as 20th century interpreters, experience both familiarity and strangeness with respect to a number of instances of causal *doen* in older texts. We are now in a position to see the motivation for its use, which means that we are now in a position to integrate the 'strange' cases into one coherent story with other cases, including modern ones. The analysis allows us, now, to assign a coherent interpretation to certain features of older texts, one which is furthermore coherent with the way we Dutch speakers interpret present-day usage events; in a way, we have extended *our* network for *doen*, so as to include a substantial set of older cases. So this particular empirical problem, involving a certain kind of intuition, has been solved by means of this analysis. This fact both supports the analysis, and shows that intuitions about actual usage events may be an integral part of a usage-based approach.

Notes

1. It is generally assumed that permission is the original meaning of *laten*, the causative uses being derived later. If that is correct, the change must definitely have occurred before the period considered here. The data in Landré (1993) clearly indicate that the whole range from permissive to causative uses of *laten* is present in the same way in 18th as well as 20th century Dutch. As for older periods, the Middle Dutch Dictionary (Verwijs and Verdam 1885-1952) also lists causative besides permissive uses of *laten* in the Middle Ages (of Old Dutch hardly anything remains). Interestingly, Verwijs and Verdam state the following concerning Middle Dutch: "*Laten* expresses more the passive, and *doen* more the active type of causation, but sometimes this difference is hardly noticeable. Compare new Dutch *doen weten* and *laten weten*..." (Middle Dutch Dictionary IV:184, my translation). It seems that *laten*, at least in combination with an infinitival complement, but probably also in other uses, can be used both for the specific concept "permission" and for its 'superordinate' "indirect causation." It is well known that this type of semantic shift is quite common, but more detailed evidence is required for the claim that it has occurred in the actual history of Dutch *laten*. In view of the available evidence so far, it might also be the case that this polysemy has been a stable property of the semantic structure of *laten* for an extended period of time.

2. Instances of volitional causation as meant in Figure 1 are situations of humans acting on the physical world, i.e. of making or allowing natural forces to change things. In several of these cases, *laten* is used (in situations of 'letting something fall,' or 'letting the bathwater flow away'), indicating that the relation between the initiating force and the result is conceived of as indirect. In other cases *doen* is used, especially to mark the non-communicative aspect of a situation (cf. example (6)); see Verhagen and Kemmer (1997), for further discussion.

3. In fact, it is a kind of affective causation as meant in Figure 1; a general subtype of such events are perceptions (cause in the physical world, effect in the mental world), which are, in the 'folk model of the mind' (D'Andrade 1987) thought of as directly caused by the outside world, and not controllable; hence these are also marked by *doen*. I will return to this specific subtype in Section 5.2.

4. The initial description of the data to be discussed is given in Landré (1993). I want to thank Nienke Landré for her help in the collection and initial classification of these data.

5. Normalized to frequencies per 120,000 words; 2/3 fiction, 1/3 non-fiction. This amount was mostly sufficient to get a corpus with 75 instances of each causal verb for each century. This number seemed reasonable for an investigation of possible developments in the distribution of different kinds of noun phrases in both types of causative constructions (cf. Sections 4.2 and 5). In some cases, less or more than this amount of text was searched, especially for *doen*—hence the normalization. Another manipulation of the data was that all cases of *laten zien* ('let see,' = 'show') were ultimately left out: especially for the recent periods, this specific combination vastly outnumbers the others, to a degree that would have made any comparison highly problematic. A disadvantage of this decision is, of course, that the data no longer allow for immediate comparison with other corpora, especially the Eindhoven Corpus of Modern Dutch. As we will see below, however, it is possible to extract certain trends from the data and to compare these with the independently established trends in certain other corpora.

6. The Eindhoven Corpus in the version that is available at the Free University of Amsterdam. It contains language data from the early 1970s (cf. uit den Boogaart 1975, and also Renkema 1981).

7. In causeeless causatives with *laten* the portion of inanimate causers is not so extremely small as in the subset for which Table 5 gives the relative distribution. Their greater frequency in causeeless causatives seems to be mainly due to constructions with reflexives, of the type *De cassette **laat** zich gemakkelijk inbrengen* [lit.: The cassette lets itself insert easily], meaning 'The cassette may be inserted easily.'

8. Note that this does not alter the fact that 'animacy' as such is still an inhibiting factor for *doen*. In other words, this constraint-satisfaction approach allows us to state that the meaning of *doen* is not changed by

the mere fact that it is being used with an animate subject NP. See Verhagen (1997) for a more general discussion.

9. Note the preposition *aan* marking the causee in this case. This does not occur with causative *doen* in Modern Dutch, for which an explanation has been proposed in Verhagen and Kemmer (1997). According to that analysis, the usage of the dative-like marking implies relative autonomy of the causee, which is compatible with *laten*, but not with *doen*. Cases having *aan* are therefore predicted to be among the first to have lost the possibility of *doen*, since their specifications are least compatible with the increasing preference for use of *doen* with non-animate, non-autonomous causees.

10. Note that the figures for the 20th century in Table 7 exhibit the same tendencies as observed in the Eindhoven Corpus (cf. Table 5), but that they do not match exactly. In terms of percentages, the skewing of *doen* and animate/inanimate is 23/77 here, vs. 42/58 in Table 5; with *laten* the ratios are 87/13 and 99/1, respectively. The differences are due to at least the following factors. First, the Eindhoven Corpus contains a sub-corpus of formal political texts ('officialese'), which, as pointed out above, is the only one in which *doen* outnumbers *laten*; this is an important factor in the differences involving *doen*. Second, Table 5 is based on a comparison of (in)animacy of causers and causees (cf. Verhagen and Kemmer 1997). The consequence is that Table 5, unlike Table 7, only concerns cases with an explicit causee, thus excluding such cases as *De acta van het concilie* ***laten*** *duidelijk zien dat*...('The council's proceedings clearly show [lit.: let see] that...'), and *De cassette* ***laat*** *zich gemakkelijk inbrengen* (lit.: The cassette lets itself insert easily; 'The cassette may be inserted easily'). The inclusion of such cases in the data for Table 7 appears to be the main factor responsible for the differences with *laten*. Finally, the present data contain a relatively larger portion of fiction, and this produces some special effects as well, particularly for *doen* (cf. Table 3, and the discussion in Section 5.2).

11. I wish to thank Huub van den Bergh for his help in laying out the relation between the data, as presented in the table, and the conceptual content of the analysis. The difference between the 18th and the 20th centuries is in full accordance with the hypothesis proposed here, because there is an almost exact parallel between the two centuries in the ratio of animacy with *doen* to that of authority. The data from the 19th century do not fit the hypothesis completely: the figures in the column 'animate' do not decrease as much (with respect to the 18th century) as

those in the column 'authority.' Several factors could be responsible for this 'anomaly.' One possibility is the artificiality of the boundaries between the periods; another, perhaps more interesting one is that 19th century texts show less independent evidence for 'authority,' while this feature actually still played an important role in the writers' and (intended) readers' views of causality.

12. This network conception of the meaning of *doen* is discussed in more detail in Verhagen (1998).

13. In order to be relevant for this particular count, it was necessary that the sex of both causer and causee could be established unambiguously. Many cases of interpersonal causation contained at least one indefinite or plural participant, for whom sex could not be determined, and these were therefore excluded from the count. Hence the relatively small number of cases in Table 8.

References

Croft, William A. 1991. *Syntactic Categories and Grammatical Relations: The Cognitive Organization of Information*. Chicago/London: University of Chicago Press.

Boogaart, Pieter C. uit den. 1975. *Woordfrequenties in geschreven en gesproken Nederlands*. Utrecht: Oosthoek, Scheltema and Holkema.

D'Andrade, Roy G. 1987. A folk model of the mind. In Dorothy Holland and Naomi Quinn (eds.), *Cultural Models in Language and Thought*, 112-148. Cambridge: Cambridge University Press.

Duinhoven, Anton M. 1994. Het hulpwerkwoord *doen* heeft afgedaan. *Forum der Letteren* 35, 110-131.

Kemmer, Suzanne and Arie Verhagen. 1994. The grammar of causatives and the conceptual structure of events. *Cognitive Linguistics* 5, 115-156.

Landré, Nienke. 1993. Wat *doen laten*-causatieven wat *doen*-causatieven *laten*? Ms., Utrecht University.

Langacker, Ronald W. 1988. A Usage-Based Model. In Brygida Rudzka-Ostyn (ed.), *Topics in Cognitive Linguistics*, 127-161. Amsterdam: John Benjamins. [Reprinted 1991 in Ronald Langacker, *Concept, Image, and Symbol*, 261-288. Berlin: Mouton de Gruyter.]

Renkema, Jan. 1981. *De Taal van "Den Haag:" Een Kwantitatief-Stilistisch Onderzoek Naar Aanleiding van Oordelen over Taalgebruik*. 's-Gravenhage: Staatsuitgeverij.

Sanders, José. 1994. *Perspective in Narrative Discourse.* Tilburg: Katholieke Universiteit Brabant doctoral dissertation.

Talmy, Leonard. 1988. Force dynamics in language and cognition. *Cognitive Science* 12: 49-100.

Verhagen, Arie. 1997. Context, meaning, and interpretation, in a practical approach to linguistics. In Leo Lentz and Henk Pander Maat (eds.), *Discourse Analysis and Evaluation: Functional Approaches*, 7-39. Amsterdam: Rodopi.

Verhagen, Arie. 1998. Changes in the use of Dutch *doen* and the nature of semantic knowledge. In Ingrid Tieken-Boon van Ostade, Maria J. van der Wal, and Arjan van Leuvensteijn (eds.), Do *in English, Dutch and German. History and Present-Day Variation*, 103-119. Amsterdam/Münster: Stichting Neerlandistiek/Nodus Publikationen,

Verhagen, Arie and Suzanne Kemmer. 1997. Interaction and causation: A cognitive approach to causative constructions in Modern Standard Dutch. *Journal of Pragmatics* 27, 61-82.

Verwijs, Eelco and Jacob Verdam. 1885-1952. *Middelnederlandsch Woordenboek.* (11 volumes.) 's-Gravenhage: Martinus Nijhoff.

Investigating Language Use Through Corpus-Based Analyses of Association Patterns

DOUGLAS BIBER
Northern Arizona University

1. Introduction

In recent years, language use has come to be recognized as an important aspect of linguistic study, with equal status to the study of language structure. This development marks a return to the priorities of certain schools of linguistics in the 1950s, most notably Firthian linguistics (see, for example, the papers in the volume edited by Palmer 1968).

Studies of use are concerned with actual practice, and the extent to which linguistic patterns are common or rare, rather than focusing exclusively on potential grammaticality. As such, adequate investigations of language use must be empirical, analyzing the functions and distribution of linguistic features in natural discourse contexts. In descriptive lexicography, which is concerned with the actual use of words, new meanings are discovered only by examining the use of a word in actual discourse contexts. Grammatical structures can also be compared from a use perspective, by studying the ways in which seemingly similar structures occur in different contexts and serve different functions. In addition, a use perspective is required to in-

287

vestigate the stylistic preferences of individuals, the differing linguistic preferences of groups of speakers, and the ways in which 'registers' (or 'genres') favor some words and structures over others.

Corpus-based analyses are particularly well suited to such investigations. Over the past decade there has been a dramatic increase in corpus-based language studies. For example, the bibliography of corpus-based studies provided by Altenberg (1991a) includes well over 600 entries, and many more studies have appeared in the last five years (see, for example, the edited collections by Aijmer and Altenberg 1991; Armstrong 1994; Johansson and Stenström 1991; Svartvik 1990, 1992). The essential characteristics shared by these corpus-based studies are:

- they are empirical, analyzing the actual patterns of use in natural texts;
- they utilize a large and principled collection of natural texts (i.e., a 'corpus') as the basis for analysis;
- they make extensive use of computers for analysis, using both automatic and interactive techniques;
- they depend on both quantitative and qualitative (interpretive) analytical techniques.

One major advantage of a corpus-based approach is that it enables a scope and reliability of analysis not otherwise feasible. Corpus-based analyses can be based on an adequate representation of naturally-occurring discourse, including analysis of complete texts, multiple texts from any given variety, and inclusion of multiple spoken and written varieties for comparative purposes. Using computational techniques, it is feasible to entertain the possibility of a comprehensive linguistic characterization of a text, analyzing a wide range of linguistic features (rather than being restricted to a few selected features); further, computational techniques can be used to analyze the complex ways in which linguistic features interact within texts. For quantitative analyses, corpus-based analysis results in greater reliability and accuracy: computers do not become bored or tired—they will count a linguistic feature in the same way every time it is encountered. Finally, corpus-based analyses enable the possibility of cumulative results and public accountability. Subsequent studies can be based on the same corpus of texts, or additional corpora can be analyzed using the same computational techniques. Such studies can test the results of previous research, and findings can be compared across studies, building a cumulative linguistic description of the language.

Even more important, corpus-based techniques enable investigation of new research questions that were previously disregarded because they were considered intractable. In particular, the corpus-based approach makes it possible to identify and analyze complex **association patterns**: the systematic ways in which linguistic features are used in association with other linguistic and non-linguistic features.[1]

Association patterns can be regarded as an extension of Firth's notion of **collocation** (e.g. Firth 1952). Collocations are characterizations of a word in terms of the other words that it typically co-occurs with. Firth also paid attention to the relationship between collocations and the 'context of situation', focusing primarily on the different purposes for which a word might be used.

The notion of association pattern extends the concept of collocation in several ways. First, association patterns are identified empirically from analysis of a representative corpus; many stereotypical collocations do not in fact represent strong association patterns, while other unanticipated collocations are identified by empirical analyses of association patterns. Second, association patterns represent continuous relationships that must be analyzed in quantitative terms. Given a large, representative corpus and the appropriate analytical tools, association patterns can be specified in precise quantitative terms, identifying the extent to which a particular type of relationship is found. Finally, association patterns are used to characterize grammatical features as well as words, with respect to systematic co-occurrence patterns with other words, other grammatical features, or non-linguistic characteristics of the context.[2]

As Table 1 shows, association patterns are used to investigate two major kinds of research question: the variablity of a linguistic feature, and the variablity among texts.

A) Investigating the variability of a linguistic feature (lexical or grammatical)
    i)   Non-linguistic associations of the feature:
        • distribution across registers
        • distribution across dialects
        • distribution across time
    ii) Linguistic associations of the feature:
        • co-occurrence with particular words
        • co-occurrence with grammatical features
B) Investigating the variability among texts
    • 'dimensions' = co-occurrence patterns of linguistic features

Table 1. Kinds of Association Patterns

Investigating the variability of a linguistic feature in terms of its association patterns has two major components: 1) non-linguistic associations, and 2) linguistic associations. Non-linguistic association patterns describe how certain linguistic features are differentially associated with registers, dialects, or historical change.

There are two main types of linguistic association patterns: lexical associations and grammatical associations. Both individual words and grammatical constructions can be studied with respect to their association patterns. For a corpus-based study of an individual word, the lexical associations are the collocations of the target word (other words that the target word frequently co-occurs with). The grammatical associations of the target word describe structural preferences, for example, whether a particular adjective typically occurs with attributive or predicative functions, or whether a particular verb typically occurs with transitive or intransitive functions.

Corpus-based studies of a grammatical construction can similarly include both lexical and grammatical associations. In this case, the lexical associations are the tendencies for the target grammatical construction to co-occur with particular words. For example, what matrix-clause verbs typically occur with a *that*-clause, and do a different set of matrix-clause verbs typically occur with *to*-clauses? Grammatical associations in this case identify contextual factors associated with structural variants. For example, are *that*-clauses used in extraposed constructions as often as *to*-clauses?

All of these linguistic association patterns interact with non-linguistic associations. In fact, corpus-based analyses show that linguistic association patterns are generally *not* valid for the language as a whole. Rather, linguistic and non-linguistic associations interact with one another, so that strong linguistic associations in one register often represent only weak associations in other registers.

One final type of association pattern is important when the research goal is to describe texts and registers rather than individual linguistic features: the ways in which groups of linguistic features commonly co-occur in texts. For example, frequent nouns, adjectives, and prepositional phrases commonly co-occur in academic prose texts, working together to provide a dense integration of information. Textual co-occurrence patterns such as these are important in characterizing the salient linguistic characteristics of registers and styles.

What is just now coming to be realized is how extensive and systematic the patterns of language use are. Such association patterns are well beyond the access of intuitions, and yet these patterns are much too systematic to be disregarded as accidental. While future research is required to determine the theoretical underpinnings of these patterns (and the extent to which they can be attributed to cognitive, situational, or textual factors), we are now in a position to document the extent and nature of these patterns much more fully than has heretofore been possible.

The following sections provide example analyses of each type of association pattern: association patterns for individual words are illustrated in Section 2; association patterns for grammatical constructions are illustrated in Section 3; and register analyses with respect to textual co-occurrence patterns are illustrated in Section 4. The analyses are carried out on a 10 million-word subsample from the Longman/Lancaster Corpus (ca. 5 million-word samples from fiction and academic prose), supplemented by a 5 million-word sample of conversation from the British National Corpus. In the conclusion, the paper outlines some of the future investigations needed for an integrated description of linguistic structure and use.

2. Association Patterns for Individual Words

Over the past 10 to 15 years, lexicographic researchers have been at the leading edge of work that applies corpus-based techniques to standard linguistic research questions. There are now many concordancing packages that are commercially available for doing lexicographic research, and the most important new dictionaries (e.g. by COBUILD, Longman, and Cambridge) are all based entirely on corpus analysis. (In contrast, there are few adequate commercially available tools for doing grammatical research on a corpus, and most publishers continue to rely on traditional methods for developing new grammars.) When coupled with a concordancing program, a corpus provides a wealth of examples for any given word, allowing lexicographers to more accurately identify and characterize the range of meanings for the word (see, for example, Sinclair 1987, 1991).

However, the usefulness of corpus-based lexical analysis is not limited to dictionary making. For example, several studies identify and characterize the use of relatively fixed lexical expressions (e.g. Altenberg 1991b, 1993; Kjellmer 1991; Renouf and Sinclair 1991). In addition, statistical measurements of word associations have been developed to further clarify the senses of words and identify the most important patterns of use (Biber 1993a, Church and Hanks 1990, Nakamura and Sinclair 1995).

One type of corpus-based investigation that is particularly interesting is the investigation of seemingly synonymous or near-synonymous words (e.g. Biber, Conrad, and Reppen 1994 on *certain* and *sure;* Kennedy 1991 on *between* and *through*). Dictionaries and thesauruses often list such words as equivalent in meaning. However, corpus-based investigations of association patterns show that there are important, patterned differences in the ways that native speakers use seemingly synonymous words. To illustrate, I briefly compare the association patterns for a pair of near-synonymous adjectives: *happy* and *glad.*

First, Table 2 shows that these adjectives are used to differing extents across registers:

	Conversation	Fiction	Academic Prose
happy	******	********	*
glad	***	*****	-

Each * marks approximately 20 occurrences per million words
- represents less than 10 occurrences per million words

Table 2. Distribution of Adjective Pairs Across Registers

To understand why these register differences exist, it is useful to study the associated words that typically co-occur with each adjective, that is, the **collocations.** Table 3 displays the most common nouns that occur as right collocates of each adjective. This table reports the strongest lexical associations as identified by *t*-scores computed for each collocational pair (see Church, Gale, Hanks, and Hindle 1991; Stubbs 1995).

happy	+	Nouns:	*man, family/families, couple, one, life, face, days*
		Punctuation:	*. , ? ! ;*
		Prepositions:	*with, as, about, at, in*
glad	+	Pronouns:	*I, you, he, she, we, they*
		Complementizers:	*to, that*
		Other:	*the, there, of*

Table 3. Preferred Right Collocates of *happy* versus *glad*

Table 3 shows that each of these adjectives has a distinct pattern of lexical association. However, these lexical associations can also be analyzed as reflecting different grammatical associations. Thus, *happy* has a strong lexical association with several following nouns, indicating that it is relatively common as an attributive adjective; for example,

> He was a *happy* man.
> ...like one big *happy* family.
> She led a full and *happy* life there.

In contrast, none of the strong right collocates of *glad* are nouns, suggesting that this adjective is not common in attributive position. In fact, analysis of the grammatical distribution of *happy* and *glad* shows that both adjectives are much more common in predicative position rather than attributive position: the adjective *happy* occurs about 80% of the time in predicative position, while *glad* is almost always used in predicative position (over 98%).[3] For example:

(1) I was comfortable and very happy.
(2) You look *happy!*
(3) She was *glad* to go.
(4) He was *glad* that he could rest.

However, more detailed examination of the grammatical associations for these two adjectives uncovers a fundamental difference: although both adjectives usually occur in predicative position, *happy* is often used as the entire predication, and thus it is commonly followed by clause-final punctuation (as in examples 1 and 2 above). In contrast, *glad* is commonly followed by a *to*-clause or a *that*-clause, which specifies what the person is glad about (as in examples 3 and 4 above).

In fact, nearly all of the preferred right collocates of *glad* represent a grammatical association of a following complement clause. For example, this pattern accounts for the strong lexical association that *glad* has to following pronouns (e.g. *I, you, he/she*) These cannot be analysed as attributive constructions, since pronouns cannot normally be modified by an attributive adjective. Instead, these are almost always the beginning of a following *that*-clause with the complementizer omitted, as in:

> I'm *glad* I'll never finish it.
> I'm so *glad* you could make it.
> I'm *glad* she's here.

The collocate pairs *glad* + *the* and *glad* + *there* represent the same grammatical association (of *glad* followed by a that-clause):

I was just *glad* the abortion was over with.
I'm glad there isn't a radio.

The preferred grammatical associations of *happy* are quite different. As noted above, *happy* is frequently used as a predication standing on its own, as in SOMEBODY BE HAPPY. However, when *happy* does take a complement, it most commonly occurs with a prepositional phrase instead of a complement clause (thus accounting for the lexical association with following prepositions such as *with, about,* and *at).* For example,

She used to be *happy* with her.
I'm not *happy* about this signature.
She did not appear *happy* at finding herself where she was.

This example illustrates the case where seemingly synonymous words actually have quite different patterns of use, reflected in their differing lexical and grammatical associations. A more complicated type of lexical-grammatical association involves words that are grammatical in the same range of structures; despite identical potentials, such words often have quite different typical associations.

	SV	SV+O (NP)	SV+O (COMP-clause)	SV+IO +O (NP)	SV+O +IO	SV+IO +O (COMP-clause)	SV+IO
tell							
Conv	-	-	-	***	-	****	***
Acad	-	**	-	*	-	*****	*
promise							
Conv	*	*	****	*	-	***	-
Acad	-	**	*****	*	-	*	-

Each * represents ca. 10% of the tokens for that verb
- marks patterns that occur less than 10% of the time

Table 4. Percentage of Verb Tokens for *tell* and *promise* Occurring with Intransitive, Monotransitive, and Ditransitive Valency Patterns in Conversation and Academic Prose

For example, the verbs *tell* and *promise* are grammatical in the same valency patterns: intransitive, monotransitive, and ditransitive. In actual use, though, these two verbs typically occur in quite different grammatical patterns, as shown in Table 4.[4]

The most striking difference between the grammatical associations of these two verbs concerns their use in a monotransitive pattern followed by a complement clause: this is the most common pattern for *promise* but the rarest pattern for *tell*:[5]

Academic prose:
> In return the student *promises* to campaign for the politician.

Conversation:
> I *promised* that I wouldn't play it.
> We still *promised* to go to aunty's.

The intransitive pattern is also more common with *promise* than with *tell*, especially in conversation:

> No I'm not gonna use it—I've *promised*.
> I won't laugh—I *promise*.

In contrast, ditransitive valency patterns with an indirect object are most common with the verb *tell*:

Academic prose:
> The central mark *tells* us which region we are in.
> The first law of thermodynamics *tells* us that energy may be converted...

Conversation:
> I'll *tell* you what it is.
> I *told* him it might need a new switch.
> She would *tell* me.

These association patterns seem to reflect a fundamental difference between the typical discourse functions of *tell* and *promise*: With the verb *promise*, the content of the promise (given as the direct object) is the most important consideration, while the person to whom the promise was made is often irrelevant. In contrast, the person being addressed is much more important with the verb *tell*, while the content of the speech act is in some cases irrelevant. As a result of these typical discourse functions, the grammatical associations of these two verbs are strikingly different, even though they have identical grammatical potentials.

Obviously, findings such as these require further interpretation, based on a fuller consideration of the individual patterns and a detailed analysis of individual instances in their discourse contexts. While it is not possible to undertake such an analysis here, these examples have illustrated the importance of lexical and grammatical association patterns in describing the meaning and use of individual words.

3. Association Patterns for Grammatical Features

Corpus-based analyses can also be used to investigate grammatical issues, addressing research questions such as: What discourse functions does a grammatical construction serve, and how are related constructions used differently? How rare or common are related constructions? Are particular constructions used more or less frequently in different registers? Are there particular words that a grammatical construction commonly co-occurs with? What factors in the discourse context are associated with the use of grammatical variants?

There are a number of book-length treatments reporting corpus-based grammatical investigations: for example, Tottie (1991) on negation, Collins (1991) on clefts, Granger (1983) on passives, Mair (1990) on infinitival complement clauses, Meyer (1992) on apposition, and several books on nominal structures (e.g. de Haan 1989, Geisler 1995, Johansson 1995, Varantola 1984). In addition, there have been numerous research papers using corpus-based techniques to study English grammar (see many of the papers in collected volumes such as Aarts and Meyer 1995; Aijmer and Altenberg 1991; Johansson and Stenström 1991).

Many of these studies use corpora to analyze the influence of contextual factors on the distribution of structural variants. Both lexical and grammatical association patterns have been shown to be important. For example, Mair (1990) identifies a number of individual verbs that are particularly common with various infinitival constructions; de Haan (1989) identifies the association of relative clauses with head noun phrases having different grammatical roles.

To illustrate association patterns of this type, I briefly describe certain aspects of the grammar of complement clauses in English. The two most common types of complement clause are *that*-clauses and *to*-clauses. In some contexts, these two are similar in meaning. For example, compare:

I hope that I can go.
I hope to go.

However, corpus-based study shows that the actual use of these two structures is quite different. First, in terms of their overall distribution, *that*-clauses are very common in conversation but not so common in academic prose. In contrast, *to*-clauses are moderately common in both conversation and academic prose:

	Conversation	**Academic Prose**
that-clauses	**************	****
to-clauses	********	*********

Each * represents 500 occurrences per million words

Table 5. Overall Distribution of *that*-clauses and *to*-clauses in Conversation and Academic Prose

This difference in overall distribution can be related in part to the differing lexical associations of the two types of complement clause. That is, while a few verbs can control both *that*-clauses and *to*-clauses (e.g. *hope, decide,* and *wish*), most verbs control only one or the other type of complement clause. For example, the verbs *imagine, mention, suggest, conclude, guess,* and *argue* can control a *that*-clause but not a *to*-clause; the verbs *begin, start, like, love, try,* and *want* can control a *to*-clause but not a *that*-clause.

These differential patterns of lexical association are even stronger when we consider relative frequency. Thus, Tables 6 and 7 below show that the most common verbs controlling a *that*-clause constitute a completely separate set from the most common verbs controlling a *to*-clause, even though some of these verbs are grammatical with both types of complement clause.

Some of these verbs (such as *want* and *try*) are grammatical controlling only one type of complement clause, and they have strong lexical associations with that structural type. Other verbs—such as *think, say,* and *know*—can control both types of complement clause; however, these verbs have strong association patterns with only one type of complement clause.[6] Thus, although there is some overlap between the two types of complement clause in the controlling verbs that are grammatical, corpus-based analysis shows that there is in fact very little overlap in the commonly occurring lexical associations.

	Conversation	Academic Prose
think	*******************	*
say	************	**
know	*********	*
see	**	**
show	*	***
find	*	**
believe	*	*
feel	*	-
suggest	-	**

Each * represents 100 occurrences per million words
- represents less than 50 occurrences per million words

Table 6. Most Common Verbs Controlling a *that*-clause

	Conversation	Academic Prose
want	**********	-
try	***	*
like	**	**
seem	*	*
tend	-	**
appear	-	**
begin	-	*
attempt	-	*
continue	-	*
fail	-	*

Each * represents 100 occurrences per million words
- represents less than 50 occurrences per million words

Table 7. Most Common Verbs Controlling a *to*-clause

Further, *that*-clauses and *to*-clauses are productive in different ways. *That*-clauses combine with relatively few verbs, from only a few semantic domains—mostly mental verbs (e.g. *think*, *know*, *feel*, *hope*) or communication verbs (e.g. *say*, *suggest*). However, a few of those verbs are extremely common controlling *that*-clauses, especially the verbs *think*, *say*, and *know* in conversation. The verb *say* controlling a *that*-clause is also extremely common in written registers such as fiction and news reportage.

In contrast, apart from the verb *want* in conversation, no individual verb is extremely common controlling *to*-clauses. However, there are a large number of different verbs that can control a *to*-clause, and those verbs come from many different semantic domains: mental verbs (e.g. *expect, learn*), communication verbs (e.g. *ask, promise*), verbs of desire (e.g. *want, like*), verbs of decision (e.g. *decide, intend*), verbs of effort or facilitation (e.g. *try, attempt, allow, enable*), aspectual verbs (e.g. *begin, continue*), and likelihood verbs (e.g. *seem, appear*).

These differing patterns of lexical association help to account for the overall differences in register distribution between *that*-clauses and *to*-clauses. Conversational partners tend to use a relatively restricted range of vocabulary, but it is almost always appropriate to report one's own thoughts (*I think that…, I know that…*) or the speech of others (*he/she said that…*). Because of the extremely heavy reliance on a relatively few combinations of this type, *that*-clauses are generally very common in conversation.

In contrast, the more frequent use of *to*-clauses in academic prose can be attributed in part to the wide range of different verbs controlling *to*-clauses. That is, academic prose is characterized by a much higher degree of lexical diversity than conversation. Thus, although no single verb is extremely common with *to*-clauses in academic prose, there are a large number of different verbs from different semantic domains used in combination with *to*-clauses. As a result, the overall frequency of *to*-clauses is higher than *that*-clauses in academic prose.

That-clauses and *to*-clauses also differ in their grammatical associations, and these differences also contribute to the overall register association pattern. One reflection of this difference is their use in extraposed versus non-extraposed constructions. Both types of complement clause have the grammatical potential to occur in either extraposed or non-extraposed constructions:

That-clauses
    Non-extraposed:
        I think that you might be wrong.
    Extraposed:
        It's possible that it'll happen again.
To-clauses
    Non-extraposed:
        I want to sleep here.
    Extraposed:
        It's possible to adjust the limit upwards.

However, *to*-clauses are in fact used much more commonly in extraposed constructions than *that*-clauses, especially in academic prose:

	Conversation	**Academic Prose**
Extraposed *that*-clauses	**	******
Extraposed *to*-clauses	**	***************

Each * represents 100 occurrences per million words

Table 8.   Use of *that*-clauses and *to*-clauses in Extraposed Constructions

It further turns out that over 80% of the extraposed *to*-clauses in academic prose are controlled by adjectival predicates rather than verbs, as in the following examples:

It is also possible to make more subtle combinations...
It is important to note that it is formed from tissue...
It is therefore essential to insist that true communities must be bare communities as well.
It is hard to resist the temptation...

These grammatical association patterns further explain the overall differences in register distribution between *that*-clauses and *to*-clauses. Extraposed *to*-clauses are by definition impersonal, since they do not have a referential subject. Further, extraposed *to*-clauses controlled by an adjectival predicate are typically used to present a static stance that is not directly attributed to any human agent, as in the above examples. These characteristics fit well with the static, impersonal presentation of information typical of academic prose. In contrast, non-extraposed *that*-clauses controlled by verbs more commonly include dynamic predicates attributed to a personal agent or experiencer, and these functions fit well with the typical communicative purposes of conversation.

In sum, both lexical associations and grammatical associations influence the extent to which a grammatical feature is used in different registers, depending on the extent to which those associations fit the typical communicative characteristics of the register. Although patterns such as these must be interpreted much more fully, the present section has illustrated the systematicity and importance of these association patterns in describing the use of related grammatical features.

4. Using Textual Co-occurrence Patterns to Analyze Register Variation

Research on discourse and the linguistic characteristics of particular varieties tends to be empirical, based on analysis of some collection of texts. There is a long tradition of such research on 'registers', 'genres', and 'styles', dating from the work of Ferguson, Halliday, Leech, Crystal, and others in the early 1960s. In recent years, most analysts studying registers have begun to use corpus-based techniques; recent edited collections with studies of this kind include Ghadessy (1988) and Biber and Finegan (1994).[7]

In addition to descriptions of a single register, a corpus-based approach enables a variationist perspective. Using computational (semi)automatic techniques to analyze large text corpora, it is possible to investigate the patterns of variation across a large number of registers, with respect to a wide range of relevant linguistic characteristics.

Research into the patterns of register variation is based on a different kind of association pattern: sets of linguistic features that tend to co-occur in texts. In previous studies, I refer to each grouping of linguistic features as a **dimension**.

Studies of this kind (e.g. Biber 1988, 1995) have shown that there are systematic patterns of variation among registers; that these patterns can be analyzed in terms of underlying dimensions of variation; and that it is necessary to recognize the existence of a multidimensional space in order to capture the overall relations among registers.

In Biber (1988), six major dimensions of variation are identified from a quantitative analysis of the distribution of linguistic features in the LOB and London-Lund Corpora. Each dimension comprises a distinct set of co-occurring linguistic features; each defines a different set of similarities and differences among spoken and written registers; and each has distinct functional underpinnings. One of the major findings coming out of this study relates to the marking of discourse complexity: contradicting the view that complexity is a homogeneous construct, early multi-dimensional studies showed that complexity features were distributed across several dimensions of variation.

To further investigate the association patterns comprising the dimensions of discourse complexity in English, Biber (1992) used confirmatory factor analysis to analyze the distribution of 33 linguistic markers of complexity across 23 spoken and written registers. Confirmatory factor analysis is a theory-based statistical approach: different models are hypothesized on theoretical grounds and then compared statistically to determine which best fits the observed patterns of variation. This study showed that discourse complexity is a multi-dimensional construct, that different types of structural elaboration reflect different discourse functions, and that different kinds of texts are complex in different ways (in addition to being more or less complex).

In particular, a five-dimensional model was identified as the most adequate representation of the associations among these complexity features. Each of the dimensions is labeled to reflect its functional and grammatical underpinnings: Reduced Structure and Specificity, Structural Elaboration of Reference, 'Framing' Structural Elaboration, Integrated Structure, and Passive Constructions.

To illustrate, Table 9 presents the defining linguistic features for two of the complexity dimensions: **Integrated Structure** (Dimension C) and **Framing Elaboration** (Dimension D). Each of these dimensions represents a text-based association pattern. That is, the groupings of features listed for each dimension represent linguistic characteristics that commonly co-occur in texts.

Dimension C: Integrated Structure
    nouns
    prepositional phrases
    attributive adjectives
    nominalizations
    phrasal coordination
    word length
    type/token ratio

Dimension D: Framing Elaboration[8]
    Wh-complement clauses
    that-complement clauses controlled by verbs
    conditional adverbial subordination
    causative adverbial subordination
    sentence relatives
    (*that-clauses* controlled by adjectives)
    (infinitives)
    (concessive adverbial subordination)

Table 9. Summary of the Linguistic Features Grouped on Dimension C and Dimension D (based on Biber 1992: Table 5)

The linguistic features grouped on Dimension C represent integrated structure. Features such as nouns, prepositional phrases, attributive adjectives, and nominalizations reflect a high informational focus and a relatively dense integration of information in a text; long words and diversified vocabulary (i.e. high type/token ratio) reflect a careful, precise word choice. Together, these features represent a dimension marking integrated structure.

The linguistic features grouped on Dimension D are all dependent clauses that represent framing elaboration. (Framing dependent clauses should be distinguished from postnominal modifying clauses, which comprise a separate dimension.) These clause types can be considered 'framing' in that they commonly serve one of two major functions: they either provide a discourse frame for a portion of text (as in the case of many types of adverbial subordination; see, for example, Thompson 1983, 1985; Ford and Thompson 1986); or they provide an overt assessment of the speaker/writer's stance (in the case of sentence relatives, *that*-complement clauses, and *Wh*-clauses; see Beaman 1984, Quirk et al. 1985, Winter 1982).

Dimensions C and D represent two quite different parameters of discourse complexity, with respect to both their defining linguistic characteristics and their underlying functions. These differences can be studied further by considering the kinds of texts that make extensive use of each complexity dimension.

To compare registers with respect to each of these text-based association patterns, it is necessary to compute 'dimension scores' (explained in Biber 1988: 93-97). Dimension scores for each text are computed by summing the occurrences of the linguistic features grouped on each dimension; then mean dimension scores for each register can be compared to analyze the salient linguistic similarities and differences among spoken and written registers.

To illustrate register comparisons of this type, Figure 1 presents the differences among twelve spoken and written registers within the two-dimensional space defined by Dimension C and Dimension D. The distribution of scores along the vertical axis represents the Integrated Structure Dimension (C). Registers with large scores along this dimension have frequent occurrences of nouns, prepositional phrases, attributive adjectives, long words, etc. This dimension distinguishes the expository (informational) written registers—which show a very frequent use of integrative features—from all other registers.

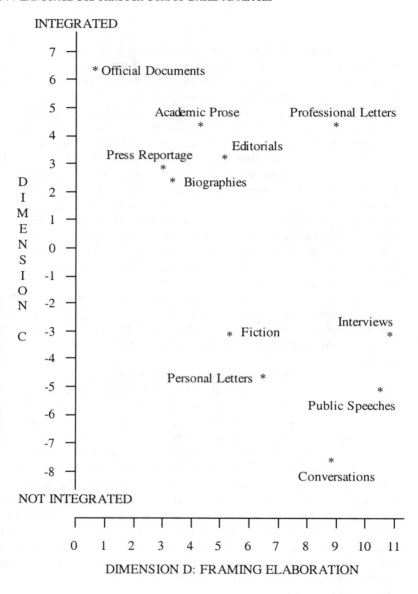

Figure 1. Linguistic Characterization of Eleven Spoken and Written Registers with Respect to Dimension C: Integrated Structure, and Dimension D: Framing Elaboration

The extremely dense use of Integrated Structure features in written informational prose is illustrated by Text Sample 1 (from an official document). These features include frequent nouns, often in noun-noun sequences (e.g. *family income, tax reliefs, family allowances*), attributive adjectives (e.g. *average, incomplete, younger, lower*), and phrasal coordination (e.g. *indices of domestic food expenditure per head* **and** *quantities purchased by older* **and** *younger couples* **and** *families*). The extensive embedding of prepositional phrases is indicated by italics in the text excerpt.

Nevertheless, average net family income was appreciably higher *in* families *with* several children than *in* those *with* only one, many *of* which were incomplete families *of* younger parents *with* lower earnings, and of course *with* lower tax reliefs and no family allowances....Table 24 gives indices *of* domestic food expenditure *per* head and quantities purchased *by* older and younger couples and families *with* different numbers *of* children, *with* 1954 *as* the base year.

Text Sample 1. Excerpt from Official Document

All non-expository registers show an infrequent use of Integrated Structure complexity; these include all spoken registers, as well as fiction and personal letters. With regard to the spoken informational registers (e.g. speeches and interviews), production constraints apparently limit the extent to which information can be carefully integrated. With respect to the non-informational written registers (e.g. fiction and personal letters), the primary communicative purposes do not require a dense integration of information.

The distribution of scores along the horizontal axis in Figure 1 represents the 'Framing' Structural Elaboration Dimension. Registers with large scores along this dimension have frequent occurrences of *Wh*-complement clauses, *that*-complement clauses, and various types of adverbial subordination. This type of complexity is most common in those registers that promote the expression of personal attitudes, justifications, and feelings: interviews, public speeches, conversations, and professional letters. Interestingly, many of these registers are spoken and interactive. Framing complexity features are much less common in those registers having informational, impersonal, 'factual' purposes, such as press reportage, biographies, and academic prose. These features are especially rare in official documents, which are typically direct statements of 'fact' with no acknowledged author (see Text Sample 1 above).

Text Sample 2 illustrates the use of framing elaboration features in a public speech; Sample 3 illustrates these features in a type of interview (court testimony), and Sample 4 illustrates these features in a professional letter. These samples differ in spoken versus written mode, but they share a focus on the expression of personal attitudes and opinions with justification for those positions. Framing elaboration features are italicized.

If you look at the steel industry, you see *that* the steel industry, *when* nationalized, was not nationalized on a basis that...

Text Sample 2. Excerpt from a Public Speech

My wife phoned the doctor *when* we arrived, *because* my mother said to my wife will you phone Richard, *because* she wanted *to* go into a nursing home, and the doctor said *[0]* it wasn't necessary.

Text Sample 3. Excerpt from Court Testimony

...Any such drastic change would ultimately require the action of the board of directors *because* it would involve a change in the constitution...and *because* any such change would in turn require a vote...*If* it is not possible *to* add your concern this year, it would certainly be possible *to* add it next year...Please understand *that while* I am sympathetic to what you are trying to achieve, and *that while* I understand *that* certain XYZ populations are...impacted..., I am not at present entirely in sympathy...

Text Sample 4. Professional Letter

Several of the framing functions of these elaboration features are illustrated in these text samples. For example, conditional clauses and *Wh*-clauses are used to contrast various possible actions or points of view (e.g. *If you look at the steel industry, If it is not possible, when nationalized, while I am sympathetic, while I understand*). Causative adverbial clauses are used to justify attitudes or actions (e.g. *because my mother said, because she wanted to go.* Similarly, in the professional letter sample, causative adverbial clauses are used to explain the opinion that: *any such drastic change would ultimately require the action of the board of directors because it would involve a change in the constitution...and because any such change would in turn require a vote. That*-complement clauses are often used to overtly frame an attitude or position relative to a 'stance' verb or adjective (e.g. *you see that*...from the public speech; and *I understand that*...from the professional letter). Thus, although these elaboration features vary in their particular functions, they share general 'framing' uses common in more personal, attitudinal registers.

Similar analytical techniques have been used to study the dimensions of register variation in other languages (e.g. Besnier (1988) on Nukulaelae Tuvaluan; Biber and Hared (1992) on Somali; and Kim and Biber (1994) on Korean). All of these studies focus on text-based association patterns—i.e., the linguistic co-occurrence patterns defining the multi-dimensional space of variation among texts and registers in a language. Biber (1995) synthesizes these earlier studies to investigate the possibility of cross-linguistic universals governing the patterns of register variation.[9]

A comparison of text-based association patterns cross-linguistically shows that structurally complex features can serve a number of different functions, associated with both oral and literate registers. There are, however, systematic generalizations concerning the marking of discourse complexity that hold across the four languages compared in Biber (1995) (see especially Chapter 7). For example, relative clauses, and nominal modifiers generally, are characteristic of literate registers, being used for informational elaboration. In contrast, adverbial subordination is used most commonly in oral registers, often to mark some aspect of personal stance; adverbial clauses often co-occur with involved, reduced, or fragmented features. Complement clauses and infinitives occur frequently in both oral and literate registers, but they frequently co-occur with other features marking personal stance or persuasion.

Overall, such comparisons clearly show that it is not adequate to treat structural complexity as an undifferentiated whole. Rather, there are different kinds of complexities having quite different distributions and functional associations. Corpus-based analyses of linguistic co-occurrence patterns—i.e., text-based association patterns—enable register comparisons of this type, resulting in a more adequate understanding of the interacting discourse systems that define the range of register variation in a language.

5. Conclusion

One fruitful area for future research is to integrate the methodologies developed for corpus-based research with those developed for quantitative studies of sociolinguistic variation. That is, the inter-relations among linguistic association patterns, together with an assessment of their relative importance, could be studied in more detail using variable rule methodologies (see, for example, Sankoff 1987). Although most sociolinguistic variation studies have been restricted to phonological variants that are semantically equivalent, a number of studies have extended these methods to consider lexical, grammatical, and discourse variables that represent 'equivalent-in-discourse' relations (e.g. Sankoff, Thibault, and Bérubé 1978, Tottie 1991, Dines 1980, Horvath 1985, Helt 1996). These techniques provide probabilistic estimates of the extent to which each contextual factor favors or disfavors a linguistic variant, when considered relative to the influence of other factors.

As the present paper shows, the study of linguistic variability can also be extended to include systematic text-based association patterns. In this case, texts and registers are characterized and compared, rather than the variants for a linguistic feature. For both types of research question (linguistic and text-based), quantitative corpus-based analyses regularly uncover important patterns of use that are highly systematic but often inaccessible to intuitions. Such language use patterns must be interpreted functionally, with respect to a number of interrelated influences, including:

- production and processing factors
- communicative purpose and topic
- situational context and interactiveness
- social identity
- textual connectivity

Recent linguistic theory has generally favored discrete/categorical descriptions over those that allow for continuous/quantitative relations. In large part this is due to the preconception that individual linguistic competence cannot accommodate systematic tendencies in addition to discrete categories and structures. Further, language competence has been regarded as an independent mental faculty that is not influenced by situational, social, or textual factors.

However, these exclusionary views are not well-grounded: First, there is no empirical evidence suggesting that mental processes cannot involve systematic tendencies. Second, there is no a priori reason to suppose that mental competencies concerning situational/social appropriateness or textual connectivity should not interact with linguistic production. Finally, neither the categorical formalisms found in generative linguistics nor the specific probabilities identified in variation studies are likely to have any direct representation in actual mental processes. However, it is reasonable to suppose that both types of description correspond to aspects of linguistic competence (cf. Sankoff 1988).

Obviously, future research is required to investigate the relative importance of use factors, and the ways in which particular functional considerations relate to particular kinds of association patterns. The goals of the present paper have been more modest: to set out a framework for describing the various kinds of association patterns, and to illustrate the highly systematic nature of each type.

Notes

1. A carefully designed, representative corpus is crucial for studies of this type. Some projects have used extremely large corpora, with relatively little consideration for the kinds of texts included; other projects have used a very careful corpus design (regarding the kinds of text) but relatively small sample size. Both types of skewing are likely to influence research findings. That is, a representative corpus must pay equal attention to both composition and size. (See Biber 1990, 1993b; Leech 1991; Fries, Tottie, and Schneider 1994 for more detailed discussions of corpus design issues.)

2. Similar research goals have been investigated in sociolinguistic variation studies, and variable rules can be regarded as a formal statement of association patterns for 'equivalent' variants (see, for example, the discussions in Sankoff and Labov 1979, Sankoff 1987, 1988, and several papers in Sankoff 1978).

3. The grammatical associations for these two adjectives are determined from automatic analysis using a grammatical tagger; these counts were confirmed and adjusted slightly based on interactive analysis of 200 randomly selected tokens for each adjective.

4. These percentages are based on interactive analysis of 200 randomly selected tokens for each verb.

5. This pattern is attested for the verb *tell*, as in:
   You can *tell* she's from London. (Conv)

6. Although rare, these verbs can take a *to*-clause as well as a *that*-clause. This pattern is most often found when the matrix verb is in the passive voice; for example,

> The follow-up action can be taken if the initial response *is thought* to be unsatisfactory.
> Volvo *is known* to be keen to strengthen its manufacturing base.
> The deal *was said* to enable LTCB to gain information and knowledge in international asset management.

7. Within computational linguistics, research on 'sublanguages' uses corpus-based analyses to address many of these same issues, with the ultimate goal of automatically processing texts from particular varieties with a high degree of accuracy (see Grishman and Kittredge 1986; Kittredge and Lehrberger 1982).

8. The linguistic features listed in parentheses on Dimension D do not have strong positive loadings on this dimension. Two other features—present participle adverbial clauses and other adverbial subordination—had negative loadings on this dimension, indicating that they do not function as hypothesized.

9. Multi-dimensional register comparisons have also been used to study diachronic register variation (e.g. Biber and Finegan 1989, Atkinson 1992).

References

Aarts, Bas and Charles Meyer (eds.). 1995. *The Verb in Contemporary English: Theory and Description*. Cambridge: Cambridge University Press.

Aijmer, Karin and Bengt Altenberg (eds.). 1991. *English Corpus Linguistics*. London: Longman.

Altenberg, Bengt. 1991a. A bibliography of publications relating to English computer corpora. In Johansson and Stenström (eds.), 355-95.

Altenberg, Bengt. 1991b. Amplifier collocations in spoken English. In Johansson and Stenström (eds.), 127-147.

Altenberg, Bengt. 1993. Recurrent verb-complement constructions in the London-Lund corpus. In Jan Aarts, Pieter de Haan, and Nelleke Oostdijk (eds.), *English Language Corpora: Design, Analysis, and Exploitation*, 227-46. Amsterdam: Rodopi.

Armstrong, Susan (ed.). 1994. *Using Large Corpora*. Cambridge, MA: MIT Press.

Atkinson, Dwight. 1992. The evolution of medical research writing from 1735 to 1985: The case of the Edinburgh Medical Journal. *Applied Linguistics* 13, 337-374.

Beaman, Karen. 1984. Coordination and subordination revisited: Syntactic complexity in spoken and written narrative discourse. In Deborah Tannen (ed.), *Coherence in Spoken and Written Discourse*. Norwood, N.J.: Ablex.

Besnier, Niko. 1988. The linguistic relationships of spoken and written Nukulaelae registers. *Language* 64, 707-736.

Biber, Douglas. 1988. *Variation across Speech and Writing*. Cambridge: Cambridge University Press.

Biber, Douglas. 1990. Methodological issues regarding corpus-based analyses of linguistic variation. *Literary and Linguistic Computing* 5, 257-269.

Biber, Douglas. 1992. On the complexity of discourse complexity: A multidimensional analysis. *Discourse Processes* 15, 133-163.

Biber, Douglas. 1993a. Co-occurrence patterns among collocations: A tool for corpus-based lexical knowledge acquisition. *Computational Linguistics* 19, 549-556.

Biber, Douglas. 1993b. Representativeness in corpus design. *Literary and Linguistic Computing* 8, 1-15.

Biber, Douglas. 1995. *Dimensions of Register Variation: A Cross-Linguistic Comparison*. Cambridge: Cambridge University Press.

Biber, Douglas, Susan Conrad, and Randi Reppen. 1994. Corpus-based approaches to issues in applied linguistics. *Applied Linguistics* 15, 169-189.

Biber, Douglas and Edward Finegan. 1989. Drift and the evolution of English style: A history of three genres. *Language* 65, 487-517.

Biber, Douglas and Edward Finegan (eds.). 1994. *Sociolinguistic Perspectives on Register*. New York: Oxford University Press.

Biber, Douglas and Mohamed Hared. 1992. Dimensions of register variation in Somali. *Language Variation and Change* 4, 41-75.

Church, Kenneth and Patrick Hanks. 1990. Word association norms, mutual information, and lexicography. *Computational Linguistics* 16, 22-29.

Church, Kenneth, William Gale, Patrick Hanks, and Donald Hindle. 1991. Using statistics in lexical analysis. In Uri Zernik (ed.), *Lexical Acquisition: Exploiting On-Line Resources to Build a Lexicon*, 115-164. Hillsdale, NJ: Lawrence Erlbaum.

Collins, Peter. 1991. *Cleft and Pseudo-Cleft Constructions in English*. London: Routledge.

de Haan, Pieter. 1989. *Postmodifying Clauses in the English Noun Phrase: A Corpus-Based Study*. Amsterdam: Rodopi.

Dines, Elizabeth. 1980. Variation in discourse: "And stuff like that." *Language in Society* 9: 13-31.

Firth, John R. 1952. Linguistic analysis as a study of meaning. In Palmer (ed.), 12-26.

Ford, Cecilia and Sandra Thompson. 1986. Conditionals in discourse: A text-based study from English. In Elizabeth C. Traugott (ed.), *On Conditionals*. Cambridge: Cambridge University Press.

Fries, Udo, Gunnel Tottie, and Peter Schneider (eds.). 1994. *Creating and Using English Corpora*. Amsterdam: Rodopi.

Geisler, Christer. 1995. *Relative Infinitives in English.* Uppsala: Uppsala University doctoral dissertation.

Ghadessy, Mohsen (ed.). 1988. *Registers of Written English: Situational Factors and Linguistic Features.* London: Pinter.

Granger, Sylviane. 1983. *The be + Past Participle Construction in Spoken English: With Special Emphasis on the Passive.* Amsterdam: Elsevier Science Publishers.

Grishman, Ralph and Richard Kittredge (eds.). 1986. *Analyzing Language in Restricted Domains: Sublanguage Description and Processing.* Hillsdale, NJ: Lawrence Erlbaum.

Helt, Marie. 1996. *A Corpus-Based Approach to Defining Discourse Markers.* Ms., Northern Arizona University.

Horvath, Barbara. 1985. *Variation in Australian English.* Cambridge: Cambridge University Press.

Johansson, Christine. 1995. *The Relativizers* whose *and* of which *in Present-Day English: Description and Theory.* Uppsala: University of Uppsala doctoral dissertation.

Johansson, Stig and Anna-Brita Stenström (eds.). 1991. *English Computer Corpora: Selected Papers and Research Guide.* Berlin: Mouton de Gruyter.

Kennedy, Graeme. 1991. *Between* and *through*: The company they keep and the functions they serve. In Aijmer and Altenberg (eds.), 95-127.

Kim, Yong-jin and Douglas Biber. 1994. A corpus-based analysis of register variation in Korean. In Biber and Finegan (eds.), 157-181.

Kittredge, Richard and John Lehrberger (eds.). 1982. *Sublanguage: Studies of Language in Restricted Semantic Domains.* Berlin: Walter de Gruyter.

Kjellmer, Goran. 1991. A mint of phrases. In Aijmer and Altenberg (eds.), 111-127.

Leech, Geoffrey. 1991. The state of the art in corpus linguistics. In Aijmer and Altenberg (eds.), 8-29.

Mair, Christian. 1990. *Infinitival Complement Clauses in English.* New York: Cambridge University Press.

Meyer, Charles. 1992. *Apposition in Contemporary English.* Cambridge: Cambridge University Press.

Nakamura, Junsaku and John Sinclair. 1995. The world of woman in the Bank of English: Internal criteria for the classification of corpora. *Literary and Linguistic Computing* 10, 99-110.

Palmer, Frank R. (ed.). 1968. *Selected Papers of J. R. Firth, 1952-59.* Bloomington: Indiana University Press.

Quirk, Randolph, Sidney Greenbaum, Geoffrey Leech, and Jan Svartvik. 1985. *A Comprehensive Grammar of the English Language.* London: Longman.

Renouf, Antoinette and John Sinclair. 1991. Collocational frameworks in English. In Aijmer and Altenberg (eds.), 128-143.

Sankoff, David (ed.). 1978. *Linguistic Variation: Models and Methods.* New York: Academic Press.

Sankoff, David. 1987. Variable rules. In Ulrich Ammon, Norbert Dittmar, and Klaus Mattheier (eds.), *Sociolinguistics: An International Handbook of the Science of Language and Society*, 984-997. Berlin: Walter de Gruyter.

Sankoff, David. 1988. Sociolinguistics and syntactic variation. In Frederick Newmeyer (ed.), *Linguistics: The Cambridge Survey*, Vol. 4, 140-161. Cambridge: Cambridge University Press.

Sankoff, David and William Labov. 1979. On the uses of variable rules. *Language in Society* 8, 189-222.

Sankoff, David, Pierrette Thibault, and Helene Bérubé. 1978. Semantic field variability. In Sankoff (ed.), 23-43.

Sinclair, John (ed.). 1987. *Looking Up*. London: Collins.

Sinclair, John. 1991. *Corpus, Concordance and Collocation*. Oxford: Oxford University Press.

Stubbs, Michael. 1995. Collocations and semantic profiles: On the cause of the trouble with quantitative studies. *Functions of Language* 2, 23-55.

Svartvik, Jan (ed.). 1990. *The London-Lund Corpus of Spoken English: Description and Research*. Lund: Lund University Press.

Svartvik, Jan (ed.). 1992. *Directions in Corpus Linguistics: Proceedings from the Nobel Symposium 82, Stockholm, 4-8 August 1991*. Berlin: Mouton de Gruyter.

Thompson, Sandra A. 1983. Grammar and discourse: The English detached participial clause. In Flora Klein-Andreu (ed.), *Discourse Perspectives on Syntax*, 43-65. New York: Academic Press.

Thompson, Sandra A. 1985. Grammar and written discourse: Initial versus final purpose clauses in English. *Text* 5, 55-84.

Tottie, Gunnel. 1991. *Negation in English Speech and Writing: A Study in Variation*. San Diego: Academic Press.

Varantola, Krista. 1984. *On Noun Phrase Structures in Engineering English*. Turku: University of Turku.

Winter, Eugene. 1982. *Towards a Contextual Grammar of English: The Clause and its Place in the Definition of Sentence*. London: Allen and Unwin.

Usage, Blends, and Grammar

MICHAEL BARLOW
Rice University

1. Introduction

The extract in (1)[1] contains a short sample of language in use, an orthographic representation of part of an exchange between two American speakers set in an academic environment.

(1) a. Why is it chapter 3?
     b. Well, that's the thing to talk about.

While the representation in (1) clearly omits a considerable amount of information, extending from the phonetic realisation of the utterances to their discourse context, it does nevertheless provide empirical data relating to an actual speech event, and as an illustration of language usage it will serve as a useful starting point for the discussion of usage-based grammar[2] presented here. We can take some comfort from the fact that example (1) represents an actual exchange, if small one, between two speakers. However, if we look to the example for insights into usage-based grammar, we see the difficulty of bridging the gap between the particular, the utterance itself, and the general, the grammatical representation that ultimately underpins the production and comprehension of the utterance—differences between production and comprehension notwithstanding. The strategy adopted here is simply to examine multiple utterances (or sentences) in a corpus, looking for regularities in usage. The relationships drawn between multiple instances of utterances and linguistic generalisations have some parallels in the connection between usage data and the form of a usage-based grammar in that, as we will see, both relationships involve data-driven pattern extraction. Even a cursory inspection of a corpus reveals recurrent regularities in the data, the most obvious of which are collocations or recurrent word associations (Firth 1957, Sinclair 1991).[3] We find, for example, that the word *thing*, which appears in (1b), is used very frequently (in both spoken and written discourses) and occurs in a number of collocations such as *the thing is* and *the...thing to do*. With appropriate usage data (i.e., corpus data) at hand and keeping in mind the parallels alluded to above between corpus-based generalisations and usage-based grammar, we can make some progress towards answering a question posed (somewhat rhetorically) in Bolinger (1961: 381):

> Is grammar something where speakers produce (i.e. originate) construct-ions, or where they reach for them from a pre-established inventory, when the occasion presents itself?

Obviously, the answer to this question is not going to simply appear out of thin air once we have the requisite corpus data. Consequently, we have to look for clues to the relationship between frequent collocational patterns and their representation in a usage-based grammar, and then consider the implications for less frequent collocational patterns such as *the thing to talk about* in (1b), which is not a particularly strong collocation.

The prevailing view of syntax is that at its core it comprises a set of rules or constraints which account for the creative use of language, and that secondarily or peripherally, the grammar (or lexicon) contains a list of multi-word idioms and other set phrases. I claim that this is exactly backwards: The main component of grammar instead comprises a large set of redundantly specified schemata, both abstract and lexically-specified, and the role of rules or constraints (or highly abstract schemata) is to provide the glue or mortar to combine these prefabricated chunks.[4] Exploring this alternative view, I investigate the relation between instances of usage illustrated by the fragment in (1) and a usage-based grammar, paying particular attention to the role of blending as described in Turner and Fauconnier (1995), Fauconnier and Turner (1996), and Turner (1996) *inter alia*. I aim to show that what looks like creativity in language is in many instances the result of blending of prefabricated units rather than the output of a set of generative rules.

The structure of the paper is as follows: I first examine the consequences of the pervasiveness of collocations for the structure of grammar, turning in Section 3 to an exploration of the nature of syntax in a collocation-rich grammar. The main part of the paper, Section 4, demonstrates the use of corpus data to investigate the extent of blending of prefabricated forms in language production.

2. Collocations and Usage-based Grammar

We can describe how a usage-based grammar might differ from a standard grammatical description by considering the following contrasts. Adopting a generic X-bar syntax framework, one could view the utterances in (1) as bracketed structures or tree-structures in which the main category represents a sentence containing phrasal categories (such as NP, N', etc.) which, in turn, contain or dominate lexical categories (such as N). Only the latter categories are linked to individual lexical items, and therefore the control of connections among words is achieved only indirectly through restrictions on the combination of syntactic categories. From this perspective, syntax is a set of constraints governing the combination of phrasal and lexical categories.[5] And, as is well-known, the typical data used in this tradition is grounded not in actual usage but rather in intuitions about sentences and specifically judgements of the grammaticality of sentences.

A model of syntax that aims to explain the distribution of syntactic categories, say AP and N' (rather than lexical items themselves), clearly has value as a way of capturing the range of possibilities of association (as famously illustrated by *colorless green ideas*), but it is bound to be unsuccessful in accounting for frequent collocations such as those involving the cooccurrence of particular adjectives (e.g., *broad*) with particular nouns (e.g., *daylight*). In other words, an X-bar framework can only account for relations between syntactic categories and is unable to represent the lexical or collocational dimension of syntagmatic structure. The ubiquity of dependencies among words (as opposed to dependencies among syntactic categories) is self-evident once corpus analyses are undertaken, suggesting the need for some kind of collocational grammar. And while no such grammar has been produced, the extent of collocations is extensively documented in dictionaries and other reference works such as Benson, Benson and Ilson (1997), Kjellmer (1994), and Moon (1998), which provide extensive lists of collocations. Moreover, the degree of attraction (collocational strength) between any of the words in a particular corpus can be estimated by statistical measures such as mutual information, t-score, cost and entropy.[6] Collocations are not only a feature of corpora; speakers know about collocations, and collocations come in different strengths in terms of how well routinised or entrenched they are in speakers' linguistic systems.

Does it matter that X-bar syntax fails to capture certain aspects of what it means to know a language? In one sense, no, it does not. If syntax is taken to be an idealised view of those aspects of language structure related to conjectural learnability issues rather than a model of day-to-day language use, then one might say that the details associated with cooccurrence patterns and frequency of occurrence are peripheral and of little or no importance. On the other hand, if we focus on usage and usage-based grammar, we find that it is the idealised syntax which is of secondary importance and plays a background role in speaker's knowledge, as explained in the discussion below.

Using corpora to examine patterns of usage reveals the important role that lexical units larger than a word perform in language production and shows that much of language in use is not creative in the Chomskyan sense, but is based mainly on the use of prefabricated or semi-prefabricated chunks. I argue that the creativity or the expressive dimension to language comes in large part from the modification of prefab structures, rather than the novel combination of lexical categories.

Well-entrenched collocations like *broad daylight* and other examples of fixed and semi-fixed structures such as those shown in (2) are instances of syntagmatic units that can be described in terms of schemata or constructions.[7]

(2) a. one thing
     b. the thing is
     c. the right thing to do
     d. sort of thing
     e. it is one thing to ... it is another thing to ...

The building blocks of a usage-based grammar are not lexical items dominated by lexical categories, but are form-meaning pairings of differing degrees of complexity and different degrees of specificity. Adopting this view of the units of grammar, we see that, in fact, the building block metaphor is not the best for this approach. (See also Langacker, this volume.) For one thing, the "blocks" have both a formal and a meaning side; and some of the blocks come already partially assembled. Nevertheless, some sort of "building block model" is necessary to capture the compositional nature of syntax/semantics. The sort of model required, however, must allow for the composition and blending of units large and small.

The connection between usage and usage-based grammar is not a simple one, but we can attempt a basic description as follows: repeated exposure to collocations leads to the entrenchment of collocational patterns and their associated meanings in the grammar.[8] This process applies not only to strong lexical collocations such as *broad daylight*, but also to looser collocational links between words as in [*it is one thing to* X, *it is another thing to* Y]. The existence of a cline from strong to weak collocational links among words and the presence of links between collocations (collocations of collocations) are amenable to treatment in a usage-based grammar that, by definition, is structured in a way that reflects input. Additionally, appropriate conditions of language usage are clearly a part of a speaker's knowledge of language and the connections between grammatical units and register, genre, and other types of situational information must also be part of the grammatical representation, but such associations are not pursued here.

3. Combining and Modifying Collocations

If we take the position that chunks represented by schemata are the fundamental units of syntax, then we must face up to a couple of problems. One concerns the modification of chunks. How are fixed or semi-fixed expressions such as *close, but no cigar* modified? If they are unanalysed chunks, then it would not be possible for them to (ever) take modifiers or to allow word substitutions. And it is in solving this problem that something akin to X-bar syntax[9] may be useful as a guide to the internal structure of chunks, which is a necessary step in the creation of modified structures. A phrase like *close, but no cigar* may be represented in the grammar with a category label for the whole phrase, but with little identification of internal structure. However, a syntactic template may be imposed on the structure if a speaker wants to create a modified structure, as in *close, but no banking cigar*[10] or *close, but no goal*. The characterisation of this procedure in terms of an imposition of a syntactic template is, perhaps, an overly dramatic description. Chunks in the grammar have differing degrees of internal structure and sometimes the internal structure will be quite transparent, as in *broad daylight* and *the thing is* but in other cases, rather opaque, as in *one fell swoop* and *easy does it*. Focussing on usage-based grammar at this level of detail, we also face the fact that individual speakers will vary, perhaps quite markedly, in the internal structure assigned to different fixed and semi-fixed expressions. Individual variation aside, some kind of analysis of chunks can always be made, but given the fundamental role of collocational units, then inevitably higher order syntactic categories play a secondary role. Further issues relating to the modification of chunks will be explored in detail in Section 4.

The second problem can be stated as follows. We have made the claim that collocations are an important aspect of syntagmatic structure and yet do not fit within traditional syntactic approaches. However, if collocational units are taken to be fundamental units of syntax, then we need a mechanism to account for the combination of these units. Here once again we can turn to abstract schemata to provide the glue allowing combination of syntagmatic units, although the structures involved will have to reflect the organisation of spoken discourse and hence may differ from traditional tree structures, which are perhaps better suited to written discourse. In a similar vein, we should note that collocational units do not necessarily correspond to traditional syntactic categories. And without promising a complete resolution of these issues, we can make some progress in understanding form/meaning composition by examining evidence from corpus data concerning usage and cognitive representations, focussing in particular on the role of blending.

To illustrate these notions, let us look at a couple of examples. In the sentence taken from a spoken corpus shown in (3a), we see the common collocation *the thing to do* forming a part of the utterance. Based on an inductive view of language learning, the frequency of this construction in corpora might lead one to suggest that the internal representation of this string will have a cognitive reality as a set phrase or grammatical unit. On the other hand, we might ask what is to be made of the occurrence of *a worthwhile thing to footnote* in (3b). This latter example seems, on the face of it, to be a good illustration of the need for a generative grammar in which syntactic processes control the combination of lexical categories. Certainly *a worthwhile thing to footnote* is going to be so rare in usage as to count for all intents and purposes as a unique utterance.

(3) a. And I think probably **the thing to do** is have a group write that ....

  b. I think at some point that might be **a worthwhile thing to footnote**, ...

There are a variety of ways in which this pair of utterances could be handled. For instance, it might be argued that *the thing to do* is a more or less prefabricated chunk, whereas *a worthwhile thing to footnote* is created according to a rule-like compositional system. Adopting this approach is equivalent to saying that there are two main ways of constructing sentences: adopting a bottom-up metaphor, we can say that one way is from the word up, and that the other is from the word up, except for those parts for which a prefabricated chunk exists. Little, if any, discussion is given within general syntax to the manner in which the two construction methods can co-exist so as to ensure that a prefabricated chunk such as *the thing to do* meshes with a syntax based on the combination of syntactic categories.[11] Disregarding the collocational connections between the chunk and other words in the sentence, we still have the problem of how a grammar in which phrasal nodes dominate either other phrasal nodes or lexical categories can cope with a complex four-word expression like *the thing to do* or with variants such as *the best thing to do*.

Alternatively, some might argue that if a rule-like syntactic system is needed in any case for (3b), then in the interests of parsimony the string in (3a) should also be accounted for by the same rule-like system. To the extent that the utterance in (3a) can be generated by the same kinds of rules as (3b), this seems reasonable. However, this approach is implausible because we are then left with the gulf between, on the one hand, a fully compositional syntax and, on the other hand, usage data that indicates the extensive presence of prefabricated chunks which have unit status on syntactic or semantic/pragmatic grounds.

Let us examine a third possibility, which is that a prefabricated chunk is involved in some way in both (3a) and (3b). This third option, explored in detail below, rests on the notion that some of the apparent creativity in language is in fact the result of merger or modification of lexical prefabricated chunks—a partial creativity based on the re-use or re-purposing of prefabricated structures, rather than complete from-the-bottom-up assembly. That is not to say that a bottom-up assembly based on the combination of lexical items never occurs, only that it is the exception rather than the rule. In other words, I argue for the view that strings such as *a worthwhile thing to footnote* are the result of blending of stored cognitive representations. Thus we can explore the idea that in meeting the needs of a particular communicative situation, there is a merger, or mixing, or blending of form-meaning pairs which leads to an output that may be much more variable than even the full range of underlying or stored cognitive representations, including all entrenched collocations. In the following section we examine the mechanisms of this blending process.

4. The Role of Blending

Blending is a general cognitive process involving the merger of formal and conceptual structures to produce new structures that contain partial projections from the input domains, along with new emergent properties specific to the blend (Turner and Fauconnier 1995, Fauconnier and Turner 1996, and Turner 1996). Metaphors and figurative language can be taken to be one type of blending, but there are many other kinds of blends in literary and everyday language, and in non-linguistic domains such as advertising images. A series of Absolut Vodka advertisements, for example, have for several years been based on visual blends which entice the viewer to marvel at the integration of the shape of the Absolut bottle with a view of a famous landmark or scene, and which, at the same time, invite the retrieval or isolation of one input to the blend: the vodka bottle itself. Absolut London, for instance, appears to be a common photograph of the Prime Minister's official residence, 10 Downing Street. Looking closely, however, you see that the outline of the famous door combined with a strategically placed lantern represents the vodka bottle. And in another example, Absolut Amsterdam, the scene is of three tall, narrow Dutch houses next to a canal, but the middle house, which has the same texture and same facing as its neighbouring houses, has taken on the shape of the vodka bottle. These particular examples illustrate a situation in which the formal blend does not correspond to a conceptual blend. In the Absolut ads, there is no conceptual blending that accompanies the visual blending of the vodka bottle and the Prime Minister's residence; there is no blending that goes beyond the blend in the visual image itself. The ad does not suggest, for example, that the Prime Minister drinks vodka at home by the bottleful.

Turner and Fauconnier (1995: 202) discuss the potential disconnection of conceptual and formal blends, noting that formal blends can occur in the absence of conceptual blends (as illustrated above). We will return to this disengagement of concept and form below.

An important motivation for blending is the push to consolidate several events into a single unit. Noting the pressure to integrate conceptual structure, Fauconnier and Turner (1996: 117) give an example of a non-integrated sequence of actions: 'Jack sneezed. The napkin moved. It was on the table. Now it is off the table.' They point out that English allows the same content to be expressed with the form *Jack sneezed the napkin off the table*, which represents an integrated conceptual structure. This integration occurs by conceptual blending in which one input is a [NP V NP PP] structure, representing an integrated caused-motion event of the type 'John threw the ball into the basket,' and a second input, which is the sequence of actions given above. Thus while the two inputs to the blend are different, they are similar enough to support a partial merger into an integrated conceptual structure expressed through a particular syntactic configuration.[12]

Turner and Fauconnier (1995: 184) state that:

> interestingly, and rather unexpectedly, conceptual blends in thought are seldom mirrored by formal blends in language. Language has other means for prompting us to perform conceptual integration.

The motivation for this statement comes from a particular view of language that most linguists would agree with, which is that language only hints at intended meaning. An utterance can be thought of as providing signposts which the language user can take note of, and within a particular context, exploit to retrieve or construct the intended meaning. One illustration of this view comes from the fact that the mere juxtaposition, rather than formal blending, of two words is generally sufficient to lead the hearer to the appropriate meaning. In other words, given the requisite background knowledge, the simple contiguity of *dolphin* and *safe* is enough to guide the hearer to the conceptual integration necessary to understand *dolphin-safe tuna;* similarly, the occurrence of *land yacht* can be seen as an instruction to create an appropriate conceptual blend of spaces associated with *land* and *yacht* (Turner and Fauconnier 1995). The precise relations between the linguistic components of the compound are severely underspecified. Language appears to us to be rich in meaning, but much of that meaning is in the context of the words being used, and, ultimately, of course, it is in the minds of language users rather than in the words themselves.

Are there situations in which conceptual blends are commonly matched by formal blends? The answer depends on where you look. We have already mentioned some noun-noun compounds analysed by Fauconnier and Turner such as *dolphin-safe tuna* and *land yacht,* in which formal blending does not occur. What about grammatical structures? When Fauconnier and Turner talk about blending and grammar, they refer to schemata such as [NP V NP PP] and [NP(x) be NP(y) of NP(z)][13] and are thus focussing only on abstract clausal and phrasal constructions, which are also discussed extensively by Goldberg (1995). However, a considerable component of grammar consists of units larger than noun-noun compounds like *land yacht* or *fire station* and which are, at the same time, less abstract than clausal structures such as [NP V NP PP]. I maintain that it is at this intermediate level of granularity that formal blends are much more common than Fauconnier and Turner seem to suggest. In short, I am arguing that if we look to the semi-lexical, semi-syntactic structures such as *[the main/best/first thing is]* and their associated meanings, we will find the locus of a considerable amount of formal blending.

Let us explore this idea further. As we saw above, Fauconnier and Turner state that one fundamental reason for the occurrence of blends is the need to merge conceptualisations of events to form an integrated structure. At the heart of what I am proposing is a different kind of merger: the blending of general, stored schema-meaning pairs to fit the particular—the current thought or intention. A thought or intention may fit well with a stored representation, in which case the word or phrase can simply be recruited, and presumably, this is what happens in the use of utterances such as *thank you, good morning,* etc. Longer and more complex phrases, however, are more likely to be the result of not only concatenative processes, but blending or modification of suitable prefabricated chunks.

This kind of blending is an abstract process not open to inspection, but it is not unreasonable to propose that there is within a grammar a set of form-meaning pairs with different degrees of entrenchment and that in expressing an idea certain chunks can be recruited and perhaps modified or blended. One way to look at this is to view the utterance to be created as a blended space in which stored form-meaning pairs are not simply concatenated, but are merged.

There is an obvious difficulty in investigating this topic that can be referred to as the concrete mixer problem. We have much more of an idea of the nature of the stuff that comes out of the mixer than we do about what goes into it. Blending by its nature obscures the input to the blend; and so finding empirical evidence of blending is difficult. The strategy I pursue here is to look for examples in which the input to the blends is retrievable, and then study the properties of the blending process. The assumption is that the same blending processes are operating whether or not we cannot identify the inputs to the blend. In other words, instead of having a two-part model of grammar in which there is a generative, word-based component supplemented by the listing of some fixed expressions, we have instead a unitary, coherent system in which the speaker can exploit a variety of lexical resources and combine them using concatenative and blending processes.

4.1 Lexical Blends

The fact that we tend to think of words as among the more stable and tangible elements in the universe of linguistic entities suggests that blending within words is rare. A blend, when it does occur, will be obvious—at least as long as the blend remains novel. Thus a word such as *automobilia* clearly results from the process of blending. In the production, and probably also in the comprehension, of *automobilia* two separate units are activated: *automobile* and *memorabilia*. It is reasonable to assume that the inputs to the blend are these two words, and that similarity in the form of these words (and perhaps other properties that they have) facilitates the production of a blend when the communicative situation calls for an intimate linking of the meanings associated with the two words.[14]

Let us briefly examine another example and consider the blend *digerati*. In this case, the lexical items merged in the blend are harder to discern; one component is probably *literati* with the other being a word something like *digital,* although the precise form remains unclear. And again, in comprehending *digerati* many hearers will activate a 'literati' meaning and a 'digital' meaning.

For some speakers, *automobilia* may actually have the status of a unit with only minimal activation of the associated contributing units, just as *smog* is treated as an independent lexical item (although wordsmiths may not be able to prevent the associated words *smoke* and *fog* from rising into consciousness). The main point of these examples, however, is to show that for many speakers the existence of a lexical blend and typically even the identity of the elements contributing to the blend are obvious. (See Kemmer forthcoming for discussion of the properties of component words that facilitate blending.) The blends are new enough to be identifiable as such and it is the very stability of words which makes the occurrence of lexical blends easy to recognise. The more difficult task to which we now turn is to search for evidence for syntactic blending.

4.2 Syntactic Blends

The constructional character of syntax means that while we may expect blending to occur, or even to be commonplace, evidence of blending is going to be difficult to find, since the units of syntax and the process of syntactic composition itself are hidden from view. In looking at the sentence or utterance—the output of constructional processes—it is difficult if not impossible to discern the elements used in the compositional process. We can see what the words making up the utterance are, and we can usually give a possible tree structure for the utterance, but beyond that, for a given usage event, it is hard to say definitively whether units larger than the word were part of the input. For example, if the output string is series of lexemes represented by $a\ b\ x\ y\ z$, we can then ask, are the basic units lexical categories associated with $[a][b][x][y][z]$, as commonly supposed; or $[a\ b\ y]$ which is merged in some manner with $[x\ \_\ z]$; or $[a\ b\ x\ w\ z]$ with y

replacing *w;* or any number of other alternative combinations? It is difficult to say, and yet it is a fundamental question if we wish to understand the nature of syntax.

Let us review the characteristics of language described above in Section 3. On the one hand, we have a standard view of syntax in which syntactic composition makes reference only to syntactic categories, not lexical items. This results in a grammar well able to account for some of the creative aspects of language, but not the collocational patterns that are found in language usage. On the other hand, the frequency of occurrence of some collocations suggests that on psychological grounds these collocations have a unit status within the grammar; similarly, the semantic or pragmatic idiosyncrasy of some collocations offers no alternative other than to assume that they are listed whole in the grammar. The presence in the grammar of numerous prefabricated units means that it is unclear what the appropriate building blocks of syntax are; hence the nature of syntactic composition must be re-examined.

Two further characteristics are worthy of note. One is the absence of a marked division between strong and weak collocations, which makes a creative/fixed dichotomy difficult to maintain. The highly frequent shorter collocations would be most likely to be inserted as a whole chunk, with modification or blending being possible, but less likely. And the looser (and longer) the collocation, the more likely it will be that compositional, blending processes will play a role.

The second, related, characteristic is that collocations sometimes appear with novel lexemes embedded in them, as in *a good thing to footnote*. Thus it is just as necessary to account for the novel items in fixed phrases as for the occurrence of fixed phrases themselves.

These properties suggest that some sort of blending of schema-meaning pairs may play a major role in syntactic composition, and so we will now turn to look at blending in more detail.

4.3 Evidence of Blending

As we have noted, while it is difficult to see the result of blending processes in general, we should still be able to find some evidence of blending in syntax. One possible indicator of blending is the occurrence of idiosyncratic combinations of syntactic categories. In many cases the blending of chunks will result in structures which are analysable by X-bar syntax and are therefore unremarkable. However, if phrasal chunks are blended, we might expect to find some cases in which the parts don't follow the expected syntactic patterns. Let us look at an example. The phrase *very much* has both a typically prenominal adjectival use (along with *very many*) and an adverbial use, as illustrated in the examples in (4a) and (4b).

(4) a. the result is not going to be of very much interest ...
   b. I agree very much with what you said.

How then do we analyse the use of *very much* in (5)?

(5) So thanks very much to my Steering Committee.

The adverbial use of *very much* appears to have become attached to the nominal *thanks*, and this odd combination of syntactic categories may indicate that this now fixed construction originated as a blend. Historically, the inputs to the blend were perhaps something like *many thanks* (or *thanks for X*) and *thank you very much*.

Other examples of odd word-class combinations noted by Moon (1998: 81-82) as expressions "that cannot be parsed according to normal syntactic rules" include *for free* and *the back of beyond*. There may be several ways to explain the occurrence of forms such as these, and here I simply mention them without further comment as possible candidates for blended structures.

Further evidence of blending may be gleaned from historical changes in syntactic structure and here we focus on a single change in the use of the verb *claim*. The examples in (6) taken from the OED show the typical use of *claim* in the eighteenth century in which the verb subcategorises for a noun direct object.

(6) a. Both sides claimed the victory (1722)
   b. These instances of kindness claim my most grateful acknowledgments. (1775)
   c. Heroines of such a cast may claim our admiration. (1776)
   d. Much learned dust involves the combatants; each claiming Truth.(1784)

Examples illustrating the use of the verb *assert* from around the same period in (7) show that, unlike *claim*, *assert* can occur with a *that-*complement.

(7) a. Because a Council of the other Side asserted it was coming down. (1712)

    b. As they confidently assert that the first inhabitants of their Island were fairies, so do they maintain that these little people have still their residence among them. (1726-31)

    c. No man should have even a colour to assert that I received a compensation. (1765)

    d. He asserts that he not only invented polyphonic music, or counterpoint, but the polyplectrum or spinet, ... (1782)

The historical evidence shows that *claim* never occurs with a *that*-complement early in the eighteenth century, but when we look at the use of *claim* in the nineteenth century, we see a change in behaviour that could be interpreted as the result of a blend of schemata associated with *claim* and *assert*. The sentences from the nineteenth century in (8) show that *claim* began to appear with a *that*-complement.

(8) a. He claimed that his word should be law. (1850)

    b. Watt claimed that Hornblower...was an infringer upon his patents. (1878)

    c. I claim that we are before them in the matter of uncapping machines [for honeycombs]. (1886)

    d. He was afraid to bet and crawfished out of the issue by claiming that he didn't drink. (1888)

Another phenomenon that may be an indicator of blending is the double copula (*is is*), as illustrated in (9).

(9) a. And my question is, is he going to do that?

    b. She said, all it is, is a bunch of riddles.

    c. Then what we would take a look at is, is this thing scorable by this kind of a rubric?

    d. What essentially it is, is Jim and Don want us to fix the discussion on that item.

    e. So the thing is, is that's the kind of level of comparison that you get, like it or like it not, at the fourth grade level.

    f. My point is, is that their objection is a red herring.

The examples in (9a)-(9d) are syntactically unremarkable; each instance of *is* plays a distinct role in each clause. However, the double copula in (9e) and (9f) is more unusual and the second *is* seems redundant, although there are different opinions on the status of these constructions. In an extensive discussion of the source of these forms, Tuggy (1996: 715) states that "parallelism with legitimate *is is* structures" may be one source for these sentences. Tuggy suggests that source of these double copula sentences is a blend or "intersection" of utterances of the type shown in (10a) and (10b).[15]

(10) a. So the thing is, it's not a diagnostic.

b. Yes, the important thing is that the long informational would be way too much for them.

Examples like (9e) and (9f) tend to be treated as errors arising out of similarities in structure, and are thus seen as the syntactic equivalent of slips of the tongue; here we will avoid passing judgement on the well-formedness of these sentences and simply take them to be evidence not only that blending occurs in language production, but that such a blend can itself become entrenched as a new constructional form.

The unusual combination of syntactic categories in *thanks very much* and *for free*, the change in the subcategorisation of *claim*, and the repetition of the word *is* in *the thing is, is* are worthy of further discussion and analysis, but here I simply put them forward as examples in which the operation of a blending process can be discerned.

4.4 The Fat Lady

Let us turn now to a more extensive corpus-based analysis of blending and examine set expressions such as *it ain't over 'til the fat lady sings* and *make hay while the sun shines*. The strategy employed is to examine usage data in corpora to find out how these set expressions "surface" in use in order to uncover evidence of blending and provide insight into the role of formal and conceptual blending in the production of these utterances.[16] The obvious advantage of working with set expressions, assuming that they truly are set expressions, is that any blending that occurs will be apparent and therefore we can use these expressions as a test bed to determine the extent and nature of blending in general and to assess the likelihood that semi-fixed expressions such as *a good thing to do* take part in blending processes. We find cases ranging from unchanged fixed expressions to minimally changed expressions to expressions that deviate markedly from the original, but which can still be seen as modifications of the fixed expression.

Let us start by examining the phrase *it ain't over till the fat lady sings*. How is this phrase actually used in an utterance? Is the phrase plucked from memory and inserted whole, or is it sometimes one input to a blended structure? Since we are discussing blending, it will be no surprise to learn that we will concentrate on its role in blended structures. When we talk about the phrase as being an input to a blend, we have to consider both the formal and conceptual aspects of this blend. As we will see in the examples below, the use of this phrase is complex and is often, but not always, involved in both formal and conceptual blending. The main focus of the present paper is on formal blending, but, as will become obvious, this phrase, in particular, seems to serve as a catalyst for conceptual blending, a full description of which is not attempted here. The numerous sentences presented below provide an extensive sampling of the use of the phrase and give a good indication of the nature of formal and conceptual blending involved.

The set phrase occurs in its full canonical form fairly frequently, as illustrated in (11).

(11)   "**It ain't over till the fat lady sings**," he said. (Times/ST 96)

The reference to a fat lady singing suggests the conclusion or end to some process, but it also evokes a frame or series of events (typically described with reference to an opera or other performances) that lead up to the finale. In the examples below there are several cases in which the conceptual blending between the finale of the opera and the situation being described is not matched by an intimate formal blending. For example, the set phrase may be followed by a conjoined phrase in which links are established to the current situation, as in (12), where the set phrase is simply conjoined with a description of a celebration that ended with a performance by Kate Smith (a fat lady singer).

(12) **It ain't over 'til the fat lady sings** and Columbus's 14th annual Fourth of July celebration, Red, White and Boom, ended just that way. (NAN 94/95)

In some of the examples there is not only the association of a fat lady with the end of a process, but, by extension, the presence of the fat lady is taken to be a necessary condition for the conclusion of the event. In the examples in (13) the set expression is again given in its full form and then followed by a conjoined phrase that provides the appropriate connections to the current situation. It is the formal juxtaposition along with some cohesive links that invite a conceptual integration of two events, and in these two examples there are also links between the fat lady in the set expression and individuals in the current situation being described.

(13) a. "However," Wagner says, "there is a basic problem. You know, **it isn't over until the fat lady sings** ... but in this athletic crowd, there are no fat ladies." (NAN 94/95)

b. "**It's not over until the fat lady sings** and there's no music coming out of Blanca's office yet," Harrison said Monday. (NYT 94)

In the following examples in (14), the fat lady does not have an actual counterpart in the situation described, but she acts within an imaginary space in such a way as to convey information about the current situation. There is no formal blending in these examples; all the action described in the sentences occurs in a constructed "opera world."

(14) a. But **it's not all over 'til the fat lady sings** and she's not even on stage yet. (Times/ST 96)

b. Of course, **it is not over until the fat lady sings** and she has yet to approach the piano. (Times/ST 96)

c. Well, Grandpa, **it's not over until the fat lady sings**, and she hasn't been called back for an encore. (SJM 91)

The remaining examples, (15)-(20), are similar in overall form to the sentences given above, but in these cases there is also some evidence of formal blending. For instance, the first sentence in (15a) contains an inserted comment and in the following sentence the fat lady acts as a protagonist in the world of Big Ten football. In (15b) and (15c), the noun phrase *opera* replaces the *it* in *it ain't over*. The explicit mention of opera in these examples is motivated by the need to evoke the opera frame so that the additional comment (e.g., *I think I heard her walking to the microphone*) can be interpreted by the hearer. The result in all these cases is a rich conceptual blend in which aspects of the opera world, crucially including a fat lady, are merged with aspects of the situation being described.

(15) a. **It will not be over,** as sports folk say, **until the fat lady sings.** Though at this rate, if the fat lady is knowledgeable about the Big Ten and handy with a blue pencil, she might want to stick around. (LATWP 95)

b. "It's been said the opera **isn't over until the fat lady sings,**" Gephardt said. "Last Saturday in Michigan I think I heard her walking to the microphone." (AP 88)

c. "The opera **ain't over 'till the fat lady sings,**" it said. "And we're not going to let her sing." (AP 90)

The example in (16) is similar to those in (15) except that the subject is *competition,* or rather *no competition,* and here we see some evidence of a simple formal blend in which a new noun phrase is placed into the schema.

(16) No competition is **over until the fat lady sings.** The current status of the battle over the megaplex location suggests she is only in rehearsal. (NYT 95)

Example (17) is complex, but interesting, and while it would be an exaggeration to say that the process of constructing this utterance is open to view, it is not hard to get a good sense of how it was constructed. The speaker, DeHihns, picks up on the previous speaker's description of a project as being dead and integrates that notion in a blend with the fat lady chunk to yield *Nothing is dead until the fat lady sings.* And then, in addition, there is a link between the metaphorical fat lady and an actual person.

(17) Asked at a news conference if the project is now effectively dead, DeHihns replied, "Nothing is dead **until the fat lady sings,** as they say. LuJuana is not fat, but she will make the final decision." (AP 90)

The following sentence is so intricately blended that it is perhaps indicative of a carefully constructed sentence of the type typically found in a journalistic style of expression. If all the examples were of this kind, one might be justified in considering blends to be an interesting aspect of a particular genre, but most of the examples do not give a sense of being contrived in this way.

(18)   In the federal government, it's never **over until the fat lady** rereads the fine print, and she moves her lips. (LATWP 95)

The form of the fat lady set phrase probably has a less direct influence on the examples listed in (19) and (20). The phrase evokes an opera scene and this opera world is transformed or blended with the current situation to produce some kind of blend involving the *fat lady* and perhaps singing, plus material indicating the described situation. These examples do not involve a merging of chunks of the sort we saw in (16) and (17).

(19) a. The **fat lady** may not be treading the Portuguese doorstep as readily as it seems. (Times/ST 96)

   b. In any event, **the fat lady** was not ready to **sing**. (Times/ST 96)

   c. "The **fat lady isn't singing** yet, but she may be warming up," South Carolina state chairman Chris Verenes said (AP 88)

   d. ... Census Bureau director for seven months, stressed that the tally isn't finished and "**the fat lady** has not **sung**." (AP 90)

   e. they resumed normal business with the resilient message that **the fat lady** is still a long way from breaking into **song**. (Times/ST 97)

   f. And **the fat lady** is warming up. (Times/ST 95)

In the following the fat lady is a signal of the end of a process and this may be further interpreted in terms of consequences, possibly negative consequences.

(20) a. "They incurred the debt, and it's time for **the fat lady** to **sing**." (AP 88)

   b. "Believe me, when **the fat lady sings**, the 1991 deficit will be higher than it was in 1990," says James C. Miller, co-chairman (AP 90)

   c. Sen. Ed Davis said that it is time for the Los Angeles police chief to step down.   "I think **the fat lady** has sung," said Davis, R-Northridge. (SJM 91)

   d. The **fat lady** burst into **song** far too early last Sunday, when referee Pat McEnaney ... (Times/ST 96)

From the examples in this section, we see that the saying *it ain't over till the fat lady sings* participates in a variety of blends and also evokes a rich semantic field which leads to complex and colourful conceptual blends. The reality of syntactic blending appears quite clearly in the corpus data. All parts of the set expression seem to be available for modification or substitution under the appropriate circumstances and there were even examples in the corpus in which *fat lady* was modified, as in *it ain't over 'til the fat guy sings.*

4.5 Make Hay

Let us turn now to the somewhat less spectacular case of *make hay while the sun shines*. This chunk is one example of a large inventory of well-known sayings, which can be considered to be a part of a native speaker's knowledge of English. In this section we investigate how *make hay while the sun shines* is used, looking once again for indications of the nature and extent of formal blending.

Let us consider the simple representation of a schema for this basic idiom given in (21). Here the formal part of the idiom is represented as an unanalysed phrase labelled only as a sentence, S, with the approximate literal and figurative meanings rendered in capital letters. This is not to say that this particular expression even in its idiomatic interpretation is completely unanalysed, but here we are merely representing the fact that the phrase is known as a unit and has a particular meaning as a unit.

(21) $_S$ [make hay while the sun shines]

| MAKE HAY WHILE | TAKE ADVANTAGE OF |
| THE SUN SHINES | FAVOURABLE CONDITIONS |

The relation between the string *make hay while the sun shines* and its meaning is here represented in isolation, but presumably it is a part of a network of "take advantage" forms and meanings. The literal meaning of the *make hay* expression is shown (on the left) in (21) since the existence of a temporal component to the meaning seems to feed into many of the blends.

Insight into the process of utterance planning, starting with an intention to express an idea and moving on to the production of language, is beyond the reach of corpus analysis and here I simply want to argue that the process, whatever its nature, must be analysed in terms of chunks and blending rather than lexical categories and an X-bar style of syntactic composition. For illustrative purposes we can give the following account. We know that the output is a form-meaning pair, which is a blend of two or more input form-meaning pairs. One of the inputs is the string *make hay while the sun shines* with its associated meaning. The other input relates to the speaker's intention to express a particular situation in which "X is taking advantage of Y" and we can assume that in this input there are potentially also some words or chunks associated with X and Y.

In the large corpora that were searched, there were, in fact, no instances of the *make hay while the sun shines* schema in its imperative form, although the examples in (22) are very similar and include the canonical form as an embedded clause.

(22) a. "We have got to **make hay while the sun shines**," he said. (Times/ST 95)

b. "I've got to **make hay while the sun shines**, so to speak." He is behind in harvesting his barley, he said ... (NYT 95)

c. **Make hay while the sun shines** was the message going out from Merrill Lynch... (Times/ST 97)

d. Long-shot Oscar nominees often try to **make hay while the sun shines**, lining up as many projects as possible between the announcement of their nomination and probable disappointment on Oscar night. (NYT 95)

These sentences are, of all the examples, most akin to the basic schema. We can see the process of blending or at least the results of blending in these utterances, with the information relevant to the current situation typically being introduced in the portion of the discourse preceding *make hay*, thereby giving information about who or what is taking advantage of current favourable conditions.

The example in (22c) shows a nominalisation of the fixed expression which is used sentence-initially to introduce a topic, with amplification of the topic following in the subsequent discourse. In (22d), as in most of the other sentences, novel material precedes the set expression, but in this particular example, information about the current situation is also given in an appended participial phrase. One could imagine a more intimate blending along the lines of "Oscar nominees try to make hay while the world waits for the results of voting," but this may have been avoided because of constraints on information flow in the discourse and/or because the description of a time slice between the two identified events does not fit so well with a *while* phrase.

It is interesting to consider that even though the basic schema corresponding to *make hay while the sun shines* appears to native speakers to be well-entrenched, the expression in its canonical form is rare. It is reasonable to suppose, however, that the schema may have been introduced and firmly established during childhood and that while the schema is not much used directly in the language, its presence in the grammar is maintained and even reinforced by instances such as those above. In other words, from the speaker's point of view, the string is used as a prefabricated unit to structure the discourse, but does not emerge intact. And from the hearer's perspective, *make hay while the sun shines* is evoked more than it is actually heard.

Minor modifications consisting of changes to tense/aspect marking can be seen in the examples in (23) below, which are otherwise similar to the sentences in (22).

(23) a. Could it be that Raymond Blanc, with his recently acquired three Michelin stars, is **making hay while the sun shines**? (Times/ST 95)

   b. ...Gary Lineker, the former Tottenham and England striker lately **making hay while the sun shone** with Grampus 8 in Japan. (Times/ST 95)

These examples differ only in minor ways from those in (22), but they are listed separately because they indicate more clearly than the previous examples that there must be some kind of internal analysis of the set expression. An X-bar analysis or labelling of some sort must be applied to the idiomatic string in order to modify the canonical form to fit the current circumstances. Some analysis of the string, indicated by bracketing in (24), is needed to motivate the modifications of the fixed expression that occur in (22) and (23).

(24) $_{VP}$ [make [hay] [while [the sun [shines]]]]

More typically, the expression is altered or blended to a more intimate degree to package both the 'take advantage' meaning of the idiom with elements of the actual situation being described. The range of examples in (25)-(28) below illustrate a "progressive obscuring" of the original form of the idiom by the introduction of increasingly larger chunks relevant to the particular situation.[17]

The first group of examples in (25) all contain a temporal phrase containing *while* and have a similar phrasal structure to the original; some of the examples also retain a reference to metaphorical weather conditions, but no reference to the sun.

(25) a. The Chiefs aren't the only NFL team that hasn't **made hay while** their **quarterback shined**. (NYT 95)

   b. Now is the season of savers' discontent, though borrowers should **make hay while** the warmer climate remains. (Times/ST 95)

   c. Hewden Stuart's plant hire business **made hay while** the rest of the construction industry suffered from a drought. (Times/ST 95)

   d. ... American cable companies are **making hay while** British Telecom fights to protect its market share with one hand tied behind its back. (Times/ST 95)

   e. Republicans strained in their attempts to **make political hay while** Democrats were obsessive in their defensive blocking. (NYT 95)

   f. the big food groups are opening selected stores 24 hours a day in a bid to **make hay while** consumer confidence continues to improve. (Times/ST 96)

   g. **While** Mr Soros apologises, the ladies of Beardstown are **making hay**. (Times/ST 95)

In these examples the favourable conditions expressed idiomatically by *while the sun shines* are replaced by a description of the actual event such as, from (25f), *while consumer confidence continues to improve*. Thus there is a more intricate blend, with information from the current situation being added in both the subject position and in the temporal phrase.

All the examples in (26) contain *make hay* plus a temporal phrase, but the temporal phrase in these sentences is not introduced by *while*.

(26) a. Opponents of the Tory Right have **made hay since** the Conservative leadership election last month. (Times/ST 95)

   b. Leeds **made hay in the first half** ... (Times/ST 95)

    c. **During his life**, they **made hay**. No piece detailing the marriage of the millionaire chairman of Hanson and the former model Miss Tucker was complete without carping references to the four decades separating them. (Times/ST 95)

    d. ...packaging companies have **a small window in the cycle** in which to **make hay**. (Times/ST 95)

    e. one of the areas where the group has **made hay in recent years**. (Times/ST 95)

    f. ...This field is wide open to Labour. If Tony Blair cannot **make hay** in such **political sunshine**, how will he fare when winter comes? (Times/ST 96)

Still other examples do not have any temporal component at all and instead focus simply on the meaning 'take advantage.' In these cases there is some suggestion of a more complex blending based not only on *make hay while the sun shines* but also on expressions such as *make money* (27) and *make runs* (at cricket) (28).

(27) a. ...one of the areas where the group has **made hay** in recent years. (Times/ST 95)

    b. ...France, which has seen her neighbour **making hay** on the back of a weak currency (Times/ST 95)

    c. ...one of the areas where the group has **made hay** in recent years. (Times/ST 95)

    d. In the meantime, the banks continue to **make hay**. (Times/ST 97)

    e. ...those companies with money to spend will **make hay**. (Times/ST 97)

(28) a. However, they survived to **make hay** against far less experienced operators. Butcher hit 20 fours and a six in his... (Times/ST 96)

    b. Slater will **make hay** against county bowling if he conquers his impetuosity on green-tinged mornings... (Times/ST 96)

In some examples, there is an idea of taking advantage politically and, in fact, *make political hay* is a collocation. This usage, illustrated below in (29) and (32), seems particularly common in the American corpora.

(29) a. A rabble-rousing Scottish parliament could **make hay with** Tony Blair's refusal to turn the clock back. (Times/ST 97)

   b. Still, Labour is hardly in a position to **make hay**. (Times/ST 97)

   c. And they accused Dole of using a critical foreign policy issue to **"make political hay,"** as White House press secretary Mike McCurry put it. (LATWP 95)

   d. Old Labour **makes hay** in Brussels (Times/ST 96)

The types of sentences illustrated in (27)-(29) are so far removed from the source expression and are perhaps being influenced by these other phrases (*make money, make runs,* etc.) to the extent that it is not at all clear that the expression *make hay while the sun shines* plays a role. A schema covering examples (27)-(29) associated with a simple 'take advantage' meaning is given in (30).

(30)   VP [make [hay] [ADJUNCT]]]

The many examples listed above are interesting in themselves, but it is worth reiterating that the main point to be drawn from these sentences is that blending is clearly a part of sentence construction. If we find widespread blending in which an idiom such as *make hay while the sun shines* combines with other form-meaning pairs, then we have no reason not to expect that blending also occurs in those situations in which the input to the blend is harder to identify.

On a final note on *make hay*, we see that in American usage (as exemplified by the examples from the New York Times and other U.S. newspapers) there is much less focus on the temporal aspect, less focus on the weather, and more of a focus on the process of making hay from or out of something. In other words, the *hay* part of *make hay* in American usage is much more likely to be seen as a product and part of an almost industrial process. The example in (31) illustrates very well this manufacturing view of making hay.

(31)   The GOP intends to **make hay with** whatever **sunshine** the committee provides. (AP 89)

Other typical uses from American newspapers are given in (32). Some of these sentences include the phrases *make hay out of* or *make hay of,* which are totally absent from the British examples and may be influenced by a schema along the lines of *make wine out of grapes*. Here again it is not clear whether there is, in these cases, a strong connection with the full idiomatic expression *make hay while the sun shines*, or whether these are now independent constructions, linked only tenuously to the full idiom. The example above in (31) might be taken as an indication that there is some connection between the shorter *make hay* construction and *make hay while the sun shines*. On the other hand, many of following examples in (32) are associated with the accrual of a political advantage mentioned above—an overtone that is not a part of the longer form of the fixed expression.

(32) a. But his political adviser, Lee Atwater, warns that rivals who try to "**make hay**" at Bush's expense "may find it backfires." (ACLDCI)

   b. The Democrats, who generally oppose term limits, did their best to **make hay of** the Republicans' multiple measures on term limits, ... (NYT 95)

   c. And not only are respected public figures calling for an amnesty; some politicians have even **made hay of** their Stasi ties. (LATWP95)

   d. ...now find themselves subjected to the repugnant spectacle of their national leaders angling to **make hay out of** the tragedy. (NYT 95)

   e. they realize that the president could **make political hay out of** any Democratic effort to repudiate Gramm-Rudman. (ACLDCI)

The above discussion shows the potential of using corpora of different speech communities to elucidate the differences between the linguistic systems of those communities. A closer look at the American vs. British corpora might reveal some very subtle differences between the usages of otherwise very similar-looking expressions.

In this section we have seen a broad range of examples involving the use of two well-known idioms and on the basis of these results we can say that blending is an important constructional process. The details of the blending process, as well as cross-dialectal variation, provide scope for deeper investigation. Another issue worth pursuing is potential differences between blending processes associated with specific expressions. For example, while the corpus examples showed that both of the sayings we investigated were involved in formal and conceptual blending, there were clearly differences between the two. The *make hay* saying appears to take part in formal blends to a greater extent than the *fat lady* expression, but it does not evoke a general hay-making conceptual domain that matches the rich opera/performance world associated with *the fat lady*.

5. Conclusion

In this paper we have adopted a perspective on a corpus as a record of language usage events and explored the view that corpus analysis can lead to insights into the nature of usage-based grammar. One characteristic of corpus data is the ubiquity of collocations of various kinds, and it is reasonable to assume that these frequent word combinations have some degree of unit status or cognitive reality in a usage-based grammar. The question explored here is the source of strings such as *a worthwhile thing to footnote* which clearly cannot be analysed as some sort of chunk, but which may be the result of a blending process, with one of the inputs being a construction or some kind of more or less fixed expression such as *a good thing to do*. In order to approach this topic we looked at the way that the fixed expressions *it ain't over 'til the fat lady sings* and *make hay while the sun shines* "surfaced" in usage and the results demonstrate that while the processes involved are complex, it is reasonable to conclude that formal (and conceptual) blending of stored units plays an important role in accounting for the creative aspects of language in use.

Notes

I am grateful to Suzanne Kemmer for comments on earlier drafts of this paper.

1. The usage examples that are not explicitly identified all come from the Corpus of Spoken Professional American English (CPSAE) (Barlow 1998), a 2 million word corpus based on spoken transcripts. To find examples of the idioms discussed, hundreds of millions of words of corpus data were searched. The data sources used in addition to CPSAE were the following:

NYT	*New York Times*
Times/ST	*The Times* and *Sunday Times* (of London)
AP	Associated Press
NAN	North American News (major U.S. newspapers)
LATWP	*Los Angeles Times* and *Washington Post*

ACLDCI   Brown Corpus and *Wall Street Journal*
Each year of *The Times/Sunday Times* contains around 40 million words. Much of the data was accessed at the LDC Online site (www.ldc.upenn.edu/ldc/online/index.html)

2. See Langacker (1987, 1988, this volume) for discussion of the relation of grammar and usage.

3. There is a considerable terminology for recurrent word patterns: collocations, idioms, sayings, fixed expressions, prefabricated units, chunks, lexical phrases. In this paper the distinctions among types of recurrent word patterns are not relevant and hence these terms are used more or less interchangeably. See Moon (1998) for discussion of terminology in this area.

4. The view of grammar as consisting of a stored set of language units or routines has been proposed by researchers working in a variety of paradigms. See, for example, Aijmer (1996), Bybee and Scheibman (forthcoming), Croft (1995), Haiman (1994), Hopper (1987), Langacker (1987), Peters (1983), and Sinclair (1991). Sinclair (1987: 319-320) makes a distinction between the open-choice principle and the idiom principle. The open-choice principle refers to the choices in terms of words and structures available to speakers in constructing utterances. Sinclair notes (1987:320) that "the open choice principle does not provide substantial enough restraints" and proposes, in addition, the idiom principle: "the language user has available [...] a large number of semi-preconstructed phrases that constitute single choices, even though they appear to be analysable into segments."

5. Sag and Wasow (1999: 416) state: "Most contemporary syntactic theories have preserved the most important innovations of the Standard Theory, namely, syntactic features, recursive phrase structure, and some sort of semantic component."

6. See Church et al. (1991) for discussion of t-score and mutual information, Kita et al. (1994) for their "cost" measure, and Manning and Schütze (1999) for an account of entropy and other measures.

7. Different kinds of description of schemata are presented in Langacker (1987); Barlow and Kemmer (1994), Barlow (1996), Fillmore et al. (1988), among others.

8. See, for example, Bybee (1999), Bybee and Scheibman (forthcoming), Croft (1995), and Haiman (1994).

9. I assume that X-bar syntax, which is organised to some extent on semantic grounds, is similar to the more abstract forms of schemata proposed here. Jackendoff (1994: 22, quoted in Goldberg 1996: 8) states "one might want to view the 'core rules' of phrase structure for a language as maximally underspecified constructional idioms." See also Langacker (this volume).

10. Example taken from the *New York Times*, Oct. 22, 1999.

11. Sag and Wasow (1999: 265-269) discuss some idioms such as *take advantage* and *kick the bucket* and in their HPSG representations it is, in fact, quite clear how the idiom is combined with other syntactic components. However, one problem with the HPSG analysis is that these phrases cannot be modified. Thus it seems that the grammar would not be able to generate *take full advantage* or *kick the proverbial bucket* except by listing them as completely separate from their non-modified equivalents. But more seriously, the extent to which collocational expressions must be accounted for within a realistic grammar is not acknowledged. However, the view of grammar as a collection of "signs" in HPSG is promising and suggests that the theory could potentially handle rich collocational connections.

12. There are also meta-blending processes of various kinds, such as the proposal by Kemmer and Verhagen (1994) that causative structures are based on other more basic structures such as transitive clauses.

13. [NP V NP PP] is from Fauconnier and Turner (1996: 117) and [NP(x) be NP(y) of NP(z)] is from Turner (1996: 104).

14. Turner and Fauconnier (1995) mention lexical blends such as *chunnel*. See Kemmer (forthcoming) for a schema-based account of lexical blends at both the conceptual and formal level.

15. According to Tuggy's terminology, the example in (10a) is a Focus formula (Tuggy 1996: 724) and example (10b) illustrates a one-"be" construction (Tuggy 1996: 713). The examples in (9) and (10) are taken from CPSAE.

16. The examples used in this section are all from written corpora, although some of the examples are quotes. We will have to wait for the creation of very large spoken corpora to fully determine the prevalence of blends based on fixed expressions.

17. The reasons underlying the choice of relatively unaltered idiom versus a relatively obscured idiom remain to be elucidated. A more integrated or

highly blended structure is denser in terms of information content, and this may be appropriate for some situations. In other situations the relatively unadulterated, unblended idiom may be useful as a way of introducing a general proposition, the particular details of which can then be fleshed out as the discourse develops.

References

Aijmer, Karin. 1996. *Conversational Routines in English: Convention and Creativity*. Harlow, Essex: Addison Wesley Longman.

Barlow, Michael. 1996. Corpora for theory and practice. *International Journal of Corpus Linguistics* 1(1), 1–37.

Barlow, M. 1998. *Corpus of Spoken Professional American English*. Houston: Athelstan.

Barlow, Michael and Suzanne Kemmer. 1994. A schema-based approach to grammatical description. In Roberta Corrigan, Gregory Iverson and Susan Lima (eds.), *The Reality of Linguistic Rules*. Amsterdam: Benjamins.

Benson, Morton, Evelyn Benson, and Robert Ilson. 1997. *The BBI Dictionary of English Word Combinations*. Amsterdam: Benjamins.

Bolinger, Dwight. 1961. Syntactic blends and other matters. *Language* 37(3), 366-381.

Bybee, Joan. 1999. The emergent lexicon. Ms. University of New Mexico.

Bybee, Joan and Joanne Scheibman. Forthcoming. The effect of usage on degrees of constituency: The case of *don't* in English. In Susana Cumming (ed.), *Constituency and Discourse*. Amsterdam: Benjamins.

Church, Kenneth, William Gale, Patrick Hanks, and Donald Hindle. 1991. Using statistics in lexical analysis. In Uri Zernik (ed.), *Lexical Acquisition: Exploiting On-Line Resources to Build a Lexicon*. Hillsdale, New Jersey: Lawrence Erlbaum.

Croft, William. 1995. Intonation units and grammatical structure. *Linguistics* 33, 839-882.

Fauconnier, Gilles and Mark Turner. 1996. Blending as a central process of grammar. In Adele E. Goldberg (ed.), *Conceptual Structure, Discourse, and Language*, 113-130. Stanford: Center for the Study of Language and Information (CSLI).

Fillmore, Charles J., Paul Kay, and Mary Catherine O'Connor. 1988. Regularity and idiomaticity in grammatical constructions: The case of *let alone*. *Language* 64, 501-38.

Firth, J. R. 1957. A synopsis of linguistic theory. *Studies in Linguistic Analysis*, 1-32. Special volume. Philological Society.

Goldberg, Adele E. 1995. *Constructions: A Construction Grammar Approach to Argument Structure*. Chicago: The University of Chicago Press.

Goldberg, Adele E. 1996. Jackendoff and construction-based grammar. *Cognitive Linguistics*, 7(1), 3-19.

Haiman, John. 1994. Ritualization and development of language. In William Pagliuca (ed.), *Perspectives on Grammaticalization,* 3-28. Amsterdam: Benjamins.

Hopper, Paul J. 1987. Emergent grammar. *BLS* 13, 139-157. Berkeley: BLS.

Jackendoff, Ray. 1994. The boundaries of the lexicon. Unpublished manuscript. Brandeis University.

Kemmer, Suzanne E. Forthcoming. Lexical blends. In Hubert Cuyckens, Thomas Berg, Rene Dirven, Klaus-Uwe Panther (eds.), *Motivation in Language: Studies in Honour of Günter Radden.* Amsterdam: John Benjamins.

Kemmer, Suzanne and Arie Verhagen. 1994. The grammar of causatives and the conceptual structure of events. *Cognitive Linguistics* 5, 115-156.

Kita, Kenji, Yasuhiko Kato, Takashi Omoto and Yoneo Yano. 1994. Automatically extracting collocations from corpora for language learning. In Andrew Wilson and Anthony McEnery (eds.), *Corpora in Language Education and Research.* UCREL Technical Papers, Vol. 4, 53-64. Lancaster: Department of Linguistics, Lancaster University.

Kjellmer, Goran. 1994. *A Dictionary of English Collocations: Based on the Brown Corpus.* Oxford: Oxford University Press.

Langacker, Ronald W. 1987. *Foundations of Cognitive Grammar,* Vol. 1: *Theoretical Prerequisites.* Stanford: Stanford University Press.

Langacker, Ronald W. 1988. A usage-based model. In Brygida Rudzka-Ostyn (ed.), *Topics in Cognitive Linguistics* (Current Issues in Linguistic Theory 50), 127-61. Amsterdam: Benjamins.

Langacker, Ronald W. This volume. A dynamic usage-based model. In Michael Barlow and Suzanne E. Kemmer (eds.), *Usage-Based Models of Language.* Stanford: CSLI.

Manning, Christopher D. and Hinrich Schütze. 1999. *Foundations of Statistical Natural Language Processing.* Cambridge, Mass: The MIT Press.

Moon, Rosamund. 1998. *Fixed Expressions and Idioms in English: A Corpus-Based Approach.* Oxford: Clarendon Press.

Peters, Ann M. 1983. *The Units of Language Acquisition.* Cambridge: Cambridge University Press.

Sag, Ivan A. and Thomas Wasow. 1999. *Syntactic Theory: A Formal Introduction.* Stanford: CSLI.

Sinclair, John M. 1987. Collocation: A progress report. In Ross Steele and Terry Threadgold (eds.), *Language Topics: Essays in Honour of Michael Halliday,* Vol. II, 319-331. Amsterdam: Benjamins.

Sinclair, John M. 1991. *Corpus, Concordance, Collocation.* Oxford: Oxford University Press.

Tuggy, David. 1996. The thing is is that people talk that way. The question is is Why? In Eugene H. Casad (ed.), *Cognitive Linguistics in the Redwoods: The Expansion of a New Paradigm in Linguistics,* 713-752. Berlin: Mouton de Gruyter.

Turner, Mark. 1996. *The Literary Mind.* New York and Oxford: Oxford University Press.

Turner, Mark and Gilles Fauconnier. 1995. Conceptual integration and formal expression. *Metaphor and Symbolic Activity* 10(3), 183-203.

Index